MARION GREENWOOD

MARION GREENWOOD

PORTRAIT AND SELF-PORTRAIT

A BIOGRAPHY

JOANNE B. MULCAHY

THE UNIVERSITY OF ALABAMA PRESS

Tuscaloosa

The University of Alabama Press
Tuscaloosa, Alabama 35487–0380
uapress.ua.edu

Copyright © 2025 by Joanne B. Mulcahy

Inquiries about reproducing material from this work should be addressed
to the University of Alabama Press.

Typeface: Arno Pro

Cover image: Portrait of Marion Greenwood by Winold Reiss; courtesy of the Reiss Archives
Cover design: Lori Lynch

Cataloging-in-Publication data is available from the Library of Congress.
ISBN: 978-0-8173-2226-7 (cloth)
ISBN: 978-0-8173-6198-3 (paper)
E-ISBN: 978-0-8173-9548-3

For Bob, always, and in memory of Alyn Fenn

Contents

Illustrations

Abbreviations

AAA—Associated American Artists

AD—Adolf Dehn

ALP—American Labor Party

AP—Associated Press

BP—Robert (Bob) Plate

CBI—China-Burma-India

CF—Charles Fenn

CM Inc.—Cannon Mills Inc.

EA—Elizabeth Ames

ER—Edward B. Rowan

FAP—Federal Art Project

GBT—Lawrence L. Gordon, Harry Bernard, Frank Tan

GG—Grace Greenwood

GGA—Grace Greenwood archives

G.R.D—Gladys Roosevelt Dick Studio, New York

HUAC—House Un-American Activities Committee

IWW—Industrial Workers of the World (Wobblies)

JH—Josephine Herbst

LEAR—Liga de Escritores y Artistas Revolucionarios (League of Revolutionary Writers and Artists)

MG—Marion Greenwood

MGA—Marion Greenwood archive

MO—Morale Operations

MoMA—Museum of Modern Art

MS—Marc Sandler

NRA—National Recovery Administration

NYPL—New York Public Library

OS—Oscar Stonorov

OSS—Office of Strategic Services

PS—Philip Stevenson

PWAP—Public Works of Art Project

RP—Rebecca Pitts

SU—Syracuse University

TVA—Tennessee Valley Authority

UNESCO—United Nations Educational, Scientific and Cultural Organization

UT—University of Tennessee

WAA (M)—Woodstock Artists Association (Museum)

WPA—Works Progress Administration

Prologue
"A Realist Woman Should Jump"

THE SPIRAL RAMP RISES NINETY-SIX FEET TO A DOMED SKYLIGHT, AN iconic feature of the Guggenheim Museum. When Frank Lloyd Wright's temple to modernist art opened in 1959, Marion Greenwood stood at the top of that dizzying pathway to the stars. She surveyed the art afficionados below. They'd come to see the other stars, the modernist pantheon. An equal draw was the building, celebrated as a work of genius and reviled as resembling an upside down cupcake. Either way, visitors seemed captivated by Wassily Kandinsky's *Blue Circle* and Jackson Pollock's *Ocean Greyness*.

Marion was not enamored. The work was all abstract, which shouldn't have been a surprise. The Guggenheim collection's previous title was "The Museum of Non-Objective Painting." As a realist and a portrait painter, Marion had plenty to say about the rise of abstraction, none of it good. She was equally dismayed but hardly shocked that men dominated the winding displays.[1] Although she had garnered the era's ultimate compliment, that she "painted like a man," she continued to battle the art world's sexism.

From her towering perch, Marion turned to her friend artist Gladys Brodsky and said, "This is the night that a realist woman should jump." Marion's partner, Robert Plate, who was with her, described her as "the most alive person I've ever known." Even to register her fury, she would not jump.

Marion had a less destructive but still audacious idea: she held her cocktail glass over the ramp and tipped its edge. According to Gladys, "Everyone was looking up. They've never served drinks from anywhere but the bottom since."[2]

Attendees at this invitation-only early viewing at the Guggenheim included many of Marion's friends. They knew her to be emotional, searingly honest, and sometimes outrageous. Her tipped glass likely amused them. But strangers, after they'd escaped the dripping cocktail, surely wondered: who was she?

≡≡

"Who was she?" was my question when I discovered Marion Greenwood's work in 2013. I'd come to Morelia, Michoacán, Mexico, through a Fulbright fellowship to teach creative writing. My friend Elinor Langer alerted me to the presence of a mural done by a key player in the life of her biography subject, Josephine Herbst. I hunted until I found it at El Colegio de San Nicolás, part of La Universidad Michoacana. The beauty of the images on an eighty-six-by-fourteen-foot, second-story wall stunned me: indigenous women wrapped in blue striped rebozos grinding corn, and fishermen in white pants, dipping nets into a turquoise Lake Pátzcuaro. I found a barely legible "Marion Greenwood" in the lower right hand corner.

There was no plaque to honor the artist.

I'd seen dozens of murals during nearly twenty years of visiting and living in Mexico. I had regularly passed El Colegio, part of one of the oldest universities in the Americas, with no awareness of its interior wall. I asked Mexican and North American friends in Michoacán about Greenwood. None had heard of her. How had we missed this mural and its creator?

Trained as an ethnographer, I had long felt that Purépecha art and culture deserve wider recognition. But here was proof that an artist with a very non-Mexican name had once been moved to depict the beauty and richness of this part of Mexico.

Who was she? This question reaches deep for feminist scholars excavating the lives of forgotten women. I've spent much of my career writing the stories of women who deserve to be known and celebrated. My instinctive reaction was that Greenwood had been such a person.

Then, one of my first interviews sealed my determination to find out. My questions about Greenwood's art met with the response, "Wasn't she a femme fatale?" This label would turn up in other contexts. The image of the siren leading men to ruin set my feminist antennae buzzing.

Marion Greenwood was both blessed and cursed by her looks. Everyone who met her commented on her stunning beauty. She was curvaceous, with waves of chestnut hair and large green eyes. Her statuesque frame stood in size ten shoes. Her deep, resonant voice was sometimes compared with that of the legendary actress Tallulah Bankhead, a tone described as "steeped as deep in sex as the human voice can go without drowning."[3] Add a New York accent and Greenwood matched Bankhead. Men pursued her and she encouraged them. Why not? If she had many lovers, so too did the male artists of the time. Considering the femme fatale charge, was her sex life the issue or simply her gender? Was it an issue of then or now?

As I dug into research, I learned that Greenwood had been revered as one of America's greatest twentieth-century women artists. After rising to prominence for her Mexican murals, she painted walls for New Deal projects in the United States and then traveled the world doing easel paintings, sketches, and lithographs. She won awards from the Carnegie Institute, the National Academy of Design, and many other institutions; more than thirty museums collected her art. At the time of the Guggenheim opening, even though realism had fallen from favor, Marion Greenwood was still well known. Yet outside of art historians specializing in Depression-era or Mexican art, few people today recognize her name.

Questions multiplied. How is artistic reputation formed? What had erased hers? How would Marion Greenwood have viewed the femme fatale label? What would she have wanted written if there were a plaque commemorating her Morelia mural?

I likened my search for facts about her life to an archeological dig. But digging sometimes turns up more dust than treasure. Archival evidence about lives, especially women's, can be maddeningly elusive or distorted. I couldn't access some materials whose owners were unwilling to open them to me.

The bigger problem was one faced by many biographers. How to conjure the dead? In an essay about historical novels, Hilary Mantel quotes St. Augustine: "The dead are invisible, they are not absent." Richard Holmes calls the biographical quest "a haunting." Mine began the day I stood under the Morelia mural, long before I uncovered Greenwood's history.

Who was she? There are so many Marion Greenwoods. Portraits of her by other artists and photographers abound. Max Beckmann, Lola and Manuel Alvarez Bravo, Alexander Calder, Isamu Noguchi, Harry Sternberg, and Winold Reiss, among others, tried to capture her allure and beauty. The world saw a joyous, intrepid bohemian, a gifted, sexually liberated artist traversing a world often menacing to women. She was all of that. Yet her letters and self-portraits reveal a different persona. She was sometimes conflicted, lonely, and locked in emotional and financial struggles. With age, she needed greater security than bohemian life offered. The myth of the femme fatale gives way to that of a hard-working artist making a living.

If I was in thrall to Greenwood's life, I was equally compelled by the places and eras in which she lived and worked: the romance of the 1920s and 1930s in New York and Mexico, the hope and possibility of New Deal programs in Roosevelt's America, China and Hong Kong after World War II, the 1950s in Woodstock. I wanted to probe how it felt to be an artist during challenging times—the Great Depression, postwar recovery, and the crushing conformity and Red Scare of the 1950s. As Abstract Expressionism rose to prominence, Marion Greenwood remained a realist and a portrait artist. Against all odds, she stayed true to herself.

That night at the Guggenheim, her bravado hinted at something ineffable— the interior life that animated the body. That spirit set me firmly on the biographer's path, searching for traces of Greenwood's ghost.

MARION GREENWOOD

PART I

Foundations
(1909–1936)

CHAPTER 1

"The Greatest Living Women Mural Painters"

To chart Marion Greenwood's ascent as an artist, we need to imagine her amid the political fervor of 1930s Mexico. The country thrummed with the postrevolutionary zeal of Mexican artists committed to creating a new national identity. Exiles from Cuba and other Latin American countries joined them, followed by a steady stream of American intellectuals, political refugees, artists, and writers. They clustered in cafés to debate ways to achieve a glorious, more egalitarian society. What role should art play?

Marion and her sister, Grace, arrived in Mexico City on October 1, 1934, after traveling from New York via Havana and Veracruz. They'd been hired to create murals in the Abelardo Rodríguez Market, one of the era's most remarkable public art projects. The sisters found an apartment close to the market at 86 Calle República de Columbia. They knew they would stagger exhausted from scaffold to bed each night.

That fall, Marion wandered Mexico City, coffee and cigarettes in hand, while the market project awaited final government approval. The capital was a thriving metropolis of more than a million people. Marion could walk to the Zocalo, Mexico's central plaza. Beige-capped organ grinders played in the shadow of the towering Metropolitan Cathedral. Model Ts and horse-drawn buggies competed with electric tramway cars. Police in white uniforms orchestrated the flow of pedestrians and traffic on streets named for revolutionary heroes Francisco Madero and José María Pino Suárez. "El Angel," the bronze statue built to commemorate Mexico's 1821 independence from Spain, towered over Paseo de la Reforma. The wide avenue emulated the Champs-Élysées, but Mexico City had eclipsed Paris as *the* place for artists.

With time on their hands, the Greenwood sisters hosted parties at their apartment. The place was likely spare. On the ship to Mexico, Marion and Grace could have carried trunks filled with clothes and art supplies. However, the sisters didn't have much. The outfit in Marion's closet was one she wore when not in her painting overalls: a simple knee-length skirt and chenille sweater. She sometimes added a polka dot scarf. Their parties surely featured drinks, if not food. Marion for one never cooked. Whatever she and Grace offered would have been meagre. They lived on little more than the promise of mural income.

Marion and Grace had journeyed south at the urging of American artist Pablo O'Higgins, who lived a kilometer away at 43 Calle de Belisario Domínguez.[1] He'd moved to Mexico in 1924 to apprentice with Diego Rivera. He had, in Marion's words, "gone Mexican," becoming a citizen and loyal communist. The endlessly generous O'Higgins taught the Greenwoods the fundamentals of fresco. He then advocated for them to join the Rodríguez Market team that ultimately grew to six Mexican and four American artists.[2] The Public Works Department had created the project to revive downtown life, modernize the working-class El Carmen barrio, and generate jobs during the Depression. Murals were integral to the building's design.

The Greenwoods' ambitions had blossomed in a family of artists and would-be artists, life in bohemian New York, and study at the Art Students League. At twenty-five, Marion was far more accomplished and recognized than the thirty-two-year-old Grace. By 1934, Marion had connected to several Mexican muralists when they were in the United States, including *los tres grandes* (the big three)—Diego Rivera, José Clemente Orozco, and David Alfaro Siqueiros.

Rivera, as the Rodríguez Market project artistic director, had approved Marion's hiring. In 1929, she had painted a portrait of Orozco in New York, and Siqueiros had visited her family's home in Brooklyn a few years later. These artists held power and opened doors into which Marion had thrust one foot. Each influenced her work. But Marion also established herself on her own terms. She was so lionized that when Spanish-born artist Juan de Diego arrived in Mexico City, everyone asked him, "Do you know who Marion Greenwood is?" She had, he said, created a wonderful aura.[3]

Renowned photographers Manuel and Lola Álvarez Bravo captured Marion's aura in photos from 1935–1936. In one, she stands in the foreground dressed in a satiny, wide-sleeved white robe. Both arms raise to push back her hair, a gesture brimming with Greta Garbo–style drama. She gazes out at some imagined horizon. What she sees is her future: greater fame for an already celebrated artist.

Marion's meteoric rise had begun during previous sojourns in Mexico. As explored in part II ("Mexican Awakening"), each stay enriched her life and art. In 1932, she'd crossed the border with Josephine ("Josie") Herbst, a writer with whom she'd begun a relationship at Yaddo. John Hermann, Josie's husband, rounded out the trio headed south. The three-way combination would prove complicated, the politics far simpler. All three chased the promise of revolution, with Josie and John as Marion's tutors. When they decamped to the popular tourist town of Taxco, the Hotel Taxqueño commissioned Marion to paint a fresco on its walls. She thereby became the first woman to paint a public mural in Mexico. Her 1933 mural in Morelia boosted her growing reputation.

Rivera had hired some of Mexico's many talented women artists as assistants. None had yet painted their own mural. Marion's claim to these "firsts" title rested on luck, her status as a foreigner, charm, tenacity, and assistance from Josie, John, and O'Higgins. She also had the physical stamina to tackle true fresco. Painting on wet plaster demands endless hours, neck craned and arms aching, to create images before the walls dry. Marion held as inspiration the great Italian Renaissance muralists whose artistry her Mexican companions had resurrected. Joining the mural world would realize a dream.

Named for Mexican President Abelardo L. Rodríguez (1932–1934), the market is still a vital community center. Locals sell clothing, sides of beef and pork, colorful piles of fruit, tacos, and pan dulce. To visit the market today, a visitor would walk about a mile from the Zocalo, passing through a working-class neighborhood with shrines to Santa Muerte. Locals revere the purple-cloaked skeletal figure, a folk saint believed to protect devotees, heal the sick, and grant requests.

In 1934, the project artists could have used Santa Muerte's help to urge the government forward. Funding had stalled for months as officials bickered over the market project and its images. The conflict highlights the central role of artists following the 1910 revolution that ousted longtime dictator Porfirio Díaz. More than a million people died in the ensuing civil war. In the aftermath, Mexico faced a collective reckoning with identity. The postrevolutionary government of Álvaro Obregón (1920–1924) ushered in land reform and created greater stability. Yet even economic reforms couldn't unify a diverse and often illiterate population. The newly envisioned country needed symbols.

Enter muralists, the reigning rock stars of the Mexican art renaissance of the 1920s and 1930s. In images on monumental walls, they celebrated workers sweating in steel mills, indigenous women grinding corn, and farmers hauling wheat from the fields. The artists' message to the populace seem to match that of the government supporting their work: Mexico was united after a decade of violence and upheaval.

The reality was more complicated. Between the end of the Obregón administration in 1924 and the Rodríguez project a decade later, funding for murals waxed and waned. Artists wanted to stir public debate about this postrevolutionary world, even at the risk of conflict. The government wanted stability, even at the risk of freedom. The state enlisted the muralists to portray a mythic version of the revolution, hoping to bury the schisms.[4]

They would not stay buried. Divisions played out among the artists. How should they depict "true revolution"? Rivera and Siqueiros's disputes were the most glaring. They had once been friends. In 1920s Paris, they'd joined the café crowds to debate the future of Mexican art. Before long, their visions of art and politics splintered. Once a vein opened, the bad blood flowed freely.

Rivera's *The History of Mexico* and other murals aligned more closely with the government focus on revolutionary success. Some younger artists scorned this vision. They embraced Siqueiros's belief that art should reveal ongoing conflict and inequality, rousing the populace to create art collectively.[5]

Siqueiros was not Rivera's only adversary. According to art critic Anita Brenner, the Mexican press so often prefaced Rivera's name with *discutido*—disputed, discussed—that it was practically a title.[6] The other muralists resented that he alone continued to receive commissions when the government cut support for the arts, though he sometimes worked without pay. In the United States and much of Mexico, he was the best-known muralist, his mastery of fresco widely acknowledged.

Art, power relations, and cultural heritage—passionate debate on these issues fueled social life in the emerging Mexican state. The Greenwood sisters' radical politics were newly minted. Where should they stand?

The project delays dragged on. Marion put aside political questions to create sketches on the government's suggested mural themes of nutrition and food distribution. She roamed the streets near the market and in the Jamaica Terminal. Men and women balanced birdcages or baskets of produce, maneuvering around cars and cattle. Milkmen carried wooden beams on their shoulders, a half dozen bottles suspended from each side. Mexico City was alive with great material, if only she could start painting walls.

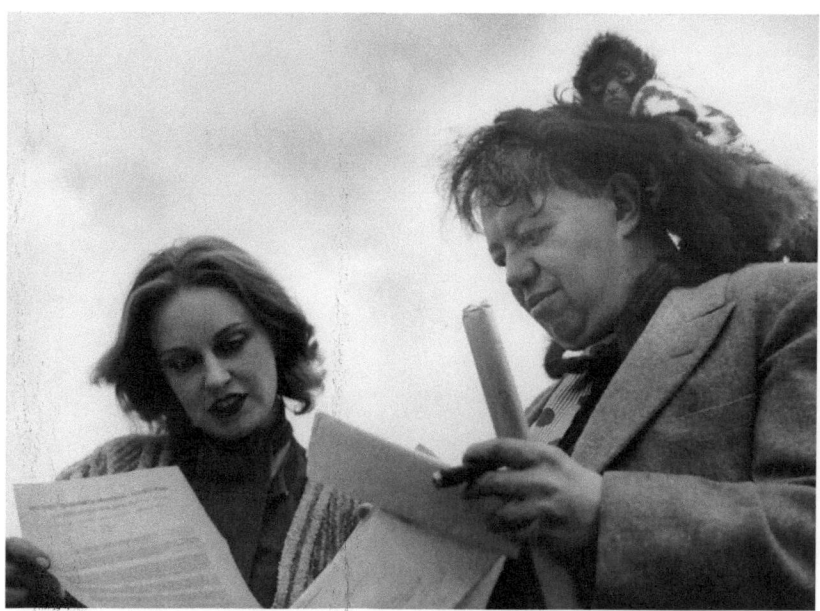

FIGURE 1.1. Marion Greenwood and Diego Rivera, circa 1936. (Photograph courtesy of L.D. Kirshenbaum, Alfred Honigbaum Archive, Kirshenbaum Family Collection.)

By December 1934, Marion was out of money and desperate. She wrote to Josie that one bright spot in her life was the arrival of two cats, a big girl and a little girl "who walked in one day . . . they love each other very much because they've only got each other to love." "Animals," she wrote, "are very comforting. Human beings are nerve-[w]racking."[7]

Was Diego Rivera one of the "nerve-wracking" humans? Marion had been visiting him on the scaffold at the National Palace, where he was painting "like a hungry woman before a meal she couldn't eat." She believed that as project artistic director, he could speed up the process. He was, she wrote, "very 'sweet' to me and said if the situation becomes too difficult, to remember he's always my friend." Marion sought Rivera's help, sure he could appeal to the head of the market. "He promised me he would do this."[8] Written documentation of their evolving relationship, if it exists, might not reveal as much as the photos.

In one shot, Marion's head rests on Diego's shoulder, their arms linked. He wears a polka dot tie and jacket. Missing are the usual overalls, sombrero, and legendary pistol. A monkey perches above his left shoulder. Marion's hair is swept back, and she wears a striped sweater, neck scarf, and dark lipstick. Their

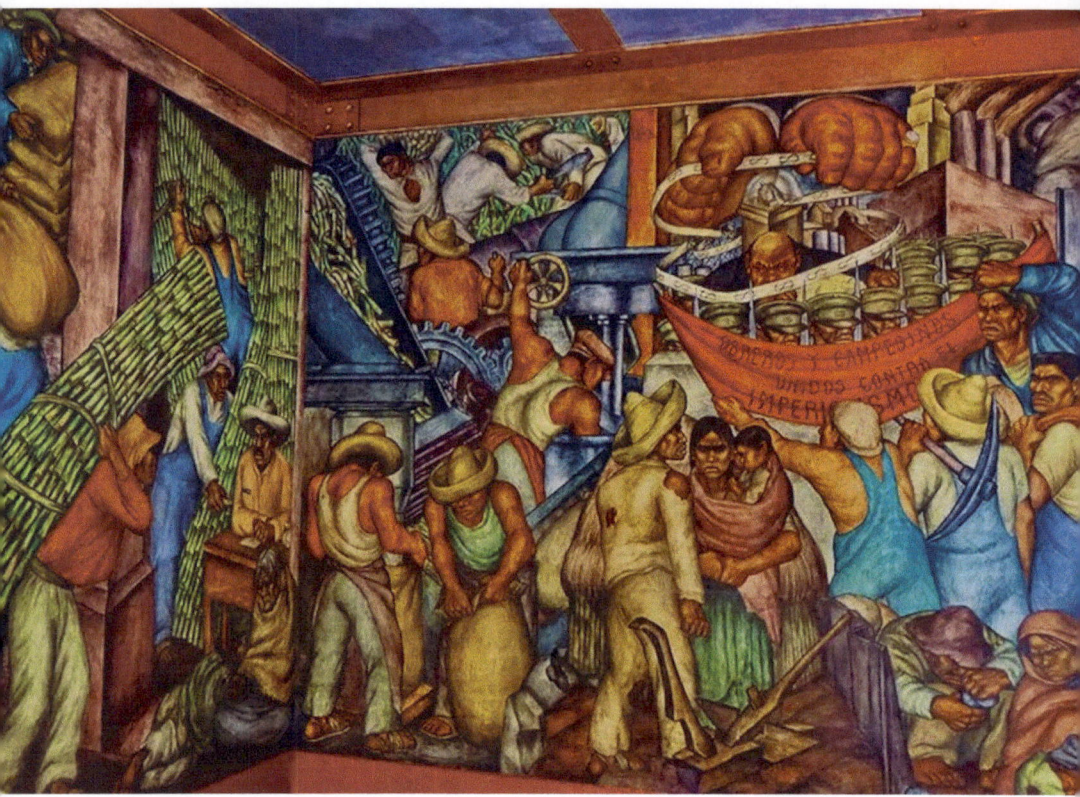

FIGURE 1.2. *The Industrialization of the Countryside* (detail), by Marion Greenwood, Abelardo L. Rodríguez Market, Mexico City, 1935. (Photograph by Joanne B. Mulcahy.)

smiles are wistful. In the next image, Marion's upturned face is hidden by her kiss with Diego. Another more serious photo shows them surveying a sheaf of papers, including a letter from the Guggenheim Foundation addressed to Diego. It may have been related to Marion's application for funding.[9]

In a silent film clip from the same encounter, Marion lights a cigarette, talking in animated fashion until something Diego says convulses her with laughter. When she throws back her head, the joyful spirit her friends described bursts from the screen.[10] Marion's encounters with Diego reveal both her joie de vivre and her ambition. She once told her mother she had learned to deal with all kinds of people to get where she wanted to be. By the winter of 1935, she wanted to be painting walls in the Rodríguez Market.

Whether or not Rivera influenced decisions, by February the political freeze had thawed. On a bright winter day, the sisters ascended the scaffold. At over 7,300 feet, Mexico City's unheated buildings deepen winter's chill. Marion layered wool shirts under overalls as she and Grace began separate murals on adjacent walls. The scaffold was high and rickety enough that rushing up and down posed risks. They couldn't descend every time they needed a bathroom so they used a can, asking their male comrades to turn their backs. Undoing overalls on a frigid day, hoping to hit the can—such was the life of a woman muralist. Yet the Greenwoods were thrilled to be on the scaffold, a place forbidden to women when the Renaissance painters the sisters so admired created their magnificent frescoes.[11]

Marion started painting in the market foyer, drawing workers unloading sugarcane, lettuce, and other produce. The mural proceeds up a wide stairway to the second-story landing. The brilliant color and density of the scene create the feeling of standing in the center of a Mexican market. Then the pastoral vision shifts. During the project, Marion and the other artists departed from food-oriented themes to political critique. Below a balding "fat cat," farmers, fishermen, and steelworkers raise a red banner of resistance. Above him, two giant fists hold ticker tape adorned with dollar signs, a recurrent symbol of capitalism.[12]

The mural then took an international turn. Marion linked Mexico's social unrest during the Depression to the rise of fascism with images of soldiers, tanks, and a Nazi flag. The composition, complexity, and sheer number of figures on the staircase and walls dizzy the viewer. In a final image that tied her wall to Grace's, Marion painted a worker and a campesino holding up a banner with the classic call: "Workers of the World Unite."[13]

Praise for the Rodríguez Market murals poured in. That a group of artists created such extraordinary work in the face of volatile political change, artistic infighting, and the economic devastation of the Depression remains a stunning achievement. The Greenwood sisters broke new ground as women and foreigners. Rivera called them "the greatest living women mural painters."[14] Art historian James Oles described Marion's frescoes as among "the most successfully resolved and visually complex murals ever completed by an American artist."[15] Her place in the limelight grew and brightened.

The Rodríguez Market experience strengthened Marion's political commitment as well as her artistic reputation. She was proud of her murals as vital revolutionary propaganda. The local response heartened her. She noted, "I was liked and appreciated, and my frescoes and my sister's were wonderfully received by the Mexican people. You know, students and professors and everybody would come watch and talk and especially the Indians."[16]

Friends encouraged Marion to stay in Mexico City to work on future mural projects. She surely would have gained commissions, but a profound sense of isolation had seized her. She wrote to Josie: "I'm glad of what I've accomplished but I'm very unhappy and incomplete and lonely here in Mexico. I could never feel part of it."[17] Throughout her life, Marion would travel to other countries for inspiration yet remain anguished by her outsider status. The tension between longing to transcend her own culture and aching to belong took root in Mexico.

Brooding over next steps, Marion visited Orozco. She considered him "a philosopher-artist which I think is one of the greatest kinds of artists one can be."[18] When Marion presented her dilemma, he advised her to head north. He might have intuited that she was not committed to the kind of transformation O'Higgins had made in "going Mexican."

The Federal Art Project also drew Marion back. In Álvarez Bravo's photo where she gazes into the distance, she may have glimpsed herself on a New York City scaffold. She longed to transfer her revolutionary zeal to images of the poor and oppressed at home. The food lines in Depression-era New York and her family's cramped home in Brooklyn would not deter her commitment. The struggle, she wrote to Josie, "is greater and nearer to me in the states."[19]

Josie wrote numerous articles celebrating Marion's work. She described the murals as touched by a unique sensitivity. Although Marion was an outsider and a city dweller, bred "on jazz music and electric lights along Broadway," she bore witness to Mexican life "not as a tourist, or as a critical foreigner, but as an acute observer." Josie compared Marion with another Brooklynite embraced by Mexicans, Walt Whitman. Like the poet, Marion celebrated a broad range of human experience. As Josie wrote, "Her nature and intuition make the understanding of oppressed races come as naturally as breathing."[20]

Josie had long implored Marion to return north: "I want to see you do one of the thousand things that are here to be done—it is exciting here—this is your country, and whether you are conscious of it or not, your roots are here."[21] Those words now fired Marion's imagination. Soon after descending from the scaffold in Mexico City, she was en route back to her family's home—a source of both comfort and dread.

CHAPTER 2

The Real Bohemians

"THE GREENWOODS ARE ALL A BIT MAD," DECLARED MARION'S LONG-TERM partner, Robert (Bob) Plate.[1] Many of her friends and lovers agreed. They found the family exasperating and sometimes destructive to Marion. Although she deplored their demands, Marion remained forever bound to her clan of eight.

Whether or not the Greenwoods were mad, one fact is beyond dispute: they were crazy for art. Few other families in Brooklyn's working-class enclave of Sheepshead Bay harbored artists and would-be artists. Elaine de Kooning, another exception who grew up there, called the largely immigrant neighborhood "a cultural backwater."[2] But within the bohemian Greenwood household, art and culture were life's core. Marion once described their Brooklyn home as an art gallery. Her mother declared that the family lacked even one normal child. For her, abnormality was clearly the preferred state.

Little formal documentation of the Greenwoods' early years exists. Yet with shards from archives, diaries, letters, and cracked photographs, we can imagine scenes from daily life. Picture the Greenwood dinner table circa 1915. "Papa" eyes his fishing rod—an instrument of escape from the din. His loquacious wife, nicknamed Musy, reads her Theosophy-inspired poetry. The eldest son, Walter, describes dance moves for his role in a Broadway production. Irwin wonders at the mysteries of the stars and planets. Charming Lester sips juice, still innocent of the alcohol that will be his downfall. Raymond, the last boy, takes it all in with wide-eyed wonder. The girls, Grace and the "baby" Marion, observe from the edge of the table.

Marion Kathryn Greenwood was born on April 6, 1909, in a booming Brooklyn. The 1890 census records nine hundred thousand people, making it the country's fourth-largest city before joining New York City eight years later. Electric lights hadn't yet replaced gas lamps lit by workers with flaming wicks that created a romantic glow. Horse-drawn trolleys and carriages filled the streets. They competed with recently arrived Yellow cabs and Model Ts. The clip-clop of horses' hooves might wake a family to the milkman making rounds. The metallic clicks of buggy wheels announced rolling shops that sold fruits and vegetables. Trolley and car horns blended into a background cacophony. Neighborhoods were changing from rural to urban through tax dollars for new bridges, subways, and elevated trains. Still, nearly a decade after Marion's birth, half the land in Sheepshead Bay had no sewers. Gas lamps might have softened that visual reality, if not the stench.

The Greenwood family's passion for water matched their devotion to art. They swam in the bay or nearby Brighton Beach and made canoeing expeditions to Rockaway in Queens. A fashionable set from Manhattan flocked to nearby beaches to swim or fish. Horse and later auto racing drew additional tourists. The venerable waterside restaurant, the Tappan House, was *the* place to dine during those years.

The Greenwoods, though, couldn't afford to eat there. Their artistic aspirations were middle class; their economic reality was not. Like many of Brooklyn's working families, they struggled. "Given the borough's economic profile," wrote one native son, "it was hardly possible for most Brooklynites to marry *beneath* their station, unless you meant the one on the el."[3]

Walter Sr., Papa, was born in 1871 in Brooklyn to a family with New England roots. He painted houses to support the children who arrived in quick succession within two decades of his marriage to Musy on March 24, 1891. According to his daughter Grace, he was a fine painter but financial pressure crushed his artistic goals. Those aspirations had likely been encouraged by his mother. Caroline Henshaw Greenwood was a self-taught landscape artist in the Hudson River style, and her work was known to other artists if not the public.[4]

In voluminous letters Marion later wrote to her mother, she sometimes added "give my love to Papa." Otherwise she rarely mentioned him. Years later when she departed for Mexico, she told her traveling companions that she didn't seek his advice or permission because he never approved of her choices.[5]

In contrast, Marion was tightly bound to her mother. Kathryn C. Boylan, "Musy," was born in New York to Irish parents in 1875 or thereabouts; census figures vary.[6] To Marion she passed on her large, deep-set eyes, aquiline nose, and Irish spirit. Marion once advised her mother to resolve a conflict by fighting back: "Remember girl your [*sic*] Irish and your baby's Irish too."[7] As an adult, Marion wrote to her mother nearly every day from far-flung places, often addressing her as "the love of my life." Her sign off was "Baby" or "Your golden heart."

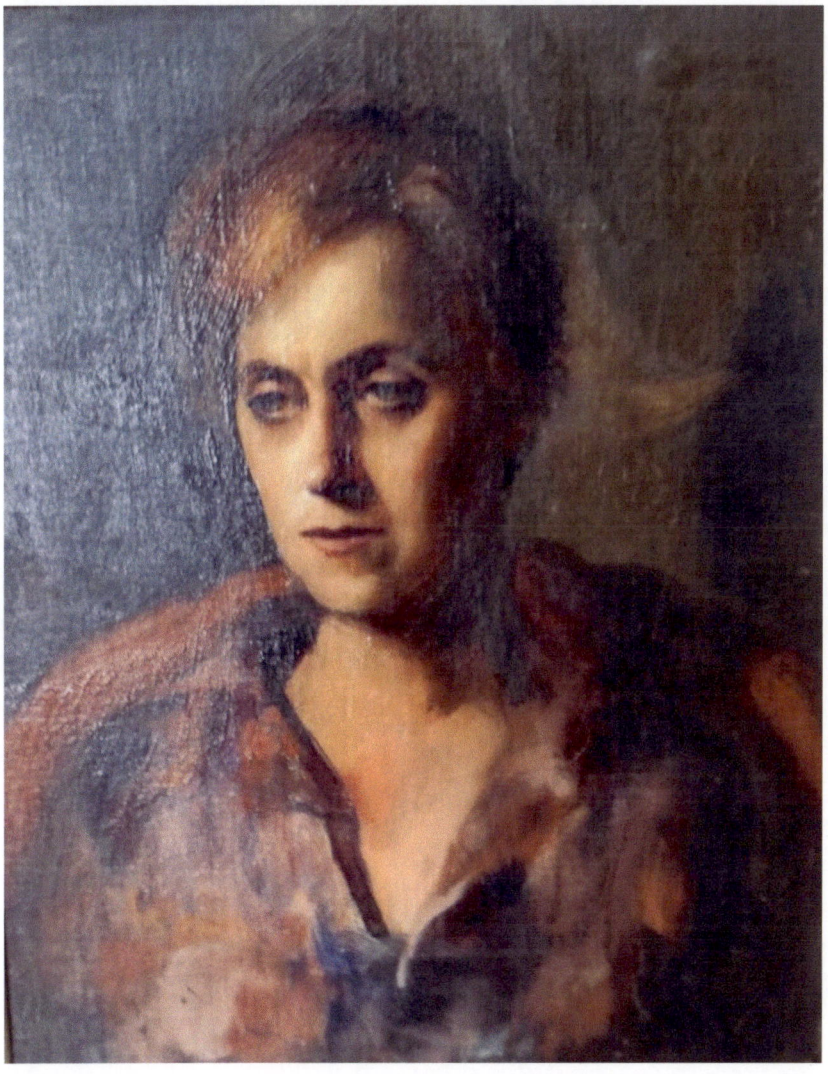

FIGURE 2.1. Portrait of Katherine Boylan Greenwood ("Musy"), by Marion Greenwood. (Photograph © and courtesy of the estate of Marion Greenwood.)

In a photo of Marion and Musy on the beach, they lean against a craggy rock in identical 1920s bathing costumes of shorts and scoop-necked tunics. Beneath the dark cotton, the bodies speak. Marion, short hair bobbed, long legs crossed, smiles coquettishly. Her mother's gray ponytail is long and tangled, her half-smile reluctant, her substantial legs covered by stockings that extend up the thigh. She wraps her right arm around Marion's waist, locking them together. Their love was mutual, intense, and complicated. Musy constantly pulled on Marion for emotional and financial support while "the baby" often bemoaned how trapped she felt.

Musy consistently shaved several years off her age. Maybe she hoped that exaggerating her youth would make her a "New Woman"—an umbrella term for the modernist sisterhood that included Emma Goldman, Margaret Sanger, and Ida B. Wells, who added the fight against racism to her agenda. A New Woman fought for the vote, workers' rights, and autonomy for women.

Tied to all those movements was one essential for Musy: spiritualism. Seances, tarot cards, and communing with spirits flourished in the nineteenth and early twentieth centuries. Women's "mind-cure" spiritualist treatments appeared in mainstream magazines like *Good Housekeeping* and *Ladies Home Journal*.[8] But the movement's importance for women was more than fluff. Marrying the spiritual and political was a savvy move. A powerful woman on the podium promoting birth control and voting rights threatened the status quo, but no one blinked when the spirits directed her to do so.

Having rejected her Catholic upbringing, Musy delved into Christian Science, yogic thought and practice, and astrology. Picture Marion's family clustered about Musy's astrological charts or the mainstream craze of Ouija boards. On May 1, 1920, a Norman Rockwell cover of the *Saturday Evening Post* features a woman in a lace-collared dress glancing up to the heavens as her male partner plies the board with questions. For those who'd lost loved ones in World War I, the spiritual quest was serious.

Musy was especially devoted to Theosophy. In New York City in 1875, Russian immigrant Madame Blavatsky established the Theosophical Society, combining Eastern religions and Western esotericism. Theosophists sought universal human connection, including equality for women. Rapid industrialization had shaken the social and political foundations of the West, leaving many people in search of meaning. Who better than artists to point the way to new paradigms? Realism failed to evoke a higher reality, and Theosophy attracted abstract artists whose colors, lines, and geometric forms reached beyond the material world. The movement influenced Wassily Kandinsky, Piet Mondrian, and many other artists whose paths would cross Marion's.

On Sundays, Musy took her daughters to local hotels to hear Theosophist speakers. She liked to mix her spirits, heading from lectures to local taverns. While she nursed a beer, men crowded around her daughters, especially the dazzler, Marion. She learned early that beauty was a source of power. Who could blame her or other women for exploiting their assets? Any woman born in the early twentieth century, with doors slammed shut to their aspirations, would use whatever resources they had. Musy's frustrated ambitions sent a message to her daughters: harness your power to fight for a place in a world ruled by men.

Along with spiritual pursuits, Musy wrote melancholic poetry. She took her writing seriously enough to join the Writer's Club of Brooklyn. She dedicated "The Dance of the Hours" to "Sweetsie," one of her nicknames for Marion. "Do you remember the music? / how it held us—and we got / lost in the beauty of it. . . . There are hours we love / and hours we hate / . . . We awake—and find we are / imprisoned in bodies. / For bodies are little houses holding us."[9] She often signed her poems "Kay Cecille," forging an identity apart from her children's demands.

Perhaps all mothers create a secret self, every child a distinct family history. Stories splinter through a kaleidoscope in patterns that shift with the teller and over time. Sometimes, the best we have are competing portraits.

Such is the case for the oldest son, Walter Frederick, born in 1891 a few months after Walter Sr. married the pregnant Musy. One version of the youthful Wally comes from photos Grace saved.[10] Here he is as a handsome young actor in the chorus of a Broadway musical. Dashing in a billowy white shirt, black tie, pants, and cummerbund, he smiles at his dance partner, who, tutu-clad and poised on toe shoes, gazes up at him. The duo brims with youthful promise. At eighteen, Walter lived at home and clerked in a shoe store, likely to support his acting. He later worked for a printer, Sidney Hollaender. In 1913, he married Lenora Frances Dressel, who died in 1928 at age thirty-five. In letters to Musy, Marion later referenced another partner, Ruth. Wally was successful enough by the 1920s to have a summer home in Pennsylvania that Marion often visited when she was young.

Here's a clashing version of Walter: "He dressed in a way befitting a prosperous undertaker," wrote Robert Plate, who knew him as an adult. "He loved flowers, hated people, wrote letters expressing hopes that a hurricane menacing New York City 'would wipe out a lot of the vermin.'"[11] He did not mean rats.

He signed his letters to Marion formally with "Walter J. Greenwood." Marion seconded Plate's portrait of her adult brother, describing him as a perennially unhappy soul. This image of the grown-up Walter so differs from the promising young actor that he, too, seems mired in his parents' world of unrealized dreams.

Irwin came next, a successful commercial artist who did designs for ad agencies. His accomplished landscape paintings—magnificent, according to one friend—still sell at auction. He, too, may have hoped for a career in fine art. Yet he joined other family members in pressuring Marion to use her budding talent in the commercial realm. Irwin's other contributions, according to Plate, were his enthusiastic and eccentric lectures. His bellicose voice would suddenly proclaim the cosmic awe he glimpsed more clearly after a few drinks. "Forces, forces, mind you . . . mysterious, unknown. We're not even worms! This earth isn't even a grain of sand!"[12] His marriage to Ruth Allen from Woodstock launched the family's part-time life in the thriving arts colony. They later separated, and Irwin's second wife, Jessica, was a stabilizing force who helped him support the Greenwoods.

The next brother, Lester, was Marion's favorite—handsome and charming. He served in Europe during World War I, then became a commercial artist successful enough to support his wife, Marie, and three children, Robert, Peter, and Suanne. The little girl, about eight at the time, disappeared during a family vacation in Florida. She was never found.[13] Whether scarred by his daughter's disappearance or the war, he found solace in alcohol. His frequent trips to Bellevue Hospital to dry out came at great emotional and economic cost to him and his family.

Another tragedy afflicted the Greenwoods in 1916, when the last son, Raymond, died at the age of seventeen. The cause is unclear, but his death left Musy in a state of permanent lament. Her poems abound with grief, nostalgia, and longing. In "Separation," she wrote directly to Raymond: "The night you went away / The stars blurred out. / And then the angels spread / Their wings across a vault of blue. / And every sense turned cold / Because I could not go with you."[14]

According to Plate, Musy used the tragedy to "establish dominion over her children by instilling a sense of guilt."[15] They felt responsible for their mother's frequent weeping and despair at having her wild poetic spirit trampled. Musy perfectly embodied Yeats's quote: "Being Irish, he had an abiding sense of tragedy, which sustained him through temporary periods of joy." She would have been a model 1960s hippie, Plate believed. Instead, she struggled, face pressed against the glass of promised opportunities for the New Woman. She never cracked open that window. Instead, she passed her hopes on to her daughters.

Grace was the next child, seven years older than Marion, delivered by a Christian Science practitioner. She was a lovely, dark-haired girl with a slight limp left from a childhood bout with polio. That didn't hold her back from successful artistic pursuits, frequent travels, numerous love affairs, and multiple marriages.

The sisters were close early in life. Imagine them at the beach together as children, then on the streets of Manhattan when both studied at the Art Students League, later still working side by side on scaffolds in Mexico City. Both would earn praise for their Mexican frescoes as well as their New Deal murals. However, Grace's feelings toward Marion grew complicated with age. Her love mixed with resentment, perhaps because she bloomed late and never achieved Marion's level of recognition.

Grace also suffered from mental health problems. As an adult, she paid for psychiatric treatment in New York with paintings. Her friend Irene Sirugo, wife of abstract painter Sal Sirugo, recalls Grace as sometimes difficult and irrational. Yet she also had "glorious" traits, including "a childlike sense of wonder" and enormous generosity. Once, after winning a $100 art prize, she insisted on taking the Sirugos and their daughter, Carol, out to dinner. The family knew that money wouldn't go far in Woodstock. They convinced her to take them to McDonalds, where Grace raved about the food. "Grace, at her best, always talked in superlatives."[16] Her enthusiasm was contagious.

When Grace was in Mexico in 1935, Musy sent her advice based on her astrological chart. Grace must overcome Saturn's influence, she wrote, to awaken her "great powers and talent."[17] Musy loved her "little wren," but Grace seemed a pale bird against Marion's bright plumage.

Perhaps the seeds for division were planted with Marion's birth, the beloved baby displacing Grace as the only girl. A dreamy child, Marion loved dogs and cats, fairy tales, and making images. She began sketching before she was six, already sure of her future. Her school reportedly solicited her work to illustrate their pamphlets and newspapers.[18]

At age nine, Marion's first portrait featured Cleopatra preparing her suicide. This might seem an odd choice for a child, particularly for a person often described as intensely alive. A friend, artist Gladys Brodsky, characterized her as "a force of nature."[19] However, the portrait subject was not surprising for someone resolved to direct her own fate. Painting the exotic Cleopatra in faraway Egypt—Marion might have seen Theda Bara's kohl-lined eyes and shimmering costumes in the 1917 silent film—reveals her early longing for worlds far from Sheepshead Bay.

Marion also echoed Musy's spiritualist leanings. Not quite as ardent as her mother, she nursed various beliefs throughout her life. She told a 1961 interviewer that Asian philosophy, together with studies of Buddhism and Christianity, helped her to "attain an intangible feeling attuned to the rhythm of life."[20]

Among Marion's papers is the obituary of Annie Besant, a prominent Theosophist and a champion of women's rights. Alongside it rests a booklet in which Theosophy philosopher Jiddu Krishnamurti echoed Besant's call to transcend the self: "Those who seek the path of pure understanding are not drawn away . . . by the multitude of desires."[21]

Herein lies one of the many contradictions in Marion's life: while seeking enlightenment, she dove headfirst into "the multitude of desires." Her partner, Bob Plate, described her this way: "Always with strong appetite for life, Marion ate too much, drank too much, even worked too much, and loved too much."[22] "Loving too much" is open to interpretation, but, clearly, men pursued Marion. However, her beauty was sometimes a handicap, Gladys Brodsky said. The nine-year-old Marion painting Cleopatra preparing to die might have intuited that beauty is a duplicitous tool.

If Marion worked too much, passion and family expectation drove her. She often cited the legacy of her painter grandmother Caroline, the strivings of her father, and the artistry of her brothers and sister Grace. Her family presumed she would make a living as an artist. Since women artists today still don't have the same recognition or economic heft as male artists, what drove such an assumption in the 1920s and 1930s? Marion had rejected her brothers' path into commercial art, so how could she proceed? Through diligence and hard work. Pain would reap rewards for the committed artist. The Greenwood gospel affirmed that creative people rest at the pinnacle of human achievement. In this they were united.

So the family soldiered on, painting, writing poetry, acting in plays, cavorting on the beach. Neighbors in Sheepshead Bay may have considered them eccentric or bohemian. Yet the Greenwood sisters rejected that label, railing against Greenwich Village artist wannabes. Those so-called bohemians were layabouts who drank in the ambiance of art and culture but created nothing. To signal that stance, the sisters wore overalls and ate sandwiches like workers on the job.

In fact, Marion's life reveals that artists slaving in a studio are the *real* bohemians. The identity born of the early-nineteenth-century romantic movement seeped into New York in the early twentieth century. Brimming with contradiction, the bohemian was "both a genius and a phoney, a debauchee and a puritan, a workaholic and a wastrel, his identity always dependent on its opposite."[23] If faux artists could claim the title, Marion renounced it. Yet she would perfectly realize the bohemian's heady mixture of "art, hedonism, and dissent from bourgeois life."

That artists would be poor was preordained by the "bohemian plot."[24] Creators live for art, unfettered from the maw of the capitalist machine. It was a belief that Marion would pursue, sometimes at great cost, for the rest of her life.

CHAPTER 3

The Art Students League and the Woodstock Colony

IN 1906, ANTHONY COMSTOCK, SECRETARY OF THE NEW YORK SOCIETY for the Suppression of Vice, raced toward Fifty-Seventh Street between Broadway and Seventh Avenue. Flanked by police, he headed for the top floor of a landmark French Renaissance–style building. Like a hound sniffing for prey, he followed the scent of paint. Amid the easels and sketchpads in the Art Students League, he found his target: reproductions of nudes. The school's catalog and magazine had likely landed in one of Comstock's notorious bonfires. The students soon had their revenge. An effigy of Comstock hung from the League's third floor, with their mutton-chopped, balding adversary described as a "sexless clown who shunned love's hallowed fire."[1]

The Comstock effigy was typical of the League's feisty students. In 1924, at age fifteen, Marion left Erasmus Hall High School in Brooklyn to join their rebellious ranks. Her decision likely surprised no one. She was already considered a prodigy. Public high school failed to stoke her intellectual curiosity or satisfy her artistic drive.

The League's motto was and remains "Nulla Dies Sine Linea"—"No Day Without a Line." In 1875, artists mutinied against the conservative National Academy of Design to establish the League. Like a European atelier, the school's teachers worked independently with no set curriculum. One of the ASL's signature strengths was and continues to be a focus on the human figure. Study from live nude models would, much to Comstock's dismay, continue to thrive. At this progressive art school, Marion found a home.

And what a home it was! Artists who studied and/or taught at the League through its long history form a who's who of American art, representing varied styles and movements. These include realists like Thomas Hart Benton and Norman Rockwell but also abstract expressionists Jackson Pollock and Helen Frankenthaler and modernists Stuart Davis and Georgia O'Keeffe, among others.

The school had no entrance requirements or grades. From the beginning, any man or woman "whose characters were approved of" could enroll in classes in drawing, painting, sculpture, and graphic arts.[2] Passion and commitment were the driving forces. Marion had an abundance of both.

She made the crosstown journey from Sheepshead Bay to the League several days a week between 1924 and 1928. If her brother Wally were headed to Broadway, they might have departed together. More likely, the adolescent Marion journeyed alone from her home on East Twenty-Seventh Street, sketchpad in hand. After walking to the Brighton line, she would cross the East River via the Manhattan Bridge and change trains to get to the school at 215 W. Fifty-Seventh Street. The roughly fifty-five-minute journey carried her into a cauldron of human energy and possibility. On the street, Marion always turned heads. Now she shifted from observed to observer. What she witnessed laid a foundation for her lifelong passions and choice of subjects.

The sheer diversity of New York City was stunning. The population exploded between 1910 and 1930 with arrivals from throughout the globe and the American South. Rapid industrialization drew immigrants to manufacturing, railroads, construction work, and the garment world. Russian Jews escaping pogroms sold herring from pushcarts on Hester Street while their intellectual brethren published Yiddish newspapers. Italian families socialized on stoops in the hot summer air. African American families moved from the Tenderloin to Harlem. Greenwich Village brimmed with bohemians hawking radical newspapers.

Equally remarkable was the city's range of diversions. After classes, Marion could choose from movies, jazz clubs, and bars. If prohibition was a joke in many cities, in New York it was absurd. Puritan John Winthrop's famous "city upon a hill" transformed in local parlance to "city upon a still." Comstock's vice-free fantasy couldn't keep New Yorkers down. Those who had survived the Great War rallied to celebrate.

Alongside all that pleasure seeking were scenes that piqued Marion's social consciousness. Strikers in picket lines clamored for an eight-hour workday and an end to child labor, meagre pay, and often life-threatening working conditions. As president, Woodrow Wilson initially oversaw progressive era reforms but soon launched a full-scale attack on workers, immigrants, and people of color. The same anti-immigrant, anti-labor stance marked Calvin Coolidge's presidency. Workers, supported by the radical intelligentsia in Greenwich Village, fought back.

Marion may have stopped there to visit her sister, Grace, on West Eleventh Street. Nearby was the site of one of the most cataclysmic events in US labor history. In 1911, fire swept the Triangle Shirtwaist Factory. Despite previous warnings, the owners had taken no safety precautions. Trapped workers, mainly immigrant women between the ages of sixteen and twenty-three, fled to fire escapes to find them locked. New Yorkers watched panicked workers leap from ninth-story windows. Their charred remains on the street fueled outrage and a growing union movement.

Workers' rights met feminist causes in women carrying placards demanding the vote and reproductive autonomy. Lack of birth control had thwarted Marion's mother, who married as a pregnant teenager. Musy might have wished she'd read Emma Goldman's cautionary note: "Dante's motto over Inferno applies with equal force to marriage: 'Ye who enter here leave all hope behind.'"[3] It was too late for Musy, but the young Marion rejected the bourgeois link of romance to marriage. She would not be forced into a union as her parents had been.

Musy's spiritualism offered personal, not social, empowerment. The spirits proved no match for the legal ban on birth control. Hanging Comstock in effigy at the League didn't trounce the ace he held: the 1873 federal Comstock Act. Contraception was deemed filthy and immoral. Sending "obscene" material related to abortion or birth control through the US mail could lead to five years of hard labor. As a fifteen-year-old making her way to the Art Students League, Marion didn't yet know how Comstock's ban would create nearly fatal consequences for her within a few years.

Marion admired writer, activist, and birth control pioneer Margaret Sanger and her painter/architect husband, William. With a nod to the artist-activist Sangers, Marion once called her own clan a "sort of Sanger family."[4] She might have seen Margaret's writing on birth control, "What Every Girl Should Know," in the *New York Call*. Comstock had the column banned, but the progressive community rallied to her defense. Sanger's combination of "bohemian slouch, feminist eros, and Wobbly sabotage" offered Marion a powerful model.[5]

One wonders what a young artist as driven as Marion would have done had she been born earlier. Before the nineteenth century, many art schools were closed to women. Only rebellious types wandered outside the allowable "feminine arts." Into the twentieth century, decorative and applied arts were more welcoming than the fine art world. At the time of Marion's birth, art had joined nursing and teaching as an acceptable profession for women. By the mid-nineteenth century, the National Academy of Design did admit women, but few art schools brought them to the table as equal creative partners.[6]

From the League's earliest days, women sat at the table. Late nineteenth-century photos show students in ankle-length dresses poised confidently before easels. Many soon ditched their corsets for loose-fitting sheaths and bobbed hair tucked under a cloche cap. Its bell-shaped simplicity rebuked the flowered, feathered excess of wide-brimmed Gainsborough hats. Women studied alongside men, although drawing classes with nude models remained gender segregated until the 1930s. The League's Board of Control always included women; fewer were faculty members.[7] Women's success stories were important to Marion. Friends from her later life described her as bold and outspoken, but at fifteen, she needed role models.

If Marion exemplified new opportunities for a woman artist, she was also unique. Her star shone from the start. In 1924, Marion gained entry on her first try to a class with George B. Bridgman, the legendary teacher of anatomy and figure drawing. To be accepted, candidates had to draw a live model. The first forty applicants came on a Monday, the next forty on a Tuesday, until the list of hopefuls was exhausted.[8]

Bridgman, a "short, stocky, cigar-smoking aesthete who swore liberally," was famously tough.[9] He ranked students' drawings on Friday afternoons, stoking competition for the number one spot. He reportedly awarded Marion the first certificate of excellence he'd given in twenty years and facilitated her scholarships. The school's class fees seem modest now—thirteen to fifteen dollars a class—but they would have stretched the Greenwood family budget. Marion was responsible for the twenty-five-cent locker charge.

In her second year, Marion added a painting class with Frank Vincent Du-Mond. He had attended the League in the 1880s, gone to Paris, and returned to New York to teach at his alma mater. With Bridgman, he helped shape Marion's lifelong focus on the human form.

Along with classical training, the ASL exposed Marion to new art currents. In the early 1900s, the art establishment still looked to Europe. A trustee of the Metropolitan Museum of Art declared in 1909, "There is nothing American worth notice."[10] League artists proved him wrong. Many turned to the streets to depict ordinary people in distinctly American ways. John Sloan was among them.

In 1928–1929, Marion enrolled in a class with Sloan, a member of the Ashcan School. More a loose affiliation than a school, "ashcan" was a tongue-in-cheek reference to the group's unsentimental images of urban life that critics called so many "ash cans." Philadelphia painter Robert Henri is credited with launching this Whitmanesque focus on the grittier side of city life. As art critic Robert Hughes described, "Henri wanted art to be akin to journalism. He wanted paint to be as real as mud, as the clods of horse-shit and snow, that froze on Broadway in the winter, as real a human product as sweat, carrying the unsuppressed smell of human life."[11]

Sloan's paintings met the Ashcan call to depict urban reality. *Sunday, Women Drying Their Hair* shows three women on a rooftop shaking out their tresses. A breeze ruffles freshly laundered clothes on the line behind them. The pleasure in routine is palpable. Sloan painted immigrants, exemplified in the Irish patrons of McSorley's, the famous New York watering hole. In those images, Marion glimpsed her family and Brooklyn neighbors.

The Ashcan artists and Musy's Irish heritage inspired Marion's devotion to "ethnic types." She would become known for her Chinese, Haitian, and Mexican subjects, but a Jewish tailor on the Lower East Side offered equal inspiration. *Little Tailor* portrays a balding man bent over his sewing machine, coke-bottle glasses sliding down his nose, gnarled hands inching the fabric under the needle. In a cramped workspace, he wears a suit and tie, a marker of dignity that Marion saw as essential to portraiture. She labored to find each person's uniqueness. Portraits opened a portal to something luminous beneath the surface.

Marion studied with Sloan for a shorter period than her other instructors. "I wish I had stayed with him longer. He was a wonderful teacher," she later told an interviewer.[12] He was a socialist and onetime art editor of the *Masses*, a magazine embraced by the city's progressives. The publication featured Ashcan artists along with essays by Dorothy Day, Upton Sinclair, and John Reed. Within a decade, Marion would provide illustrations for its successor, *New Masses*.

While Marion sketched models in Bridgman's class, evolving modernist currents swirled around her. "Modernism" includes wide-ranging responses to the vast social changes wrought by industrialization and rejection of nineteenth-century Victorian values. Modern art aimed to break down hierarchies, challenge existing beliefs, and embrace a wide range of styles. The label fit Ashcan artists as well as the newly arrived European avant-garde.

In his 291 Fifth Avenue gallery, photographer Alfred Stieglitz had already featured modernist American artists, such as Arthur Dove and Marsden Hartley, and Europeans Picasso, Matisse, and Cézanne. However, the avant-garde's widely recognized public debut dates to February 17, 1913. The "International Exhibition of Modern Art," better known as The Armory Show, featured European and American artists, including fifty women. The crowds came for the show stealers from abroad. Visitors streamed down Lexington Avenue and East Twenty-Sixth Street on foot and alighted from Model Ts outside the cavernous Armory building. For some attendees, Matisse's *Red Studio* and Marcel Duchamp's *Nude Descending a Staircase, No. 2* signaled the end of the civilized world. For others, civilization had finally arrived. Either way, Cubism joined the vocabulary of artists and viewers in the United States.

By the time Marion arrived at the Art Students League in 1924, experiments in modernism lived alongside more traditional versions. Marion's early portraits were realistic, yet she sought something in each individual that revealed their character. Realism goes beyond mimicry, argues critic Linda Nochlin. It involves "a taste for ordinary experience in a specific time, place, and social context," offering far greater depth than "the passive reflexivity of the mirror image."[13] Realists "re-present" the world in new form.

Art, Marion and many others believed, could transform society and challenge the predominant racism. Like others in her circle, she welcomed the growing and dynamic influence of Black culture. Between 1910 and 1930, approximately 1.6 million African Americans headed north in the Great Migration that would continue for decades. They created groundbreaking work in all genres: jazz, the blues, visual art, and literature. Some of Marion's finest work would portray Black dancers, artists, and Harlem residents engaged in daily life.

While white New Yorkers enjoyed Harlem's cultural richness, Black residents who crossed racial boundaries often suffered consequences. Yet there were places where different racial and cultural groups mixed. The Art Students League admitted a small group of African American as well as international students. Painter and educator Theresa Pollack, whose student years overlapped with Marion's, said that there was "an easy mingling here [in the League lunchroom] of models, students, instructors, and visitors, irrespective of race, sex, creed, or differences in lifestyle."[14]

At fifteen, Marion leaped into this swirl of artistic and cultural crosscurrents. She was hungry to learn and still unformed as an artist. What path would she follow? She loved the natural world, yet she rejected the landscape painting of her grandmother and brothers. "That didn't mean they were bad," she said of her family's work.[15] She later experimented with art deco and other styles; she befriended many Theosophy-inspired abstract artists. Yet she would find her own way, driven by an affinity for diverse human faces and forms. Trust in her own judgment would steady her through the art world's upheaval.

The League's broad education, openness to women, multicultural setting, and location in a rapidly changing city shaped Marion's life as well as her art. By 1928, after nearly four years at the ASL, she was a different New Yorker.

⇉⇇

A little over a hundred miles up the Hudson River, another art scene beckoned. In 1922, Marion's brother Irwin married Woodstock local Ruth Allen. Marion and Musy and assorted siblings began making the journey to the Hudson Valley for the summer.

In early photos of Marion in Woodstock, she revels in bucolic splendor. Here she sits on a craggy outcropping near a creek accompanied by two dogs and an unidentified man. She wears a midriff-baring top, shorts, and a contented smile. In another, she perches on a wide flat rock above a gushing stream, a color palette and paintbrush in hand. Woodstock's watering holes and rivers turned her into a lifelong swimmer. This country idyll became as central to Marion's life as New York City.

Long before its fame as the site of the legendary 1969 festival, the town's majestic setting in the Catskill Mountains drew artists and dreamers. A 1922 travel guide captures the allure: "The seething city's deafening noise / Grows dim and then no more. / The moving palace glides away—a new world lies before."[16] That new world included places like Overlook Mountain House. At 3,150 feet, it offered grand vistas of verdant farmland, shimmering lakes, and the Hudson River—a deep source of artistic inspiration. Woodstock became one of the country's most important art colonies.

It is unlikely the Greenwoods had a car or would have chosen to drive north. Steamy road trips could take up to seven or eight hours. Kids along the route sold pails of water for a dime so travelers could douse themselves or their overheated radiator. More likely, Musy chose a bus or one of the increasingly efficient trains from the city to the West Hurley station. The Hudson River steamers, popular for their scenic views, were another option.

The family seemed born for Woodstock life. The town dated to 1787, but the world the Greenwoods embraced was the "Woodstock Colony" or "The

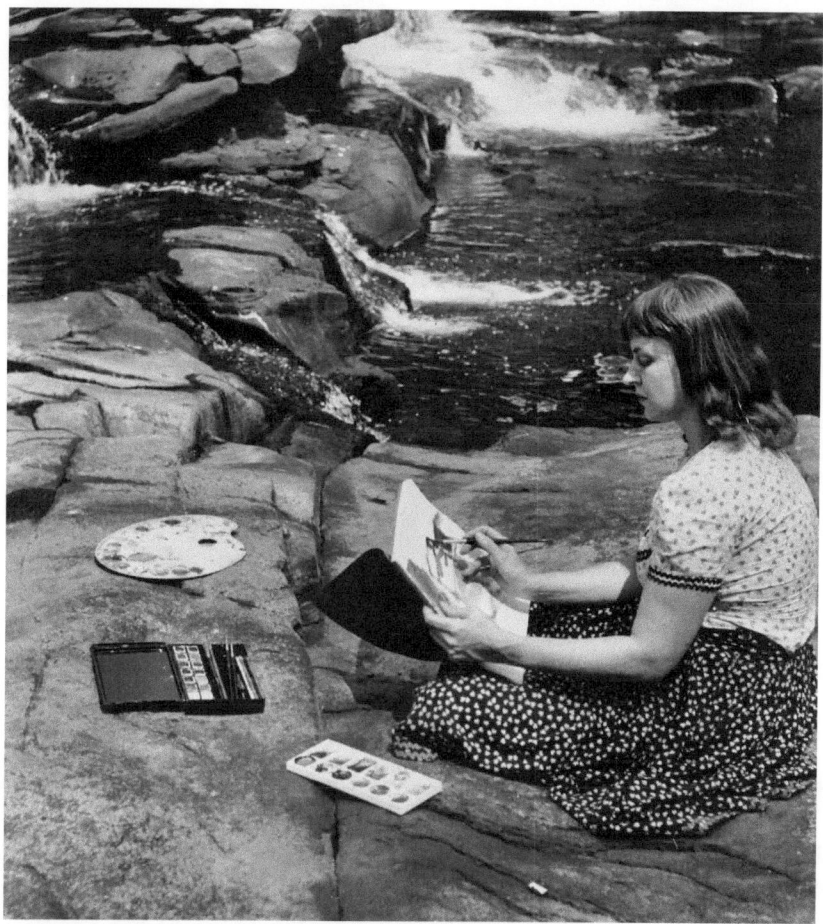

FIGURE 3.1. Marion Greenwood painting near a stream in Woodstock, circa 1926. (Photograph © and courtesy of the estate of Marion Greenwood.)

Village," a gathering of sometimes ragtag but always creative people. Its genesis was Byrdcliffe, a utopian community founded in Woodstock by Ralph Radcliffe Whitehead in 1902. His vision lay in the Arts and Crafts movement's revolt against industrialization and its discontents.

A British dreamer, Whitehead had studied with one of the movement's founders, John Ruskin, who linked social reform, nature, craftsmanship, and morally upstanding citizenry. Whitehead had little affection for the United States until 1890, when he met Philadelphia native Jane Byrd McCall during her European travels. She shared his dream of a utopia devoted to Arts and

Crafts principles. They spread the message to Americans seeking spiritual renewal and political reform, both of which Marion would embrace.

Charlotte Perkins Gilman, author of the feminist classic "The Yellow Wall-Paper," introduced Whitehead and McCall to a young social worker and writer named Hervey White. With tousled hair, scraggly beard, and home-dyed clothes, he embodied the wandering seeker. Bolton Brown, a furniture maker and lithographer, joined them. The group hunted for a rustic site near a population center where they could grow grain and grapes. After several failed West Coast attempts, Brown found a captivating landscape in the mountains outside Woodstock.

There were snags. Whitehead had to overcome his antisemitism, fearing a Jewish influx from nearby resorts.[17] The virulent antisemitism of fin de siècle Europe had bled into the US fear of immigrant "others." Such prejudice would weaken, though not disappear, when important Jewish artists and intellectuals arrived in flight from war in Europe. Whitehead, who was footing the bill, finally agreed on the site. Thirty-five buildings for artists soon filled the side of Mount Overlook.

The art scene that the Greenwoods entered was rich and varied, mixing tradition and innovation. In 1906, the Art Students League established a Woodstock outpost and school of plein air landscape painting. Impressionism's natural light replaced the Hudson River School's gauzy views of nature. The European avant-garde gained a foothold in Woodstock via Konrad Cramer and Andrew Dasburg. Cramer, who immigrated from Germany, forged important links between his natal country and American modernism. The Paris-born Dasburg was an early proponent of Cubism. Both had work exhibited in the Armory show. Traditional painters sometimes clashed with these modernists. However, the Woodstock Artists Association (WAA), established in 1919, nurtured a range of styles.[18]

As soon as Marion's family arrived, she submitted a portfolio to the WAA. Her drawings and paintings likely featured portraits of friends, family, and certainly animals. Cats were her lifelong companions, more reliable than their human counterparts. Her acceptance at age fourteen reputedly made her the youngest person ever admitted to the association.[19]

As Marion found her place in the community, a new artistic ecosystem was evolving. Lithography, a medium Marion would pursue for life, became a central element. Marion studied with German-born artist Emil Ganso, excited by the possibilities of lithographs: "I found out I could scratch with a razor blade and get marvelous effects—almost sculptural effects and wonderful graze with it and rubbing."[20]

Among Marion's Woodstock portraits is a striking sketch of Ganso. He stares at the viewer through wire-rimmed glasses, a cigarette hanging from a mustachioed upper lip. His look is tough but sympathetic. Her Woodstock images echo *Little Tailor* and the Ashcan call to portray the uniqueness of each person.

Marion created mosaics with modernist Ukrainian painter and sculptor Alexander Archipenko. He was one of the first artists, after Picasso, to apply Cubist style to sculpture. Arriving in Woodstock from Paris in 1924, he was already known as an innovator and contributor to the Armory show.

If the Greenwoods' arrow aimed them toward Woodstock's freewheeling, sometimes zany atmosphere, the bull's-eye was the Maverick Art Colony. When the founders of Byrdcliffe split over divergent philosophies, White left to create the Maverick retreat in the woods. Artists lived in primitive houses for ten dollars a month. Each featured water from a nearby well, a fireplace, and an outhouse.

White's contributions to the town's art scene still resonate in the Maverick concert series he established in 1916. More seductive for Marion's family was the outdoor Maverick Festival that ran from 1915 to 1931, formative years in her upbringing. To raise money for a well, White staged a theater performance in a stone quarry. Those without costumes had to pay double, so attendees gleefully donned peasant smocks and pirate gear. Dressed as Pan, a leafy wreath on his unruly hair, White joined locals to roast hotdogs on makeshift campfires.[21] Held on the night of an August full moon, the party hosted circus performers and characters out of Arabian Nights. The Greenwoods flourished amid the riotous, often drunken, and endlessly creative scene.

Photos from the Maverick archives showcase an evolving cast of art world characters Marion came to know. Ashcan-affiliated painter George Bellows wears a drooping fake mustache and sailor's outfit standing among a group of children in Dutch costumes. Peggy Bacon, known for her humorous drawings and caricatures, sports a headdress with elaborate pom-poms and dripping jewelry. A handsome, androgynous Alexander Archipenko is disguised by a long wig and mustache, his shirt open to the waist as he raises a glass.

In a festival photo, Marion cavorts in a wooded glen with her sister, Grace, and a group of unidentified friends. Marion laughs with the kind of effervescence her friends described. Her patterned bolero pants are slit to the thigh, topped by a satiny top. Grace wears a turban, a black strapless top, and black

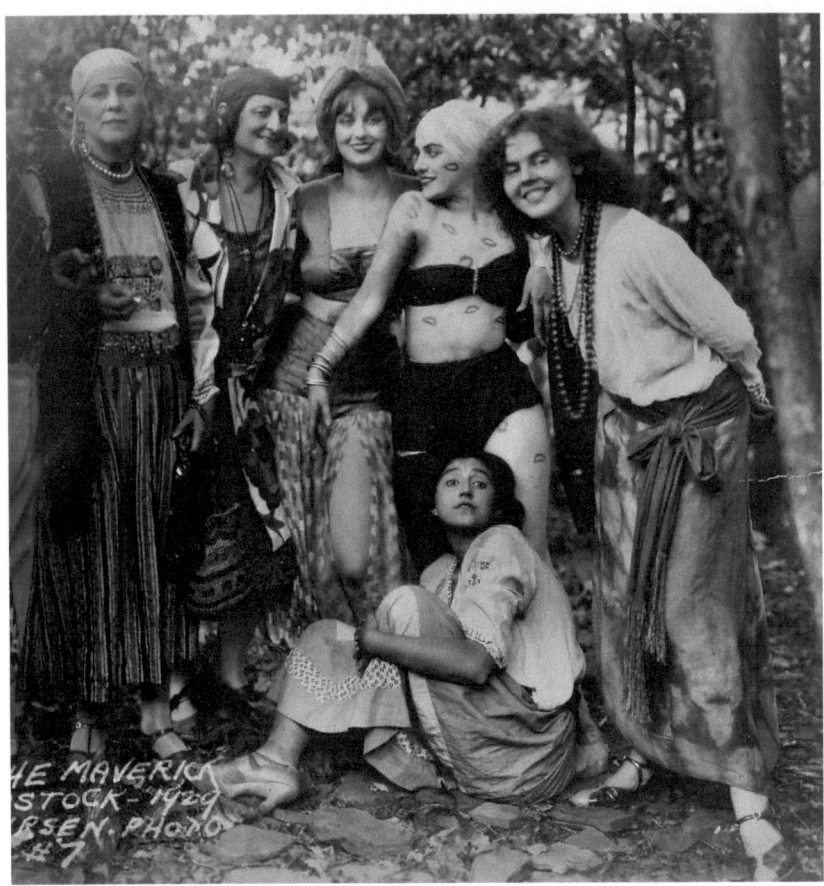

FIGURE 3.2. Marion Greenwood (center) with Grace Greenwood (to her right) and unidentified friends at Woodstock's Maverick Festival, 1929. (Photograph courtesy of the Center for Photography at Woodstock.)

pants, her exposed midriff full of lipstick kisses. In one of the archival photos, Marion is identified as "the beautiful woman on the left," while Grace is described as "Marion's sister . . . also a painter." A note on the back quotes Musy: "Marion isn't a bad girl, she just gets lonely at night."[22]

Musy's comment begs interpretation. Did the mother who could not harness the sexual freedom of the New Woman encourage her daughters to do so? However we read Musy's words, Marion the budding sensualist clearly joined the fray with gusto. Comstock be damned.

Marion came of age in the two "villages," Woodstock and Greenwich. When not traveling, she would move between these two sites throughout her life. The city's clamor for social change and feminist revolt kindled her social consciousness while Woodstock offered natural beauty and madcap revelry. In both settings, teachers of painting, drawing, and printmaking shaped her work. It's easy to imagine why those mentors celebrated and encouraged a student so charismatic and prodigiously talented. George Bridgman's belief in Marion proved formative. In 1927, he wrote a recommendation letter extolling her character and extraordinary gifts. The response would launch the next stage of her development.

CHAPTER 4

"My University"
Yaddo and the Gateway to Europe

YADDO, THE NOW-FAMOUS ARTISTS' RETREAT, WAS IN ITS SECOND SEASON in 1927 when Marion arrived. George Bridgman's recommendation to Director Elizabeth Ames stated, "Miss Greenwood has studied at this institution [the Art Students League] under me some two years. I know of no one, as a student—who has greater ability—and no one who works harder than this young lady. A scholarship taken last year at the League proves that the board and faculty think the same as myself."[1]

Marion wrote a grateful response to the Yaddo invitation. Ames, an arts lover and savvy businesswoman who dominated the colony for more than four decades, would develop strong ties to Marion. But she was initially taken aback by one of Marion's requests: that Musy accompany her daughter to Yaddo. "Due to a recent bereavement she has undergone," Marion wrote, "and also the mutual interest of art, I feel I owe her my companionship as much as possible, especially in summer, when I generally study without instruction and therefore have more time to devote to her." Thus were mother and daughter's lives intertwined. When Marion added, "I assure you that no one would be more appreciative of such a beneficial opportunity or enjoy it more," she spoke for Musy and herself.[2]

Yaddo didn't allow family members unless both were working artists. Despite her mother's lack of achievement as a poet, Marion perhaps argued that Musy fit that category. She wrote, "In regard to the creative work you mentioned, I might say that my Mother has written poetry for years and was a member of the Writer's Club of Brooklyn."[3]

Whether due to the "working artist" argument, Marion's youth, or the colony's relative newness, Ames relented. Musy could stay in a nearby, affordable accommodation. Less than two weeks later, Marion wrote again to thank Ames for this concession. However, she arrived at Yaddo alone because of Musy's health problems. This was surely a boon for Marion's independence and growth.

Her residency ran from July 29 to August 15, the first of what would become multiple stays. She departed from New York City brimming with excitement. From the train station in Saratoga Springs, a driver chauffeured Marion across winding, tree-lined roads to the four-hundred-acre estate. A stone wall surrounded the fifty-five-room Victorian mansion fronted by terraced gardens. White marble water nymphs cavorted in a bubbling fountain. Pine trees edged an abundant rose garden. For an eighteen-year-old who shared a bedroom with her mother in Brooklyn, Yaddo was an excursion into unimaginable and sumptuous space. The retreat's many splendors—thick bath towels, meals ample enough to match her appetite, and the proverbial room of her own—deepened the wonder.

Yaddo was among the retreats created at the turn of the century to shelter artists from the turmoil of city life. Joining MacDowell in New Hampshire and Byrdcliffe in Woodstock, Yaddo combined creative solitude with the founders' goals of social betterment. Women were critical as founders and cofounders, fighting to increase support for the arts in American life.

Yaddo holds a storied place in American art history. The year Marion attended, the *New York Herald Tribune* celebrated the retreat's ability to nurture "the spirit and its works in what we are told ad nauseam is a materialistic age. One sonnet would justify the whole experiment and render it immortal."[4] Resident artists, writers, and musicians have collectively won a Nobel Prize, MacArthur Fellowships, Pulitzer Prizes, and National Book Awards, with more announced each year.

Yaddo's founders, Spencer and Katrina Trask, bought the estate in 1881 to recover from the death of their first child. They had three more children. All died between 1888 and 1889, two from diphtheria that they contracted from their mother. In 1891, the mansion burned to the ground. The ever resilient Trasks rebuilt and began work on the artists' retreat. When Spencer died in 1909, his partner, George Foster Peabody, married Katrina. Together, they brought Yaddo to life.

When the retreat opened in 1926, Elizabeth Ames declared it like a small house party, where guests could work or play. For Marion, there was plenty of both. Just waking to morning light in her own bed and cream in her coffee would have induced rapture. But as her partner Bob Plate later wrote, Yaddo offered much more—"a new world . . . a luxury cruise, a university and an entrance into an exciting society of extremely accomplished and creative people."[5]

Lively dinner conversations circulated around the mansion's long, elaborately carved table. James Rorty, radical writer and one of the founding editors of *New Masses*, surely prompted political talk. Marion impressed the older, more accomplished artists and intellectuals. Along with youth and beauty, her intelligence, diligence, and fearless approach to learning impressed other residents. Based on her recollections, Plate described a typical Marion prompt. "'Let's talk about Plato,' she would say for instance, to Erwin [sic] Edman and the [philosophy] professor from Columbia, flattered as well as amused, would hold forth."[6] Given Marion's spare formal education—her spelling and grammar would remain erratic—Yaddo exposed her to new political and artistic worlds.

Marion sketched and painted every day, creating portraits of fellow residents that she often gave away. After returning to the city, she wrote to Elizabeth Ames that "the quiet and beauty, and most of all, the appreciation that has been shown me, have done wonders for my art." She added, "You have certainly helped me along the road to becoming what you want me to be."[7]

"What you want me to be" requires a second look. Who was the eighteen-year-old Marion apart from the desires and needs of others? She'd begun to search for a distinctive artistic style. That quest already clashed with the need to fill her family's coffers and expectations. Marion also wanted to please Elizabeth Ames. Years later, her letter of gratitude would ricochet in strange fashion when she complained that Ames had created a myth of who she was "because that's what she wanted me to be."[8]

Marion might have grown despondent returning to her family's home after the residency. Instead, an exciting option soon emerged. George Foster Peabody asked her to create a portrait of founder Spencer Trask. She quickly agreed, laboring over the details of Trask's face based on a small photograph. Trask had a long straight nose, full dark beard and mustache, and receding hairline. His thoughtful eyes reveal the generous nature of a patron of the arts, education, and new technologies. In her cramped room at home, amid her distracting family, Marion created a compelling image that must have pleased Peabody. He soon sent her a check for $1,000. It was an enormous sum for a young artist.[9]

Marion wrote to Ames about how "generous Mr. Peabody was to me." She added, "Now this is important news—I am going to Europe at last. My mother, sister and I sail on the 'Saturnia' May 5th for Marseille, France, where friends tell us, we can rent a cottage for only ten dollars a month, in the small art colony on the Mediterranean, called 'Cagnes Sur Mer.'"[10] This trip was a fantasy long deferred. Paris was de rigueur in an artist's training. Marion's teachers, George Bridgman and Frank DuMond, had studied at the École des Beaux-Arts and the Académie Julian, respectively.

When the Greenwood women embarked, Marion was nineteen, Musy was fifty, and Grace twenty-six. It may seem curious that the strong-spirited Marion would bring a family entourage on such an adventure. However, recall that Musy almost played chaperone to Yaddo when the Greenwood baby dipped her feet into the waters of independence. The trip was also a gift for Musy. Her doctor had recommended an ocean voyage for health reasons, but Musy deferred going until Marion could accompany her. The Yaddo commission arrived like manna for all three.

On ocean voyages to Europe, first-class passengers could choose to play games, gather in smoking parlors, or lounge in spacious sleeping cabins. The Greenwoods were likely in the middle-class tourist area, but just getting to Europe was adventure enough.

The French southern coast had long drawn writers, artists, and musicians. Mythic light on the crystal blue sea, terra-cotta rooftops, ancient ruins, and sleepy fishing villages beckoned to Europeans Francis Picabia, Pablo Picasso, and Jean Cocteau. Many North American artists joined them. Marion initially chose Cagnes-sur-Mer, complete with a medieval castle, based on stories she'd heard. Pierre-Auguste Renoir lived in Cagnes for twelve years before his death, in 1919. She surely knew his work, perhaps magnetized to the region by the muted orange and gold *Landscape near Cagnes*.

Marion, Musy, and Grace ended up thirty kilometers away from Cagnes in Villefranche-sur-mer. The town's industrial veneer drew a bohemian crowd in the 1920s, including the celebrated artist and muse of Montparnasse, Kiki Man Ray. Unlike the glitzier Riviera spots, no one went to Villefranche to gamble or take the curative waters.[11]

The Greenwood women were wonderfully productive there. Marion and Grace painted while Musy wrote poetry. One poem appears on the back of a photo of Musy in a wide-brimmed hat standing in front of an ancient stone fortress. "We dance again," she wrote, "to old melodies of romance / I feel the Tang of the sea." Other poems are melancholic. "AntiWar," dated July 1928, begins "I am dreaming of an old house in Villefranche." The poem moves to images of fall foliage, a cold and dark Mediterranean, and a "strange quiet old lady sits sleeping / in a chair / Dreaming of a loved one back again . . . All seems peaceful and safe / but O God—the empty room—the wakeing [sic] and the pain."[12] Perhaps Musy blended this dirge for her dead son Raymond with memories of World War I, still lingering in collective consciousness in 1928.

The trio moved to Paris later that summer. If Marion's Yaddo money stretched, they might have luxuriated in sleeping cars on "le train bleu" that ran from the Riviera to Paris and Calais. Since the turn of the twentieth century, artists, writers, musicians, and all manner of bohemians saturated Paris with innovations in art and culture. The birth of the modern, the assault on conformity, the dancing, drinking, frivolity, and elevation of art—all fulfilled the Greenwood women's dreams.

Marion, Musy, and Grace arrived amid the "années folles," the decade between 1921 and 1931. Americans were the biggest group of expatriates to leave their mark on the Paris scene. Many were "le type transatlantique"—a foreigner creating a new identity via another culture. "Le type" wasn't simply an expat living elsewhere but rather someone who carried "the ideas and values of one culture into the heart of another."[13] American "transatlantique" artists Marsden Hartley, Alexander (Sandy) Calder, and Man Ray joined Gertrude Stein and Josephine Baker. Americans had moved from being the stepchildren of Europe to making their own contributions.

Musy, Marion, and Grace lived in a studio at #50 Rue Vercingétorix, "a great old alley of studios" and a hub for artists. They shared the space with artist Max Steinbook, who became Grace's lover and, later, traveling companion to Rome.[14] Stuart Davis lived on the same street that summer, a setting he captured in the oil painting *Rue Vercingétorix*. So many Woodstock artists were in Paris that year before the stock market crash that they were "virtually a colony in exile."[15]

Marion left the studio each day to attend one of two schools: the Académie de la Grande Chaumière and the Académie Colarossi. Both bypassed the more conservative École des Beaux-Arts to create a relaxed venue for adventuresome art students. Marion drew live models and then headed with friends to Le Dôme and other cafes. Musy, always game for a drink and lively conversation, often joined them. Years later, writing from Mexico, Marion would mention running into an old friend from Paris, Iberio, who asked about "the Mama of Montparnasse."[16]

By August, at least one Parisian was besotted with Marion. M. Fernand Huré published a rhapsodic article in "Ambassades et Consulats," an organ of the international diplomatic community. A portrait of Marion, her short hair flipped, eyes staring straight ahead, adorns the first page. Huré writes, "Oh! Diana, why did you reincarnate yourself—tall, supple, harmonious . . . an angel, who came down from a window, or better, from a dream. Goddess, with your huge green eyes that have no limit. Your eyes are like these vast fountains where, on depths of wavy greens the skies reflect themselves."[17]

This extravagant homage repeats familiar stories about Marion. How she came of age in a family of artists. How she excelled at the Art Students League and thrived at Yaddo. Her attraction to Hindu thought and a description of the studio she used in Woodstock as "Irresistible Cottage." He ends with "Oh, miracle of candor! Miracle of eternal beauty. Sagacity, gracefulness, talent form a radiant crown upon your pure brow. If they had known you, Dante would not have loved Beatrice, nor Petrach [sic] his Laura."[18]

In the middle of Huré's exhaustive celebration, he praises Marion's industriousness. She painted and sketched furiously in Paris. In a photo captioned "Baby & model," Marion strikes a jaunty pose. One hand tops her detailed, realistic portrait of the classic old Frenchman beside her. With her artist's smock and beret, she is the prototype of an American artist in Paris.

Marion experimented artistically, inspired by the buzz of modernism. In the first decade of the twentieth century, Paris became a world where, in Picasso's words, "a fruit bowl in art and a fruit bowl in life had nothing in common."[19] He exploded the dominance of Western art's single perspective with *Les Demoiselles d'Avignon*, a painting of five women in splintered planes. Matisse's loose brushstrokes in *Le Bonheur de Vivre* added fuel to the combustion. He, Georges Braque, and other artists of les Fauves (the wild beasts) flooded canvases with vibrant color. These movements are now so well-known that it's challenging to recapture their newness or the critical fury that followed every break from tradition.

Some of Marion's paintings depart from the realism of her portrait of the old Frenchman. *Notre Vendeuse de Journaux* depicts an old woman news vendor on a Paris street. She gazes at the viewer, eyes blurry, half smiling. The name of the newspaper she clutches is obscured except for the word "Peuple." *L'Ami du Peuple* was both a contemporary publication and Jean-Paul Marat's radical paper of the French Revolution.

Marion's choice of the news vendor and other subjects from the streets reflect her Ashcan School training. The loose brushstrokes and the woman's exaggerated features reveal elements of European expressionism. Marion responded especially to the work of Käthe Kollwitz. The German artist began as a realist but turned to expressionism in response to the suffering of the working class, women, and children. Marion later said, "At times I've been at my best, I verge on expressionism."[20]

Another Paris portrait features an artist Marion met in Paris, Georges Karma. He wears a formal black jacket, his bow tie and white collar as askew as his crooked smile. Two shadowy figures of women hover in the background, suggestive but not realistic. These two portraits were among Marion's work featured in a group show that fall at the Galerie René Zivy, 57 Avenue Montaigne, in the heart of Paris. The exhibit showcased "les jeunes," including Karma. Four of Marion's works sold—quite an accomplishment for a young, recent arrival.[21]

Friendships and connections forged that year would shape Marion's future life. In France, she encountered Mexican modernist artist Adolfo Best Maugard. At La Grande Chaumière, she met sculptor Isamu Noguchi, who would remain a friend and sometimes lover in New York, Woodstock, and, later, Mexico.

Noguchi had come to Paris in 1927 en route to India on a Guggenheim fellowship. His friends, among them dancer Michio Ito, Ezra Pound, and Jules Pascin, wrote introductions for him. On his second day in Paris, Noguchi met a friend of modernist sculptor Constantin Brancusi. India receded as he settled in as Brancusi's assistant.

Noguchi was born in Los Angeles in 1904 to Yone Noguchi and Léonie Gilmour. Yone left for Japan, created a new family, and remained absent for much of his son's life. Léonie moved to Japan with Isamu when he was two. When he was thirteen, his mother sent him to high school in Indiana. He faced culture shock, loneliness, and racism. After suffering through those formative years, bohemian Paris liberated him. Noguchi went from having few friends to meeting people "that I could accept or who could accept me." "After all," he said, "this business of discrimination . . . didn't exist there."[22]

In Paris, Noguchi's community included Stuart Davis, Alexander Calder, the Greenwoods, and other expats who hung out on Rue Vercingétorix. Isamu's charm and good looks magnetized women. He had numerous affairs in Paris, one reputedly with the famous Kiki de Montparnasse. He and Marion forged an enduring connection.

Marion's and Isamu's youthful radiance would have captivated even a world as beauty saturated as Paris. They were a stunning couple. In a later photo taken in Woodstock, they lie on their backs, eyes closed. Each extends one arm overhead to create an arch, their other arms linked at their sides. Isamu

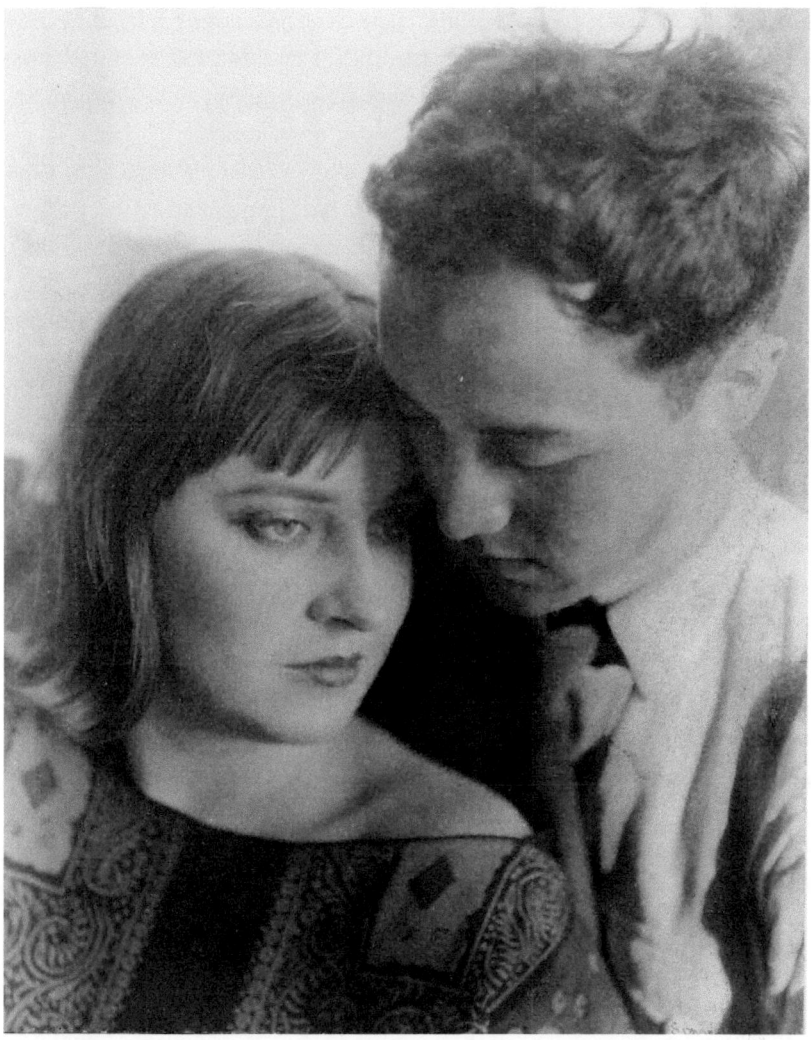

FIGURE 4.1. Marion Greenwood with Isamu Noguchi, circa 1930. (Photograph © and courtesy of the estate of Marion Greenwood.)

is bare-chested, Marion's body spills out of a black bathing suit. The image is sensuous and ecstatic.

At different times, the two artists created images of one another. Noguchi's 1929 captivating bust of Marion now rests in his eponymous museum in New York. He exaggerated her wide eyes, elongated nose, and set mouth to give her a strong, determined look. "He was in love," wrote Noguchi biographer Hayden

Herrera, noting one letter to Marion: "I have been finishing your head and now it's perfect—looking at me—and as I worked, I saw you, and even now I feel you in the room. It seems as though I have stolen some essence—calling you back—I wonder whether you felt me kiss you on your brow?"[23]

Marion painted a striking, expressionistic oil portrait of Noguchi in 1928. His expressive eyes stare ahead, a cigarette dangling from his lips. A 1929 crayon and pencil sketch captures Isamu's mischievous look, one eye closed as if winking at the viewer.

Marion surely had other affairs in France. For years after she returned to New York, letters from the forlorn arrived. One writer struggled with English to express his longing: "Dearest Liebling, It's a long time I had not had any news from you. Today I am to Genova to see my mother but I will return very soon to Villefranche. Darling, write my very soon. Will you come bac to Eropa? I hope but years comes and goes without you. Loves, T."[24] One wonders how Marion had time to keep Musy and Grace company, paint productively, and leave behind so many lovesick men.

When fall set in, the trio decided to return to New York. Marion and Musy sailed from Le Havre on the *Carmania* on September 29, 1928, arriving on October 8. Grace sailed from the same port on the same day but on a different ship, the *Rochambeau*, arriving on October 9. Perhaps Grace had gone off on her own. Sometime during her European travels, she visited Italy. The ship's record lists thirty passengers, the *Rochambeau* only three, so maybe the *Carmania* filled before she could sign up. However, the separate departures might be another sign of Marion and Musy's interdependence.

In the spring of 1928, before she left for France, Marion wrote to Elizabeth Ames describing a new art teacher, German immigrant artist Winold Reiss. Marion also listed him as a reference for admission to Yaddo. Reiss had ties to the arts colony, having visited in 1925 before the residency opened. She might have met him even earlier in Woodstock where he founded a summer school in 1919.

Reiss wrote to Marion ("Dear Greenwoodlein") in Paris during the summer of 1928. He fondly recalled a road trip to Sheepshead Bay, where he visited with her family. Marion had expressed frustration with getting French peasants to pose. He encouraged her to keep trying. When she grew lonely, he advised, "if the trains pass you on their way to Italy, take your brushes and paint—paint—paint your longing, paint your desires and paint your beautiful young thoughts."[25]

When she returned to the United States, Marion's "beautiful young thoughts" would, under Reiss's tutelage, turn to painting the diversity of American life.

CHAPTER 5

Representing "Others"

Winold Reiss, "Ethnic Types," and the American Southwest

MARION'S PURSUIT OF CULTURAL DIFFERENCE LIKELY BEGAN WITH HER yearning to escape Sheepshead Bay. Imagine her at age nine, discovering a mysterious world as she painted Cleopatra's kohl-lined eyes. Add her mother's goal of transformation into someone "other." Musy once told Grace, "I chose the wrong parents, the wrong race and creed, even the wrong color so karma is giving me growth."[1] Consider how Musy kindled Marion's spiritual pursuits, especially the Theosophical belief in an unseen world beyond the reach of Western science. Mix in bohemian New York's celebration of its vast, immigrant population. All combined to drive Marion into realms outside her own. There she found subjects that would "arouse empathy" in herself and others.[2] Her quest to understand and depict human diversity deepened through friendship and study with Winold Reiss.

A pioneering designer and portrait painter, Reiss started a studio/school in New York soon after he emigrated from Germany in 1913. He arrived just as the Armory Show shook the art world. He would move his studio around Greenwich Village five times during his long teaching career. From 1927 to 1940, the studio filled a warehouse at 108 W. Sixteenth Street, providing a bustling center of cross-cultural incubation. He painted the building a marine blue, his name in vermillion above the door. The studio functioned as a workshop, showroom, art school, and living space.[3]

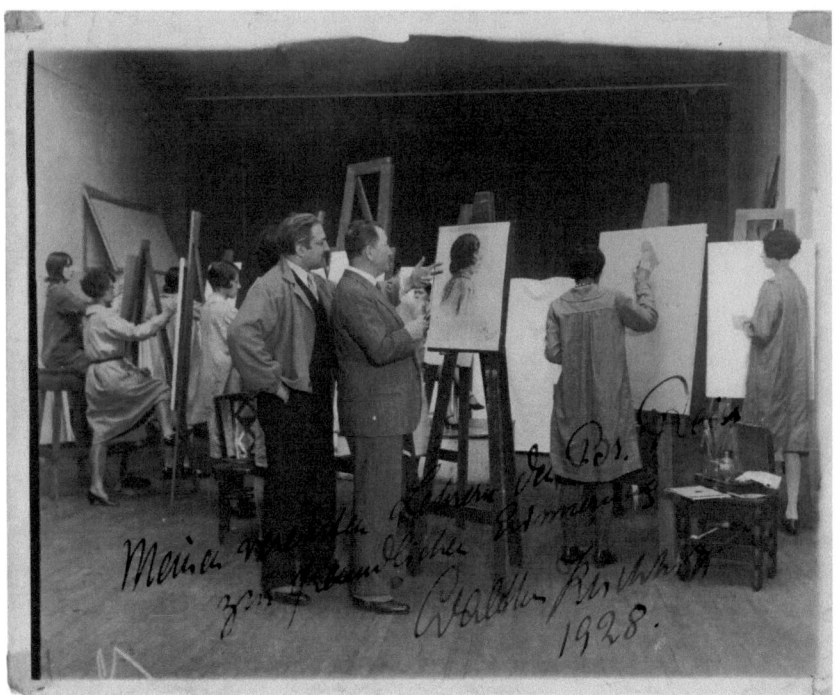

FIGURE 5.1. Marion Greenwood (far left, seated) in Winold Reiss's studio, 1928. (Photographer unknown, courtesy of the Reiss Archives.)

After returning from Paris, Marion made her way to Reiss's studio. In one photo, she sits with her back erect as she draws a model in the background. She wears her signature smock, chin-length hair flipped up in back. The only men, Reiss and Walther Kirchhoff, a friend and celebrated German opera tenor, stand amid a cluster of students. Throngs of young women flocked to Reiss as "a romantic and exotic figure."[4]

Winold loved all forms of art. Jazz or classical music filled his studio. Ailes Gilmour, Isamu Noguchi's half-sister and a member of Martha Graham's modern dance company, sometimes performed Indian dances. She noted that "the artist Marion Greenwood was always there."[5] Noguchi often joined them, reigniting the spark with Marion lit in Paris. All thrived in the heady atmosphere of the Village gathering place.

Reiss was cultured, handsome, and intense. In a conté-crayon portrait, Marion captured his bushy mustache and eyebrows, the widow's peak that parted a shock of dark hair, and a long nose he stared down with searing focus. One

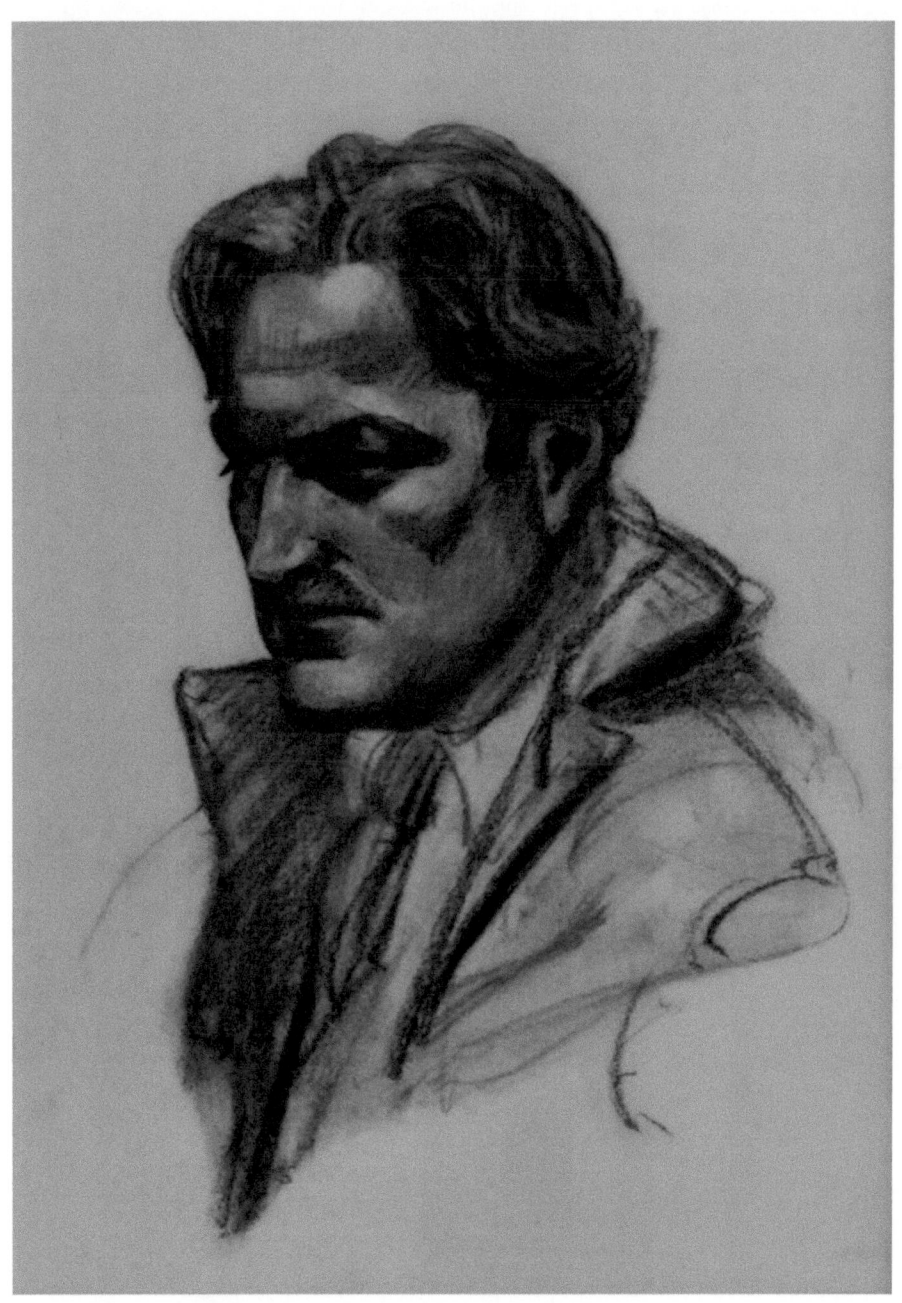

FIGURE 5.2. Portrait of Winold Reiss, by Marion Greenwood, circa 1930. (Photograph ©
the estate of Marion Greenwood; courtesy of the Reiss Archives.)

student recalled his European flair, the scent of his cologne and cigars, his fedora and spats. When he entered a room, the energy changed.[6] His intensity included an ability to engage with anyone. This capacity enabled a lifetime of friendships with a wide range of people. Marion shared this adaptability and found in him a kindred spirit.

Reiss arrived in New York carrying a childhood dream. Growing up, he'd read novels by James Fenimore Cooper and German writer Karl May. The central character in May's books was "Old Shatterhand." His Native American companion, Winnetou, following the logic of fiction, spoke German. Reiss devoured travelogues about an ethnically diverse America, longing for the day when he would come to paint Indians.[7]

Reiss's passion for diversity had roots in German history. He was born in 1886, fifteen years after the country's separate territories united into a nation-state. Until then, Germans' identities were seeded in being "Prussian" or "Bavarian"—a distinction akin to an "ethnic type." Reiss crisscrossed the country with his father, Fritz Reiss, who painted various peasant groups. The Arts and Crafts movement's romantic spirit infused the work of both father and son. Two of Fritz's beliefs shaped his son and would in turn influence Marion: that ethnically different groups, the poor, and the masses were worthy of portraits and that to find one's true subjects, an artist must travel.[8] These ideas, along with the Art Students League's philosophy, crystallized Marion's growing drive to depict nonelites and diverse people.

Reiss studied decorative and fine arts amid Munich's thriving European modernism. In New York, he established a design business, lectured at the Art Students League, and cofounded the Society of Modern Art and the magazine *Modern Art Collector*. He created covers for Scribner's and other magazines, poster art, furniture, and fabric; he also painted murals, portraits, and landscapes. Reiss's astonishing versatility led one critic to call him a "modern Cellini" after the gifted sixteenth-century sculptor, writer, and goldsmith.[9]

The bright colors and folk motifs of Reiss's designs filled New York City's hotels, offices, bars, and shops. One restaurant in the Longchamps chain displayed Reiss's stunning art deco portrait of Marion. Her folded hands seem demure, her off-the-shoulder turquoise-and-pink dress a modernist complement. She stares directly ahead, lips set. The image also appeared on the cover of *Town & Country* on August 15, 1928. Reiss paid her fifty dollars to pose.[10]

Also in 1928, Marion created a self-portrait, one of the earliest examples of the image she wanted to project. Her flipped hair and black-lined eyes match those in Reiss's portrait, but she made it her own by adding a necklace and altering the hair. A nearly identical image appears in a photo she sent Reiss, probably from France. She sits on the staircase of a crumbling building, dressed in a skirt and striped sweater. The eye travels from the made-up eyes down to welts and bites covering her legs. With mischievous humor, Marion wrote on the back, "Can I forget the mosquito bites?" Was she rejecting the focus on her beauty by showing a more flawed, human, and vulnerable side? For her entire life, Marion lived in the crosshairs of others' never-ending gaze. Although she embraced this source of power, she yearned to flip the mirror outward. She turned it toward people unlike her.

Among the people whose differences she celebrated were Native Americans. Reiss's drive to depict indigenous cultures deeply marked Marion's vision. A 1928 photo from the West Sixteenth Street studio shows a man in a traditional headdress posing for a group of art students. For Marion and Reiss, beliefs about Native Americans began as romantic and sometimes simplistic but evolved for both.

Reiss's evolution began with his journey west in January 1920. At age thirty-three, he boarded a train to Browning, Montana, en route to the Blackfeet reservation. Arriving at 3:00 a.m., he stumbled into a full hotel. Desperate, he cajoled the clerk to let him join the bed of a sleeping cowboy. He awakened to find his bedmate gone but outside were "eight or ten very tall Indians in Buffalo coats and huge fur caps standing silently in the snowy enclosure before the hotel." Reiss realized he had no plan for facing real people, not characters in books. Reverting to impulse, "I walked up to the tallest brave and slapped him on the back to his utter astonishment."[11]

Things might have gone badly. The man whose back he slapped, Turtle, was a feared young hunter. "He was lucky not to have been throttled," Blackfeet leader and historian Paul Raczka said of that first encounter. But when an English-speaking tribal member asked what Reiss wanted, he recalled, "I said I had come all the way from Europe to make the acquaintance of my Indian brother." The interpreter's explanation brought a handclasp, smile, and nods that passed all down the line."[12] Turtle embraced this naive outsider as a friend.

In 1927, Reiss returned to the Blackfeet reservation to paint portraits. Funding came from the Great Northern Railway, whose creation radically altered the landscape of the American West. The Blackfeet felt the effects acutely. The rail lines ran along the border of Glacier National Park and the Rocky Mountains, which the tribes called "the backbone of the world." Reiss chose portrait subjects, then Railway employees selected images for calendars and menu cards for the train's dining car. His sponsor wanted to see the Blackfeet in traditional dress. The general public shared the railway's desire to capture "authentic" Indian life. This aesthetic colored the work of many artists, including photographer Edward S. Curtis. It was characteristic of "well-meaning but ill-informed whites whose interest in Indians was more romantic than realistic," writes Jeffrey C. Stewart. "That approach to Indian culture froze Indians in time for whites who felt ambivalent about modernization."[13]

At the same time, US government policy attempted to destroy the "authentic" in the interest of assimilation. The Indian Appropriations Act of 1851 created the reservation system to control indigenous culture, movement, and lands. In 1871, the United States made Native Americans, seen as intellectually and culturally inferior, wards of the federal government. "Uncivilized" individuals were surely not worthy of nuanced portraits. Yet those are what Reiss soon created, moving beyond stereotypes. He showed the Blackfeet in both traditional and Western-style dress. Ethnographic details combined with the colors and abstraction of his design work to powerful effect.

Reiss taught his students to respect the complexity of individuals in all cultures. This attitude was crucial to his summer school in Glacier Park that ran from 1934 to 1937. He closed it in part because of tensions between his goals and those of the Great Northern Railway.[14] Throughout her life, Marion would face similar struggles between her artistic agenda and the compromises making a living sometimes demanded.

How can we read Reiss's portraits of Native Americans and how they influenced Marion? While the government declared indigenous people inferior, some artists envisioned them as spiritually advanced. You can catch a whiff of the nineteenth-century noble savage and romantic primitivism—the "other" uncorrupted by civilization. However, Reiss inherited another nineteenth-century philosophy—the German idealism of Johann Wolfgang von Goethe, Heinrich Heine, and Wilhelm Dilthey. "Reiss's art," writes Jeffrey C. Stewart, "reflected what these better known intellectuals extolled in their writings—that unity in diversity was one of the highest goals of modern civilization."[15]

As Marion came of age artistically, a new consciousness about race, ethnicity, and culture was emerging in the United States. Another German immigrant, ethnographer Franz Boas, challenged the then-dominant view of human differences as biological, debunking the supposed superiority of certain racial and ethnic groups, notably white people. If this now accepted idea hardly sounds

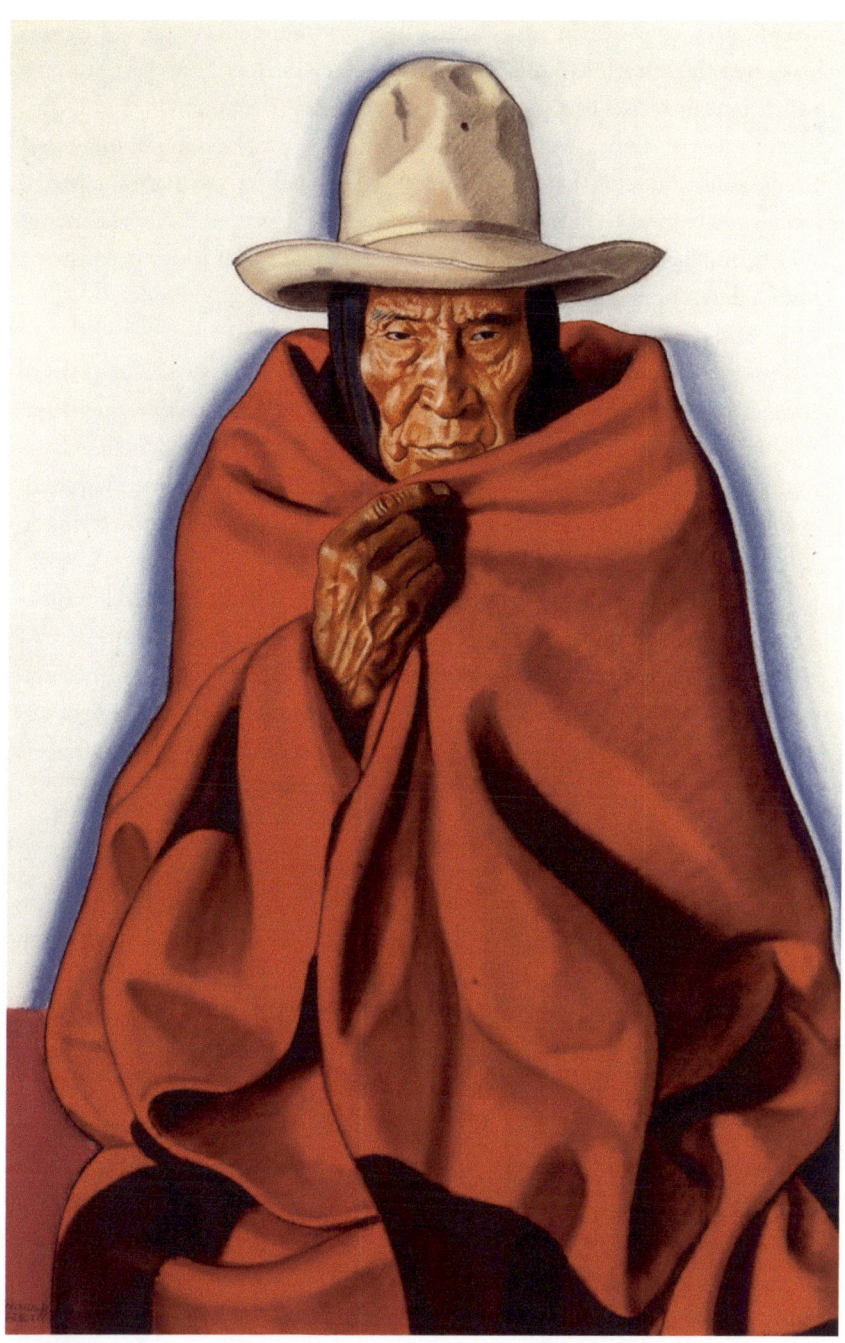

FIGURE 5.3. Winold Reiss portrait of Dan Bull Plume, 1948. (Photograph © and courtesy of the Reiss Archives.)

revolutionary, consider the landscape of the early twentieth century. Museums showcased the linear movement of racial hierarchies from "primitive" to civilized. Scientific racists used head measurements called craniometry to support eugenic theories embraced by the New York Zoological Society, among other groups. Fairs and zoos displayed ethnic "others" such as Ota Benga, a Mbuti man from what was then the Congo Free State. Boas battled pseudoscience at every turn. His careful fieldwork demonstrated how social patterns construct cultural differences. In doing so, he and his followers created modern anthropology and revolutionized intellectual life.[16]

Reiss recognized a kindred spirit in Boas's groundbreaking work. He invited him to his 1928 exhibit of Native American portraits in the Belmaison Galleries of New York's Wanamaker department store.[17] It's unclear whether Boas attended or ever met Reiss. But the artist followed ethnographic principles in his focus on fieldwork. He learned from the people he painted while trying to understand their perspectives.

The two men, like their German forebearers, argued for a common humanity. Yet they both recognized and celebrated rather than erased cultural difference. Reiss was "transnational" not only in bringing German modernist design to American portraiture but also in acknowledging immigrants and indigenous nations within the United States. These German intellectuals were humanists—a label that Marion would also adopt for her life and work.

≒≒

In Reiss's studio, Marion met a lifelong friend, Grace MacFarland. Marion became "Zaddo" to Grace's "Mac"—intimate nicknames they would use through life. Grace, six years older than Marion, had left her prosperous Illinois family to study art in the East. As her friendship with Marion deepened, she proposed a road trip.

They took off in the late summer of 1930 in an open touring car. California was the stated destination, but Marion left no record of that state. The Southwest, especially Taos with its multistoried adobe dwellings, captivated the young women.

Along the way, the duo collaborated on what they called "Whitmanesque poems." The stunning landscapes prompted "Rock," written in Acoma, New Mexico, in August: "We are the record / All this has been. / Angels moving down the air / and dark-winged-beasts / and amazons and giant-chiefs." Whitman's lustiness inspired "Friendship": "Amigo! I want to give you all myself /

See, my sanctuary is open to you. / I would hide nothing from you; / the gates are wide, come! / O love me and let me love you. / It is so easy."[18]

Both were on a spiritual journey. The artist's quest for enlightenment was in the air. Kandinsky's *On the Spiritual in Art* (1912) was especially popular. Although not strictly a Theosophist, Kandinsky lauds Madame Blavatsky, the movement's founder. In the Southwest, the travelers rode horses and danced in the rain. Their poem "Freedom Song" celebrates the mystical in the natural world: "Be let loose in the open sky of life! / sing the soul, winging at last / . . . Far, far, I am eddied into the open arms / that have no within, no without / I take flight on a new journey! / I can look into the face of all that lives. / I listen to what each say he is / and I receive it."[19]

For Marion and her family, art was both means and end. Greenwich Village, Woodstock, Paris, and Yaddo each offered different models of artistic community. Taos amplified those visions. Traditional Pueblo artists had long thrived in the Southwest, painting inside kivas and on hides. Writers, painters, and musicians from elsewhere arrived in the nineteenth century, drawn by the magnificent landscapes and allure of indigenous and Hispanic folk art. Salon host and arts patron Mabel Dodge turned up in 1917 and married a Taos Pueblo tribal member, Antonio Lujan. She changed the spelling of her adopted name to "Luhan" and re-created the gatherings she'd held in New York. Alfred Stieglitz, Georgia O'Keeffe, and Paul Strand's wife, Rebecca, joined the community at different times.

Marion's and Grace's exuberance about Taos was infectious, and the art community welcomed them. They met British painter Dorothy Brett, who'd come at the invitation of D. H. Lawrence and stayed. Brett had been cosseted as a child in a well-to-do political family in England. Like Reiss, she developed a childhood fascination with American Indians, in her case prompted by Buffalo Bill's touring Wild West Show.

Marion also befriended Dane Rudhyar, a French writer, modernist composer, and Theosophist. Rudhyar had been born Daniel Chennevière but changed his name when he became a US citizen. The inspiration was a Sanskrit word, *rudhirá*, for the "red planet" Mars and "the electric power released during storms."[20] He saw dissonance as the basis for meditative listening in Asian-inflected, multicultural music that challenged European forms. Rudhyar was a formative influence on the Theosophy-inspired Transcendental Painting Group that later emerged in Santa Fe. Like their east coast abstract brethren, these artists wanted to transcend the material world yet found spiritual inspiration in the desert landscape. Rudhyar wrote tomes about Theosophy, astrology, and human brotherhood, a magnetic pull for "Mac" and "Zaddo." During later periods of Marion's life, he would send her advice based on detailed astrological projections.

Zaddo and Mac moved across the Navajo nation from Taos to Monument Valley, where they met artist Edward Biberman. On one golden September day, he and Marion roamed the desert hunting for prehistoric ruins and rock formations. Other times, the three friends journeyed together. In one photo, they pose next to an abandoned trading post framed by sandstone buttes. Biberman stands between Grace and Marion, whose face is obscured by a wide-brimmed black hat. To their right, a Navajo man, likely their guide, sits on a horse. On the back of the photo, Marion wrote, "In Monument Valley—Utah—where I painted the Navajo Boy."

Throughout the trip, Marion had sketched horses and portraits of different Pueblo peoples. But it was the Navajo she longed to portray. She repeatedly crossed the reservation in search of a willing subject. Her guide nixed portraits as a violation of their traditions. Then, on an excursion into the desert, they encountered a ten-year-old shepherd. Marion, with the guide's help, bribed him with a chocolate bar to pose. In the painting, a headband wraps around the boy's long dark hair. He faces the viewer, unsmiling, arms crossed. Today, it's hard to read his stance as anything but resistance.

We now see Marion's bravado and breach of cultural norms as deeply offensive. Not so for white viewers in 1930. When she and Grace returned to New York, *Navajo Boy* was among the works selected by the G.R.D. Studio for a group show. One reviewer called it the "strongest work" in the exhibition, "a boldly expressed brown face seen against brown hills." Another critic applauded Marion's "brilliant, southern study of an Indian boy with black hair against orange cliffs."[21] The *New York Evening Journal* featured an article titled "NY Girl Artist First to Paint Navajo." A photo of Marion holding *Navajo Boy* accompanies the story. The writer began, "With a five-cent bar of candy and the exertion of her feminine wiles, a pretty twenty-one-year old artist has overcome an age-old Navajo Indian tradition that forbids anyone of that tribe being portrayed."[22]

The caption under the photo of *Navajo Boy* deepens the offense: "The first time a Navajo Indian has been captured by a painting brush and held prisoner by colors." Art historian James Oles points out that the language of "capturing" the boy on canvas recalls the imprisonment of Native Americans in the nineteenth century.[23] Marion seemed unaware of her glaring error and of the power dynamics that led the guide to collaborate. Yet the painting and Marion's attitude were not only accepted but celebrated.

If Indians were exotic, the landscapes and cultures of the American Southwest were especially so. Folklorist Barbara Babcock has argued that the Southwest is the "Orient" of the United States—an idea drawn from Edward Said's "Orientalism," the term for Western cultures' imperialist views of "the East" and all the power imbalances they imply.[24]

Like Reiss, Marion yearned to fathom and depict the beauty of diverse cultures. By the time she and Grace journeyed west, she had not yet gleaned Reiss's essential lesson: respect was paramount. Artists must accept that some people would never pose for them. Like all complex individuals, they had boundaries, expectations, and needs. For Native Americans, these issues were compounded by centuries of US government repression.

Reiss awakened Marion's incipient search for difference, spiritual understanding, and the role of the artist in these quests. Unlike the older and more experienced Reiss, she had not yet moved beyond ethnic stereotypes and her own ambition. Reiss had developed greater sensitivity to cultural norms and individual differences. So, too, would Marion. She would have to journey to Mexico and beyond to achieve that understanding. But in 1930, her education would first deepen in another diverse world closer to home.

CHAPTER 6

Uptown and Downtown

Letters from friends in the Southwest followed Marion back to New York. One sent notice of a summer school with Hungarian-born modernist painter Emil Bisttram, cofounder of the Transcendental Painting Group. Like Dane Rudhyar, he found spiritual sustenance in the Southwest. "Practically all the Taos artists have been studying with him," her friend wrote. "How nice it would be if you could come for the summer." Artist Edward Biberman recalled his excursion into the desert with Marion to hunt for prehistoric ruins: "Would that we might be doing it again today. . . . I visited the little bridge, the rocks, the cave, and all the scenes of our last year's wanderings—alone—sad to say."[1]

Marion rejected appeals for her return. Despite an auspicious beginning at Yaddo, an exhibition in Paris, and connections in Taos, she was still a twenty-one-year-old unknown from Sheepshead Bay. She had to carve out a place in the art world and somehow make a living just as the Depression shook the country.

She needed new subjects for portraits, which soon emerged in Reiss's studio. The Greenwich Village hangout was multiracial, multiethnic, and international. Reiss's German family—his sculptor brother Hans, ex-wife, Henriette, and son, Tjark, often joined the group. Mexican artist, writer, and ethnologist Miguel Covarrubias, famous for his caricature covers of the *New Yorker* and *Vanity Fair*, found his way there. The artists often depicted one another. Covarrubias sketched Reiss, giving him a single knowing eye—"the very sense organ most crucial for a painter."[2]

Mexican artist Adolfo Best Maugard, whom Marion had met in Paris, likely stopped by. He and Covarrubias had taught painting together in Mexico City and were roommates in New York. Best Maugard also introduced Covarrubias to his wife, dancer Rosa Rolanda, whose portrait Reiss painted. Her traditional Mexican dress of wide skirts and giant sombreros rivaled Frida Kahlo's sartorial marvels.

In 1920 or 1921, Reiss had commissioned another regular, the Hungarian-born photographer Nickolas Muray, to photograph the studio scene.[3] He showed men and women, Black and white, sketching nude models who were sometimes people of color. For different races and genders to draw nude models together was revolutionary, a practice prohibited in many art schools. Perhaps the retrospective glance always casts a sepia tint, but Marion seemed to have landed in a rare site of egalitarian and modernist creativity.

Reiss's studio hosted Mexican artists he'd met on a life-changing trip in 1920. His detailed diary of the odyssey south of the border opened with "Forward into the Promised Land. I want it all." From October 5 to December 10, he traveled from village to village drawing portraits of Zapatista revolutionaries, indigenous people, and mestizo festivals. Friends advised him to carry a gun; he replied that his sketchbook would suffice.[4] His journey was curtailed by illness, but he returned north renewed.

Reiss met writer Katherine Anne Porter in Mexico. She'd also arrived in 1920, prompted by her close relationship with Best Maugard. She had not yet written the celebrated *Ship of Fools* but was gaining attention for her short stories. Back in the United States, she featured Reiss's portraits in "Mexico: A Promise," a special issue of the politically progressive magazine *Survey Graphic*. Editor Paul Kellogg highlighted diverse countries and cultures.

Black artists were pivotal to the mix in Reiss's studio. Baritone, actor, and activist Paul Robeson sometimes sang and played the piano. Charles H. Alston, later the first African American administrator for the WPA's Federal Art Project, attended classes. Painter Aaron Douglas transformed from student to trailblazing artist and, later, founder and chair of Fisk University's Art Department.[5]

Survey Graphic soon led to a more important collaboration. In 1924, Kellogg invited Reiss to work on a special issue featuring African American arts and culture. He collaborated with Alain Locke, a philosophy professor at Howard University and emerging literary critic. "Harlem: Mecca of the New Negro" provided portraits of prominent African American artists and leaders of what we now know as the Harlem Renaissance. The issue featured well-known writers Jean Toomer, Zora Neale Hurston, and Langston Hughes and Reiss's portraits of "Harlem types." Images of ordinary working and middle-class African

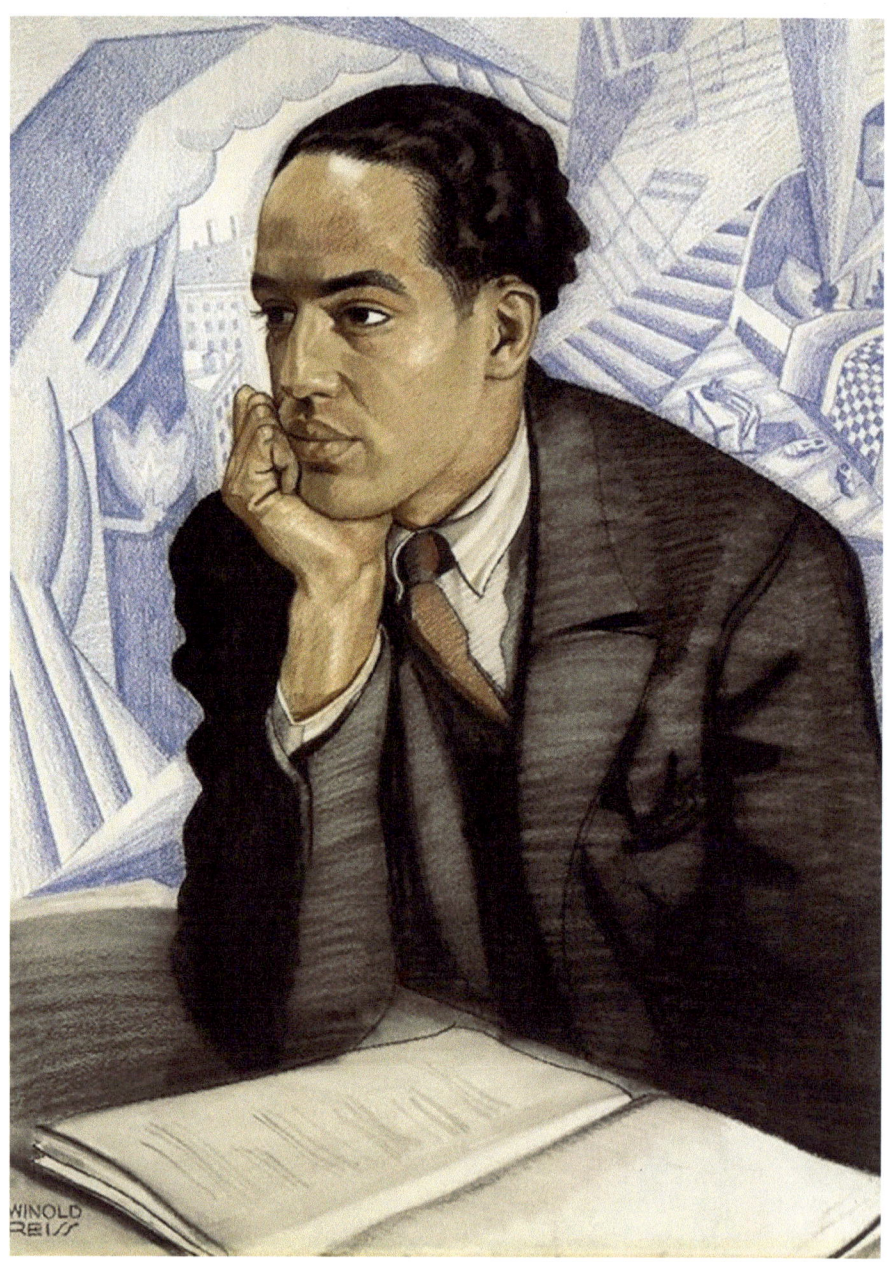

FIGURE 6.1. Winold Reiss portrait of Langston Hughes, 1926. (Photograph © and courtesy of the Reiss Archives.)

Americans joined those of lionized figures like tenor and composer Roland Hayes, whose portrait graced the cover. Two print runs of the March 1, 1925, issue sold out immediately, making it the most successful *Survey* publication to date.[6]

The response to that issue and the spiraling energy in Harlem prompted another Reiss-Locke collaboration: *The New Negro: An Interpretation.* Critics then and now objected to aspects of the book. Still, it's hard to overstate the importance of this seminal work of literature and social and political analysis. Most of the thirty-eight contributors were African American, among them Zora Neale Hurston, W. E. B. Du Bois, Countee Cullen, and Claude McKay. Reiss and Douglas provided the images.

As with his Blackfeet portraits, Reiss infused his individual portraits with brilliant modernist design. He saw "New Negroes" as key players in the creation of American modernism, "dignified individuals deserving of respect from the larger culture."[7] But Reiss's portraits were more than images of distinct people. They brought to life the cultural awakening born of the Great Migration north.

Reiss's consciousness about race, ignited during his Mexican sojourn, kept growing. He had personal experience with bias. To escape anti-German prejudice during World War I, he moved his then-wife, Henriette Lüthy, and son, Tjark, to Woodstock. Henriette was born in Liverpool to Swiss parents. She could make work-related calls on his behalf without fear of provoking anti-German sentiment. Woodstock had hosted several anti-war plays during the war and proved more hospitable than New York City. But the assault on Germans alerted Reiss to the virulence of prejudice.

Not everyone appreciated Reiss's work. When the Harlem branch of the New York Public Library held an exhibit, some local naysayers condemned the realistic depictions of darker skin and natural hair. Others railed against the choice of a white artist. Locke fiercely defended Reiss. In "To Certain of Our Philistines," he argued that the critics had internalized Caucasian notions of beauty, while Reiss showed the depth and complexity of Black "types."[8] Artist Aaron Douglas agreed: "We are possessed, you know, with the idea that it is necessary to be white, to be beautiful. . . . It takes lots of training or a tremendous effort to down the idea that thin lips and a straight nose is the apogée of beauty."[9]

Reiss was particularly keen to show the complexity of Black women's lives. Ironically, a Mr. Williams of Harlem claimed that two schoolteachers Reiss had painted looked menacing—this about two professional women holding a book and wearing their Phi Beta keys. One of the teachers, Miss Price, shot back that she was sorry that she would frighten Mr. Williams but she found the portrait to be a "pretty good likeness."[10]

Critics in the white-dominated art world praised the work, as they had Reiss's Blackfeet portraits. Galleries were another story. Despite the allure of "romantic primitivism," only one gallery had exhibited the Blackfeet paintings. They promptly sold out. The Harlem images couldn't garner any enthusiasm. "No gallery," Tjark Reiss later recalled, "wanted all of Harlem coming down and traipsing through their gallery. Very simple. They wouldn't exhibit the pictures."[11] Reiss's devotion to multiracial images marginalized him, as did his focus on portraiture. Though attention to his work is growing, he still remains unaccountably absent from many contemporary art histories.

Reiss's vision of Black culture as a fulcrum of the American experience offered Marion a model. She adopted his ethnographic practice of closely observing people before sketching. His Harlem portraits and connections to Mexico inspired her choice of subjects, including compelling depictions of many African Americans. One painting, *Mississippi Girl*, later earned second prize in the Carnegie competition. Marion learned from Reiss how little an artist controls reception to images, despite that person's intentions. But all of that was yet to come.

⇒⇐

While frequenting Reiss's studio, Marion worked feverishly to establish her reputation. The G. R. D. Studio group show that included her paintings from the Southwest generated publicity and sales of several paintings. One depicted Verna Carleton, a close friend and writer with a strong interest in the arts. *Creative Art* magazine lauded *Portrait of Verna* as well as *Gene at Work*. One reviewer claimed that in this group show, Marion alone "shows her artistic strength in no uncertain terms." *Gene at Work*, the critic added, "dismantled the myth that women painters could do nothing but 'limpid watercolors.'" Gone was the "line of demarcation between 'men painters' and 'women painters.'"[12] Soon women would achieve the success in the plastic arts that they had found with literature. Marion surely didn't envision imminent equality, but at least she was garnering attention.

More followed. Marion's sketched and painted leading figures like George Gershwin and Buckminster Fuller, whom she met through Isamu Noguchi and Ailes Gilmour. In the early 1930s, she worked for the theater section of the *Sunday New York Times*. Here was a chance to express her genre-crossing interests

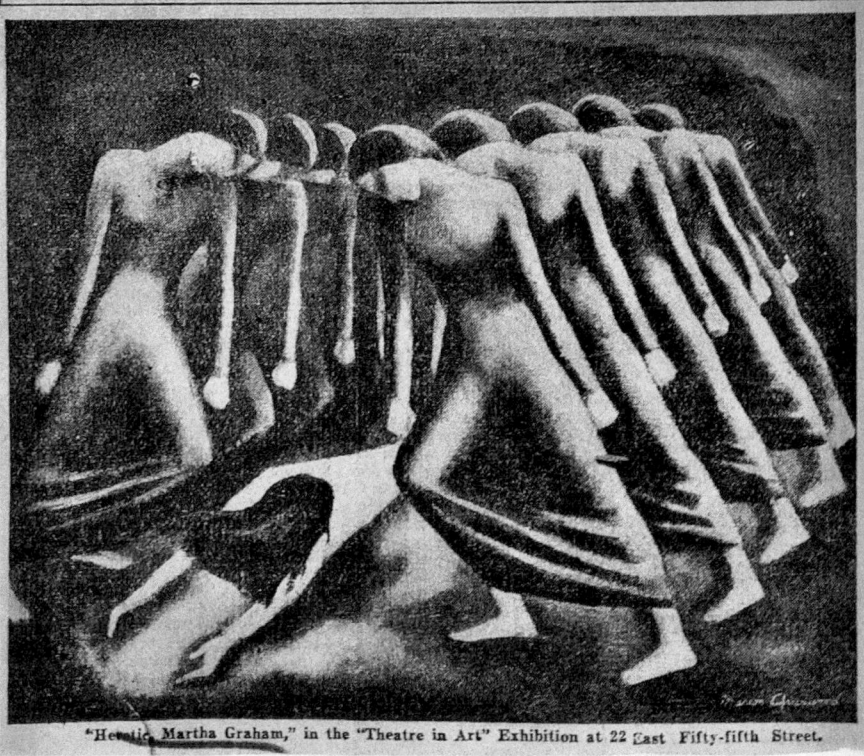

"Heretic, Martha Graham," in the "Theatre in Art" Exhibition at 22 East Fifty-fifth Street.

FIGURE 6.2. Sketch of Martha Graham's *Heretic*, by Marion Greenwood, featured in a 1932 "Theater in Arts" exhibit. (Photograph © and courtesy of the estate of Marion Greenwood.)

in music, dance, and theater to match those in literature and visual art. Drawings of opera singer Lily Pons, actor Melvyn Douglas, and a visiting troupe of Russian dancers splashed her name across the breakfast tables of the newspaper's readers. For a time, Marion also worked in a studio close to Martha Graham's on lower Fifth Avenue. She would carry her sketchbook over to capture the dancers' movements. One drawing shows Graham seated, overseeing the rehearsal. Other times, Marion joined the dancers. It's easy to imagine her as a fluid dancer. Not all her partners from those years matched her skill. She once described being with Piet Mondrian as like "dancing with a stick," which is curious given his reputation as the once lively partner of a young Lee Krasner.[13]

One striking painting reveals Marion's early experiments. *Heretic, Martha*

Graham features two columns of angular, featureless dancers. Between them lies a woman, her body and long dark hair flung onto the ground. Marion based the painting on Graham's groundbreaking performance as the white-robed "heretic" amid twelve dancers in black body-length dresses. Graham said, "I felt at the time that I was a heretic. I was outside the realm of women. I did not dance the way other people danced."[14] The outsider message resonated for Marion. She resisted the call to traditional education, marriage, family, and the limits on women's lives.

Heretic was included in the 1932 *Theater in Art* exhibit at the Sidney Rose Gallery at 22 E. Fifty-Fifth St. The painting hung with Miguel Covarrubias's caricature of Broadway theatergoers in tuxedos, top hats, and furs, Thomas Hart Benton's *Burlesque*, and José Clemente Orozco's *Coney Island Side-Show*.[15] Marion must have relished sharing space with Orozco, especially since the geometric symmetry of *Heretic* nods at *Zapatistas* (1931). Orozco's painting portrays the final battle of the revolutionary hero Emilio Zapata and his followers. A row of women in white robes and men in wide sombreros carrying scythes march toward their deaths. Their red-and-white clothing and hats contrast with a stark black background. Orozco inspired her move in a more expressionistic direction.

Could Marion's interests have developed into something other than realism? The Depression intensified her family's economic woes. Whenever she moved away from lucrative work, they hounded her. Musy wrote that Lester, Marion's favorite brother, declared her adherence to fine art "only a way of escape and selfish." Musy added a cryptic note, "And when I am drained, there is always the Ocean and you two [Marion and Grace] will be awakened."[16] We probably need a Ouija board to decipher Musy's ominous-sounding message. Marion's dream of courting the muse kept receding as she focused on realistic work that would sell and support her family. This tension would plague her for life. Whenever forced to accept commissions, something in her rebelled.

⇒⇐

Marion couldn't afford to move out of her family's home in Brooklyn, but she escaped to the Village at night. One evening at the Grand Ticino Restaurant, men flocked around her. Against the dark interior and white-clothed tables, a fight erupted. Artists Arshile Gorky and Joe Pollet came to blows over who would sit with Marion. Gorky ended up on the floor, left to "struggle in the sawdust" while Marion strolled away with "a cooler-headed third man."[17]

Joe Pollet may have been the "tall, cultured European artist" Marion was seeing during the winter of 1931–32.[18] Multiple men were courting her, leaving open the identity of the player in the drama's next act. Whoever the artist was, he was married and unsympathetic when Marion discovered she was pregnant. She hid her situation from Musy, with whom she still shared a bedroom.

Abortion was illegal, the landscape littered with tragedies dating back to the 1873 Comstock Law banning the use of US mail for materials about reproduction. It hadn't always been so. The seventeenth and eighteenth centuries' tolerance for abortion shifted in the 1850s when physicians conspired with legislatures to criminalize the procedure. Medical professionals would control pregnancy, stifling competition from midwives. Still, licensed doctors continued to perform abortions—an estimated 800,000 a year during the 1930s.[19] Some were reputable providers sympathetic to women's plight; others were frauds women sought out in desperation. Abortions often took a great financial and physical toll.

Such was Marion's case in spring 1932. It's unclear who performed the abortion. But soon afterward, she developed a life-threatening infection. Her family rushed her to the hospital, though only Grace knew the real reason for the rescue operation. Many years later, Marion would rebuff a gallery director who wanted to sleep with her. "We can't get intimate," she said. "I've got scars that are too embarrassing to show."[20] She would reference that eight-inch scar on her lower abdomen in letters and stories for years to come.

Were those scars only physical? Musy had urged her daughters toward the sexual freedom they embraced, one enhanced by the era's liberatory attitudes. Yet Marion's sex life was constantly scrutinized, while the affairs of her male counterparts were not only tolerated but celebrated. Much of the critique of her sexuality was yet to come. The arrows directed at the youthful Marion had been the Cupid variety, but the stinging weapon of the double standard would soon find her.

Marion was recovering at home in April when a letter from Elizabeth Ames arrived. Marion was, Ames claimed, one of those few guests for whom Yaddo had special regard. A return invitation welcomed her for a month or longer during May and June, with another stay in late summer or fall. Marion was elated by this "godsend." "Most of all, I am thankful to you, dear lady, for your kind interest in me and your rare understanding and sympathy." She added, "I am so eager to get away, the thought alone is lending wings to my recovery."[21]

Ames knew about Marion's "operation," if not the cause. To aid healing, she installed a comfortable cot in the studio for Marion to rest between hours at the easel. Guests were unwelcome, Ames stressed, perhaps to head off a visit from Musy. The Yaddo director fiercely guarded residents' time and privacy.

Marion arrived at the train station in Saratoga Springs on May 12, 1932. A Yaddo driver ferried her back to the estate. Marion anticipated productive hours of painting but surely not the life-changing events that awaited her.

CHAPTER 7

"A Large Dose of 'Painful Brooding'"

By 1932, the Dow Jones had fallen 90 percent from 1929. Bread lines snaked through the streets of New York City. The homeless crammed into shelters known as "Hoovervilles," and one of the largest filled a lawn in Central Park. Unemployment hit one in three city residents; half of the manufacturing plants had closed. The Communist Party created Unemployed Councils to rally desperate workers. Rent strikers fought evictions. Neighbors convened to carry furniture back into the apartments of the expelled.

Away from the despair, Yaddo beckoned with its abundant green lawns, rose gardens, and water nymphs in gurgling fountains. Marion could ascend the mansion's winding staircase like one of the nobility. A proverbial room of her own awaited. If she faced one of her frequent bouts of insomnia, she wouldn't wake Musy. Dostoevsky or one the other writers she'd discovered at Yaddo five years before would keep her company.

If Marion sought retreat from the world, the other Yaddo residents brought her back. She painted portraits of many of these politically committed artists, writers, and composers. In one photo of the Yaddo group, *New Republic* associate editor and activist Malcolm Cowley sits in the front row. His hands curl into fists as he leans forward as though ready to pounce. Later that year, he and fellow resident Waldo Frank will journey to Kentucky as union-sponsored observers to a miners' strike. Frank, standing to the right in the second row, will be threatened and beaten by the mine's owners. His writing about the spiritual strength of Spain and Latin America will captivate Marion. Modernist composer Aaron Copland stands at the center of the back, tall and dapper in a suit and tie. His creation of vernacular American music will soon emerge in *Billy the*

Kid and *Fanfare for the Common Man*. Below Copland, between two unidentified women, sits Marion. She wears a long skirt, white lace blouse and sweater, black-and-white pumps. Her legs are crossed at the ankle, hands folded demurely on her lap. The modest, tranquil presentation belies the turmoil ahead.[1]

One figure central to that turmoil is absent from the photo: Philip Stevenson, a leftist writer later blacklisted during the McCarthy era. He and his wife, Gladys, hoped to arrive at Yaddo together. They had met at a sanatorium while recovering from tuberculosis. Gladys, an aspiring musician, had to forego a residency so she could stay in Santa Fe and care for their children. When Philip accepted the Yaddo residency, he responded to Ames's standard cautionary note about the need for serious work. Nothing would distract him, for "time and privacy are what I need."[2]

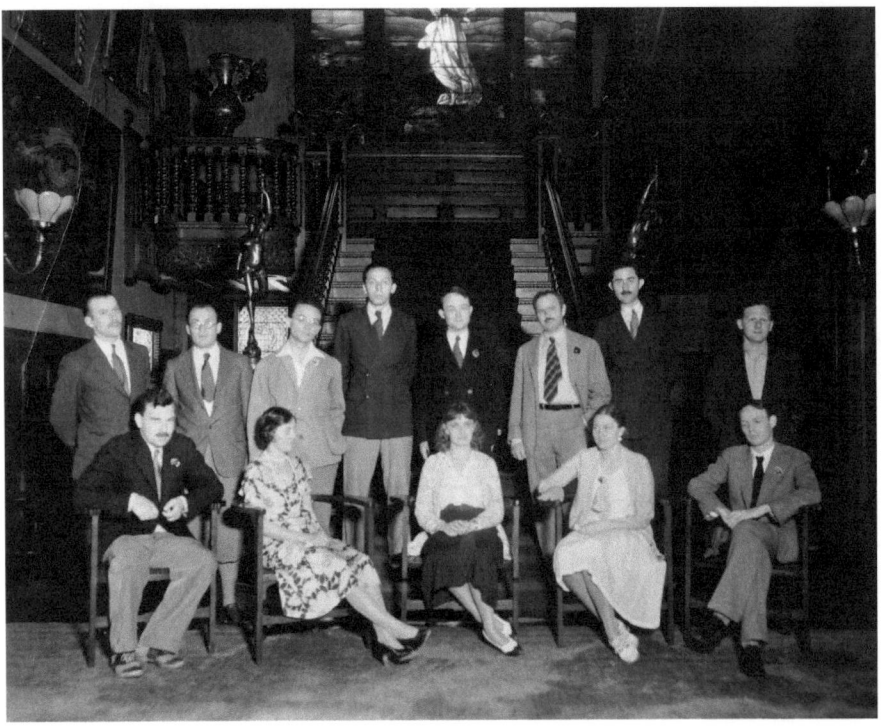

FIGURE 7.1. Yaddo residents, 1932. Back row: Ernst Paul Fiene, Joshua Kunitz, Leonard Ehrlich, Aaron Copland, George Milburn, Waldo Frank, Morris L. Ernst, Joseph Vogel. Front row: Malcolm Cowley, unidentified woman, Marion Greenwood (center), and unidentified woman and man. (Photograph courtesy of the Manuscripts and Archives Division, the New York Public Library.)

Perhaps he should have heeded Ames's warning. He and Marion were soon romantically entangled. Her portrait depicts him reading, his handsome face bisected by a dark mustache. Streaks of gray hair graze either side of a widow's peak. Through the summer, he alternately embraced and rejected Marion. His desire for her clashed with the need to write and remain responsible to his family. His vacillation sent her into emotional tumult.

Marion had clearly emerged as a promising artist. She was also young and beleaguered by this off-and-on affair with Stevenson, money worries, and her family's demands. The Depression hadn't driven them from their Brooklyn home, but Papa had trouble finding work as a house painter. Marion needed someone to share her troubles. Enter the older, established and sympathetic Josephine Herbst, who arrived a few weeks after Marion.

"Josie," also missing from the photo, was a serious, accomplished writer of two novels and extensive journalism. She had originally moved to New York from the Midwest and worked for H. L. Mencken, writing for the *Smart Set* and other publications. As a journalist, she later covered Cuba and the Spanish Civil War. She would go on to write numerous novels and nonfiction works.

Josie shared a stone farmhouse in rural Erwinna, Pennsylvania, with her husband, writer John Hermann. They bought the house, which had no electricity or plumbing, and fifteen acres for $2,500. Simplicity equaled focus on their writing. The homey front porch with its caned chairs hosted Ernest Hemingway, Nathanael West, and other New York literati needing a weekend escape to Bucks County. In due time, Marion would find her way to that porch.

Josie and John had met in Paris in 1924. She spied him at a table alone in the Café du Dôme nursing a hangover. Josie was in Europe to escape an escalating depression and to recover from an affair with writer Maxwell Anderson. At the time, he was married and intended to remain so. Anderson spared little sympathy for her surprise pregnancy. Josie had pondered keeping the baby, but his rejection swayed her toward an abortion.

John was the son of a Michigan businessman. An aspiring novelist, his book *The Big Short Trip* tied with Thomas Wolfe's *A Portrait of Bascom Hawke* for the *Scribner's Magazine* short novel prize in 1932. Despite some success, his reputation never matched Josie's.

Josie and John were mismatched in other ways. He was nine years her junior and lacked her ambition. According to Elinor Langer, Josie's biographer, he preferred "the company of the cafés and she preferred the solitude of the typewriter, he had confidence in his charm but not in his book and she had confidence in her book but not in her charm."[3] He would join the Communist Party, while Josie steered clear of outright affiliation, although she shared his political commitments.

They married in part to satisfy his conservative parents. That the decision was never fully their own may have foretold problems. In February 1932, they were mired in marital conflict when invitations to Yaddo appeared in their mailbox, prompted by Malcolm Cowley's recommendation.[4] Here was a miraculous if temporary solution to the tensions. In the end, John opted to return to his family's home in Michigan. He dropped Josie off in Saratoga Springs in mid-June.

Josie later described her first glimpse of Marion: "I watched you coming back across the room, and what there is about your face and body, whether it is your skin or heavy eyes or what, but just to see you brings back in me in some way all I ever loved and lost, the dreams a child has of a world that never quite comes true."[5] In Marion, Josie saw her beloved sister, Helen.

In 1920, recently married and pregnant, Helen was living in their childhood home in Sioux City, Iowa. Like Josie, she was a writer with dreams, not ready for a child. Agonizing over the abortion decision, she sought Josie's advice. Find a good doctor, her sister urged, not one of the "hypocrites." In the same letter, Josie included an eerily prescient poem by Maxwell Anderson called "Grief Castle": "I keep my darkness though. This cloud is mine. / This memory of a sun that passed and turned. / If you had told me then there would be one spring / and then no more spring—no, for the whole earth burned, / And the sky was a flame, and winter was shriveled away—/ I would not have believed. But now I believe and know."[6] By the time Josie's letter reached Sioux City, Helen was dead from a botched abortion.

Josie's abortion after the affair with Maxwell Anderson, Marion's two recent "operations," and Helen's deadly infection underscore the suffering wrought by Comstock and his legions. For all the celebration of the New Woman and emerging freedoms, women had to navigate landmines to create an independent life, especially a creative one.

Josie would forever grieve the loss of Helen. Meeting Marion offered a seemingly miraculous reprieve. In the young painter, she saw not only Helen but other "loves now dead and gone and somehow terribly sweet because they are now gone forever."[7]

Josie and Marion were as incongruous a couple as Josie and John. Marion was twenty-four, Josie forty, though she often shaved off years in formal

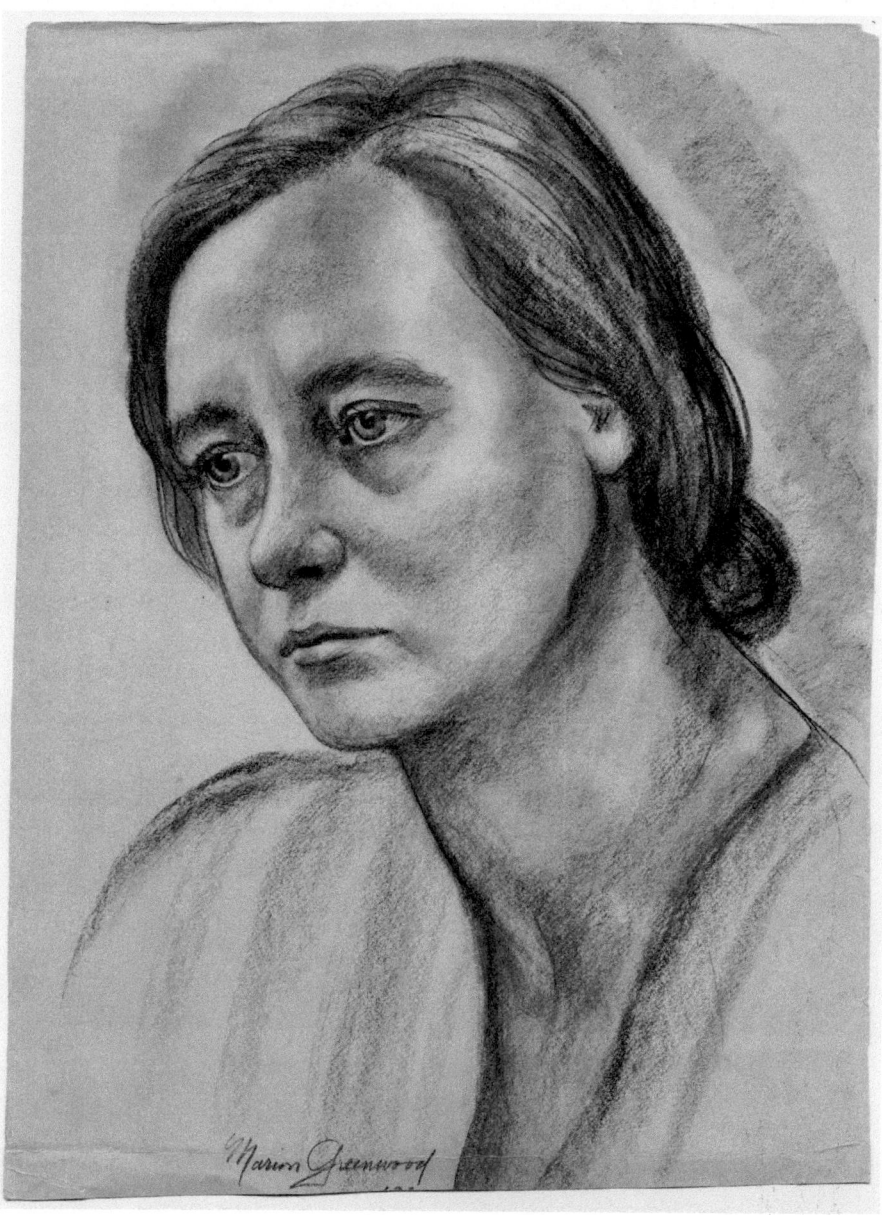

FIGURE 7.2. Portrait of Josephine Herbst, by Marion Greenwood, 1932. (Photograph ©
the estate of Marion Greenwood; courtesy of Josephine Herbst Papers, Yale Collection of
American Literature, Beinecke Rare Book and Manuscript Library.)

documents. For all her literary achievements and connections, Josie remained ill at ease, "shy, awkward, uncomfortable in her body."[8] Marion was a sensualist and celebrant of the flesh.

Marion's bawdy humor fills letters to her many lovers. She once wrote to the artist Adolf Dehn, who would remain a lifelong friend, "I'm freezing to death—can't get warm. Poison ivy has crept slowly but surely into 'the secret recesses of my innermost being.' Yes, just there! No one knows but Jesus! . . . Dear, carnal rogue, come here and be chilly with me."[9] In another letter to Dehn, she described being "away from the brutalities and carnalities of rogues such as you, I can once more be my own spiritual untouched self." She follows with "Bite your finger very hard for me, between the first two knuckles—then cut if off, put it in a holder and send it to me and I'll use it for a smudger while sketching—as a little souvenir of warfare waged between 72nd Street and Brooklyn."[10] Marion was a tease and adventuress, ready for everything life might offer.

It's easy to imagine the two women growing closer as they wandered the leafy paths of the Yaddo estate, how they might have first joined hands walking under a full moon, how that physical and emotional closeness turned them from the garden to the bedroom, from friendship to love. And turn it did, in ways that would change both their lives.

What did this relationship mean to them? Marion offered Josie vitality, release from tensions with John, and reconnection to her beloved sister. Josie offered Marion refuge and counsel. Both sought sexual as well as emotional intimacy, though connections to women would prove more powerful and enduring for Josie. At a Yaddo residency years later, she formed a long-term relationship with Jean Garrigue, a younger poet. There's no hard evidence that Marion had other women lovers.[11]

In the early twentieth century, the landscape for women loving other women was a mixed tableau. Feminists in Greenwich Village lived openly as lesbians, while others created less overt "Boston marriages" outside traditional partnerships. Society often ignored relationships between teachers and other working women who lived together.

In the late nineteenth century and into the twentieth, American and European sexologists began to study same-sex relationships between people they called "inverts."[12] For some, including Havelock Ellis, that term was not negative; he was sympathetic to a range of human sexuality. Other researchers created the stigma that dominated Marion's time. Many women whose "romantic friendships" had been accepted were ostracized.

Marion sometimes called gay men "fairies" or "swishy boys," but with affection. At Yaddo in 1932, Marion befriended and painted a portrait of Newton Arvin, whose story reflects the era's entrenched homophobia. He was young, balding, and bespectacled, the prototype of an accomplished academic and literary critic. He taught at Smith College and was a frequent guest at Yaddo and a board member from 1939 to 1961. In 1960, Arvin suffered a tragic fall from grace when he was arrested for possessing magazines deemed "pornographic," including *Trim: Young America's Favorite Physique Publication*. Smith College forced Arvin into retirement and the Yaddo board removed him. Such indignities, even in the supposedly tolerant art and academic worlds, underscore the power of homophobia and conservative New York business interests on Yaddo's board.[13]

The "Lavender Scare" is not as well-known as the anti-communist "Red Scare," but one bled into the other. During the McCarthy era, both gays and communists were portrayed as "subversives" who threatened the fabled American way of life. Many were hounded and ousted from government service and other jobs.

When Josie met Marion, that period had yet to unfold. Yet both were circumspect about their relationship. Marion told her family that Josie was a friend. From Yaddo, Josie described Marion to John in cryptic fashion. Still, he knew. Clearly Josie had met someone who made her, he said, "feel on your own two feet and not feel like you felt with me." He worried that "my way of loving you was bad for you."[14] His suddenly passionate letters to Josie tried to resolve the pre-Yaddo tensions.

John and Josie reunited in Pennsylvania but soon departed for Canada. Josie's longing for Marion grew with every mile. She wrote from Montreal, "Be patient, my sweet thing, and life is going to be as good to you as I should love to be. We will have good times together this winter. John likes you; with a strange intuition he has talked about you. I'm going to tell him all about you someday."[15] When John got to know Marion, Josie was sure he would feel included. She admitted that he remained miserably in the dark.

In August, Marion moved from the main estate to Triuna, a small group of Yaddo-owned islands in nearby Lake George. She wrote to Josie in Sioux City, Iowa, where she'd gone to cover a farmers strike. Philip Stevenson had driven there with Mary Heaton Vorse, a prominent journalist and labor activist. Like Malcolm Cowley, Waldo Frank, and many of Marion's Yaddo companions, they sought justice for workers as the vise of the Depression tightened.

Josie reported that despite Philip's genuine feeling for Marion, he would remain married. "He will try," Josie wrote, "to keep you whole in his heart. You will make a mistake if you do not keep him whole, too." Marion ricocheted between desire for Philip and longing for Josie, creating emotional turmoil all around. One night Josie saw Philip "walk off and look up at the moon. That's your moon and his," she wrote to Marion, "But the stars are mine."[16] For years afterward, the moon and stars would figure in Josie's memories of Marion, triggering fear of losing her.

Back in Brooklyn, Marion's letters vacillated between invitation and indifference toward Josie. She goaded her with the story of an artist who wanted Marion to marry him and live on his Woodstock farm. "I said 'No sah!' Just catch me," she wrote, adding, "You delight me. You irritate me. I love you. Write me here, this cliff dwelling in Brooklyn, where I live with my Mommy and Poppy, like a mouse that won't leave the trap."[17] Entrapment included evenings with her parents, "which means long arguments about money, art, life in general, and then the familiar stony silence, in which I am able to write you, and glance over and feel sorry for the poor, tired old head of my father reading the paper and my poor tired little mother, sad as usual, but enjoying a cigarette."[18]

Marion's family triggered her dark side. She bemoaned their crushing unhappiness, especially that of her frustrated mother. Grace had found a studio with money from a musician she'd been seeing, someone Marion dismissed as dumb. These comments might read like a young person's typical complaints about family. Yet Marion took seriously the responsibility to care for her clan. Little wonder that she pondered escape. At Yaddo, she and Josie talked about a trip to Mexico with John.

That fantasy soon took back burner to a new worry. "The full moon has come and gone without having the slightest effect on the tides of my blood," she wrote to Josie as she surveyed the long red scar on her belly from her earlier operation—the scar now "pointing accusingly toward my poor little~~~~~~which was used not wisely but too well." She described this new pregnancy as holding "the makings not, mind you, of a long lean melancholy grey streaked templed man but an impudent, red-faced yodeling brat of stout Swiss peasant stock."[19] Philip Stevenson was likely the "grey-streaked templed" man she would have preferred as partner to the pregnancy. The identity of the Swiss "yodeling brat" remains a mystery. Marion wrote to "the Swiss" to say she didn't blame him since she felt that she should have known better.

Marion planned to use an assumed name to see Mary Holton, a woman who gives "'a poke' in the right place and brings on the menstruation." She begged Josie, "For God's sake keep this quiet. If my mother ever found out she'd curl up and die but not before shooting me and the whole Swiss nation."[20] Musy's bohemian attitudes extended only so far.

Less than a week later, Marion thanked Josie for a seventy-five-dollar loan, presumably for the abortion. She described enormous relief and gratitude. It was the first of many times Josie and John would rescue Marion. Emotions grew entangled with finances: "I never asked you to do all that you did and when I try to tell you how grateful I am, how I appreciate it in the marrow of my bones, how I won't forget you and these good actions till my dying day, you shut me up and say it sounds as if I were writing [to] Mrs. Ames [at Yaddo]." Marion insisted she never asked for assistance but "help always came. And I've always payed it back in some way, too, and will in this case."[21]

The details of "the poke" remain murky, but Marion claims to have learned her lesson. Her mother could not understand why her otherwise social daughter was now home every night. "If you can't be good, be careful," was Marion's new mantra. "Sublimation not fornication and so to bed with my mother."[22]

Refraining from sex did not end Marion's problems. Another infection soon raged. She returned to the doctor who had performed the operation the previous spring. He advised her to wait it out and hope her body would fight the infection. The cramping, vomiting, and fear left her morose. Marion hid the problem from Musy. She swore dramatically that she would have taken something lethal had it been handy. She keened to Josie that life was "just one grand endurance test from beginning to end with a few measly rest periods we're supposed to enjoy, with nothing but struggle, suffering, and death to look forward to."[23] Musy's sense of Irish tragedy was front and center.

In response to Marion's jeremiad, Josie compared her with Daisy, a moody character in Edmund Wilson's novel, *I Thought of Daisy*. The story follows a young man and his romance with a chorus girl in bohemian New York. Marion rebelled. "I couldn't find one similar trait for the life of me!" "Jesus!" she added, "Will you stop trying to pigeonhole me!! Or my tastes!! I'll have you know they are not limited to 'painful brooding.'" Josie likely pointed to Marion's love of that great brooder, Dostoevsky, frequently referenced in *I Thought of Daisy*. Marion added that "a large dose of 'painful brooding'" was necessary to get to the heart of things or have anything to say.[24]

Marion's affinity for another writer who influenced Wilson's novel was growing. At Yaddo, she borrowed Josie's copy of *Within a Budding Grove*, the second volume of Marcel Proust's *In Search of Lost Time*. His melancholic musings on time and memory perfectly suited Marion's temperament. The seven-volume novel would accompany her through every stage of her complicated life. Though her idiosyncratic education left gaps in her knowledge and terrible spelling habits, Marion was intellectually alive. She embraced sophisticated literature and complex thinking. In Josie, she treasured something she'd never had in a close relationship: engaged argument over ideas and opinions. She had found a sparring partner and mentor as well as a lover.

After John and Josie returned to Erwinna from Iowa, Marion recovered enough to visit. Their spark reignited. Back in Brooklyn, Marion kept it lit via letters. They traded sympathy for their respective ailments, in Josie's case kidney problems. Confined to bed one day, Josie described how John and his friend "Pep," writer Nathanael West, were out hunting pheasant while she and Marion nursed their ailments. "Dear Little Crocodile," she began, "Here we are, in bed, but not in bed, alas, together. Could anything be funnier than the lives of women?" In their next incarnation, Josie mused, at least one of them should be male because "here are the women, always on their backs. Even in defeat, on their backs. And the men can walk upright & sound." Her tone turned teasing, "So bitch, you did not write me even a line for today, especially after I was foolish enough to ask you to be good to me. You don't need love, but a whip. After all the trips I've made to town & all the running & all the evidences you've had of real anxiety, you can't give me that much. . . . But I'll teach you yet, you little tadpole. Just a rudimentary lover, that's all you are, got all the wriggles and the tail twistings & that's all; still a tadpole. I love you anyway." She signed off with "What do you do with my letters? Tear them up."[25]

Marion volleyed back. "How is my blue-eyed buxom bitch today—and the bad bad kidney"? Marion reported on her continued infection but she was determined to recover:

> Old Greenwood will be up an at em soon. I might be able to be smacked down at present, I might be wobbly and leak like a sieve when vertical but it won't be long now and believe me baby—all the godamn males on earth won't be able to push me over without money down and a room of my own. But how I would give up all sensual pleasures if I could be free of them and not need them, if I could throw all physical desires in the sewer or the sea, how peaceful and calm and beautiful life would be—I could then give myself up wholly to the serene and contemplative study of Man's evolution thru eternity, inquire and

gain power over the most secret and occult laws of Nature. Yea, verily seated on some glacial peak of the Himalayas, having become incapable of tears, and killed out all desire, having triumphed over the painful wheel of re-birth—being and becoming—I could gaze unmoved as the aeons rolled out Man's destiny before my eyes. Great civilizations, races, cultures would rise and fall, immense continents would sink beneath the sea—shall I go on—or wait until I see you—alas you are not ready—you refuse to see the light . . . but when the pupil is ready, the master appears—I would love to see the mood that this letter has put you in, do you want to ring my neck, baby?[26]

Here are many Marions: the spiritual seeker, the "brooder" on life's pain, the playful partner who knew she would goad her lover with these spiritual meanderings. Josie was not Grace MacFarland ("Mac"), Marion's companion on her Southwest adventure. She was not likely to dance under a full moon in Taos.

During Marion's visit to Erwinna, John joined the duo. Perhaps they walked in the countryside past the region's covered bridges, branching off in twosomes, then threesomes, while they cooked up plans for travel to Mexico. Marion's letters soon included loving attention to John. He seemed to accept the three-way arrangement, despite misgivings. He could not imagine his life without Josie, while she could not choose between him and Marion.

If the potential hazards of an entangled trio were an obstacle, the lure of Mexico overcame them. Plans for the adventure brewing since Yaddo simmered through the fall. Marion dreamed about the trip while recovering. She began to sign her letters with "Adios, Chichita."

Roadblocks soon appeared. Marion's infection flared. In November, she wrote that Mexico was out. But determination spurred her recovery. "Every time I might feel like weakening I'm going to get hard," she wrote. "Females, women have to be *hard* in this world. I'm going to think of pain and get hard."[27] When Marion's bleeding finally stopped, she felt like Lazarus.

Marion's family initially objected to the trip. They worried about her health but likely also feared losing her financial contributions. She never sought her father's approval, so his resistance meant nothing. Josie wrote reassuring letters to them and Musy finally relented.

Musy became very tender toward her soon-to-depart daughter. This sent Marion back to "painful brooding" about how every separation triggers fear of the final parting: "The Executioner certainly waits at the door and sometimes he lurks in the room." The sad hour of dusk triggered similar thoughts: "It is the very nature of things near and dear to us that we must leave them." "They being born must die," she wrote, claiming those as the last words of the Buddha and her first thoughts as a child. "Amen. Oom nani padni oom"—Marion's creative spelling of *om mani padme hum*—"Praise the jewel in the lotus."[28]

The three travelers had lofty plans. John and Josie would work on their novels. Marion would paint Mexican life, a passion born in the American Southwest and Winold Reiss's studio. In the sunny south, they would live cheaply and focus on their art.

They were also in flight from economic despair north of the border. Rescue via President Franklin D. Roosevelt and the New Deal programs was a year away. Even if business titans had rallied to create jobs, many thought that would not alleviate suffering. Industrialization was part of the problem, threatening the soul of the country. Marion shared John and Josie's leftist politics, although at twenty-three, hers were still in formation. Yet each wanted their art to serve society. Each longed for a place less tethered to rampant capitalism. For artists and intellectuals from all over the world but especially the United States, Mexico was that place.

The trio left New York on December 16, 1932. An irony not lost on them was that thousands of Mexicans and Mexican Americans crossed the southern border at the same time—a massive deportation euphemized as "repatriation." Fueled by racism and the Depression's economic collapse, the expulsion included many US citizens. Although anti-immigrant sentiment gripped the United States, artists and intellectuals embraced a larger sense of the Americas unbroken by borders.[29] Armed with political fervor, Josie, John, and Marion believed their art would transform the world. At the very least, the journey would change their lives.

PART II

Mexican Awakening
(1932–1936)

CHAPTER 8

"The Enormous Vogue of Things Mexican"

HEADING SOUTH TO MEXICO FROM NEW YORK, MARION WROTE TO MUSY from every stop. She praised John's superior driving and gushed about how her companions pampered her. They insisted on hotels with hot baths for Marion—far more luxury than she had at home in Brooklyn.

Perhaps that caretaking role renewed the couple's relationship. Josie dressed in new clothes that John had bought for her, which surely depleted their funds during the Depression. Still, tensions lingered from the three-way shifting emotional and sexual liaison. Was that why they often journeyed in silence? Or had they fallen into the spell travel casts, the present obscuring past and future?

Marion was wide-eyed at the American South. They passed historical landmarks like Harpers Ferry, West Virginia, where she noted the death of the famous abolitionist John Brown. Tennessee was a snowy wonderland of hoarfrost on the trees, the Blue Ridge Mountains an exquisite landscape. In Nashville, the seven-year-old Grand Ole Opry or Fort Negley, the Civil War redoubt, or other tourist sites might have invited a visit. But Marion, Josie, and John were not tourists. They were pilgrims and Mexico beckoned.

In this they were hardly alone. As early as 1914, journalist John Reed crossed the border to meet Pancho Villa and report back. In the 1920s, political and cultural crusaders followed. Ernest Gruening wrote a piece for *Collier's* that described the "rising hum of fervor, of a people reborn, of hopes rekindled." Postrevolutionary passion reached fever pitch by the time the *New York Times* announced the "enormous vogue of things Mexican" in 1927. The floodgates opened to artists, writers, musicians, and intellectuals from north of the border.[1]

The surge of the vogue overturned the suspicion that had dominated both countries at the turn of the century. Americans thought the Mexican was "an insurgent or a bandit or, at any rate, a conspirator against his own Government."[2] Mexicans found Americans crass and money oriented with no sympathy for the arts.

Mistrust transformed to a mutual embrace by the time Marion, Josie, and John crossed the border at Laredo, Texas, on Christmas Eve, 1932. They embarked on the not-yet-officially opened Pan American Highway, an ambitious multinational project that would eventually snake over 19,000 miles. In the 1930s, it was the route of choice to the Mexican capital. In later decades, hotels, restaurants, and other comforts would emerge to meet tourist needs. But for these travelers, the road was often rough. Marion's cultural awakening more than compensated: "I wouldn't have missed it for the world."

From Tamazunchale in the state of San Luis Potosi, her romance with Mexico and its indigenous people blossomed. She described "going through the most gorgeous mountains and country I ever saw in my life, full of these wonderful Indian people pure descendants of the old Aztecs, with bamboo huts and thatched roofs, banana and orange trees, cattle all over and wonderful colors everywhere the mountains raise their heads so high they are always covered with clouds. I would give anything to stop and paint these people but they are so strange and aloof, it would be quite difficult."[3] Marion's outsider status seemed inhibiting in ways it had not when she painted *Navajo Boy*. Restraint would serve her well in the coming days and deepen her appreciation for cultural difference.

Many shared Marion's passion for all things indigenous. As the Mexican Vogue expanded, leftist intellectuals applauded the integrated economies of Mexican villages, denouncing the growing industrialization and materialism of the United States. "Romantic anticapitalism" met "romantic primitivism" in lauding spiritually evolved pueblos. A steady stream of seekers descended on Mexico.

Marion declared car travel as the only way to glimpse this new world. She recalled, "In those days when you drove, it was very, very primitive. And the scenery was marvelous and seeing the Indians working in the fields. I was just so overcome with enthusiasm. I never felt that way again, I guess. Because, after all, I was very young."[4]

Marion was indeed young, unused to separation from Musy. In Mexico City, her homesickness spiraled. A childhood memory resurfaced: waking to find Musy gone, Marion would panic. Her mother missed her terribly. "We are very much alike in temperament," Marion wrote. "Tonight I feel so alone and blue. I long for my little sweetie." She worried over having left Musy for an indefinite time. "Jo and John think you're a swell mother and very gallant the way you sent me off with smiles and everything." She encouraged her mother to avoid loneliness by going to Theosophical meetings at the Des Artistes Hotel.[5]

The neo-Gothic Hotel des Artistes on Central Park West seemed light years away from the Mexico City hotels where Marion and her companions landed. Much reminded her of Paris, "except alas, there are no outdoor cafes after all, foreign and busy narrow streets with much bustle, Indians and Spaniards and beggars, hundreds of them, and even more churches everywhere, where the priests sit in an open confessional, and black-veiled women kneel and whisper their confessions."[6]

Marion had embarked with such high expectations that mixed reactions to the city were perhaps inevitable. The brutality of a bullfight horrified her. Mexico City's plaza was like Coney Island, full of junky toys, the Indians who sold them beset by poverty. She pined for the "primitive" village life she'd experienced on the trip south.

All three wanted an environment more peaceful than a hotel. In January 1933, they moved to a more affordable boarding house on Avenida Alvaro Obregón in Colonia Roma. Wealthy Mexicans and foreigners flocked to the neighborhood's European feel and art deco housing born of a post-revolution building boom. Marion welcomed the quiet, but she froze in the unheated buildings and the food upset her stomach. She had hoped the family-run pension would force her to speak Spanish; her lack of fluency increased her isolation. All those difficulties would continue to haunt her.

Marion's awe at Mexico's splendor balanced her complaints. The group climbed the pyramids at Teotihuacán. At the Palacio Nacional, Marion finally stood face to face with Rivera's murals that depict Mexico's ancient civilizations, Spanish colonization, and contemporary life. She likely knew some Mexican history before departing. Still, shock competed with horror at the murals' depictions of how indigenous people were enslaved, their religion and culture suppressed. A trip to Cuernavaca prompted her to extoll the wonderful diversity of Mexico's climate and cultures.

In a world that magnetized artists and radicals, Marion, Josie, and John ran into many people they knew. Marion complained about the uninteresting

Greenwich Villagers and Woodstock types, "hangers on and parasites who never do anything themselves."[7] "Real" bohemians created art.

Marion failed to see that she and the "parasites" were fellow pilgrims. Through the 1920s, press about the Mexican Vogue flourished in the United States. José Juan Tablada, a poet who lived in New York for more than a decade, worked tirelessly to promote Mexico. A 1923 exhibition at Gertrude Vanderbilt Whitney's Studio Club included work by Orozco and Covarrubias. The exhibition "Mexican Arts" opened at New York's Metropolitan Museum of Art in 1930 and traveled to thirteen cities. Americans embraced these introductions to Mexico's "unspoiled culture that had escaped the trammels of industrialization."[8]

Anita Brenner's *Idols Behind Altars* (1929) stirred more excitement about Mexican art. California anthropologist and folklorist Frances Toor launched the groundbreaking journal *Mexican Folkways* to chronicle and celebrate artists on both sides of the border. Enthusiasts kept moving south: silversmith William Spratling, writers John Dos Passos and Langston Hughes, journalist Alma Reed, photographers Paul Strand, Edward Weston, and Tina Modotti, among others. Marion would cross paths with many of them during her time in Mexico.

Although Marion shunned the "hangers on," once settled into Colonia Roma, she reconnected with old friends. Mexican painter Adolfo Best Maugard, a regular at Reiss's studio, was back in Mexico. Marion's good friend from New York, writer Verna Carleton, had moved to Mexico City with Ignacio Millan, a physician. They'd met in Marion's studio. Verna was posing for a portrait when Millan, studying in New York, wandered in. Before long, they married, with Diego Rivera and Frida Kahlo as witnesses.

Friends of Verna and Ignacio organized a party to introduce Marion, Josie, and John to the city's art scene. Even with limited Spanish, Marion connected on the dance floor with Leopold Méndez, a celebrated printmaker. Ever on the lookout for romance, she pondered the handsome Méndez. He had soft features and a shock of dark hair falling over his forehead. She restrained herself, surmising that he probably had a Mexican wife and child.

At the party, she also met Pablo O'Higgins, the artist who most influenced her life in Mexico. Born "Paul Higgins," he had changed his name soon after he arrived in 1924 to apprentice with Diego Rivera. Any links to his father's name would have damaged his radical credentials in postrevolutionary Mexico. As Utah's assistant attorney general, the elder Higgins had confirmed the death sentence for Joe Hill. The leftist "Wobbly" (Industrial Workers of the World)

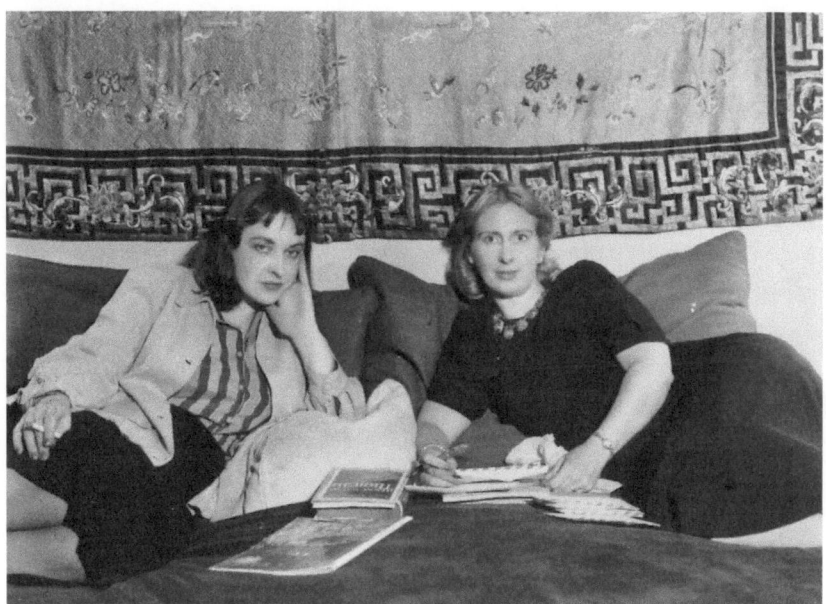

FIGURE 8.1. Marion Greenwood with Verna Carleton Millan. (Photograph © and courtesy of the estate of Marion Greenwood.)

hero and poet was widely believed to be innocent. Protesting his execution became a cause célebrè of the Left.

"Paul" to "Pablo" was logical but how to explain the addition of "O"? His maternal grandfather was a Northern Irish Presbyterian, but O'Higgins's name change suggested Irish Catholic heritage. In that identity shift, he signaled sympathy for the religion and experience of colonization Ireland shared with Mexico. "O" also hinted at *Los Patricios*, the St. Patrick Battalion of Irish immigrants who fought on the Mexican side in the 1846–48 Mexican American War. His new name "proletarianized" his identity, freeing him from his family history.[9]

In 1933, O'Higgins had returned from a journey to Europe and the Soviet Union armed with the language of "comrades."[10] Marion, after long political discussions on the journey south with Josie and John, now embraced that rhetoric. O'Higgins would accompany her as teacher and promoter through many stages of her life in Mexico. She harbored no romantic feelings, just deep appreciation for his kindness and generosity.

During the party, Marion learned from O'Higgins and Méndez about a program she described to Musy: "One thing which is swell is that painters like Leopoldo and Paul Higgins (who gives us Spanish lessons), they are all given jobs by the government to paint frescoes on walls in schools and public buildings so that they all have something to do and are given a position of some responsibility as soon as they show they can do good work."[11]

"The something to do" was the government mural project that would soon shape Marion's life. After the revolution, Obregón appointed writer and philosopher José Vasconcelos to head the Ministry of Public Education. In hiring artists to paint murals in public buildings, Vasconcelos aimed to educate and thus "redeem" the masses.[12] The broader goal was a spiritual nationalism based on *mestizaje*, a synthesis of European and indigenous cultures.[13] His parallel agenda was to erase Mexico's postrevolutionary violence under idealized murals that would steady the State and soothe international fears about instability.[14] Aztec pyramids and women weaving; Benito Juarez, Emiliano Zapata and Pancho Villa; Spanish conquistadors vanquished, workers organizing— these and similar images soon adorned the convent of San Pedro y San Pablo, the National Preparatory School, and the Ministry of Public Education. Gone were the European-focused arts programs of dictator Porfirio Díaz's regime. Muralism would shift in later years from Vasconcelos's focus on *mestizaje* to *indigenismo*, the "authentic" spirit of Mexico's *pueblo* (the people).

In 1924, Plutarco Elías Calles, El Jefe Máximo (the "Supreme Leader"), became president and Vasconcelos was forced from his post. By then, the muralists had moved in politically radical directions that the conservative Calles perceived as a threat. Funding disappeared for Siqueiros and Orozco, who sought work north of the border. Rivera continued to receive mural commissions, but he, too, eventually headed north. All left indelible marks on US public art and culture and on Marion's art.

On this first trip, Marion carried the fervor of the Mexican Vogue and was acquainted with some of its luminaries. She had painted José Clemente Orozco's portrait while he was in New York in 1929. In his early life, he'd participated in anarchist movements, but the time Marion met him, he condemned bloodshed for any cause as "butchery." Stories circulated that he had lost one hand in a violent encounter between supporters of Pancho Villa and Emiliano Zapata. He found this amusing. An accident when he was young was the real culprit.[15] Marion also embraced his broad humanism. How should a person be? She thought that Orozco knew.

Marion may have encountered Diego Rivera before her trip. Ignacio Millan had written to her in 1931 when Rivera headed to New York: "I want to tell you that Diego Rivera is coming to N. York in winter. If you are still wishing to have a share in his work, be ready."[16] It's more likely that in 1933, he was still a distant source of artistic inspiration. Within a few years, that distance would transform to intimacy.

It's equally unclear when Marion met Siqueiros. He'd been in and out of prison, fleeing north to the United States numerous times during the 1930s. His friendship with Marion was sometimes charged, but she admired his work. She later said, "He had completely different ideas, believed in keeping the image moving and he was playing around with all kinds of complicated optical problems and was fascinated with all kinds of new modern mediums like ducco (a paint used for metal and wood surfaces)."[17]

Rivera, Siqueiros, and Orozco got much of the glory, often to the neglect of other important artists. James Oles argues that Mexican muralism was "more than a monolithic movement sponsored by the Ministry of Public Education. Rather, by the 1930s it was a heterogeneous force marked by competing and overlapping strategies played out by a wide range of participants."[18]

In Mexico City and other artistic centers, Marion would encounter many of those participants. Her excitement grew in a Spanish class with O'Higgins. He knew all "the old geometric secrets of composition like the Pythagorean triangle and the Golden Mean, which the old Greeks and Egyptians used in their painting and architecture. It's just what I've been looking for as all the great artists had this knowledge."[19] O'Higgins offered to teach her to grind her own paint and, best of all, to master fresco. This was the gold she'd come to mine. Artists north of the border, Marion told Musy, lacked both the knowledge and government backing for muralism.

Mural painting offered meagre pay but opened a path to recognition and future employment. On a deeper level, Marion was thrilled to follow the great Renaissance muralists. Despite her discomfort with food she couldn't eat and buildings where she shivered, she assured her mother that her journey to Mexico was worth any cost. She urged Grace to join her, certain that O'Higgins could help them both.

Marion still missed Musy but her letters shifted from longing to advice. Write more often and send letters via air mail. Be careful and don't drink too much. Go to Florida (where her brother Wally was in temporary residence) but watch out for sharks. Don't rush across the street "like you do." Write more poems. John and Josie "think you're a real poet."[20] Her sign-offs still gushed: "I love you more than anything else in the world" or "more than life itself," always from "your baby girl" or "your Babito."

Marion recognized her debt to Josie and John. They'd bankrolled the trip and chose Mexico City as their first stop so Marion could connect to the art world. Now, Josie had a contract for her next book, *The Executioner Waits at the Door*. She and John longed for a quieter place to write. Marion claimed they had felt left out at the party set up by Verna Carleton and Ignacio Millan. All the Taos and Greenwich Village "hangers-on" made them nervous, she told Musy. "They are finished with all that."[21]

Maybe Marion wanted to honor their wishes. Maybe she was conflicted about staying in Mexico City. Perhaps a move would ease the three-way entangled relationship. Whatever the motivation, soon they were en route to Acapulco, Cuernavaca, and elsewhere as they searched for a new place. Soon, their letters were postmarked "Taxco." When the trio landed in the booming arts community, Marion's career as a muralist would finally begin.

CHAPTER 9

"A Perfect Romantic Setting"
Taxco and the Market Mural

THE JOURNEY FROM MEXICO CITY TO TAXCO TWISTED OVER ONE HUN-
dred and ten miles of labyrinthine roads. Poet and translator Witter Bynner described the colonial town as "beautiful beyond description, with cobblestoned
lanes leading always up and up into a hundred little heavens."[1] With every mile,
Marion's anticipation grew.

Starting in late January 1933, the travelers rented "Casa Sáenz," a house built
for Moisés Sáenz, the former subsecretary of education and a disciple of John
Dewey. Marion pronounced it a "palace" that rivaled the luxury of Yaddo. For
thirty-five dollars a month, their new home boasted "red stone floors, a bunch
of Indian servants, [a] courtyard blooming with flowers, in fact a perfect romantic setting," Marion wrote to Musy. "We rented it thro a writer friend here
named Bill Spratling."[2]

William Spratling, a tall, slender expat, was an architect and author. He had
arrived in Taxco in 1929 on an adventure that became permanent residence.
When writer Carleton Beals visited the same year, Spratling was the only American resident. A few years later, Beals declared the town haunted by bohemians.

This was exactly the crowd Marion, Josie, and John had hoped to avoid.
When they arrived, Taxco was already a bustling colony where artists and the li-
terati flocked to escape urban life. "The world is small," Marion told Musy. "Different people I've met here and in Mexico City all know some of my friends.
It's always the way in art colonies." She'd run into someone who knew her
brother Irwin, noting how kind and generous he was. Despite praise for a family

member, Marion reiterated her complaint about familiar faces: "The people travel but in the beaten path so that really one never gets away from the circle one first started in."[3] She was, of course, one of the circle of expats. Her attitude rested on an old story of tourists and travelers resenting one another.

Marion quickly overlooked those complaints. Beyond providing luxurious quarters, Taxco's art renaissance created the world where she would flourish. That flowering rested on Spratling's chance encounters and his ability to harness the gifts of the local community.

Spratling was a child of the American South. He studied and later taught architecture at Alabama's Auburn University, then moved to Tulane University in New Orleans. Older faculty members advised him to avoid housing in the disreputable French Quarter. He ignored their counsel. His landlady, newspaperwoman Natalie Scott, introduced him to William Faulkner, Sherwood Anderson, Oliver La Farge, and other artists, writers, and musicians flourishing in 1920s New Orleans. In 1926, he and Faulkner, who was also his roommate, published caricatures of those key players in *Sherwood Anderson and Other Famous Creoles*.[4]

At Tulane, archaeologist-anthropologists Frans Blom and Oliver La Farge encouraged Spratling's budding interest in Mexico. He soon embarked for Veracruz, then to Mexico City to write about colonial buildings for *Architectural Forum*. On the train, he struck up a conversation with a Frenchman wearing a monocle. Despite having little language in common, the two launched a lifelong friendship. René d'Harnoncourt would become an influential art critic and collector, stalwart supporter of Mexican artists, and director of the Museum of Modern Art in New York from 1949 to 1967. During Spratling's eventful first trip, he also met the editor of *Mexican Folkways* Frances Toor, Diego Rivera, and volcanologist and artist Gerardo Murillo Coronado, known as Dr. Atl. Such was the small, interconnected world of North American and Mexican artists and thinkers. After spending summers in Mexico from 1926 through 1928, Spratling moved permanently to Taxco.

Some acquaintances described Spratling as quirky and cantankerous. He also had a magnetism that attracted a wide circle of friends, including US ambassador Dwight W. Morrow. A Renaissance man and aficionado of all things Mexican, Morrow served from 1927 to 1930 and greatly improved US-Mexican relations. His respect for the country was a radical departure from the attitudes of his predecessor James Rockwell Sheffield.[5]

Spratling met Morrow and his wife, Elizabeth, during an early visit to Taxco.

The Morrows commissioned him to buy pottery for them and create drawings of their house in Cuernavaca. At the end of Morrow's stint as ambassador, he wanted to leave a gift to Cuernavaca. Spratling suggested that his friend Diego Rivera paint frescoes in the city's Cortés Palace. An avowed communist, Rivera could hardly be seen entering the US Embassy. Spratling arranged a meeting at Morrow's home.

Rivera arrived wearing a "new sharkskin suit, a Texas hat, and a forty-five." He and Morrow got on famously and launched the fresco plan. Rivera, however, fretted over how much to charge. Spratling figured the cost based on a one-meter-square oil painting Rivera had sold for a thousand dollars. At the projected size, the mural fee would be $12,000. Rivera recoiled at such an exorbitant price, but he promised Spratling a $2,000 commission if it were accepted. Morrow didn't blink.[6]

In January 1929, Spratling took his cash to the local peanut vendor in Taxco and bought a little house on Calle de las Delicias "set in a triangular garden" with "a deer, a green parrot, and a duck to keep him company."[7] The place offered Spratling a deep and enduring sense of home.

Spratling despaired at the tragic neglect of Taxco's silver industry. When he arrived, he'd found "a quiet little village, everyone was poor, the few mines open were 'high grading,' that is, working out only their richest veins, since silver was at an all-time low and could be bought for fifteen pesos a kilo."[8] That low price belied the importance silver had once held in what is now the state of Guerrero. More than seven hundred years before Taxco silver jewelry shops appeared in airports, indigenous people tapped the region's silver mines to create trade networks. In the 1550s, the Spanish hauled off the silver and abandoned Taxco.

After Morrow's ambassador position ended in 1930, he visited Spratling in Taxco. The friends discussed the state of the silver mines. Mexicans had continued to create silver chalices and *milagros*, tiny metal offerings to the saints often shaped like body parts. Except for Oaxacan necklaces and Pátzcuaro's fish earrings, silver jewelry was rare. Could new forms for silver resurrect the industry?

Inspired, Spratling convinced Artemio Navarrete and a few other accomplished goldsmiths from nearby Iguala to come to Taxco. He rented an old smelter, set up an apprentice system, and began jewelry production based on his own and others' modernist designs. Polished ebony and precious stones often enhanced the pieces aimed at high-end tourists seeking souvenirs with *Mexicanicity*.[9] Spratling was a traditional *patron*, exacting with high standards but also widely acknowledged as respectful of the artisans' talents. He later said, "We can teach [the indigenous people] nothing in the way of handicraft or artistry. The only thing I have done is to capitalize this gift."[10]

The silver industry's boost to art and tourism created the comfortable expat life Josie, John, and Marion now enjoyed in Taxco. They worked on their respective projects, settling into bed at 10:00 and rising at 7:00. A marvelous cook made healthy food, a boon to their collective health. Marion painted, took Spanish lessons, and sunbathed on the roof. Her gaze fell on "old chapels and shrines, blue mountains, Indians and burros trudging along winding roads in the sun." The Mexican night was "full of mystery outside, guitars and voices in the distance, and silent sandaled Indians with big sombreros walking in threes and fours down the cobbled streets."[11] The workers posed for her in the house so she didn't have to hunt for subjects.

She sought models anyway. Mexican life pulled Marion out of her comfortable quarters. On Sundays in the market and on the town's side streets, she watched the "young boys walk around the little square, and the girls, too, in the opposite direction, and a band plays all out of tune in the middle, and the little town with its crooked red roofed houses and steep narrow streets is like a toy stage setting."[12] She attended fiestas and rituals in the surrounding pueblos.

Marion's descriptions are filled with the contradictions of "romantic primitivism." She often called the Indians "childlike," yet she observed the indigenous rituals with admiration. Her descriptions of vibrant pueblo life have an ethnographer's objectivity. There was "dancing, fireworks, much praying and repenting, and baptizing and christenings." "Young girls who are to be confirmed dance and chant all day in front of the altars. Yesterday we went to a nearby village to watch a fiesta, and one Indian, a *penitente*, came on his knees for miles with an organ cactus with spikes on it tied to his bare back to the altar of the church, where he was absolved for his sins. The primitive Indian worship and customs underneath the veil of Christianity is very interesting."[13]

Peon's Funeral, based on a burial procession, is among Marion's Taxco oil paintings. Another, *Mother and Child*, features an Indian woman nursing her baby, a work that visiting American artists praised. One told her that she had "the most extraordinary talent for a woman that he ever came across and if I kept on plugging and didn't pay attention to anything else, I would really be a great artist someday," she wrote.[14]

Marion seemed unfazed by the "for a woman" comment. Relegating women to secondary status was, after all, the dominant attitude of the day. But easel paintings were not her goal. To learn fresco, she hoped to paint a mural inside their rented house. The owner, Moisés Sáenz, might pay her if he approved. She had already enlisted the help of local workers to mix cement and other preparations. "Aren't you proud of your little baby girl?" she asked Musy, adding, "I always seem to get people to do things for me, eh baby?"[15]

Marion encouraged Grace to come to Mexico, but she backpedaled on previous suggestions that Musy join her. When her mother complained about Florida, where various family members fled New York winters, Marion reminded her that no place is perfect. Appreciate the warmth, stay calm, and read good books. In Mexico, she warned, Musy would be sick all the time. Besides, Marion projected a return to New York soon. Before long, she told her mother, they'd be kissing and fighting again. She also discouraged Irwin, who must have expressed interest in visiting.

Who could blame Irwin and Musy for wanting to escape Depression-era New York for the life Marion had described? Who could blame Marion for wanting to protect her idyll at Casa Sáenz? She was thriving.

Marion bragged to Musy about her accomplishments, but she was also humbled by her good fortune. She would sit on the veranda after John and Josie went to bed to survey the sparkly lights of Taxco and ponder life: "For no reason at all I suddenly find myself in a country I longed to come to, and to be able to paint and live in luxury just like last summer in Yaddo and yet I haven't a cent behind me."[16]

Marion's luck kept growing. Chiltipin and Johnny Sutherland, the owners of the Hotel Taxqueño, commissioned her to paint a mural in their popular tourist lodging. Mabel Dodge Luhan had been one of their first guests, followed by Aldous Huxley, Isamu Noguchi, George Gershwin, and many others.

This was Marion's chance. Josie and John realized she would need additional help. They paid Pablo O'Higgins to come from Mexico City. Marion's gratitude mixed with her increasing political consciousness. She saw Josie and John's support as tied to their broader personal and political agenda of social transformation. Marion now envisioned a US revolution on the horizon. She assured Musy that the Depression would drive workers to revolt when class consciousness ignited the unemployed.

Pablo O'Higgins arrived on March 16 with a former assistant to Diego Rivera, Ramón Alva Guadarrama. They prepared the walls while John helped to mix lime. Marion transferred her market sketches to wet plaster, a challenging process she described to her father in a rare letter to him: "You have to be a mason first, it seems to me, and know just the right amount of lime, sand, and cement to mix together as a layer so when you paint, you have to work while it's wet, then the color is absorbed into the plaster."[17] The assembled team worked steadily, while hotel guests gaped and bombarded Marion with questions. By April 5, 1933, just before Marion's twenty-fourth birthday, the mural was finished. The hotel owners, the Sutherlands, celebrated her achievement.

Taxco Market features a lively mix of men in sombreros, serapes, and huaraches. Women draped in rebozos bustle around produce stalls. The market theme was characteristic for the era in Mexico. Markets were quintessential tourist magnets promoted by popular guidebooks. The lively, messy, colorful world of a market stood in stark contrast to the increasing gray of Depression-era America and its growing mechanization. Yet if the theme was typical, Marion's work stood out for other reasons. Dina Comisarenco Mirkin, author of a book on women muralists in Mexico, argues that the mural highlights the diversity and critical contributions of women to the economy.[18]

Marion's innovation shone in the mural design. The location on a six-square-meter wall on a narrow back stairway would have posed challenges for even an experienced artist. Yet Marion created a sense of movement, with figures staggered along the vertical steps. The design mimics the ascent of a hotel guest up the stairwell. James Oles writes, "It is almost as if the stairwell opens out into the town itself, and a market that is in permanent operation. Indeed, Greenwood's use of perspective provides the mural with a verticality and depth that mimics the steep topography of the town."[19]

The Sutherlands immediately produced postcards of the mural, and Josie began touting Marion's accomplishment. In *Mexican Life*, she noted that Marion brought to fresco "the same preoccupation with the content beneath the surface that distinguishes her portraits." Like Winold Reiss and her teachers at the Art Students League, Marion extolled ordinary working people, individuals set against distinct cultural backdrops. Josie celebrated the permanence of Marion's mural, unlike the work of artists who carried their paintings north. This placed her in the illustrious company of Rivera and Orozco. The latter, Josie asserted, was the stronger influence, with "his passionate convictions and preoccupation with the current of life beneath the outer garment."[20] Marion always claimed greater artistic allegiance to Orozco than Rivera. Her Taxco mural, though, lacked the political and historical references of either artist. In a tourist hotel in a tourist town, her traditionally themed mural nonetheless left her mark on the landscape.

The more enduring and remarkable aspect of *Taxco Market* was this: Marion

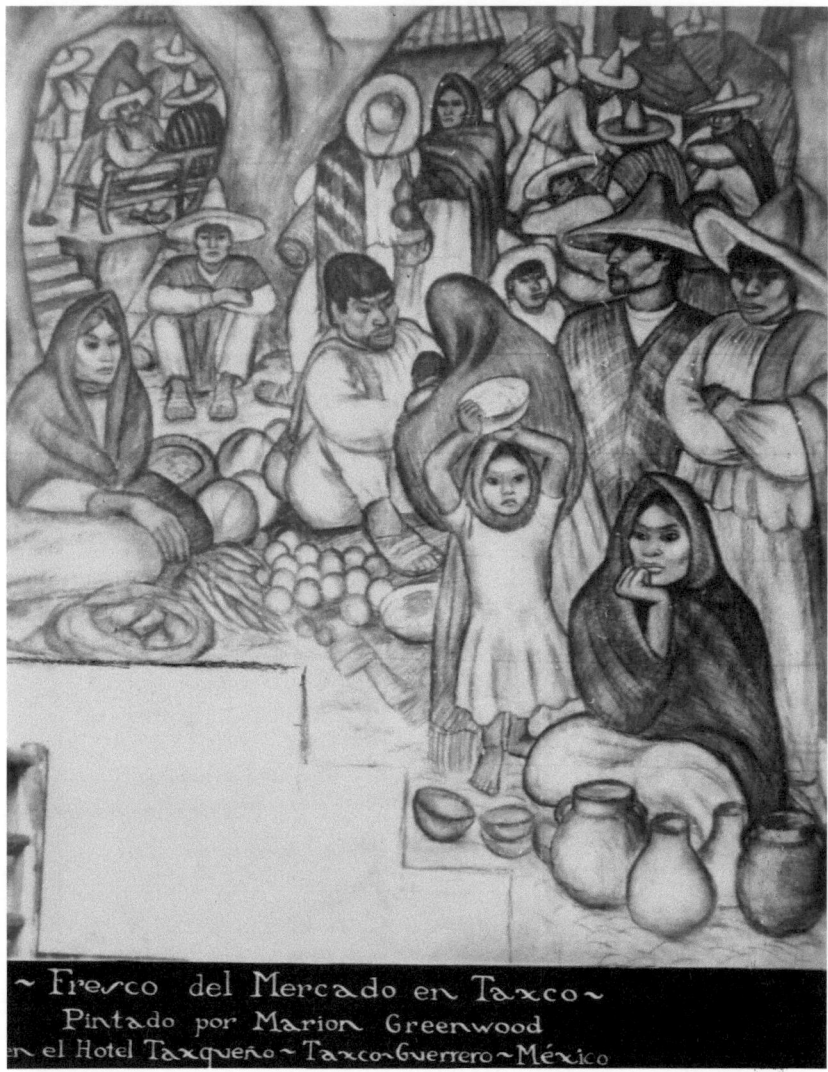

~ Fre∫co del Mercado en Taxco ~
Pintado por Marion Greenwood
en el Hotel Taxqueño ~ Taxco·Guerrero ~ México

FIGURE 9.1. Postcard of the *Taxco Market* mural, 1933. (Photograph © the estate of Marion Greenwood; courtesy of the Archives of American Art, Smithsonian Institution.)

became the first woman to paint a public mural in Mexico. "How's that baby?" Marion wrote to Musy about her newly exalted status. Other women had been assistants on Mexican murals, including Americans Ione Robinson and Maxine Albro and Mexican Isabel Villaseñor. In 1936, Aurora Reyes would claim her own "first" as a Mexican woman muralist for *Atentado a las maestras rurales* (Attack on the Rural Schoolteachers).[21] The stars aligned for Marion in part because she was a foreigner, free from the traditional bias against Mexican women painting in public places. Add to that assistance from O'Higgins, Josie, and John. Those merged with Marion's work ethic, talent, and chutzpah to get her there first.[22]

The mural affirmed Marion's decision to come to Mexico. Josie wrote to Musy to solidify that claim: "Your baby is a very good girl and is working very hard. She is a tremendous eater . . . and is looking about 500% better than when we left New York." Best of all, she was preparing for her art career in New York: "There is not a doubt in the world that so far as American painting is concerned, the movement is all toward mural and fresco." In a twist that surely rankled Marion's brothers, Josie added that many US commercial artists were unemployed, while "a good piece of work," by which she meant fine art, always found a home. Josie's letter echoed Marion's enthusiasm for Mexican life. Nights filled with the scent of a just-opened blooming cactus, birds whistled in the early morning, and the town's central square came "alive with color."[23]

Was such tranquility a true portrait of John and Josie's experience? Marion mentioned an occasional spat but mainly reported them working hard on their books while she painted. In reality, John had begun to lose focus. He neglected his writing, drank too much, and worried Josie. Marion lambasted him one night after Josie came to her shaking with anger and anxiety. The problem, as Marion saw it, was that his life had been too soft. He hadn't suffered or faced the hardships that she and Josie had.

Whatever Marion's feelings for John, Josie was her emotional anchor in Mexico, as her mother was at home. Marion once noted Josie and Musy's similar temperaments and shared astrological sign. She even remarked on their physical resemblance. It's too bad, she added, that Josie "hasn't your figure and nice narrow head."[24] Comparisons aside, Marion's stronger mooring was always her mother. She held back twenty dollars that Josie and John didn't know about so she could send it to Musy if needed.

Tensions more extreme than the occasional argument seethed under the surface. Josie's letters to friends were uncharacteristically terse, saying little about their Mexican adventure or their troubles. In February, she wrote to Katherine Anne Porter, "You say, tell me ALL. Would that I could."[25]

In the absence of written records, Josie's biographer Elinor Langer points to photos that offer a counterpoint to Marion's upbeat letters: "In most of the photographs John looks not only not happy but actively miserable, as if while she [Josie] is flowering, he is fading, and Marion looks not only indifferent, at times she looks positively glum."[26] John couldn't fathom how he found himself in this sexual and emotional triangle. His own occasional straying from the marriage was "so traditional it was practically respectable," Langer writes, "yet he fundamentally objected to the threesome."[27] During their Taxco sojourn, secret notes passed between different configurations of duos, weaving a web that would ultimately unravel.

John's discomfort added to a growing restlessness. His commitment was to communist revolution. To participate, he needed to return north. On April 5, he headed for Texas with the car. Plan A: Josie and Marion would take a train and meet him there in a month, then drive back to New York together. Plan B: John would finish his novel in Texas and return to Mexico. Neither scenario played out. Instead, Josie and Marion made plans for Mexico City.

Marion hoped that a bigger city would offer more mural commissions. Portraits were a less appealing option. A wealthy couple, the Parkhursts, had approached her to paint their rich American friends "who play bridge, the wives have their hair waved expensively—empty chatter, loads of money." She dismissed them as "the worst kind of American bores, absolutely without any sensitivity or natural culture." Most damning, they offered payment so low that it wouldn't even cover her materials. Rich Mexicans were almost as bad as their American counterparts.[28]

Marion's family prodded her to return home, but she stayed clear of their drama. Lester was struggling financially. Marion couldn't understand why his wife, Marie, didn't get a job as other wives did. Why didn't Lester and Irwin, both artists, collaborate? She realized that her family had never worked together, so likely nothing would change.

Marion's repeated urging that Grace join her went unanswered. A mutual friend, Armando, had spotted Grace at a party in New York and reported that she "was so drunk he'd never seen anything like it. It's too bad I thought she had come to her senses by now."[29] When Grace finally responded to Marion, she attributed her sister's success to luck. While luck played a role, and help from Josie, John, and Pablo O'Higgins an even greater one, Marion had also overcome numerous obstacles in completing the Taxco mural.

Marion constantly exhorted her mother to seek emotional and financial independence. Otherwise she would stay mired in the martyr complex born of residual Catholicism and Irish tragedy. Put money down on a small house in

Woodstock, Marion commanded. Build a little studio with big windows, a fireplace, and several bedrooms. Transfer your belongings and my pictures from Irwin's. Get Papa to help you move from Brooklyn. Don't let Irwin interfere. If he does, order him to give you his back studio and support you for the rest of your life. "I'm going to be utterly disgusted if you don't do it."[30]

Marion had once considered Provincetown, Massachusetts, the prominent arts colony where some of her Yaddo companions lived, as a possible part-time home. Now she argued that the familiarity of Woodstock made it the better choice. Miraculously, Musy scraped together the money and soon owned a plot of land in Woodstock.

As Marion navigated newfound success, she never forgot her mother's sacrifices. Musy still fought for time to pursue her literary and spiritual interests. From Mexico, Marion sent her a fifty-sixth birthday greeting: "Remember always, sweetie, how I love and appreciate you not only as a mother but as a person—and I want you to realize you are a person and an individual and remember that being a mother was just one function in your life, not everything. Joe [Josie] and John both said when they read your letters, it's wonderful how alive and clear cut your impressions are about everything." She encouraged Musy to keep writing because "creative work is the only thing that makes life worth living." Work for money is "merely prostitution" that leaves the artist "wondering why life feels futile and empty. Thank God I never went into commercial art, I am building my career and slowly progressing. Especially since I'm here I realize how happy I can be in just working and creating without distractions. And being in this rich, primitive country has freed many things, and I feel at last and with certainty that I have something significant to say."[31]

The complicated family narrative is all there: real bohemians persevere. Passion, not money, will triumph. In urging her mother to honor her creativity, Marion was justifying her own need to do so.

Like Yaddo, Mexico offered the university education Marion never had. In Taxco, she studied Spanish, Mexican history, and cultural issues. Her connection to master artists illuminated "the golden mean" and other secrets. "The interesting thing," she told Musy, "is that it all connects up to Theosophy—Rivera and Orozco, the two big fresco artists, are both Theosophists." That claim exaggerates their allegiance, but they were exposed to theosophical networks in Mexico and had been earlier.[32] Marion harnessed the Theosophy connection to justify her decision to stay. Surely Musy would understand the appeal of such a spiritually evolved world.

Marion also pulled out an old argument: Josie and John had invested in her and it would have been unfair to rush back to New York. She couldn't admit that she wanted to escape her family. But she related the advice of a palm reader who said she had "a great capacity for power as long as I kept following my own impulses and didn't let family or friends keep me from it."[33] Amen, Josie must have thought. Her negative feelings about Marion's family were smoldering and soon to emerge.

Toward the end of April, Marion and Josie left for Mexico City. Once ensconced in a hotel, their relationship began to fracture. Marion grew distant. She feared exposure as Josie's lover without the normalizing presence of John. For all the liberatory attitudes toward sex in the 1920s and 1930s, taboos about homosexuality endured. It's widely assumed that Spratling was gay. If so, that didn't seem to affect his stature in Mexico. Harsher judgments arrived from unexpected quarters. Katherine Anne Porter wrote to Josie about the "slimy tangle" surrounding Moisés Sáenz, a friend to many Mexican and North American gay artists and politicians. Porter denounced the world of "pederasts" and "fairies."[34]

Marion withdrew further. One day, Josie left her a note in their hotel in Mexico City: "I love you so much, too much, and too much love is never lucky. I wish you felt as I did about love, that it happened like a crater or a rock and was a phenomenon no matter where it came from. But unless it comes from a man it means so little to you, that it means now, just only beginning, to mean almost nothing to me but pain."[35]

Growing tensions with Josie tormented Marion. Uncertain of what to do next, her survival instinct rose. She put her troubles aside to fixate on possible commissions. Luck and connections soon merged to open a new path.

CHAPTER 10

Pátzcuaro and the Music in the Square

IN APRIL 1933, MARION CHARMED A GROUP OF DINNER GUESTS AT THE home of Ignacio Millan and Verna Carleton. The couple had moved from New York to Mexico City and were living with Ignacio's family. Despite limited Spanish, Marion engaged everyone in lively conversation, including Ignacio's relatives. She once told Musy that she could adapt to every kind of person to get somewhere in life. Her ability to connect was part ambition, part genuine interest in others. People in turn responded to her.

So it was for one guest, Gustavo Corona Figueroa. He was a handsome thirty-something lawyer and rector of La Universidad Michoacana de San Nicolás de Hidalgo in Morelia. Perhaps they sat side by side. Corona spoke English so they would have chatted with ease as Marion casually produced the postcard of her Taxco mural. Corona was impressed. He offered her a mural commission on the spot.[1] The university would pay for housing and materials but no salary. She eagerly agreed.

The drama of the spontaneous offer is alluring, but the mural commission may have been in the works. Corona wanted to attract artists to his university and likely knew of Marion's mural. The prestigious school begun in 1540 was one of the oldest institutions of learning in the Americas. However, the provincial capital of Morelia didn't tempt more established artists who could find better opportunities in Mexico City. Marion, in contrast, was young and hungry for experience.

Marion deeply appreciated Verna and Ignacio's support, but their life resurrected her disdain for marriage. "I'd go crazy in such an atmosphere," she said. "She has no freedom, no life."[2] She claimed that Ignacio denigrated Verna in front of guests. He praised Marion, she insisted, because she wasn't his wife. Marion distrusted Verna's professed love for Ignacio, suggesting she merely wanted a husband.

Marion's negative take on their marriage may have been unfair. Ignacio had written to her in March, voicing support for Verna's desire to write. Perhaps Marion was ambivalent about Verna. Their friendship would wax and wane over many years. Marion was "mad as a hornet" when Verna suggested the rector, Corona, as a potential love interest. She demanded that Verna "stop suggesting men for me, I would arrange my own life."[3] Verna also questioned how long her friend's financial luck would last. Marion fumed that her friend, like Grace, didn't acknowledge her diligence.

Marion's artistic focus, fear of losing her freedom, and her parents' unhappy union all shaped her conflicted view of marriage. She told Musy that Verna and Ignacio offered "an interesting glimpse into a form of life I might have lived and almost came near to doing but thank God I had sense enough to realize it would be that way."[4] "Came near" suggests a rejected marriage proposal, but does "that way" refer to all marriages?

Marion claimed to be finished with men. Then she made a classic contradictory turn after she heard that her Yaddo flame, Philip Stevenson, was frustrated with his wife and contemplated a trip to Mexico. "Who knows?" she wrote to her mother, "I may yet come back with a good husband."[5] Marion needed connection; Josie was right that her orientation was to men. Perhaps Marion's reconsideration of Philip also underscores the pressure on women to conform, even in the bohemian art world.

Marion buried those concerns to focus on mural planning. Not long after the dinner party, she and Josie left Mexico City for Michoacán. Crossed by the Sierra Madre del Sur and the Trans-Mexican Volcanic Belt, the rural state teemed with pine and juniper forests, corn and wheat fields. Although Marion would paint the mural in urban Morelia, a nearby town in the mountains enticed her. Pátzcuaro, about sixty kilometers from Morelia at approximately 7,020 feet, was an oasis of calm after Mexico City. Towering stands of eucalyptus trees lined the entrance to town. Red tile roofs dominated the aerial view and stone arches edged the central plazas. Wrought-iron balconies jutted out from second-story windows of colonial mansions hidden behind huge wooden doors. Pátzcuaro was the embodiment of authentic Mexico.

That authenticity was partially the design of Lázaro Cárdenas, a native son of Michoacán who was governor from 1928 to 1932. He took over a state still

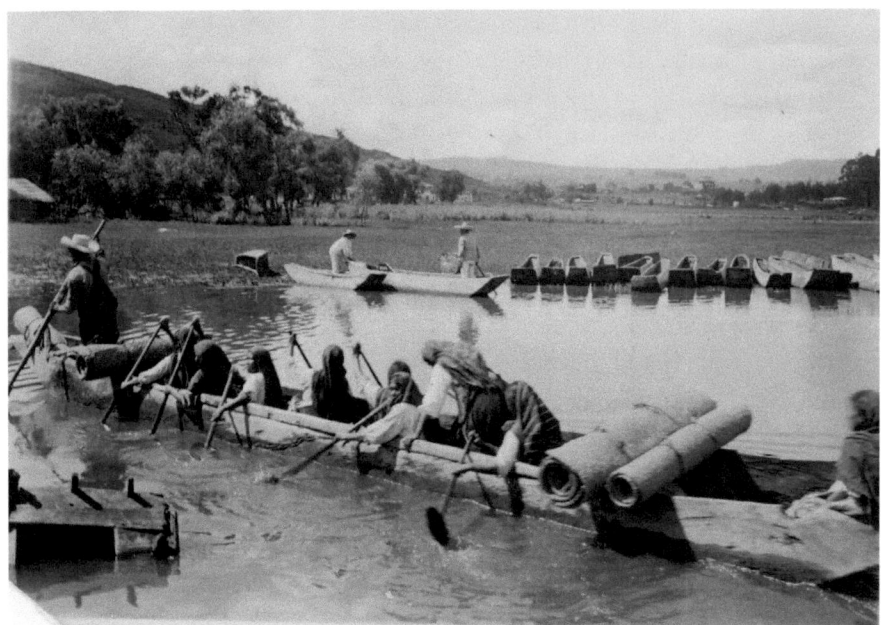

FIGURE 10.1. Fishermen on Lake Pátzcuaro in *tuparis* (dugout canoes), circa 1933. (Photograph © and courtesy of the estate of Marion Greenwood.)

convulsed by the bloody Cristero Wars. When the postrevolutionary federal government cracked down on the Catholic Church, religious rebels and farmers fought back. Shouting ¡*Viva Cristo Rey!*, they attacked government forces, who in turn tortured and killed priests. Cárdenas was determined to bring peace and prosperity.

His economic development program promoted tourism throughout Michoacán with a focus on the pueblos surrounding Lake Pátzcuaro. That project would continue into his term as revered president from 1934 to 1940. He aimed to achieve locally what the postrevolutionary government had attempted nationally: unity through shared symbols. Art historian Jennifer Jolly argues that Cárdenas made Pátzcuaro a laboratory for the creation of a Mexican national identity rooted in *indigenismo*, traditional arts, and muralism. His efforts fed the larger stream of *Mexicanidad*—"Mexicanness." *Lo tipico* Pátzcuaro was the nation, writ small.[6]

Lake Pátzcuaro and its indigenous pueblos captivated Marion. Michoacán was and remains one of the richest repositories of traditional arts in Mexico.

The Purépecha, then called Tarascan by nonindigenous people, were master artisans well before colonization. Yet the creation of pueblo-specific craft production is often attributed to the sixteenth-century Spanish Vasco de Quiroga. The first bishop of Michoacán, Tata Vasco, lives on in popular memory as a benevolent figure who created village hospitals. These were meant to provide indigenous populations with moral and artistic education (along with conversion).[7] This legacy is now contested, but during the 1930s, tourist brochures and even President Cárdenas invoked Tata Vasco's mythic status. Among the arts, Lacquerware was particularly important, but other *artesanias* included woven textiles and rebozos, carved furniture, silver jewelry, ceramic pots, candelabra, capes and feathered garments, masks, leather clothing, baskets, and straw work. Though Marion hadn't worked out the mural design, she decided indigenous life would be her subject.

Before venturing out to pueblos, Marion explored the town with Josie. They stayed at the Hotel Ocampo on the Plaza San Augustín, across from the sixteenth-century convent of the same name. Marion's vision of "real" Mexico appeared under the balcony of their room: vendors selling produce and folk arts under colonial building facades. At night, Josie and Marion gazed up at the moon, that shared symbol of love and pain from their time at Yaddo. Josie would be haunted by the "dreamlike lake and square" where "in twilight, the little lights coming out, the moving people and you hanging over the balcony looking on with your great green eyes."[8] That haunting included Josie's desire to stay with Marion.

Josie did not stay. The women's differences glared: age, artistic goals, and depth of passion and commitment. Josie saw little chance those would change. Preoccupied with Marion, Josie's progress on a second novel in a planned trilogy stalled in Mexico. She weighed Marion's mercurial emotions against her life with John. They'd built a marriage on shared passion for writing and political change. Despite a desperate love for Marion, Josie boarded a train in late May to meet John in Texas. They drove back to Erwinna, Pennsylvania, alighting on the exact day that Josie had arrived at Yaddo the previous year. Her world had transformed in those twelve months.

Marion's repeated phrase, "Now I'll be all alone," obsessed Josie as she journeyed home. She saw their aloneness as different. Marion's need didn't seem to her as tortured or complete as her own. She'd predicted, then witnessed Marion's return to men. Josie poured out her heartbreak: "If I had taken a spoon and scooped you out and crawled into your little hide, I couldn't live more completely in you. . . . Maybe it was more for Mexico than for me that you came away, but I knew I'd get you to love me just as I know now that I will see you and love you again." Until that happened, Josie's ache would resurface with every full moon. She loved "a small old moon and the young new moon but the big moon I dread and suffer to see."[9] Something in its reliable return, the endless cycle of remembrance, tormented Josie.

The two had many terms of endearment. One of Josie's for Marion was "Nealy," a beloved friend she either knew or invented as a child. On the train, she pretended "like I used to as a little girl with Nealy . . . just sit with her on that green bank under that lilac tree where I sat all alone as a little girl and where I'm sitting now waiting for Nealy to come again."[10]

Josie eased her ache through writing: "The only thing that will save me is my work and I will cling to it like a raft in a flood."[11] She urged Marion to do the same. Keep art at the forefront. Hide your problems from the university rector, Corona, who might not sympathize. Remember why you are there and don't squander this opportunity. Josie's role as cheerleader, advisor, and occasional scold would keep Marion bound to the mural project.

In Pátzcuaro, Marion pined for Josie. She saw her "Papeeta" everywhere she looked: "I'm so lonesome for you, Baby. I feel worse, much worse than when Philip left me in Yaddo. . . . I can't even write without weeping. I feel so alone. Dreamt about you all night and when I lay in bed your face is as clear, with the shiny blue eyes looking at me with such tenderness."[12] Marion's expressions of love often mixed with gratitude, a source of torment for Josie since she could not tease them apart.

After Josie left, Marion's appreciation for Pátzcuaro deepened: "The little plaza seems to come more alive and interesting each day, and there's been a great full moon lately that stayed out, while a soft rain comes down, and the Indians gather under the portals and sing when it rains and the little lights of the *puestos* (stalls selling goods or food) burn till very late."[13] She loved the spectacular drama of the summer rainy season. The sky seemed close, and she welcomed the rolling thunder streaked by sudden sunlight.

Marion wanted to create an original vision of Michoacán life untarnished by other artists' abundant images. Outsiders had long flocked to the region around Lake Pátzcuaro. In the nineteenth century, Alexander von Humbolt described the lake as one of the world's most picturesque. Into the next century, travelogues and guidebooks flourished, including a popular US tourist guide, *Picturesque Mexico*. Romantic photographs of fishermen with butterfly nets and women selling *charales* (a type of fish) in the market fueled a growing postcard industry.[14]

Among the American artists and writers who preceded Marion were Edward Weston and Tina Modotti. Anita Brenner commissioned them in 1926 to take photographs for her book on Mexican art, *Idols Behind Altars*. They had traveled the region with Miguel and Rosa Covarrubias, whom Marion knew from Winold Reiss's studio in New York.

How would Marion depart from other artists' perspectives and see the region with new eyes? Who would allow her to sketch? When she initially traveled to the pueblos, indigenous people, whom she described as "proud and contemptuous," refused to pose. They laughed at her offers of money as "too ridiculous."[15] Marion admired this lack of attachment to money. "They're very casual about spending, and they're poor, too. It's a nice quality."[16]

Marion persisted despite her frustration. She fumed about repeated attempts to hire boats and cars, annoyed by Mexican protocol, which, "after a lot of palaver," still "seems to require a great fuss first before you get anything." But by the end of May, she was traveling to pueblos via burro ("my backside is raw"); the local doctor's boat (hard to procure); or with "my muchacho," Cristophe," "nice but just a kid"; and two "little toughies who run the taxi" (potentially dangerous).[17]

For one pueblo trip, Marion traveled by taxi with Cristophe and "the toughies." On the return to Pátzcuaro, the car broke down just as a huge thunderstorm swept across the lake. The dirt roads muddied so the group settled into the taxi for the night. The toughies fell asleep snoring in the front seat. Marion huddled in the backseat with the muchacho, Cristophe, "under a coat, soaken wet, cold and hungry and pitch black." She recalled, "During the long fifteen hours we sat in the car, he got quite hot and bothered. I spent most of the night telling him 'no aprendo' when I apprendod very well that he wanted me for just a 'momentito.' The nerve. But he took it all right and didn't seem hurt." Dawn came, burros arrived, "an Indian lent me his sarape and we all jogged slowly back with the rising sun and the wet smell of the earth, it was beautiful." She seemed gleeful about the unexpected events even if she felt "that I've been buggered by a burro."[18]

Marion's adventures continued throughout June and July. In one pueblo, she had lunch with "the big hombre in the checked shirt, pistol, boots, mustache n' everything"—a man Josie had admonished her to avoid. She described him as "a gentle soul with a child's mind," refuting Josie's fears.[19] She returned to Pátzcuaro after a cockfight, the lake a deep emerald streaked with purple. She sketched men working in the fields and joined her muchacho, Cristophe, for a wonderful local wedding on the island of Janitzio. The local potters of Tzintzuntzan, the seat of the Purépecha Empire before Spanish colonization, welcomed her. She raved about the beauty of their ceramics.

In the pueblo of Erongarícuaro, Marion initially hit resistance: "The women hide their faces or run as if I were a monster and the men laugh and move triumphantly away and there I am helpless." However, by the time of the June Corpus Cristi festival, she felt more welcome. Marion described locals "dancing with fishnets and great canvas fish, burros wreathed in orchids, men showing how they make clay tiles, and agricultural products . . . appreciating the things of the earth." One image inspired comparison to a Greek frieze: "a great line of oxen wreathed in flowers around their horns and bellys and beautiful carved ancient plows with wonderful Indians behind each one." Marion called the event "wonderfully pagan," but in fact Corpus syncretizes indigenous and Catholic beliefs and practices. The church's celebration of the body and blood of Christ merge with traditional petitions to the gods for a fruitful rainy season and harvest.[20] Marion summarized the event's final hour when the Indians "threw great lumps of golden wheat at each other," ending up in front of the church where they "kneeled and the priest blessed the wheat and I wanted to weep, it was so beautiful." The next day, the reality of indigenous life hit hard. At a hacienda where she had lunch, she was appalled to learn that the Indians waiting on them were paid "only fifteen centavos a day and corn."[21]

From Erongarícuaro, Marion couldn't find transport back to Pátzcuaro. She joined another American artist, Ryah Ludins, to hire a local with a canoe to row them across the lake. The sun blazed, followed by torrents of rain. Ryah remained uncomplaining throughout, which riled Marion no end. It was just the beginning of her grumbling about her companion.

Ryah had arrived in Pátzcuaro in June. Marion initially welcomed the company of a good artist with a sense of humor. Yet she soon grew bored and resentful, perhaps jealous that Ryah exuded a confidence she lacked. Ryah was too happy all the time, Marion grumbled, and so "damn optimistic, she doesn't mind anything."[22] Such upbeat attitudes annoyed the brooding, Dostoevsky-loving side of Marion. Still, she planned to tap her companion's expertise to work out the mural dimensions. Marion justified milking Ryah's knowledge: "She's certainly been getting a hell of lot coming around with me, she saves money and gets subject matter she'd never get otherwise." Her question to Josie was strictly rhetorical: "I'm awful, ain't I, baby?"[23]

Paul Strand arrived that summer, staying at the Concordia Hotel across from Marion in the Ocampo. He was assigned to report on craft education in Michoacán.[24] With him was Agustín Velásquez Chávez, the nephew of Carlos Chávez of the education ministry. Marion sometimes dined with the group, although she complained that Strand was "avidly buying Pátzcuaro out" of the town's art, as had Weston before him.[25]

Josie fired back at Marion's grievances about other foreigners: "Please be nicer to Ryah. You shouldn't act as if Mexico was yours alone." She reminded Marion of the aid she'd received: "If I had not been able to pay Paul [O'Higgins] and Ramón [Alva Guadarrama, an assistant] to come to Taxco, where would you have been?" Verna Carleton and Ignacio Millan's connections had smoothed her path. Josie refuted Marion's contentions that he and Verna were both neurotic, their marriage a sham. Ignacio had, Josie said, "a first rate mind, and I don't give a damn what his attitude toward Verna is."[26]

Josie gave a searing report on Marion's family. She'd visited them in Brooklyn after her return north. She reassured Musy that her baby was fine and that the Mexico experience would boost career and character. But Josie had to endure Musy's endless complaints about her sons. She hated the negative way she talked about Grace. "It froze my blood," Josie said.

Josie also worried about the effect Grace and the other Greenwoods had on Marion. Her sister had arrived in Mexico with her new husband, musician Bill Ames. Josie suspected, perhaps prompted by Marion, that Grace had married for convenience: "It is kind of awful to marry just to go to Mexico. And some bitter core in her makes all her personal life just nothing to her." Grace, she asserted, had damaged Marion by encouraging her to have affairs. Her sister could "gum things up for you there, please don't let her talk too bohemian, it won't help you with those people. And don't let her see this letter, which may be very unjust to her. I like Grace for her guts and lack of hypocrisy but I don't want you ever to be like that." "Don't ever change how you are," Josie begged. "Even your mother's love," she wrote, "which is warm and beautiful, has the power to hurt you in its own need."[27] Josie's warning about Marion's family was echoed by friends and lovers throughout her life.

Perhaps Marion brushed off the criticism of Musy and Grace, but she listened regarding Ryah. She backed off her complaints, at least for their time in Pátzcuaro. They commiserated over stomach ailments and other problems that beset foreigners in Mexico, a group Marion pronounced to be nothing but a lump of symptoms.

The most prominent symptom was insect bites. Marion mused about how Domingo, the hotel housecleaner, might react to her naked body: "He's a fairy but that doesn't prevent him from peeking at me through a crack in the door when I'm undressing." Just wait until he "gets a glimpse of me in . . . all the glory of my thousand and one scars and flea bites, which seem to be increasing." She was sure Domingo would run a mile.[28]

In a photo Marion sent Josie, she wears a wrinkled cotton blouse, an A-line skirt, and battered shoes. Although conscious of her great beauty, she didn't fuss about dress and rarely mentioned clothes. With no salary for the mural, she bought only essentials. As for shoes to fit her large feet, "they don't come as big as God made mine." When she met an American tourist wearing size ten oxfords, she traded a sketch for the shoes.

On the back of the photo, Marion scribbled that she was feeling romantic—not surprising for her. After several months in Pátzcuaro without Josie, her loneliness built. She pronounced her *muchacho*, Cristophe, too young. She'd also discovered he had killed three men, one for refusing to play his favorite song in a local brothel. Not a likely romantic prospect.

Then Marion met Manuel Moreno Sanchez, a handsome young member of Michoacán's justice tribunal, when he visited Pátzcuaro. She buried her reservations about Mexican men, at least this one. He was twenty-four, accomplished, and interested in her. Marion painted his portrait. In return he gave her a copy of his *Imperialismo y el Derecho Internacional* (*Imperialism and International Law*), as well as Alma Reed's monograph on Orozco.[29]

Manuel returned to Morelia but lingered in Marion's mind. In July, she wrote to Josie, "Manuel is making no bones about saying he is falling in love with me. He's very young and untouched and reminds me of a wild colt. I'm getting to like him a lot and at least it will make living in Morelia bearable." Yet she added, "I certainly can't have an affair with him, not with the fresco to do, and in a small town like Morelia, and I don't think I'd want to marry a Mexican."[30]

Josie lost no time in responding: "Listen sweetheart and look at me. . . . You have a gigantic piece of work to do and you waste yourself as you always have. Now, this chance will come but once. Pull yourself together and get a little hard. . . . You aren't there to enjoy yourself." She interpreted the growing misspellings in Marion's letters as signs of instability. Her counsel on Manuel: "I doubt he wants to marry you, I think he wants to make you." On what life would be like if she married Manuel: "You would live in the provinces," an imprisonment worse than Verna Carleton's in Mexico City. Just having an affair would be worse. On proper behavior: "Mexicans are much more conventional than we are even in our provincial cities and you know nothing about them—all you know is the code of bohemian life and nothing could more ill equip you for Mexico."[31]

Josie's response mixed practical advice with her lingering pain. She knew Marion would leave her for a man. "I wouldn't ask you to have my fate, to love a man and yet to yearn for me as I yearn for you. . . . You will marry someone, you will get yourself involved and you will not be like me." She wanted Marion to be happy and "free from the kind of galling need that will keep me always moving from land to land. No place will be wholly good without you." She had offered her heart and Marion had let her pass from her life as smoothly as from a dream. "I am humiliated," Josie wrote, "to have shown you my great need." Her ache is palpable: "Someday the water will rush over my head, the drowning, you know, really do drown."[32]

Marion quickly responded. Manuel was just a way to spice up social life she described as "hellishly dull": "I'm not made of wood, naturally I'm going to react to Manuel. I'm made that way. I always have to have something like that going on around me." "Something like that" was sex, romance, being needed, and living on the cusp of excitement. Yet no man, Marion asserted, "could ever make a difference between me and you."[33] Belief in love was "taken out of me, by men, the only real love seemed to me to be that of a mother for a child, and then you came along and made me believe."[34]

Josie's angst was compounded by problems with John. In her letters, Marion mused about their happy Mexican sojourn. In fact, their three-way relationship had driven a wedge between Josie and John. They still loved one another, but their union teetered on a precarious edge.

Amid the emotional turmoil, Josie wrote articles to promote the mural project and allay Marion's anxiety. She had reason to worry. Political problems at the university mirrored larger tensions in Michoacán. The Catholic general Benigno Serrato replaced Lázaro Cárdenas as governor in 1932. He was seen by Cárdenas's supporters as "counterrevolutionary." The conflict played out at the university where striking students called for Corona to resign as rector. A group came to Pátzcuaro and confessed to Marion their plan to oust him. After taking her into their confidence, they still viewed her as his accomplice.

Despite fear that the students would sabotage her mural, Marion carried on with sketching the Purépecha. Indigenous people had "aroused empathy" in her going back to classes with Winold Reiss and her trip to the American Southwest. In Pátzcuaro, she showed new awareness, admitting "I'm romantic about them [Indians], I know. But they appeal to me very much." Lyrical descriptions of the landscape merged with recognition of her outsider status: "In this season, the sky a deep steel blue very dark and the mountains with blood red seams all over it, the earth is so red in the rainy season because everything else is green—and the Indian walking burdened in the mud speaking in soft Tarascan and smiling with good faces—very good faces. The Indians are so good." And, "I love them but I am apart. I shouldn't try to paint these people." She'd moved beyond her ignorance of cultural taboos when she painted *Navajo Boy*: "Why should I [paint] when the Indians themselves are such swell artists? They should be given a chance to paint walls and it would make anything else look sick."[35]

The insects, challenges of transportation to the pueblos, and loneliness—all pushed Marion toward Morelia. Student resistance wouldn't hold her back. She left Pátzcuaro on August 6, 1933, with a portfolio full of sketches and a heavy heart. She had come to love the rains drenching the lake and the countryside, pounding the plaza as she stood on her balcony at night. "You have no idea how dramatic and ominous this country becomes now," she told Josie, "with the continual rolling of thunder, and great patches of sunlight like spotlights on a stage."[36] Twelve moons had passed since she met Josie at Yaddo, three since her lover returned to John. Nostalgia, regret, and a "large dose of painful brooding" filled her letters: "The music in the square is so sad tonight—and the rain, it never stops."[37]

CHAPTER 11

"A Girl Alone" in Morelia

IN THE FALL OF 1933, MARION PERCHED ON A SECOND-STORY WOODEN scaffold at el Colegio de San Nicolás in Morelia. Local people gathered to gaze up from the courtyard's manicured gardens. What prompted their open-mouthed astonishment—that *la gringuita* painted through the sacrosanct siesta hours or that she dressed in overalls? A "girl alone," as she described herself, was brazen enough, but dressed like a man?[1]

Marion arrived in August from Pátzcuaro, crossing the verdant wheat and corn fields of Michoacán. Morelia is located at approximately 6,200 feet in the Guayangareo Valley of the Sierra Madre Mountains, a drop of about 1,000 feet from Pátzcuaro. She moved into the Hotel Casino on the main Plaza de los Mártires. From the balcony, she could survey the growing capital city where horse-drawn buggies and campesinos on burros met Fords and Buicks on the streets. The stunning buildings of pink cantera, cobblestone streets, and views of the surrounding mountains would have enticed any visitor. However, in 1933, Morelia was also a provincial capital. Women who stepped outside the gender norms of home and hearth raised eyebrows. "The Mexican woman has no more freedom than in a harem," Marion declared.[2]

Photographs fail to capture the loneliness that accompanied the creation of her mural. Political issues kept Marion holed up in her hotel room. The student strikes had shuttered the university for much of the summer, but by fall the campus was open again. Corona somehow held his position as rector. Still, student mistrust lingered, making Marion's position tenuous and stalling the start of painting. At one point, students resolved to "destroy any wall painted by an adventuress from New York."[3] One night, she received a phone call from an unidentified man. He'd heard that Marion wasn't enjoying Mexico so why didn't she just leave? Her fear intensified when someone broke the lock and entered her hotel room, although nothing was taken.

On Sundays, Marion watched the faithful flock to the magnificent eighteenth-century Baroque-style cathedral and stroll through the lively city center. Their promenades deepened her desolation. She pronounced Sunday "unbearable in every part of the world, stiff people walking around the square pathetically all dressed up."[4] The day's activities embodied all that she hated—convention, staid family life, a focus on appearances. In her utopian vision of communism, "there are no Sundays in Soviet Russia."[5] Her reaction reveals what was sorely lacking in her life: ritual, connection, and belonging. She wrote to Josie, "I've never felt more alone or had the horrors more than now."[6]

The growing independence Marion had felt in Pátzcuaro began to wane. Her stomach clutched when she woke, triggering memories of childhood when her mother was gone in the morning. Now she again faced "that horrible feeling of absolute isolation and of no point to my existence": "It all comes down to an inherent loneliness which has caused me to waste my time and body in a frantic sort of clutching with people I didn't care for. It isn't searching because I don't expect to find anything. It's an escape from myself." Marion's fear that she would never have an enduring relationship had kept her searching for lovers in New York. If one failed, another hovered in the wings. To Josie, she wrote, "I can't do that here—I'm in an absolute prison—and how I hate myself for this pettiness and pride." There was no escape. "Now I'm facing the music."[7]

Technical problems compounded political constraints. Local contractors mistakenly used the lime meant for the wall. While waiting for supplies, Marion overcame her fears to explore the beautiful colonial city. She visited an "insane asylum" with another artist. Scenes of women with shaved heads huddled in a courtyard under the baking sun horrified and fascinated her.[8] She ventured into the countryside with an odd combination comprised of Manuel's sixteen-year old nephew, a disabled writer, and a congressman. The drinking and target shooting didn't daunt Marion. But the writer, whom she described as "loco," "got sweet on me and kissed me in front of the other two. It's just the hardest thing to know how to act with these Mexicans."[9]

She read the only book she had, *Virgin Spain,* by her Yaddo companion Waldo Frank. She begged Josie to send books, which she would devour. Manuel eventually brought her James Joyce's *Dubliners* and W. Somerset Maugham's *Of Human Bondage.*

As an erstwhile "novio," however, Manuel backpedaled. He likely realized a gringa would not serve his political ambitions. He avoided seeing her alone, afraid of the optics. Marion realized how little she understood Mexican culture: "I never realized the barrier between different races till now, although I've been intimate with mostly foreigners but foreigners in one's own land is quite different." She nurtured little remorse about Manuel's rejection. She told Josie that he could go "sit on top of an organ cactus for all I care."[10]

Morelia's social scene made Marion suddenly conscious of her tattered clothes. She relied on an old red leather jacket to brave dances where the Mexican women wore floor-length gowns. Women eyed her as though "I were some strange specimen from the moon."[11] The wife of the Catholic governor, Benigno Serrato, objected to her presence. Then Marion heard rumors wafting over from Pátzcuaro that she drank and caroused. Gossip circulated that she was lazy, which surely galled her. Marion prided herself on her work ethic.

Most vexing, Marion agonized over the mural composition. She had kept Corona at bay all summer, and she now felt pressured to produce something profound. "If I were doing symbolic stuff it would be easier. The realistic approach is always the most difficult," she wrote. She described a "peculiar feeling that it's another person that does it, my work I mean. There's some knot somewhere that ought to be untied."[12]

The project so plagued her that she needed escape. She slept, smoked, and drank. But she assured Josie that she was not becoming an alcoholic like her Irish grandfather.

Maybe Marion hoped for mystical intervention with her composition. Each day, she crossed the plaza from her hotel to the Museo Michoacano on Calle Allende. In a room she likened to a monk's cell, she worked on her sketches. Religious texts in Latin gathered dust alongside plaster *santos*, angels with trumpets, and pre-Hispanic images. The ill-fated Emperor Maximilian, executed by the Mexican government in 1867, and his wife, Carlota, had stayed in the building on a visit to Morelia. It was not their ghosts or those of the Catholic saints that haunted Marion. Rather, she felt the spirits of indigenous people, "these great Indian idols." "I feel strangely connected to them," she wrote to Musy while working on sketches of their descendants. "If we could only look back into the mysteries of the ages, wouldn't it be wonderful. Someday we'll be able to—just like the radio catches the vibrations in the ether."[13] Perhaps the conjured spirits offered Musy solace for her daughter's absence.

In the museum room, Marion turned her abundant drawings into full-scale cartoons. But what should they convey? "I'm afraid that I have nothing to say," she wrote, "which has not been said before in the way of social significance and political attitudes, it's all been said very well by Orozco and Rivera and many others. I'm simply going to paint these people as I feel them in all their sadness, their apathy, and their beauty. Hammers and sickles, and historical periods and personalities have been done to death. I have only become class conscious in the last year, it would be an affectation for me to paint the usual propaganda at this period when I have nothing original to offer whereas if I paint something I *feel* it might have much more significance."[14]

What she *felt* was the dignity of working people. She would portray the daily labor of fishing, farming, and folk art production in the pueblos around Lake Pátzcuaro. To counter potential objections, Corona's secretary, Salvador Gó-mez, enlisted a group of students to assess some of her hundreds of sketches. A surprising ally emerged: a student who had attended Erasmus Hall, the Brooklyn high school that Marion left at fifteen. The focus on indigenous people must have met the group's approval. She got the green light to move forward. However, the students' blessing didn't end her anxiety.

Marion soon realized the responsibility of altering an iconic building. The Spanish bishop "Tata" Vasco de Quiroga who established Michoacán's village hospitals, also founded the Colegio de San Nicolás in 1540. In 1580, the school moved to Morelia, then called Valladolid, and was later remodeled in nineteenth-century neoclassical style. Heroes of the independence movement and the revolution studied there. San Nicolás, considered *la alma* (the soul) of La Universidad Michoacana, had already been named a national historic landmark.[15] For an "adventuress from New York" to take on creation of a fresco there was audacious.

The wall itself was daunting. At approximately eighty-six by fourteen feet, the mural site is best viewed from the courtyard below or from the entrance on Avenida Madero, named for the revolutionary hero and former president. Iron railings and stone arches interrupt the view of the wall, so the images had to be painted in segments. Marion puzzled over how to make each separate section stand alone and still offer a continuous view from different vantage points. How to fit the fishermen's canoes under the arches? Show a family mending nets? In the middle, a door to the library further interrupted the arrangement. How to utilize the small space above that door and tie it to the overall composition?

Over the summer, Agustín Velásquez Chávez, the nephew of a government official traveling with Paul Strand, suggested that Marion paint hands pouring water over the doorframe. She rejected the idea as derivative of Rivera's work. She had a breakthrough with her own idea: to depict "a massive head of an Indian (head down in perspective) straining under the weight of a block of stone . . . this will symbolize the Indian as a crushed race, and all the primitive races that have been crushed, and whether or not he will lift the burden or let it crush him utterly remains to be seen."[16]

Marion was lonely enough that the arrival of Ryah Ludins initially cheered her. Ryah had been in Mexico City, where Pablo O'Higgins taught her basic fresco technique. Now she, too, wanted to paint a mural. Marion advised her not to push Corona too much or too soon. Ryah ignored her. When Corona soon came through with a commission, Marion's competitiveness flared. She complained to Josie that Ryah "has an intensity and joy about life and her work that I envy. . . . She's shrewd and practical and frugal, with the precious proper Jewish streak of Eddie Biberman."[17]

What prompted that comment? Marion had been close to Biberman, an accomplished artist whom she met in Taos. She had many Jewish friends. O'Higgins also disliked Ryah, but I found no evidence that he held antisemitic views. Did Marion glean this rhetoric from her mother? Musy once griped about Woodstock rents and the town being "infested with Village Jews."[18] Perhaps mother and daughter both drew from the larger society's seemingly inexhaustible supply of antisemitism. Marion's flared when she felt jealous or insecure.

Consider Marion at twenty-four: alone, still striving for independence from her family, and reeling from threats to her safety. Despite her considerable accomplishments, she woke each day unsure of how to face the mural challenge. But in September, the lime arrived and wall preparation began. The time for hesitation was over.

Each day, Marion walked across the plaza to El Colegio as the city slowly came to life. Vendors hawked newspapers and coffee shops set their outdoor tables. Her assistants had chipped the wall down to the brick surface, prepared with layers of lime and marble plaster. She took the smaller design she'd transferred to a large outline on the scale of two inches to a foot, then traced onto transparent paper. Next, she layered the outline over several successive coats of wet plaster, racing against time to get the images up before the sun dried the plaster. She welcomed the continued fall rains when lingering dampness allowed painting into the evening hours.[19]

The Morelianos who gathered below the scaffold to watch distracted Marion. She preferred nocturnal painting under the stars. On those nights, she felt truly happy. Other times, she left the scaffold feeling more dead than alive. Problems multiplied. O'Higgins told her to use mine sand. When it wasn't available, she settled for river sand that required treatment to remove impurities. Even after mine sand arrived, the wall darkened in some spots and turned too light in others, forcing Marion to repaint.[20] Frustration mounted. In one dramatic letter, she told Josie her fatigue was so extreme that death would feel delicious. Josie urged her to keep going.

In September, Grace, who had been in Taxco with her husband, arrived to help. The tensions that often plagued the sisters didn't mar their time in Morelia. At night, they went to movies and explored the city. Grace seemed different in Mexico, Marion told Musy: "She's so easy to get along with, I can't get over it. She's very quiet and calm, and the people here like her a lot." Grace also seemed happier in her marriage, although she reported that she almost had an affair with Hans Hoffman. Marion described him as "pretty pent up" since "being the typical cautious German, he's been afraid to screw a Mexican."[21]

From the hotel, the sisters moved into a pension run by an undertaker. Marion dreamed of death, describing the scene to Josie. The place was populated by "old hags who wander up and down the halls, exactly like old witches in fairy tales, knotted and knarled [sic] with hunchbacks. . . . The house is full of cats who won't come near you and a thousand birds and two fat pigeons who do nothing but screw in the bathroom. . . . I wake in the morning to the sweet sound of coffins being hammered together. In life we are in death. Buenas noches, Papeeta!"[22]

In October, the sisters' white knight, O'Higgins, arrived and moved into the same pension. Marion welcomed him but found his personality puzzling. "He's so dry and impersonal . . . and romantic about Mexico," she complained, ignoring her own romantic leanings. His WASP quietude clashed with her emotional Irish nature. When he left the pension, she and Grace would "scream and yell and get bawdy."[23] Still, her quibbles paled against her admiration for O'Higgins's political commitment and generosity. He helped in all the areas where she lacked expertise: Spanish, chemistry, and the geometry she needed for mural composition. When O'Higgins left for Mexico City, Marion backpedaled on complaints about his "dryness." She reported to Musy that she and Grace missed him: "He's one of those unusual unselfish people with a great love of humanity, and a Communist."[24]

As the weather grew colder and drier, Marion missed the rainy season's great drama. She bundled up and went to the scaffold each day, urged on by Corona. She appreciated his support but suspected his motives: "He feels like Sforza

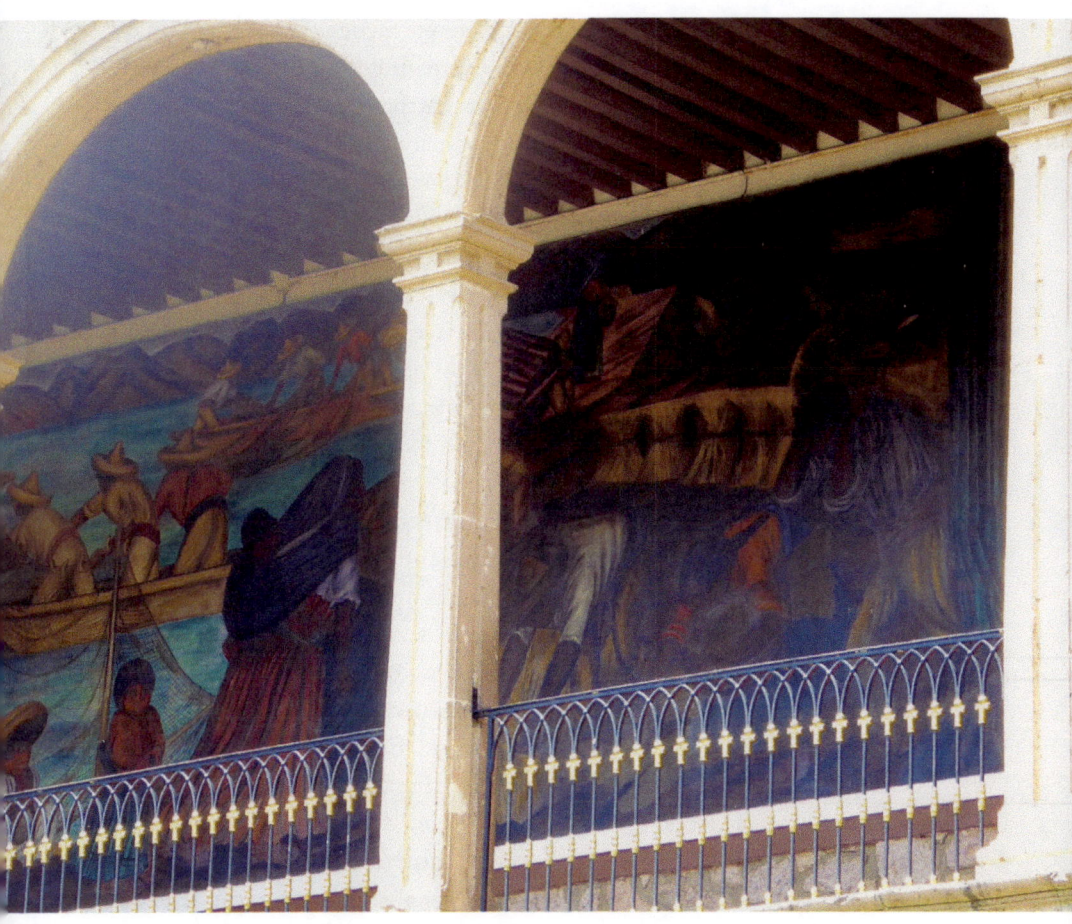

FIGURE 11.1. Two mural panels of *Landscape and Economy of Michoacán*, by Marion Greenwood, 1933. (Photograph by Joanne B. Mulcahy.)

[the Renaissance patron of Leonardo da Vinci] and wants to get a lot of other painters here, including Rivera, to cover the walls of Morelia and thus go down in history as a patron of the arts."[25] Corona likely coveted political points. Yet he also honored the university's humanist tradition. Art would link diverse people through empathy, the foundation for social transformation. Corona's philosophy was shared by Marion's teachers and would shape her extensive career.

In January, after months of sleepless nights, aching back and hands, uncertainty, and fear, Marion stood before the mural with a very satisfied Corona. The vibrant images brought the Purépecha to life. To the left of the section corresponding to one of the stone arches, a couple mends a net. The woman's coral blouse and purple skirt contrast with her partner's white cotton top and pants. Two children sit beneath them. A cross-hatched net spreads out behind the family, framed by men in canoes on an aquamarine Lake Pátzcuaro. Farmers harvest wheat above seated figures grinding pigment for pottery and preparing reeds for mats. Mountains line the back wall, while cactus and other elements of the local landscape frame the doorway. Purépecha women's pleated skirts and striped rebozos and men's white cotton pants and wide sombreros add important cultural details. Above the doorframe rests an indigenous man's head. Eyes closed, chin resting on the frame, he carries the weight of the stone on his back, the symbol of oppression Marion saw as the mural's essential element.

Earlier picturesque images and travelogues focused on Michoacán landscapes; when people appeared, they were largely passive. In contrast, Marion rendered the Purépecha as hardworking and active, refuting a common stereotype about Mexicans as lazy. James Oles suggests that if Marion's mural "rises above the merely folkloric, it is because she has not idealized or ignored the difficulties of peasant work, as did so many other visiting artists in Mexico."[26] He points to a related detail: Greenwood's signature over the skirt of the potter in the lower right-hand corner suggests solidarity with working women.[27] Art historian Dina Comisarenco Mirkin further argues that Marion avoided clichés, documented indigenous lives in a monumental format, and showed women as equal participants in labor.

Although Marion increasing tilted toward communism, she resisted overt ideological statements. She rejected several mural titles Josie suggested: "If you and John forgive me, baby, I don't like those titles. They remind me too much of cartoon propaganda. I notice that neither of you would name your books in that fashion." To come alive as art, Marion argued, a work need not be consciously revolutionary if it is a "strong vital interpretation of living realities painted with *sincerity* and love for the beauty of line, rhythm, and sound structural composition."[28] She pondered the titles *Tarascan Indian* or simply *Michoacán* before settling on *Paisaje y economía de Michoacán—Landscape and Economy of Michoacán*.

Articles in the Mexican and US press praised the mural. One critic called her an artist "of international fame." The *New York Herald Tribune* lauded the painting.[29] In *Mexican Life*, Josie highlighted Marion's focus on indigenous figures, one that reflects the era's belief in the "disappearing Native": "His ways of life are doomed also to disappear before the onslaught of the machinery age which is slower in Mexico than in the States. . . . But now while there is still time, when ways of life are almost as ancient as the Indian himself, Marion Greenwood brought it down in imperishable color, the method, the feeling, the burden and beauty of this Indian life which is a cultural heritage not to be lost, as many of the Aztec idols and cities were lost forever."[30]

Marion was less enthusiastic about a piece by Mexican journalist Francisco Antuñez. He began with praise for this "serious and understanding painter, blessed with a fine spirit of observation, an extraordinary sensitivity and with an ardent desire, above all, to understand the ideological expressions of revolutionary Mexican painting." However, he soon descended into the obsession with Marion's looks that would bedevil her for life: "tall, thin, pale, her broad forehead veiled by bangs of ashen blonde hair that falls like a mane over her erect shoulders; those big glaucous eyes with black striations, eyes that seem to carry with them the enchantment of far horizons, a sharp nose, a sensuous mouth, with a harmonious voice and a distinguished expression."[31] Marion's responded furiously to his "ridiculous pompous article about me. He has about as much idea about art or writing or anything as I have of long division." She tried unsuccessfully to block publication.

Despite her success, Marion bemoaned her aching back and red, calloused hands. Her Taxco mural hadn't demanded the same degree of physical stamina. The social expectations made her deplore her status as a woman. She wrote to Josie, "I wish I'd get hard and strong for this work I have to do in life. I wish my breasts and hips would disappear. They're in the way and look awful in pants."[32]

Josie had warned Marion that she would chafe at the restrictions on women in a provincial capital. However, Marion's complaints about Mexico echoed broader grievances. In an emotional letter to Josie, she described her as the only person she had never doubted: "I wonder if I could feel like that if you were a man. I don't think so. I am becoming more bitter with that sex every day. This damn place and all the criticism has made me more bitter about being a woman. If I were a man everything would be easier. I want to revenge myself on men. They've all treated me like hell, for no goddamn good reason."[33]

For all her complaints, Marion emerged from Morelia transformed. The family narrative returned in her note to Musy that "life has to be sacrificed for art." The outcome of that sacrifice was greater strength of character and the assurance that "now I am positive of my future and what I have to do in life and I have absolute belief in my work."[34]

Before the mural was completed, one central event ended all doubts about

Marion's triumph. Lázaro Cárdenas, campaigning for president, came to the university to meet students. He stood under the balcony in the San Nicolás courtyard, then ascended the stone stairs to publicly thank Marion for giving a part of her life to Michoacán. The leftist Cárdenas would become one of Mexico's most beloved presidents, embraced by the masses as a near saint. Since he was "the hero of Mexico," Marion reported to Musy, "now everyone thinks it's swell." Cárdenas had, she added, "said a mouthful."[35] For all that she had given to Michoacán, Marion had gained confidence, enhanced skills, and deeper cultural understanding.

CHAPTER 12

"Life Will Become One Big Wall"

IN A 1933 PHOTO, THE GREENWOOD SISTERS REST ON THE SCAFFOLD IN front of Marion's Morelia mural. A box of Kellogg's All-Bran rests between them. Grace stirs her coffee, short curly hair askew. Marion, in overalls, gulps down a drink. They look like they'd rolled right out of bed. Two talented sisters happily embarked on a novel opportunity in a foreign country. They got along so well in Mexico. Who would have guessed at their differences?

People inevitably compared them. Grace was lovely, with delicate features and dark curls, but she couldn't compete with her sister's sensational looks and magnetic aura. Renowned photographer Lola Alvarez Bravo described Marion as *muy guapa, preciosa* (very beautiful, exquisite) while Grace was *una chaparrita, común y corriente* (a "shorty," common and run-of-the-mill).[1]

Marion had long overshadowed her sister artistically, partially due to what her family perceived as Grace's lack of confidence. Writing to her mother, Marion mused, "Her work is really swell but she's too timid to attempt something by herself."[2] At the same time, Marion disparaged Grace as lazy, perhaps to guard her own status as her mother's favorite. Musy reinforced Grace's weak sense of self. She once griped to Josie that her unreliable elder daughter never did anything right, thus no one expected anything from her.

Marion half envied Grace's lack of angst and ambition. "I've come to the conclusion that she's a much happier nature than I am. Atmospheres don't seem to affect her very much, music doesn't make her sad, and she's not sentimental." No Dostoevsky-inspired brooding for Grace. In contrast, Marion had inherited her mother's dark side and dread of being alone. Why, she asked Musy, are we like that when other people are not?[3]

Musy's view of Grace added to her general gripes about life. She complained about everything: her colitis, the summer heat, her new house in Woodstock (which she called an old shack), boredom (though Irwin came daily to lecture her on "the art of being happy though married," therein the Greenwood view of marriage). All this led her to pronounce that "life is not worth living." She even groused to Josie that for her "babe" Marion, "everything is art." What did she expect? "Everything is art" was the heart of the sisters' upbringing.[4]

Whether due to lack of family support or mental health issues, Grace had trouble getting things done. That changed with the chance to paint her own mural in Morelia. O'Higgins, the sisters' champion, suggested to Corona that Grace should also get a commission. Soon she was walking across the plaza daily to the beautiful Museo Michoacano. Her assigned wall was a narrow, twenty-eight by ten-foot space just off the museum's entrance. The small scale allowed her to work quickly, completing the project in less than a month. O'Higgins and Marion helped, as Grace had for her sister's mural. Still, not bad for one seen as lazy and unproductive.

The images of *Hombres y Máquinas* (*Men and Machines*) contrast with those of her sister's mural. While Marion depicted indigenous men and women working together, Grace's figures were all male. Her theme, the tension between human labor and industrialization, was popular in Depression-era art. The mural's five workers seem enmeshed in the steel gray gears they push against. One man faces the viewer while the others gaze down into a vortex of machinery. The dizzying feeling of a downward spiral is captured in the painting's descriptive plaque: "*La clase trabajadora inmersa en la vertiginosa industrialización*"—"The working class immersed in dizzying industrialization." A viewer then or now might conclude that in the battle between men and machines, the latter were winning. Yet the workers resist the gears with immense arms that suggest equal if not greater strength.

Marion celebrated Grace's mural as "very Orozco in feeling" in depicting the struggles of the underclass.[5] Even in capitalist countries, workers could outwit machines. Art historian Dina Comisarenco Mirkin argues for the influence of the early twentieth-century Russian avant-garde, who believed industrialization would better workers' lives once they subdued the machine.[6] Grace, however, expressed uncertainty about her painting's message. On a scrap of paper, she wrote, "This is symbolic of man's struggle against the mastery of the machine (I think!)."[7]

Although both their paintings would fade with age, the sisters made their mark in Morelia. Like Marion, Grace would forever harken back to this time as

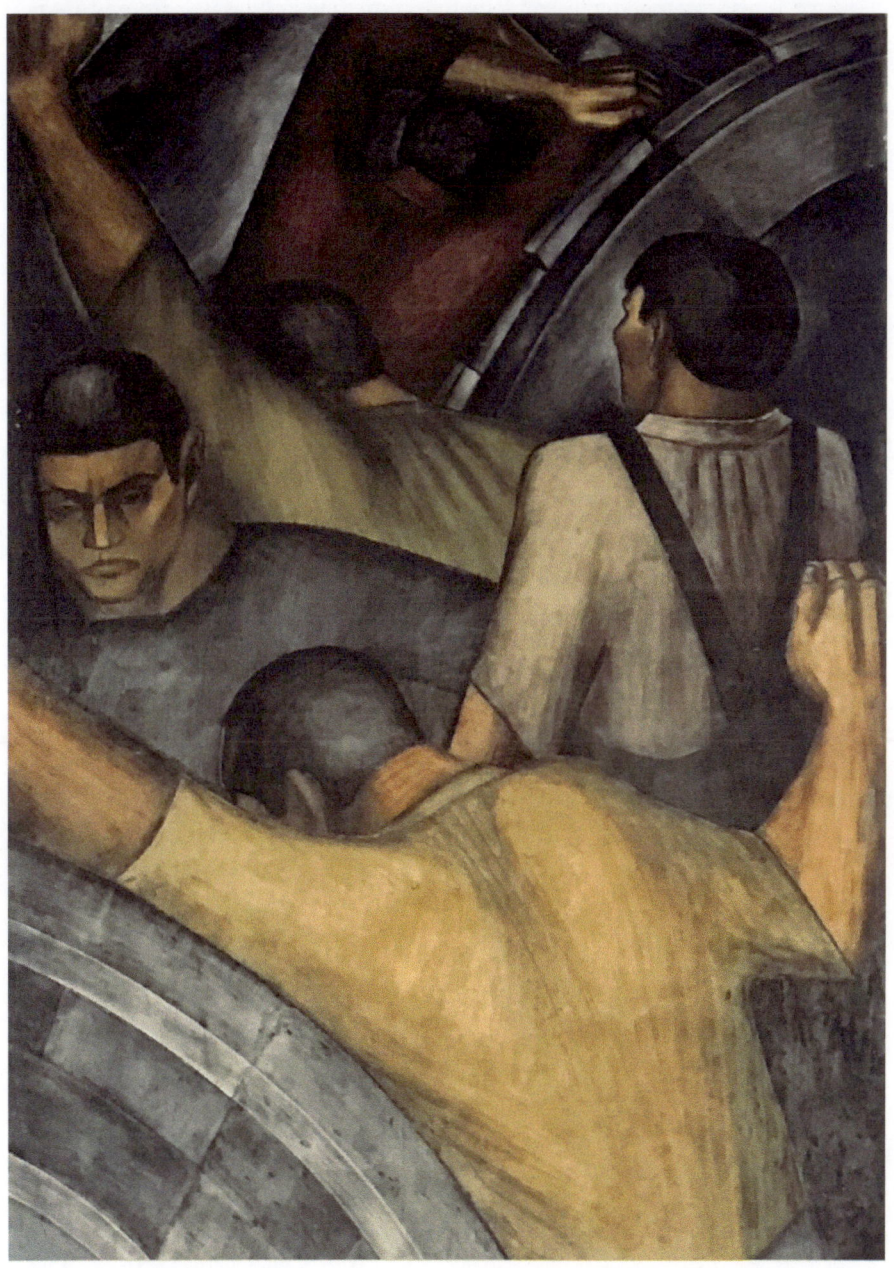

FIGURE 12.1. Grace Greenwood's *Men and Machines* (detail), 1933. (Photograph by Joanne B. Mulcahy.)

transformative: "I guess I'll be spending the rest of my life on a scaffold, too—fresco is just my medium—so life will become one large wall—from wall to wall—and paint the life instead of living it."[8] Here is yet another twist on the family narrative. One had to choose: live or paint.

Grace had promised her husband, Bill Ames, that she'd be back in the United States by Christmas. Instead she stayed with Marion through the winter of 1934. Both were itching to leave when they finally boarded a train for Mexico City in February. They hoped to head to New York in early March.

Marion was more than ready. "I've decided America is the only place for me—where a woman can be a human being—not a suppressed self-conscious female behind the bars of a balcony," she wrote to Josie.[9] Other factors affected her decision to return. She missed Musy. Her size ten shoes had holes; she longed for comfort after months of fighting loneliness and self-doubt. Muralism was the artistic future. She was sure that she could paint walls in New York.

Pablo O'Higgins doubted her hopes for US commissions. The "dumb capitalists" who owned the walls wouldn't support them.[10] Marion thought otherwise. "I'm really full of hope and ideas for the future," she wrote. "I want to do fresco of the Negroes in the cotton fields and chain gangs, etc. And I want to do the American Indians and New York subjects. Oh, I've got so much to do if I'm only able to get walls."[11]

Corona provided 500 pesos for Marion's fare home, but the sisters needed passport clearance. The pace of Mexican bureaucracy drove Marion crazy. Why did the country allow a four-hour lunch and siesta? She yearned for the rush and bustle of New York. While she and Grace killed time, O'Higgins taught them encaustic, a technique that mixes pigment with hot wax. Marion was once again grateful for his mentoring.

During their enforced wait, the Greenwoods leaped into Mexico City social life. Josie had sent Marion money for new clothes. After months in overalls and old sweaters, she stretched her legs into stockings and headed out at night. The sisters were living at the Hotel Guardiola, where Marion had spent part of the previous year with Josie and John. Haunted by memories, she happily moved a week later to the cheaper, sunnier Hotel Isabel in Mexico City's historic center. The artistic German owner furnished their top-floor room with Turkish rugs and a view of the city that Marion loved. They were close to Sanborn's, a restaurant founded by Californians. Marion craved American food, a preference that made O'Higgins shake his head. She clearly had not "gone Mexican."

Two friends squired Marion and Grace around town. Abel and Jaime Plenn,

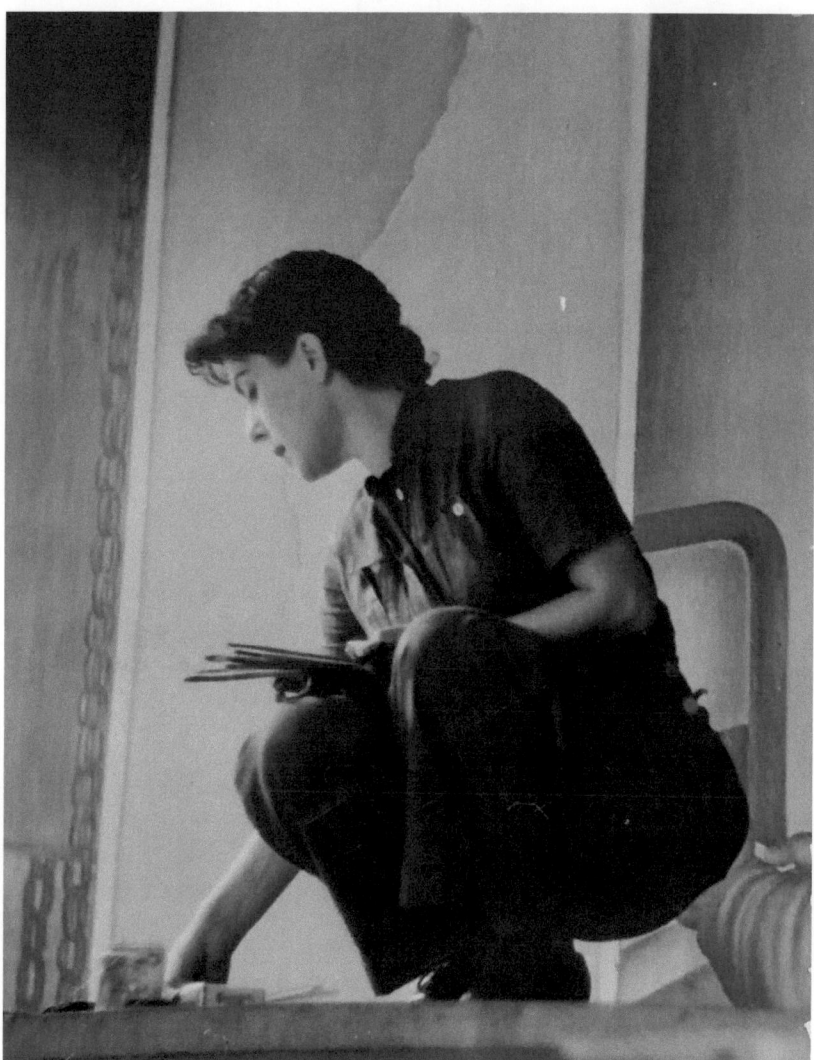

FIGURE 12.2. Grace Greenwood on a scaffold. (Photograph © and courtesy of the estate of Marion Greenwood.)

both writers, lived for extensive periods in Mexico. Jaime wrote and edited numerous books, including *Mexico Marches*. Abel would go on to write about Spain as well as Latin America, and both were well connected through their cousin, Anita Brenner. The brothers became early and lifelong champions of the Greenwoods' work. Grace and Jaime were lovers, a relationship she would regret ending.[12]

Abel took the sisters to Diego Rivera's murals that they hadn't previously seen. Between 1924 and 1927, Rivera worked in the Chapingo Chapel outside Mexico City, a site converted to the national agricultural college. Forty-one separate panels depict nature's evolution alongside social revolution. O'Higgins, whose figure appears in one mural, assisted him. The paintings, now considered among Rivera's finest works, profoundly affected Marion.

Soon afterward, Verna Carleton and Ignacio Millan invited the Greenwoods to visit Rivera in the San Ángel neighborhood. The sisters eagerly anticipated an intimate discussion about their fresco problems and future commissions. Marion had rejected offers to paint another wall at the university in Morelia or one at Lázaro Cárdenas's Pátzcuaro house. However, she asked Cárdenas's office for a recommendation letter to the education secretary in Mexico City. The cosmopolitan capital was "the only place I'd consider where at least I won't be totally buried alive."[13]

The encounter with Rivera was a bust. "What a letdown," Marion reported to Josie. "His house was full of stupid rich Americans, a precious arty atmosphere, all aware of the 'great presence' of Diego, who disappeared to talk over more business. Grace and I thought we'd be able to talk and ask him questions about our fresco troubles but we didn't try, as they were all watching us like cats, especially Frida, the wife."[14]

Verna had warned Marion not to expect too much from Rivera. Jealousy made him loath to say anything good about other painters.[15] More than one artist leveled this charge against Rivera, but in this case it seems unfair. He later praised both women as pioneers of Mexico muralism and celebrated their work. However, at this house in San Ángel, he was too busy to pay much attention to the Greenwoods.

The architect and artist Juan O'Gorman, whom Marion described as "crazy about" her Morelia mural, rallied on her behalf for a commission. Yet he could not do anything, he confessed, without Rivera's approval. Abel Plenn offered to write an article about Marion's work. Perhaps in return, Marion asked Josie to help him get into Yaddo the following year. The ever-faithful Pablo O'Higgins also advocated for them. He called Marion's Morelia mural "splendid" and "much more important than the situation that produced it." Yet she feared that others, especially Rivera and American writer and artist Emily Edwards, thought she was "trying to step in where others should be."[16] Marion carried Corona's letter of introduction to an appointment at the Ministry of Education, but nothing came of it.

One tantalizing future project emerged: murals inside the Mercado Abelardo L. Rodríguez near the Zocalo. The Greenwoods toured the site with O'Higgins. The multiblock area had been the Jesuit church and school of San Pedro y San Pablo but was soon to become a community center for the working-class neighborhood. The Greenwoods stuck with their plan to return north but kept alive this possibility. Fate would decide which side of the border would see their next murals.

Walls or no walls, Marion promised Josie she'd be back soon. Leave behind the bickering and jealousy in Mexico City, Josie argued. "Abel and Paul are very exceptional and also real revolutionaries." The United States, she reminded Marion, was her country and another possible revolution awaited her. To find work in New York, Josie encouraged Marion to contact Rene d'Harnoncourt, then assistant to the president of the American Federation of the Arts.[17]

In 1934, although the Depression ground on, many people shared Marion's optimism about social and political change. The previous spring, New Yorkers had turned out in droves to protest Adolf Hitler's rise to reich chancellor in January. Twenty-three thousand squeezed into Madison Square Garden to hear speakers, while another thirty thousand stood outside to listen via broadcast. Celebrations greeted the end of prohibition in December 1933, not that the well had ever run dry in New York City. Creativity thrived despite the economy. People flocked to the newly opened Apollo Theater in Harlem, and jazz filled clubs throughout town. Franklin D. Roosevelt had entered the White House while Marion was in Taxco. His New Deal legislation passed during the first three months of his presidency. The massive infusion of money and jobs creation, including work for artists, would soon touch the lives of Marion and Grace.

That was still ahead. In February, the sisters waited on their expired visas. Ignacio and Verna again intervened and paid the fine. March 8 found Marion and Grace back on a Ward Line ship headed north. Opportunities would open in New York, although those didn't play out exactly as the sisters had hoped.

On the ship, Marion's excitement dwindled. The thought of her family home in Brooklyn filled her with dread. She feared her shared bedroom with Musy would feel like prison after her newfound independence. "Try and lighten my burden a little," she asked Musy. "I'm not a baby anymore. I'm a sad woman but I'm not as weak as you insist I am."[18] Marion's new artistic expertise heightened her need to break free. Even her brother Irwin affirmed her choices in going to Mexico. She had been wise to avoid the pitfalls of commercialism, he said.

The ship docked on March 13. Marion's first impression of her homeland confirmed her foreboding. Misery consumed her "ever since I first watched the sky-line again. It seemed such a different and cruel world of hard stone and windows and warped lives. I hate it all but that is always my first impression after being away for a while. It's just fear of struggle, I guess, and hating to come back to Brooklyn."[19]

We can only speculate about how hard Musy pressured Marion to return. She surely missed her daughter's support. Papa seemed perennially out of work. Marion often advised Musy on the family troubles. Tell Irwin to get out of Woodstock and away from his in-laws, whose lives were filled with drama she compared to a Russian novel. Tell your sons that they should have invited you and Papa to Thanksgiving dinner. Go to Theosophy meetings and be gutsy as befits your heritage. She added her reminder: "Remember girl, you're Irish and your baby's Irish, too."[20]

As Marion left Mexico City, she received news that Musy was ill. She worried but also suspected her mother would recover once she returned. Indeed, the doctor confirmed that only Marion's presence resurrected Musy's desire to live. That melodramatic response reflected the tight mother-daughter bond that now enclosed Marion in a straitjacket of double-edged love. She made frequent trips to see Musy in the hospital and scrambled to make money to pay the bills. "*Que vida!*" she wrote to Josie.[21]

Marion felt distant from old friends and lovers. Social life was nonexistent, with "no casual screwing." Mexico seemed like a dream. She was anxious to see Josie but feared a break was imminent. Marion's alter ego Nealy, Josie's childhood fantasy friend, reemerged: "Nealy could come back to you if that feeling that she did know could be found again. But time changes things, doesn't it Josie. If you admit it to yourself, your feeling has changed. There's something there but it's not the same. . . . Poor Nealy, she's very sad and life seems to be getting more difficult for her."[22]

Tensions escalated when Josie visited Brooklyn. Marion couldn't meet her at the station because Musy was too sick to be left alone. So she said. Josie trekked to the family home only to discover the house full of people who could have attended to Musy. Backpedaling, Marion pretended she hadn't known that seeing her was Josie's only agenda. "You aren't that stupid," a furious Josie wrote. Why wouldn't Marion be her top priority? She had jeopardized her own work to support Marion emotionally and financially. Josie's fear that Marion had used her for professional gain resurfaced.[23]

Marion responded that Josie was "wrong, all wrong" in that assumption: "I never worked you, I've never been able to work anybody, I'm not made that way. Perhaps I've accepted money too lightly in my life but it's because I would give it as I take it if I had it." She promised to pay back all aid from Josie and John.

Their letters now brimmed with acrimony. Marion accused Josie of not appreciating her family. Josie fired back that Musy had damaged her daughters and poisoned their future relationships. The deeper cause for Josie's pain was that Marion tried to hide the nature of their relationship. She'd been aloof during Josie's visit. Marion assured her that if they'd met privately, she would have shown affection. But she could not. "You seem to utterly ignore the fact that two women in love is not an everyday ordinary thing," she wrote to Josie later. "To my parents it would be the most horrible shock on earth because *naturally to them* such a thing is abnormal. You ought to be broadminded enough to realize their outlook in life and not expect anything else."[24]

Further recriminations followed, then rounds of reconciliation. Josie would continue to write articles celebrating Marion's work. Marion would continue to profess love for Josie. But something tore in the taut thread that had bound them at Yaddo, tightened in Mexico, and then begun to slacken.

Marion turned to work to tamp down grief over Josie. She and Grace soon moved into the world they'd dreamed about: commissions to paint walls in the United States. In April, the Public Works of Art Project (PWAP), a government agency administered through the Treasury Department, hired them to create murals for the Immigration Building on Ellis Island. Grace's would depict indigenous life and modern America. Marion's would cover early settlement through the nineteenth century and the movement West. They worked furiously to produce drawings and sent them to Washington to meet an April 28 deadline.

In Taxco and Morelia, Marion worried that she was not revolutionary enough. The inverse worry now consumed her: her growing class-consciousness might look radical to the US government. Conservative legislators fought any politically progressive images.

Marion's worries were moot. The PWAP folded in June 1934, nixing the immigration mural. The agency had existed briefly from the previous December as a stopgap measure to address unemployment, sponsoring important projects such as the San Francisco Coit Tower murals. However, the PWAP never offered the long-term lifeline that the Federal Art Project soon would. Its demise left the Greenwoods scrambling for income. Gone was their place in the sun as celebrated and accomplished foreigners.

Pondering next moves, Marion reconnected with some of the Mexican muralists in New York. Siqueiros was back and he trekked out to Brooklyn to visit Marion and her family. Every visiting artist at some point seemed to encounter Musy. Siqueiros told "howling stories" about his brother Chucho, an actor whom Marion had sketched while in Mexico. She and Josie planned to attend Siqueiros's lecture on "The Technique of Revolutionary Art" sponsored by the John Reed Club in April.[25]

Orozco and journalist Alma Reed also made their way to Brooklyn. She was lionized in Mexico for exposing injustice in the case of seventeen-year-old Simón Ruiz. An undocumented Mexican worker in California, he had been sentenced to death on trumped-up charges. Reed's articles on his plight led to the elimination of the death penalty for minors in California. On a reporting trip to Mexico, Reed met and fell in love with Yucatán's socialist governor Filipe Carrillo Puerto. Before they could wed, he was assassinated by forces bent on protecting the Yucatán's hacienda owners.[26] The loss devastated Reed, but she never relinquished her passion for Mexican art and culture.

"Orozco was very swell—a real person," Marion reported. Both visitors were enthusiastic about the Morelia murals. Reed reminded the sisters of how warmly Mexico had welcomed them. As Orozco's informal agent, she urged the Greenwoods to extend the same welcome to him and other visiting Mexican artists. Could Marion contact Edwin Alden Jewell, the *New York Times* art critic, on Orozco's behalf? While sympathetic to the goal, Marion rejected being an advocate for others, even those she admired. She had trouble promoting her own work. It simply wasn't her personality to be "a pusher, a businesswoman, a politician and everything but an artist."[27]

As Marion grew weary of her family's needs and complaints, Mexico beckoned. All summer, O'Higgins had written with updates on the Rodríguez Market project. He exhorted Marion to "beg, borrow, or steal the money" to get back at once. To ensure she and Grace could join the team, they should stress these themes and designs in preliminary drawings: "local conditions, actual struggle, and present day reality of exploitation, misery, and social retrogression" in Mexico. Concrete events such as the recent mining strikes would be appropriate. If they got stuck, just label the work "crisis."[28]

"At once" didn't happen exactly as O'Higgins urged. Marion was approved to join the group in August, but she held back until she was assured that Grace would be included.[29] Musy's health also worsened, perhaps in response to her daughters' imminent departure. When those issues resolved, the sisters again boarded a Ward Line ship for Mexico in September 1934. Grace's husband had given her the eighty-five-dollar fare, and Marion somehow dug up the money.

Sorrow tempered Marion's excitement. She had to euthanize a favorite cat no one wanted. Loss of an animal always grieved her. Her relationship with Josie was in flux. Still, she departed from New York full of hope. Her future shimmered on Mexico City's walls.

CHAPTER 13

Comrades in Mexico City

On a late August afternoon in 1935, a crowd streamed into Bellas Artes, the Palace of the Fine Arts in Mexico City. Americans and other international visitors joined local teachers, artists, writers, reporters, and government bureaucrats for what was normally a sober education conference. Events, however, would prove anything but normal and sober.[1]

The stunning Art Nouveau building buzzed with excitement. As sun filtered through the iron and Marotti crystal roof, spectators jostled for the best vantage point on the day's promised spectacle: a face-off over art and revolution between Rivera and Siqueiros. Rivera had launched the conference with his view of art's revolutionary function. Siqueiros spoke the next day, repeating his charge that Rivera was a snob, dilettante, and "mental tourist." Who but a stooge would take funds from imperialist bureaucrats and those ultimate capitalists, the Rockefellers?

This accusation was familiar to Siqueiros's fans in the audience. Among them was journalist Emanuel Eisenberg, writing for the progressive *New Masses*. The US magazine had already published Siqueiros's attack on Rivera as a "counter-revolutionary."[2] Animosity between the two artists also hinged on differing visions of communism. Rivera stayed loyal to Trotsky, Siqueiros to Stalin. Still, no one expected events to turn as they did.

As Siqueiros wrapped up his speech, a door suddenly opened. There stood Rivera. In Eisenberg's version of events, he appeared "large, hippopotamus-like, grinning."[3] When Rivera failed to get the floor, he whipped out his pistol. Photographer Edward Weston once contrasted Rivera's ever-present "six-shooter" with his friendly smile and infectious laugh.[4] No such jollity filled Bellas Artes as Rivera demanded a chance to speak "or else." The official in charge calmed the audience with a promised follow-up the next day.

By morning, news of the confrontation filled local and international newspapers. "Mexico," wrote Eisenberg, "is probably the only country in the world where a controversial meeting of two painters, in much less than a day's notice, could be calculated to attract a thousand people."[5] Witnesses to the anticipated drama, later dubbed "The Battle of the Century," might have left disappointed when the only attacks were verbal. But the week ahead held surprises.

During one afternoon debate, Marion, almost a year into her latest sojourn in Mexico, stood. Why, she questioned Siqueiros, had he not practiced what he preached? He, too, had sold paintings to tourists and taken government funding. Siqueiros, taken aback, sputtered that he had no choice but to paint for the bourgeoisie. The imperialists had penetrated the art world.

Under Marion's challenge to Siqueiros lies the gutsy girl who left high school for the Art Students League at fifteen and tackled fresco at twenty-four. She never feared speaking her mind. But her question also reflects tensions that beset Mexican muralism, the broader national and international political battles of the 1930s, and her gradually evolving convictions. How much did Marion's response to Siqueiros implicitly support Rivera, with whom she was having an affair? Not for the first time, the personal and political intertwined during the complicated year of 1935.

When Marion and Grace joined Pablo O'Higgins on the project in October 1934, they had no notion their time in the capital would stretch to nearly two years. After arriving in Mexico City, they settled into the apartment at 86 Calle República de Columbia near the Zócalo. Their new home was soon a gathering place, likely filled with post-party, overfilled ashtrays and empty bottles. Success in Morelia, youth, and beauty made them sought-after companions.

Among those socializing chez Greenwood were members of the Communist Party, including Pablo O'Higgins. "It's become a hangout for them," Marion wrote to Josie, adding that she was "keeping a few of the secret papers" of the group: "It's all right but we don't have much privacy anymore. The party will soon become legal again here anyway—so the government says."[6] In 1925, the government had declared the party illegal, its members forced underground until leftist president Lázaro Cárdenas restored its legal status a decade later. In the interim, many Mexicans suffered, including Siqueiros. He'd landed in prison for marching in a May Day parade in 1930. Despite solitary confinement, he remained unrepentant.

Before she returned to Mexico, Marion had served as liaison between Siqueiros, who was working in New York, and O'Higgins on Communist Party matters. One letter from O'Higgins included requests for John Dos Passos's *1919*, the second in his USA trilogy, Lenin's *State and Revolution*, and a plea for Marion to "tell Siqueiros that the comrades got his communication."[7]

Through the 1920s, Mexico City's radical scene drew not only North Americans but a lively Latin American group. Chilean poet Gabriela Mistral, Nicaraguan Augusto César Sandino, and a host of others stirred political and artistic fervor in this transnational hub. Many hung out at the Communist Party headquarters on Mesones Street to help turn out the publication, *El Machete*. One group of Latin Americans moved into an old house where "The Liberator" Simón Bolívar once lived. The city's radical possibilities lingered during Marion's sojourn.[8]

Mexico-based artists aligned with the Popular Front, an international antifascist coalition. The movement brought together diverse moderate, communist, and other progressive groups to confront early twentieth-century crises, including the rise of right-wing parties in Europe. The Great Depression hastened the urgency for change. In the Americas, debates raged over how art should reflect historical reality.[9] Yet artists put aside divergent views to foment social change. The Rodríguez Market project offered Marion a clear path to join the struggle, if only they could start work.

Government support for muralism had diminished, then disappeared under conservative Plutarco Elías Calles. When his presidency ended in 1928, he continued to rule through three "puppet presidencies" known as el Maximato (from Calles's sobriquet el Jefe Maximo). One of the Calles's "puppets" was Abelardo L. Rodríguez for whom the market was named. He shared el Jefe's disdain for communism. His administration, however, recognized murals as job engines that generated national feeling and solidified group identity. Noting the importance of murals didn't translate to support. The government fear of radical agendas spurred further market project delays. Officials also balked at the inexperience of some of the artists.[10]

Herein was the root of the problem. There would be murals but what images would be acceptable? How radical were the Greenwoods? The sisters' social consciousness kept growing. O'Higgins sent Marion Russian magazines to further the political education Josie and John had begun. Once just an acolyte, Marion now fully embraced communist rhetoric. She occasionally yearned for new clothes, but individual need paled against the drive for a more equitable society. "The world is in a terrible mess," she wrote to Musy. "When people begin to have a group feeling instead of worrying about their own little lives and think they're of such importance, things will begin to straighten themselves out."[11] Marion's embrace of a radical agenda wasn't a huge shift. She was committed to painting the poor, workers, and people otherwise invisible. The Depression's devastation reinforced that commitment. Now her passion had a name.

Marion constantly urged Musy to look beyond the family to a broader collective. All her friends were communists, Marion said, "And for good reason, it's the only way out believe me I'm a radical myself since I've been here and see the conditions of poor, crippled Indians and homeless children, and the Americans dressed marvelously in swell cars riding past." She lambasted the Mexican bourgeoisie, whom she saw as imitating the crass aspects of US life. Communism gave her "a wonderfully hopeful slant on life and it's something you can grasp, something useful. Someday I may even be able to go to Russia and paint revolutionary frescos."[12] In directing Musy to buy a place in Woodstock, she insisted that "Capitalism is bound to fall absolutely in a couple of years and the city will be a hellhole."[13] Communist victory was inevitable.

Many of the muralists saw themselves as akin to workers in trade unions. In 1922, Siqueiros, Rivera, and Xavier Guerrero had organized the Syndicate of Technical Workers, Painters, and Sculptors. Robert Montenegro and Orozco joined them. In 1933, a new group emerged. O'Higgins, Leopold Méndez, whom Marion had met earlier, and other artists formed the LEAR—Liga de Escritores y Artistas Revolucionarios (League of Revolutionary Writers and Artists). The Comintern of the Soviet Union recognized the group as the Mexican section of the International Union of Revolutionary Writers. Their anti-fascist focus on universal peace, labor issues, and anti-capitalist content permeated discussion of the Rodríguez Market murals.

Commitment to the Popular Front and the syndicate's collaborative spirit didn't end tensions between artists. For Siqueiros's followers, Rivera's *The History of Mexico* and other murals whitewashed ongoing conflict and inequality. Government support, they argued, turned artists into lackeys and thwarted "real" revolution—this, despite the fact that Siqueiros also relied on the government. Marion's challenge to him surely hit a raw nerve. A competing group of young artists revered Rivera's memorializing of the Mexican revolution and national identity. Many were followers from the National Fine Arts School, where he'd been director since 1929.[14]

Marion should have had inklings that the market project might not run smoothly. O'Higgins had detailed the conflicts in his letters through the summer of 1934. He and other project artists struggled to keep Rivera at arm's length. Responding to one of Marion's letters, he laughed at her "reference to 'magnanimous Diego.'" "He's about as magnanimous as Henry Ford," O'Higgins wrote. "Tzab, Bracho [two of the other artists in the project] and I are handling him as best we can but don't write to Mrs. Millan [Verna] or ask Diego for anything. He's hypocritically trying to get your stairway and loves us all about as much as poison!"[15]

The government initially approached Rivera to direct the entire project, but he was too busy. His payment request for a hundred pesos per square meter was also too high, especially compared to the thirteen pesos the younger artists would receive.[16] Rivera suggested O'Higgins, who pulled together the diverse group that included the Greenwoods.

In the end, Rivera became artistic director. Antonio Mediz Bolio, a poet who worked for the government, would scrutinize the political content. Predictably, Rivera nixed the idea of adding Siqueiros, although he agreed to Orozco, who declined. Rufino Tamayo, whom Marion liked and respected, was also rejected.[17]

The final group met to share ideas on the government's suggested themes of nutrition and food distribution. At the biological institute, they researched plagues, parasites, and natural events that ruined food for the poor. Science would be the foundation of a socialist society. Marion reluctantly joined them. She balked at "the group's fad on the scientific approach which Paul thinks is so Marxian," she said. "It's alright in its place but it leaves the people cold."[18]

Marion's embrace of radicalism was at fever pitch, yet she rejected rigid ideology. Chalk it up to a stubborn streak, her contradictory nature, or inherent rebelliousness, which she attributed to her Irish heritage. Cracks in her professed politics also presaged doubts that would fully surface in years ahead. On the one hand, she was committed to the working class. When she was ultimately paid for her market mural, she loved standing in line with workers to receive her bags of pesos. But solidarity had limits. She resisted O'Higgins's proposed pay for market artists to equal that of workers: four pesos a day. "It may be all right for him but not for me," she complained. "He's so afraid that I won't be proletarian enough."[19]

Marion believed in letting images tell the story but without suggesting social change had been achieved—a view in line with Siqueiros's vision: "Propaganda in art is most difficult these days because if you paint revolution, people think it's already taken place": "The whole policy of the Mexican government is to use demagogic phrases and appear revolutionary. All the government buildings have the most radical posters—'Down with imperialism, Fascism—Workers of the world unite'—the result is the most hopeless confusion in the minds of the people. The only way to solve it is to state the present miserable conditions but you don't dare paint the way out if you don't want to fool the people."[20]

To create those images, Marion sketched on the streets near the market, in steel factories, and in Mexico City's Jamaica Terminal. Goods arrived there from Xochimilco, where gondola-style boat rides on its canals made it a popular tourist destination then, as it is now. In 1934, those waterways served as the main transportation network for food and other supplies. From the city, Marion ventured out to coffee and sugar plantations in Veracruz. She brandished a government letter of introduction. Even with credentials and dressed in a skirt, she would have stood out in rural communities rarely visited by foreigners, especially women.

Smoking, drinking, and debating politics, Marion and the others waited through the fall to start painting. Their submitted plans languished in bureaucratic purgatory. Previously accepted proposals were suddenly modified. Artists would be paid by square meters covered rather than a daily wage. Materials arrived only to be sent back. Contracts were drawn up, including a provision that the US artists would not request diplomatic intervention and would be judged by a Mexican tribunal if problems arose. If they objected to the terms, the record has buried that knowledge.

The projected market completion was the end of November, so Rodríguez would still be president at the opening. The date was wildly optimistic. Instead, Rodríguez and incoming President Cárdenas met to inaugurate an incomplete building on November 24.

Through December, Marion attended local festivals, including the Virgin of Guadalupe celebration on December 12. She was appalled when the police broke up the event. The Indians, she reported to Josie, had come "all dressed up from far and wide" to dance and celebrate, only to be "dispersed like rats" by the anti-clerical government.[21] Marion had embraced her mother's esoteric religions and had no great love for the Catholic Church. However, she resisted the crackdown on religion when it affected indigenous life. What might replace those festivals? she asked Josie. She seemed to answer her question with a description of the party's growing strength. If she pondered communism as a replacement for religion, she was not alone.

At least Christmas was over. Like her despised Sundays, holidays left Marion bereft, even with Grace present. Josie sent a letter from Yaddo, asking if Marion remembered a night they spent together in Monterrey. "I was born remembering," Marion wrote. "Each memory is like a burnt hole in my chest."

New worries soon eclipsed her sorrow over Josie. The government had ordered the scaffolding taken down and the payroll suspended. Marion was broke and in debt to Jaime Plenn, a good friend whom she'd met on her initial visit to Mexico City in 1933. She spent Christmas Eve at the steelworkers dance with her old Morelia boss, Gustavo Corona. He was in town looking for work after being ousted by the Cárdenas government. Miguel, her potential flame back in Morelia, was out of a job as well. He looked "perfectly awful without the surety of his high position," "very fat now and stodgy, and to think I ever wasted a thought on him."[22]

Marion got through January with sinking spirits. Perhaps that's when she sought out Rivera, who had promised he would always be "her friend." Photos of them together in 1935 show a relationship both serious—a contemplative Marion consulting with Diego—and playful—Marion laughing before a luxurious kiss. What photos can't reveal is how long their "friendship" lasted. Marion's notebooks from the era contain his phone numbers—"43733 Casa" and "23179 Palacio"—the National Palace where he was completing the monumental *The History of Mexico* fresco.[23] Perhaps their liaison was brief. Regardless, it's clear that Marion's status had changed since her 1934 visit to the San Ángel neighborhood. Then, Diego largely ignored her while Frida scrutinized the scene from the wings.

Whether he or someone else pushed the project forward, by the end of the month, the political logjam had broken. In February, a relieved Marion ascended the scaffold. *The Industrialization of the Countryside*, as the mural would be known, began on the ground floor with images of food distribution. Against the backdrop of a canal, a woman in a rebozo holds a recent catch of fish. Workers unload produce arriving at the Jamaica terminal. Boats cluster around a dock. For centuries, artists had depicted their enduring romance with Mexico City's canals and waterscapes. But Marion's unsmiling workers, bent under their loads, expose the hardships of such labor.

From the foyer, the mural proceeds up a wide stairway onto a landing wall. Images of sugarcane production transform the scene from pastoral to political. Workers in a steel mill share dense space with farmers and peasants. Symbols of exploitation are juxtaposed: a "speculator" middleman in coat and tie, a bookkeeper tracking accounts and doling out meager wages, a banker's fat

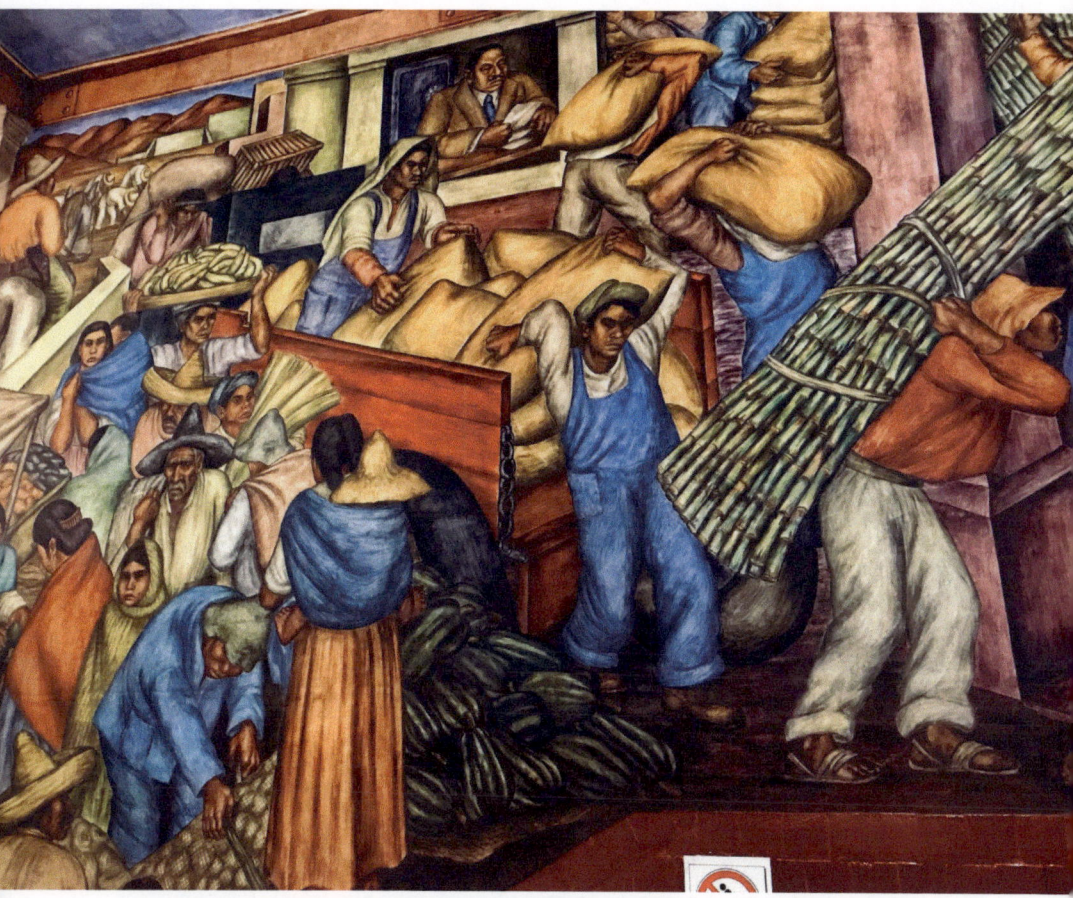

FIGURE 13.1. *The Industrialization of the Countryside* (detail), by Marion Greenwood, 1935. (Photograph by Joanne B. Mulcahy.)

fists holding ticker tape, his power enforced by a ring of soldiers. Beneath him, workers resist. One grips a pickax, another raises a tightened fist as the group hoists a red banner with the words *Obreros y Campesinos Unidos Contra el Imperialismo* (Workers and Farmers United Against Imperialism).

Marion tied the 1935 strikes in Mexico to global issues in keeping with the iconography of international anti-fascism. Soldiers drag off a stevedore protesting the unloading of war munitions. Banners read *No más materiales para la guerra imperialista / Queremos pan para los sin trabajo* (No more materials for imperialist war / We want bread for the unemployed) and *Abajo con la guerra y el fachismo* (Down with war and fascism). Images of Nazi flags link to fascist groups such as the Camisas Doradas (Gold Shirts), who were active in Mexico at the time.[24]

Marion's angular shapes underscore her adherence to Orozco's style. Rivera's influence is equally clear. Her stairwell figures parallel his Ministry of Education mural in the repetition of massive hands holding capitalist ticker tape and in the interplay of montaged figures in a compact space. Despite some of the younger artists' grumbles about Rivera, his work inspired many of the market murals. In particular, *Mexico of Today and Tomorrow* in the National Palace (1935) raised shared concerns about the plight of workers and the rise of fascism.[25] Marion's images of workers and tyrannical capitalists also mirror O'Higgins's accomplished market mural. However, Marion had progressed enormously on her own.

The overlap in muralists' images was not theft. It reflects the era's collaborative spirt and the nature of the form. Frescoes require a main artist, a group of assistants, a master mason, and apprentices. One story claims that Siqueiros went to bed one night, leaving his mural incomplete. A colleague, Guerrero, added a head to one of his panels. When Siqueiros discovered it, he declared, "Wonderful! Either I did it in my sleep or it is a miracle." The next day, he left yet another unfinished panel. Orozco did the honors that night and Siqueiros was reportedly delighted by the addition.[26] True or not, the story points to the celebration of shared creativity.

Grace, too, repeated themes Rivera and others had explored: the dark, treacherous conditions that led to mining accidents. She traveled to the silver mines surrounding Pachuca about eighty-six kilometers from Mexico City. Her plan to go underground hit resistance from the officials at the American-owned Real del Monte mine. A long-standing belief held that a miner would die if a woman entered below the seventh level. Undeterred, Grace donned a helmet and overalls and descended with a mine crew for four hours. Her chutzpah brought accolades in the US press. Her adventure provided the mural's main theme and images.

Grace's *Mining* opens on the ground floor with a tragic accident. The mural moves to Mexican and foreign bankers dipping their hands into piles of gleaming coins. Strikebreakers gather outside a munitions factory. Images of anger prevail: fists in the air and a banner declaring !*Contra el imperialism y la guerra*! (Against imperialism and war!). Workers with guns enter the factory, ready to seize control of industrialization.

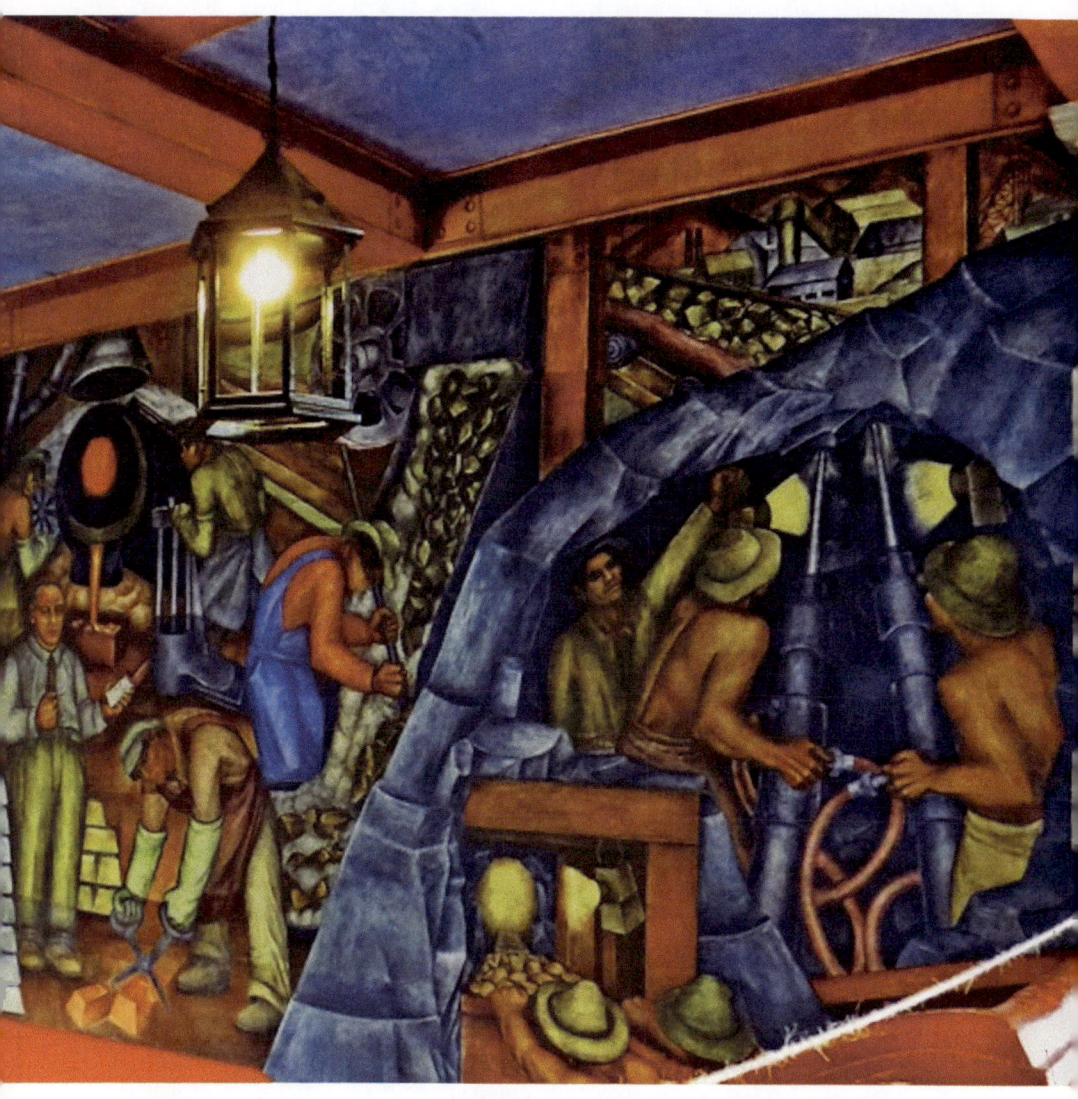

FIGURE 13.2. Grace Greenwood's *Mining* (detail), 1935. (Photograph by Joanne B. Mulcahy.)

Grace's figures are more rounded than Marion's and fewer in number. Art historian James Oles sees Marion's use of dense imagery and space as more advanced. Still, he celebrates both murals for their successful integration of images. The powerful political message leaps out at a viewer from the second-story wall they shared. On either side of a window, an urban worker and a campesino kneel. They reach up toward a red banner inscribed with the words *Trabajadores de Todos los Paises Unidos* (Workers of the World Unite). Marion had overcome her resistance to "demagogic phrases," at least for the moment. Oles sees the two kneeling workers and their clarion call to unity as an apt metaphor for the Greenwood sisters. Here were "two young Americans, artists who had adopted the overalls and wages of the working class to bring their social message directly to the people."[27]

The "two young Americans" welcomed a late addition to the market project: their old friend and Marion's former lover, Isamu Noguchi. Long after their meeting in Paris, Marion and Isamu stayed connected in New York and Woodstock. In 1935, he was in flight from racism in the US art world. Among other insults, the art critic Henry McBride denigrated one of his sculptures as a "little Japanese mistake." "Once an Oriental, always an Oriental," he wrote.[28]

The sisters urged Noguchi to join them, and convinced Rivera to offer him part of their second-story walls. Their eagerness to share was likely prompted by an overabundance of space as well as generosity.[29] Noguchi was game. In June 1935, he borrowed a car from Buckminster Fuller, the polymath architect, futurist, and designer of the geodesic dome. They had met at Romany Marie's tavern in Greenwich Village, where artists could trade art for meals. Noguchi drove the Hudson to Hollywood, where he raised travel funds by creating busts of friends and by commission. With the addition of a $600 Guggenheim grant, he headed south.[30]

What a grand time the Greenwoods must have had with Noguchi, working on adjacent walls! He used cement for his powerful bas relief sculpted mural, *History of Mexico*. Ascending the staircase, red flags and a clenched fist greet the viewer. A fat capitalist fighting a skeleton animates class conflict. Fascists with swastikas, tanks, and marching soldiers reverberate with Marion's mural, while fallen miners tie to Grace's. Einstein's formula $e = mc^2$ on one wall is Noguchi's paean to science as a driver of social change. For an explanation of its meaning, he wrote to Fuller, who replied with a fifty-word telegram. One day, a Mexican man watching Noguchi work explained the formula's "real meaning": "*estado = muchos cabrones* (the state equals many sons of bitches)."[31]

The Greenwoods welcomed Noguchi to their circle of friends, but it seems unlikely that he and Marion were lovers. Noguchi fell hard for another woman. As soon as he arrived, Noguchi contacted Miguel and Rosa Covarrubias, friends from New York and former regulars at Reiss's studio. One night Noguchi joined them in a taxi en route to a dance. With the Covarrubias couple was Frida

Kahlo. Her great passion for life, despite health and marital problems, deeply impressed Noguchi. Clandestine meetings followed. Since Noguchi truly loved her, and since everyone knew how Diego ran around, why shouldn't she? That was not Diego's reaction.

Different versions of the story compete. One claims Diego uncovered the affair when the bill for furniture Isamu and Frida had purchased for a love nest was mistakenly delivered to him. Another story has Diego arriving home to find one of Noguchi's socks in their dog's mouth. Had the culprit not escaped via an orange tree, would Rivera's famous pistol have surfaced? Said pistol appears in another story Noguchi often told. He was visiting Frida in the hospital when Diego arrived wielding his gun and said, "Next time I see you, I'm going to shoot you."[32] Whichever drama ended the romance, Isamu and Frida remained friends. Such was often the case with Noguchi and his women, including Marion. In one letter, he affirmed her work by saying, "I'm mighty pleased to hear that you are working hard and leading an asthetic life—may you fill me with amazement."[33]

Marion filled many with amazement, as did the other project artists. Some stopped work at the end of 1935 after government contracts ended, leaving several murals incomplete. But the Greenwoods' work was finished. They departed amid a sea of praise. In *Mexican Life*, Guillermo Rivas called Marion a "young and talented American idealist," describing her work as "an authentic integration within local milieu—which is in itself a prodigious feat—a firm mastery of the difficult medium, and on the whole a truly notable stride of progress."[34] Regarding Grace, Rivas noted, "It does not happen often that uncommon talent recurs in the same family." He praised Marion's "equally gifted sister" for her depiction of miners as an example of "a highly imaginative and harmonious fusion."[35]

Reactions north of the border were mixed. A critic for *Time* magazine attacked the Greenwoods' left-leaning messages: "The Indian mestizos who rule Mexico love nothing so much as a mural full of anti-capitalist symbolism, though they themselves number some of the richest men in North America." The government, the author wrongly asserted, forced artists to address the "Socialist ideology of Mexico's National Revolutionary Party." The use of parenthesis in the article's title says it all: "Mexican Market (Art)." In a rare turnabout, the writer failed to note Marion's looks while calling Grace "pretty, angry-mouthed." Marion, Grace, and Pablo O'Higgins were described as the "ringleaders of the little group" that produced such suspect "art."[36]

They were indeed "little ringleaders," those Greenwoods. During nearly two years in Mexico City, the sisters were comrades to their fellow artists. Yet Marion's views on radical thought were growing more nuanced. She began to suspect ideology as the enemy of individual expression, although the seeds of doubt would not fully flower for years. When she left Mexico, her leftist politics were sometimes contradictory but essentially intact. The time had come to return and do her part in the artists' fight for social transformation in the United States.

To gain a foothold in the struggle, Marion asked Josie for a letter of recommendation to the Guggenheim Foundation. She and Grace had proposed a joint project. They would "spend one year gathering material all through the US in mining and agricultural districts and industrial centers for projects and easel pictures. In other words, study the American scene and present it from a social angle."[37]

Her request was a message in a bottle. Marion didn't know Josie's location. She'd followed her writing in *New Masses* and other publications. Yet letters Marion sent to Cuba and other places where Josie covered international events bounced back. She worried that she had lost Josie forever. Marion's affair with Diego Rivera, her friendships in Mexico City, and Grace's presence couldn't negate her pain over Josie. The old existential brooding now gripped Marion.

In March 1936, the Greenwoods left for New York just as the purple jacarandas enlivened Mexico City. Marion had sent photos of the market murals to Mike Gold at *New Masses*. They were, she argued, far superior to the "tripe in the so-called revolutionary art number [of the magazine]. I know this stuff of ours is not only good 'art' but good 'propaganda.'"[38] Despite delays and infighting, the market project artists had produced powerful, enduring radical images.

Conflicted emotions over the tumultuous two years engulfed Marion. If she had earlier, in the words of Lázaro Cárdenas, given "part of her life to Michoacán," she gave an equal if not greater part to Mexico City.

CHAPTER 14

"The Struggle Is Greater and Nearer to Me in the States"

WHEN THE SISTERS RETURNED TO NEW YORK IN 1936, MARION WAS twenty-seven—an adult returning to her parents' house. She had been away for more than three and a half years. To find her footing, she turned to Josie. However, as she suspected, the distance between them gaped. So had the chasm between Josie and John after they left Mexico in 1933.

Back in their Pennsylvania farmhouse, Josie and John had tried to escape emotional conflicts by burying themselves in work. Josie turned to *The Executioner Waits*, the novel that had stalled in Mexico. John plunged into political organizing. Tensions escalated after John read the passionate letters Marion and Josie continued to exchange through their growing rift. While Marion was still in Mexico, John and Josie separated.

Marion felt partly responsible for the breakup. "I can't believe it's on account of those letters," she wrote. "Maybe I just can't stand to believe it."[1] Her consoling words to Josie followed the "you're too good for him" theme. "I don't think and never thought that he was ever the real man for you. . . . To me you were so much more the stronger person, more deep and more profound. I could never take a man like John seriously. For that matter, there isn't a man I ever knew or know now that I *can* take seriously. Maybe I've been hurt too much in the past or maybe something is wrong with me."[2]

Josie was at Yaddo. Marion pondered visiting or reapplying for a residency herself. Then a letter from Josie related something she had told Elizabeth Ames. Marion responded, "She'll [Mrs. Ames] never understand, being what she is.

After all she forced that myth on me because that's what she wanted me to be. I'm glad you told her, though. You never need lie on my account."[3] It's unclear what "told her" means. Josie possibly revealed the nature of their relationship to Ames. Yaddo's treatment of writer Newton Arvin, who was ousted from the board, underscores the colony's attitudes toward gays and lesbians. Yet Ames offered him a fellowship after he was dismissed. Yaddo would host many other gay writers during Ames's tenure, including Truman Capote and Patricia Highsmith. It seems unlikely that she would have censured Marion and Josie. Regardless, Marion declared she had given up on Yaddo.

She fixated on finding work. Marion contacted Oscar G. Stonorov, the Philadelphia architect who later partnered with Louis Kahn on numerous projects. He'd written to Marion in 1934 about potential government murals based on drawings Noguchi had shown him.[4] He was encouraging, asking her to "please just be patient."[5]

Marion had trouble being patient. She feared that her Mexican murals had raised US government hackles. Perhaps she'd make a mistake in sending photos of her work to Mike Gold at *New Masses.* "Since I've come out openly in my work as a revolutionary, the powers back in Washington at the head of the mural departments have recoiled in a surprising fashion—the very ones who were rooting for my work when I left last fall," Marion wrote.

One person rooting for her was Edward Rowan, assistant technical director of the Treasury Department's Public Works of Art Project (PWAP). An earlier *New York Times* article quoted him pleading for federal support for the arts: "About one thousand artists in New York City who are dependent on brush and canvas or pencil and pen for a livelihood are in serious straits if not actually starving. . . . Some are men so prominent that publication of their names would cause great surprise." When the PWAP was dismantled after less than a year, he rued that "some rising American artists like Miss Marion Greenwood of Woodstock and New York City" are being forced to leave the country to paint murals in Mexico.[6]

Now Marion, Grace, and other artists were back to join the complicated web of New Deal programs. When Roosevelt was elected president in 1933, he confronted bread lines, unemployment, and deepening despair. His three Rs—Relief, Recovery, and Reform—engendered vast public projects, including the arts, under the Works Progress Administration (WPA).[7]

Making the arts part of what Roosevelt called "a more abundant life" was visionary. Federal money rushed to destitute artists in urban and rural areas, creating an enduring and justly celebrated public art legacy. The Federal Art Project (FAP) financed approximately 2,500 murals, 18,800 pieces of sculpture, and 108,000 easel works.[8] The program ran from August 1935 through June 1943, at its apex employing more than five thousand artists in theater, music, writing, and visual art. If Marion feared rejection, it wasn't due to gender. For the first time, women were hired in closer proportion to their population. In 1935, 40 percent of artists on relief were women.[9]

A unifying theme was culture as collective experience. No longer would the capital "C" culture of opera and symphonies dominate. The director of the Federal Art Project, Holger Cahill, was committed to John Dewey's vision of art and creativity as shared in a democracy. Quilts, needlework, folk arts, posters, furniture, and many other forms became part of the abundant artistic life.

The New Deal's broader agenda was to unify the country around a cultural inheritance and "usable past." Artists would be considered workers. They were like "the farmer or bricklayer," argued artist George Biddle in a letter to then interior secretary Harold Ickes.[10]

If artists as workers and art as foundational to national identity sound familiar, it's no coincidence. After six months in Mexico watching muralists work, Biddle wrote to Roosevelt in 1933. He urged the creation of a federal arts program based on the Mexican model. James Oles called that letter "among the most frequently quoted documents in the history of US art."[11] The use of the arts to unify a nation, a profound spiritual quest, the search for an aesthetic free from European influence—all of Marion's longings that found a home in Mexico now echoed and reverberated in the United States. FAP director Holger Cahill frequently borrowed "renaissance" from the Mexican context to describe the new projects north of the border.

The United States hadn't experienced the kind of postrevolutionary violence that Mexico had. Nonetheless, the Depression unleashed an economic violence that left many destitute and desperate. The country needed its own reconstituted identity. The exchange between Mexican and North American artists created an intense cross-fertilization of ideas, images, and political messages. Marion had returned with the skills and political consciousness to contribute to the struggle she'd told Josie was "greater and nearer to me in the states."

In the early 1930s, general audiences as well as the art world buzzed with excitement about Mexican influence in the north. A cadre of Rivera's followers who had been apprentices in Mexico welcomed him to San Francisco in 1930. Frida Kahlo accompanied him, breaking new ground in her own art. Huge crowds witnessed Rivera's *The Making of a Fresco Showing the Building of a City* at the California School of Fine Arts. In New York, his one-person show at the Museum of Modern Art, only the second in the institution's history, broke attendance records (1931–32). Rivera's 1933 Detroit mural celebrating the city's industry triggered the ire of conservative Catholics affronted by nude figures. Well before his Rockefeller Center image of Vladimir Lenin in *Man at the Crossroads* stoked the fury of his patrons, Rivera was already *the* radical artist in the American mind.

Orozco came early, living in San Francisco and New York between 1917 and 1919. At his initial border crossing, officials destroyed many of his sketches and paintings. They could not, however, crush his commitment to skewering American as well as Mexican greed and oppression. Between 1927 and 1934, he created murals depicting the alienation of US cities and the violence of the Mexican Revolution. At Pomona College, *Prometheus*, a mural commission facilitated by journalist Alma Reed, drew crowds to equal Rivera's. The Titan defying the Olympian gods was a perfect theme for the anti-authoritarian Orozco. His 1930–31 mural cycle at the New School for Social Research in New York represents his philosophy of human brotherhood. The *Epic of American Civilization* at Dartmouth College (1932–34) stirred controversy as anti-American but ensured his legacy internationally. He influenced numerous American artists, among them Thomas Hart Benton.

Siqueiros's art and personal history both generated attention. In 1930, communist activity had landed him in the notorious Lecumberri Prison in Mexico City, followed by internal exile to Taxco in 1931–32. After flouting the rules of exile, he faced a return to prison or a necessary departure from his country. He headed north to Los Angeles in 1932.

In California, he lectured at the Hollywood John Reed club and completed three murals. His students from the Chouinard Art Institute helped create *Street Meeting*, which depicted workers and union organizers. Siqueiros was deported after his visa expired, but he left behind devoted followers. Those included Philip Guston (then Goldstein), Ruben Kadish, and Jackson Pollock, who participated in his 1936 "Experimental Workshop" in New York.

Racism was among the shared themes in the work of US and Mexican artists. Noguchi's *Death (Lynched Figure)*, the 1934 sculpture that Henry Mc-Bride called "a little Japanese mistake," parallels Orozco's 1930 lithograph of the lynching of African American men.[12] Both artists registered their horror in response to the same photo, "Lynched Figure," from the leftist journal *International Labor Defense*.[13]

African American artists created their own compelling depictions of racism as well as scenes from daily life. Jacob Lawrence, Charles Alston, and Hale Woodruff, who studied with Rivera in Mexico, all worked for the FAP. In government programs, they finally received pay equal to white artists—$23.50 weekly. Yet racial mixing in New Deal programs, along with nudes and political messages, proved dangerous. A white southern legislator exploded when Black artists drew nude white women as models. Some referred to the National Recovery Administration, the NRA, as the "Negro Run Around."[14] Despite the rhetoric of equality, Black artists were largely segregated in their own neighborhoods.

Marion had reason to worry that her politics might block a commission. Newspapers, particularly those owned by William Randolph Hearst, condemned the FAP as "full of tripe," "inane" work. The *Chicago Tribune* described the art as "wasteful, ugly and communistic."[15]

Marion had witnessed Noguchi's struggles. Government programs repeatedly rejected his proposals, including patriotic sculptures such as a *Monument to Ben Franklin*. One agency sent him a "thumbs down" so extreme that one official said, "They almost broke their thumb nails."[16]

Noguchi believed he knew why. His bust of the New York program's director, Audrey McMahon, was the death knell: "She hated this head. I mean she was sort of ugly as a mud fence and I guess I made her even more so."[17] Holger Cahill, in charge of the FAP, tried to intervene, promising Noguchi commissions in Seattle or Chicago or anywhere but New York. Instead Noguchi headed for Mexico and never regretted his decision to join Marion, Grace, and the Rodríguez Market crew.

Despite fears of censorship, Marion and Grace soon received commissions. Stonorov was in charge of Westfield Acres, a government housing project in Camden, New Jersey. Marion had a choice: "In those days, it was either hospitals or insane asylums or jails, and I wasn't interested in that. I'd rather paint healthy people than sick ones. And so I picked the housing project."[18]

Marion visited sites of production to generate images: canning facilities, hosiery workers factories, and shipyard docks. She had to create preliminary drawings to scale, then submit them for approval. She painted on canvas in a loft she rented on Twenty-Third Street, then transferred the painting to a still-incomplete building. Grace worked separately on her own mural.

Marion's twelve-by-fifty-foot painting shows women clustered around sewing machines, workers welding steel for ships, men filling a bin with Campbell's Soup cans, and that symbol of the industrial age, a smokestack. A gaggle

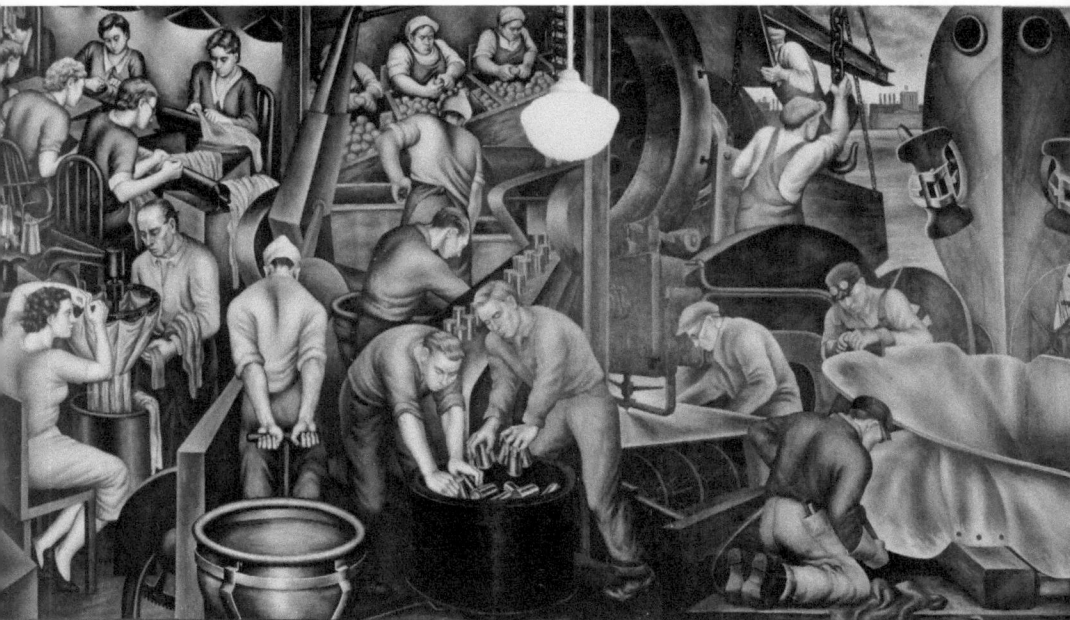

FIGURE 14.1. Westfield Acres mural (detail), by Marion Greenwood, circa 1937. (Photograph courtesy of the National Archives, Identifier 70171584.)

of families stand in front of the decrepit housing that Westfield would replace. Architects and engineers pore over their plans alongside workers carrying American flags. The combination created a visually dense if politically muted parallel to her Mexican work. Overt signs of resistance to capitalism and exploitation are absent.[19]

A 1936 letter from Stonorov to Marion explains that omission. An official who had visited the mural site objected. "The picket line in your mural should be thematically balanced by the scene of settlement, as we had discussed previously if you can remember," Stonorov wrote. "I feel that it is essential that the Administration's policy toward Labor, namely, The Right to Bargain Collectively and The Worker's Right to Strike, should be brought out in this way, otherwise criticism from the representatives of industry in Camden might become serious." Stonorov suggested a design fix: to place a piece of paper on the bargaining table that described the right to collective bargaining. That "would truly express the point of view of the administration."[20]

Marion was surely unhappy. She longed for the artistic freedom she'd had in Mexico. She also hoped to branch out stylistically. One panel features columns of steel that show movement toward geometric abstraction much like that of *Heretic*, her earlier painting of Martha Graham's dancers. But Marion stuck with the social realism the art world expected of her, fearful that experiments would be rejected. An article in the *Daily Worker* featured her mural in an ad for the exhibit "How Murals Are Made and Their Functions in Modern Life." She is identified as an ALP, American Labor Party, artist.[21]

Ralph M. Pearson cited Marion's mural as one for the "new day," combining "reality and human character" with "powerful sculptural forms of architectural design and plastic feeling." The Westfield murals were anti-elitist art free from European influence. "A national culture," wrote Pearson, "is created and measured by *productions* and not by hoarding, hero-worshipping, or copying."[22]

Stonorov promised Marion that she could join an exciting development at the 1939 World's Fair. He was drawing up plans for an ambitious three-building community center that would surpass Westfield Acres. A library, science labs, art galleries, a gym, and a swimming pool adaptable to winter ice skating would fill the building. Stonorov planned to work with the newly created Architects, Painters and Sculptors Collaborative that had set up shop at 147 E. Nineteenth Street. The group included both Greenwood sisters, Ryah Ludins, José de Rivera, and Isamu Noguchi. Enthusiasm for the project would surely blossom once viewers saw the plans at the World's Fair. Despite the Depression, utopian dreams filled the air. The MoMA exhibited a project model in the summer of 1937, and Marion demonstrated fresco technique at the actual fair in 1939. The center, however, remained a dream.[23]

Marion worked on the Westfield mural from 1936 until its installation in the spring of 1938. Sometime during those years, her relationship with Stonorov shifted. His sign offs of "Cordially" and "Yours" became "Love, O." He was, like many men before and after him, smitten by Marion. Based near Philadelphia, he traveled frequently to New York to see her. In a letter to "Dear one, Lovely," he describes burying himself in work to forget his longing, the "thunder, lightning of our meeting, the crescendo . . . pianissimos and fortissimos of our heartbeats." He added drawings of Marion on a horse and a picnic setting where they savored the "haystacks, chianti, cheese and the warm sun of Virginia." He bemoaned that they could not prolong their fleeting happiness. They had come "so close to each other that they felt a breast, a breast, a sigh, a sigh."[24] For the married Stonorov, there was "thunder and lightning." For Marion, there was the train or bus trip to Virginia, drinking chianti, and riding horseback. All were blissful relief from her family in Brooklyn.

A cynic might attribute this sexual liaison to Marion's ambition. But she was a sensual person, drawn physically and psychologically to many people. In Pátzcuaro, Marion pondered an affair with the Mexican politician Manuel because, she told Josie, she was "made that way."[25] Sylvan Cole, who later directed the Associated American Artists Gallery, described how powerfully people responded to Marion—sexually, artistically, socially. They in turn "eulogized her, sent poems and letters to her. The people who were touched by her work were touched really and deeply."[26]

Perhaps Marion's liaison with Stonorov soothed her pain over losing Josie. Letters continued to pass between the two women, but their relationship, like Josie's with John, was shattered. Each faced her individual suffering. What saved them was work—their "raft in a flood." Marion wrote to Josie, "I only know that as each year goes by my work becomes the only important thing and the 'deep secret sources of happiness' that you speak of can only come to me in moments and less and less from one individual, less and less personal."[27] Later that year, Marion would meet someone who made her reassess this assertion. Charles Fenn would also challenge her earlier statement that she could never take a man seriously.

PART III

Love and War
(1937–1947)

CHAPTER 15

Partnerships with Men and Nature

A GREENWICH VILLAGE PARTY CIRCA 1937: TWO ROOMS SWELL WITH THE crowd of artists and intellectuals into which Charles Fenn, a salesman for the Cannon Mills Textile Company, has recently drifted. He spies Marion from a distance, glowing like the sun, "not only beautiful but radiantly vivacious." The electric attraction triggers his memory of the song, "Some enchanted evening, you may see a stranger." "Magically prompted" to overcome his British reticence, he approaches and asks her name.[1] Marion seems amused as she extends a hand.

Charles worked the room to get her contact information. Their first date involved dinner and drinks. The second rendezvous was at her tiny apartment-studio on E. Twenty-Third Street, a neighborhood he considered a slum. Marion was working on the Westfield Acres project, making Federal Art Project wages of $23.50 a week. Charles bought a charcoal sketch of a Mexican girl, which surely earned him points.

On the third date, Charles, "always considerately slow in my sexual advances," finally kissed her. She drew back in surprise and said, "I never meant to let you do that!" Charles claimed it took months to get Marion into bed—an uncharacteristically shy response from her. Perhaps she held back because she intuited this relationship might be different. Charles later wrote, "I can honestly say we were in love from that moment until her death."[2]

Charles was born in London in 1907. His father was a cutlery salesman whose income, like that of Marion's father, did not support the family. His mother took in boarders to make ends meet. Charles resented that his mother had to work so hard. That grudge hardened after she died when he was about

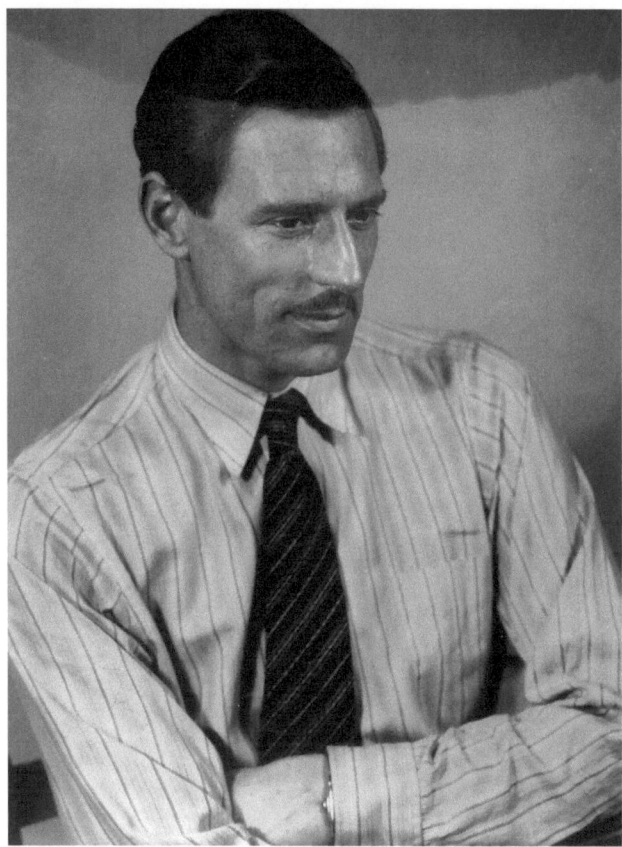

FIGURE 15.1. Charles Fenn, circa 1937. (Photograph © and courtesy of the estate of Marion Greenwood.)

twenty-two.[3] He was close to his one sibling, Bob, who became a literary agent. Ian Fleming was among his clients.

Charles initially worried about what the glamorous, celebrated Marion might see in a textile salesman who "had not only never heard of Diego Rivera but sometimes wore a bowler hat."[4] In fact, Charles was her kind of man. He was extremely handsome, tall, wiry, sandy-haired, and often mustached. Like Marion, he was an intellectually curious autodidact, having taught himself Latin and other subjects. He'd hoped to be a teacher, but his family could not afford the university education reserved for elites in early twentieth-century England. Still, he was "cultured"—knowledgeable about art, literature, and classical music. He was a talented painter and Marion would later seek his advice on her work.

A few years before his mother died, the seventeen-year-old Charles lit out to see the world as a steward's boy on the Cunard Line. Years later, he delighted children by making the "rrrrr" sound of the ship's engine. The game masked his real feeling about the work: "unbelievable slavery."[5]

Among the places the Cunard Line stopped was Cobh Harbour, Ireland. There Charles witnessed distraught families bidding goodbye, probably forever, to emigrating relatives. Those wrenching scenes did not deter him from making a similar move. He graduated from cabin boy to chief steward, but, after seven years, he could no longer endure ship life. When an American passenger offered him a job with Cannon Mills, he leaped. In July 1930, at age twenty-three, he arrived in the United States.

Charles perfected an air of seeming older so he could command respect in the hardcore business world. Soon he was wining and dining customers on bootleg gin the chemist tested first to ensure it wouldn't kill them. For cocktails, they mixed the alcohol with grapefruit juice. He would forever grimace when he drank juice, remembering the burning taste of raw alcohol.[6]

During Charles's gin-drinking years, hangovers conspired with loneliness. Just before he met Marion, he had decided it was time for a steady relationship. He later wrote, "I was helped toward this decision by meeting at the time an exceptional girl, a painter with talent, brains and beauty. What more could one ask?"[7] "An independent spirit," he might have added. Pursuing their individual creativity mattered to both. Fenn had been at Cannon Mills for seven years, but he aspired to an artistic life.

Charles shared something else with the "exceptional girl": a passion for socialism. While working on the Cunard line, he met Henry Morris, who introduced him to a book from the ship's library: George Bernard Shaw's *The Intelligent Woman's Guide to Socialism and Capitalism*. He became "Shavian inspired and favoring public ownership, equality for women, and racial equality."[8] He took from Shaw the idea of the "artist-philosopher," a label Marion later applied to Orozco. Shaw led Charles to Mozart, Blake, Ibsen, and Wagner. He grew critical of Shaw later in life, but his early encounters created a socialist lens for viewing history, literature, and economics. By the time he met Marion, he was primed for a politically like-minded mate.

Luckily, when Charles applied for US citizenship in 1930, he didn't have to disavow socialism but rather anarchism. He had only to affirm that he was not opposed to organized government and to reject polygamy.

Marion and Charles moved in together. At some point, they relocated to an apartment on E. Thirty-Fourth Street once occupied by well-known architect Stanford White. Charles continued to travel for Cannon Mills while Marion completed the Westfield Acres mural and accepted two more commissions. They were, it seemed, perfectly compatible in guarding independent lives.

In a surprising twist, the next scene in the Charles-Marion saga features him at New York's municipal building in search of the marriage bureau. A clerk sends him on his way with "good luck!" "Oh dear," says Charles, "How people take on about it! We shall have the devil of a time, that's clear!" In the elevator, a sudden qualm sends him to the wrong floor. When he finally arrives at the proper office, another clerk asks, "Where's the lady?" Charles calls Marion, who wants to delay a week. But "with promises of an extra good lunch and even a bottle of wine, I coax her into coming down at once," teasing her about the dress she arrives wearing, a "ravishing turquoise, and cut very low."

Further problems ensue. When the clerk challenges Marion's address—her studio is in an office building not considered a residence—she glares furiously. Her misgivings mount. "Oh Lord," cries Marion. "Do we actually have to go through the whole business today?" Charles calms her fears. Finally, they stand before the official clerk. Alas, they have no witnesses. Another waiting couple volunteers. Then there is the matter of a ring, or lack thereof. Charles scratches his head; Marion is ready to bolt. He fashions a ring from a cigarette package cellophane. "It gleams like beaten silver on Marion's finger." When the "I do" moment arrives, Charles says "I shall" to cue his British nationality. Marion utters, "Uh, uh." Charles gives her a hearty kiss, which she returns and pronounces the experience lovely. They depart into the sun and Marion says, "Well, darling, I feel awfully hungry." "Nothing is changed," Charles says to himself as they head for lunch.[9]

So reads Charles's irreverent recounting of their wedding on June 4, 1937. He later said it took months to persuade Marion to marry him. Her version doesn't exist, so we can only wonder whether Charles embellished the story. Was she really reluctant to leave home that day? Did she resent being taken away from her work? Given her parents' troubled union and the general bohemian ethos to bypass marriage, she had been conflicted. The question is, how conflicted? Did her love for Charles allow her to bury those fears? Despite her devotion to an independent life and Emma Goldman's admonitions to early twentieth-century women to "beware all ye who enter" into marriage, Marion was now a spouse.

Married or not, she was and would remain a working person. In 1938, a branch of the WPA commissioned her to do a mural for the post office in

Crossville, Tennessee, about sixty-five miles west of Knoxville. As with the Westfield project, Marion would paint on canvas in her New York studio and transfer the work to the post office wall. She visited the Tennessee Valley Authority's (TVA) hydroelectric dams and chose "partnership of man and nature" as her theme and the mural's title.

The TVA was among the first federally controlled regional planning agencies. The Depression had hit the Valley especially hard. The average annual income was $639.00, farms were failing, and few could afford power.[10] The government touted the dams as a success story despite conflicts over the people displaced and indigenous heritage sometimes destroyed.

In the fall of 1938, Marion wrote to thank Edward B. Rowan, assistant director of the Section of Fine Arts, for the opportunity. The commission might be a steppingstone to other projects. Rowan was the same official who had argued for a US mural program to keep artists like Marion at home. He seemed a likely advocate.

In January, she sent a proposed design. A family relaxes near a silo and barn on a pastoral landscape. To their right, a "man directs the turbulent current into a dam [the newly built Norris Dam] from which the river flows out into a peaceful, fertile Tennessee landscape."[11] Her image matched the government's message of the responsible harnessing of resources. Marion expected an enthusiastic response.

Instead, Rowan wrote a week later to say that members of the section nixed details: "It is our suggestion that you take [out] the family group under the tree with farm, etc. and on the left represent the farm and on the right use the landscape of the dam and river without symbolism."[12] The committee requested a two-inch scale color sketch with the proposed changes.

A new memo arrived from another official, T. W. Forbes: "It seems to me that the central group is a bit forced in its artiness and that the baby, especially in the head, is far from satisfactory. The man is all pose it seems to me and there is a good deal of pose in the woman too."[13]

Marion must have rolled her eyes. Her response was cordial but terse: the revisions would require a new approach. She sent a sketch with the proposed changes. More complaints followed: the farmer was "obviously forced and presented without conviction." The child was "not satisfactory due to the inadequacy of his costume."[14]

"I beg to disagree," Marion fired back. She would change the child's costume but rejected other ideas. Her sketch considered the "architectural rhythm necessary to all mural design." She wrote, "My aim throughout this design was especially that of a plastic restfulness, combined with understatement of gesture, movement stressed through counteracting lines of composition." Did they want a painting or merely an illustration?[15] Implicit is the question: who were these philistines? She wielded the sword of artistic jargon to show who was boss.

Rowan's responded, "it is noted that you do not concur with the opinion of the members of the Section." He assured Marion that "great respect is entertained here for your achievements." The passive voice masked the underlying assertion: the section was boss. The committee members, he said, were "acquainted with a number of Renaissance murals." They knew what they wanted. Please submit a full-sized version of the drawing with revisions.[16]

In a book on post office murals, the author might have had Marion in mind when he declared: "Artists tend to be a bit headstrong."[17] He failed to note the government's equal stubbornness. Marion contained her fury though the volleyed memos, signing off respectfully with "very sincerely" or "cordially yours." She would be paid $700 for the final product.

Marion warned Rowan that the committee's demands would force delays. Their correspondence ended abruptly in April 1939 and didn't resume until the following January. In the interim, Marion and Charles embarked on a trip of several months. They stopped in London to see Charles's father and brother Bob. In June, she sent Papa a postcard from Tunisia, one of the few surviving pieces of correspondence with him. She reported on their rescue from a sand dune by soldiers in tanks. In Italy, Marion marveled at the Renaissance frescoes. She said, "I looked at the frescos with such love because I had suffered in fresco myself. So I was able to appreciate so much more [about] the Piero della Francesca's."[18] The Italian master's mathematical training, which helped him create new forms of perspective, recalled her struggle in Mexico to learn the foundational elements of composition.

After the trip, Marion returned to the Tennessee mural with renewed vigor. In January 1940, she completed the four-by-thirteen-foot *Partnership of Man and Nature*. Grace had painted a mural for the Lexington, Tennessee, post office, so Marion hired the same craftsman to install her painting. The sisters had again worked on nearly parallel projects.

Marion's final composition features water flowing from the dam on the left. Its steely lines contrast with the soft human figures and rolling hills beyond. The man still at the center rests against a tree, the baby at his feet. His wife leans forward to fill a basket with apples. The unsmiling family looks downright glum. It's

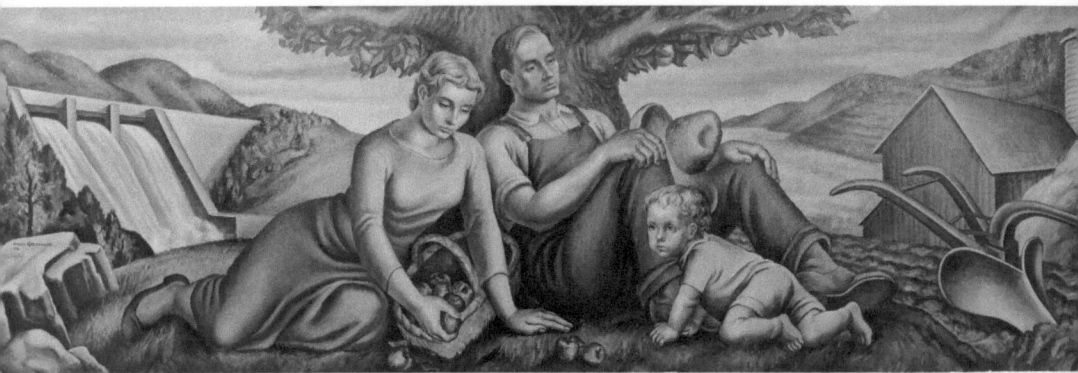

FIGURE 15.2. *Partnership of Man and Nature*, by Marion Greenwood, circa 1939. (Photograph © and courtesy of the estate of Marion Greenwood.)

therefore surprising to read the narrative that accompanied the January 30 inauguration: "Ms. Greenwood, sharing the optimism of many people of the 1930s, not only felt challenged by the hardships of the Great Depression but eager to express her ideas in her work."[19] Visitors to the post office loved the painting.

Marion did not attend the inauguration. For her, surely one of "the hardships of the Great Depression" was working with the section. For an artist Rivera had declared among the greatest living women muralists, the assault on her decisions was a slap in the face. Granted, Marion's problems with the US government didn't match those Noguchi and others encountered. Yet the section's endless demands compromised her artistic integrity. Later, she expressed sympathy for the political resistance government bureaucrats faced: "The supervisors on the mural project were certainly trying to do their best, but they had pressures on them from all sides also, and then the people were constantly criticizing the whole Federal Art Projects."[20]

The same month that Marion finished the Crossville mural, she forged a new relationship. She had met Julian Huxley while in Europe with Charles. The renowned biologist, humanist, and brother to Aldous traveled widely for his work. He had spent several years in Rice University's Department of Biology and came to New York frequently. Soon Julian and Marion were seeing one another.

On a January day in 1940, Marion walked through a magical, silent snow past Radio City Music Hall, watching a half-moon overhead. She recalled a recent visit to the MoMA with Huxley. He had shown her how to glimpse Radio City through an opening in MoMA's roof. Despite the cold, she was warmed by the happiness she'd felt with him. They shared a passion for philosophy, art, and an abiding devotion to animals. Suffering cats in particular left Marion anguished. In one letter, she told Huxley how she had rescued a stray and brought her to a local bar for a meal and hot milk.[21]

Marion knew Huxley would be sympathetic. She had devoured his *Essays of a Biologist*, where he argued we can neither prove nor disprove that animals feel emotion. He explored the mating practices of birds in Texas and Louisiana. Certain herons and egrets break into pairs. Instead of hurriedly building their nests, they "indulge in what can only be styled a honeymoon." He compared them to happy couples on a park bench in spring, hours spent in stillness. Then they suddenly raise their heads and intertwine their necks into "a real true-lover's-knot!"[22] Marion must have swooned when she read this.

She fell for the man as well as his writing. Julian was a different kind of handsome than Charles Fenn. In her 1939 portrait, he wears a suit and tie, his cheek resting on one hand as he gazes thoughtfully at the viewer through round wire-rimmed glasses. With one eyebrow slightly raised, he seems to question our thoughts and perhaps his own.

Their close ties ranged from platonic to romantic and perhaps sexual. Julian had been married to Juliette Baillot since 1919. He announced early on that he wanted an open marriage. His traditional French-Swiss wife stayed with him but then developed her own relationships. Julian had an affair with American poet May Sarton, but it was Juliette who aroused Sarton's great passion.[23]

In one letter, Marion zigzagged on whether she and Huxley should have sex. She wrote, "As you put it so aptly, 'if sleeping together is just the natural and simple expression of the more real thing, which we have now,' it would be lovely." Purely physical enjoyment, she added, might distort feelings but so could a purely mental or spiritual relationship. "Just because the physical intercourse is easier and more dangerous does not make it the less valuable. . . . Hearing, seeing, touching, tasting, and talking—have we done enough of any of those things? I'm not so sure that we have." Julian may have held back because she added, "At the same time I am really happy that you feel this way and do not desire me passionately or romantically. . . . Most of my life men have either insisted on placing me on a pedestal and treating me like some fantastic exotic creature, which even in my adolescence created great inner unhappiness, or else have misunderstood my warmth and love of life and natural need of various types of individuals to make it fuller and interpreted that for their own purely sexual desires."[24]

Marion also appreciated Huxley's spiritual bent. He considered himself a secular humanist and argued against traditional notions of God. Yet he ascribed divinity to certain awe-inspiring events. These included volcanic eruptions, sex, birth, death, intoxication, possession, and mystical vision.[25]

Huxley's "An Essay on Bird-Mind," begins with a poem, "The Birds." The first two stanzas describe the beauty of birdsong and the human envy of the freedom of flight. The ending points to the ephemeral: "But some with deeper and more inward sight / see them a part of that one Life which streams / Slow on, towards more mind—a part more light / Then we; unburdened with regrets, or dreams, / Or thought. A winged emotion of the sky, / The birds through an eternal Present fly."[26]

The last line might have come from one of Marion's Theosophy journals. A poem by Jiddu Krishnamurti asserts that a man of true purpose is never deterred from the path to enlightenment "by the multitude of desires." The poem ends with "a bird swiftly flying towards its distant home."[27]

Marion's "multitude of desires" for Julian left her conflicted. Yet by May, she had moved on. Perhaps she hadn't responded to his letters; he had hinted that he would "soon find comfort in somebody else." She urged him to do so. "Our short meeting and knowing each other was a beautiful strange little interlude in the complicated pattern of each of our lives." She felt pressed by time, work, and a life too full to add people beyond Charles and dear friends. The sign off was not "love" but "Goodbye Julien and God bless you."[28]

Marion and Julian would continue to correspond into the 1950s. In one letter, he proposed seeing her again. The intense sexual affair that each seemed to want at different points may have been short-lived or may not have happened. Years later, Marion's friend Gladys Brodsky visited Julian in London, where he showed her Marion's portrait of him. "He just sounded like he was madly in love with Marion," Gladys said. "But everybody was in love with Marion."[29]

By the time Marion bid goodbye to Huxley, World War II dominated the news. She and Charles had been in Europe in September 1939 when Hitler invaded Poland. France and Britain soon declared war. Marion didn't yet know how the cataclysm would change her life. Her immediate concern was finding new work.

Soon she was on a scaffold again. New York City's government arts project hired her to paint a mural for the Red Hook Housing Project in Brooklyn. The director, Audrey McMahon, was the person whose tensions with Noguchi had hastened his exodus to Mexico. Marion faced no such problems. She agreed to paint on-site at the forty-acre development. The ambitious project's twenty-nine buildings would house more than nine thousand people. There were outdoor gardens, a nursery school, and the community and recreation center where Marion would paint.

Red Hook was one of Brooklyn's busiest ports. Immigrant stevedores, long-shoremen, and truckers unloaded goods on its piers. During the Depression, the community's homeless created one of the city's largest Hoovervilles. Corruption and violence amid widespread poverty had traditionally plagued the area. The new housing was meant to renew and uplift Red Hook.

Marion prepared by talking to locals in industrial facilities and along the wharves. African Americans and Puerto Ricans had joined the area's earlier waves of Italian and Irish immigration. The diversity called to Marion. In the faces of the Irish immigrants, she saw her family. She sympathized with the hard lives she witnessed, creating images that she would use in the mural. Although from a different part of Brooklyn, she was embraced as a native daughter.

Marion labored over the mural from March through June. Each day at midnight, her assistants José Gutierrez and Mario Acosta laid the first layer of plaster, followed by another at seven in the morning. She climbed onto the scaffold with a pack of cigarettes, an egg sandwich, and coffee to sustain her for nine or more hours. Classes, meetings, and art events were already in full swing, and children swarmed the scaffold and demanded attention. The turmoil added to the inherent challenges of fresco. This left Marion "a rag" at night. Yet she welcomed people's responses, and she found most of their questions thoughtful.

Separate panels on three sides of the auditorium's entrance hall comprise the 325-square-foot mural. On one side, children play ball and read while a man plucks a stringed instrument. An expectant family watches workers construct their new home. Over the door, a man holds blueprints to symbolize future development. Their leisure fit the utopian vision of healthy life touted in official descriptions of the housing.[30]

The mural dedication on November 27, 1940, was part of a larger "Art Week" celebration. The considerable press coverage applauded Marion's work and gutsy personality. A *New York Post* review captioned her photo with "Marion Greenwood refutes the theory that mural fresco painting is too strenuous for a woman." The artist is described as a "hazel-eyed, chestnut-haired, 31-year-old" who "refutes the sentiment that beautiful people are likely to be stupid. Her work illustrates a lively interest in human beings, a keen power of observation, an intense awareness of form and color."[31]

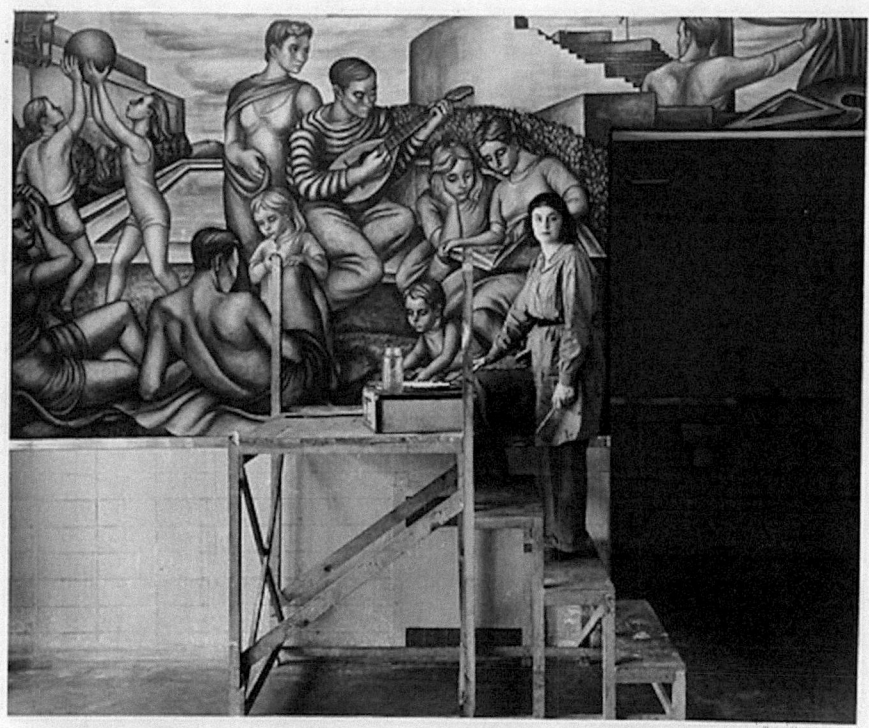

FIGURE 15.3. Marion Greenwood working on the mural *Blueprint for Living*, 1940. (Photograph by Sam Shalat, Archives of American Art, Smithsonian Institution.)

A mixed blessing, this review that blended praise for Marion's talent, commentary on her looks, and a quote perhaps erroneously attributed to Michelangelo— "fresco is man's work." Another critic mentioned Marion's "remarkably large gray-green eyes" but at least noted her lack of attention to appearance. She wore "brown slacks, green anklets, a pair of old shoes and a paint-streaked smock whose original color is practically indistinguishable."[32] Here was a woman dressed in the messy work garb worn by male counterparts like Philip Guston, whose mural design for the Queensbridge Housing Project had been approved along with hers.

Despite ongoing success, public art projects wore Marion down. After a dinner for the head of the New York City's art commission, she wrote to Huxley, "Boring speeches and watching the bowing and scraping of artists to politicians and having to flatter one's aesthetic and economic foes makes me ill." She was aghast when the officials compared the WPA murals with Italian Renaissance art. At the afterparty for artists, she drank too much. The next day, she told Huxley, "my head feels like a Bosch fantasy looks."[33] Still, she was grateful that fawning over officials kept the projects alive, at least for other artists. She'd already decided she would no longer be one of them.

Marion was full of political contradictions. She wanted to feel like a worker in overalls but disdained the meager wages. The proletariat was easier to champion from a distance. She also scorned the lack of sophistication among US viewers, even the Red Hook crowd, whom she enjoyed. Americans asked, "'Lady, why aren't they all smiling?' And I'd say, 'Well, you've only seen toothpaste and magazine advertisements. You've never even seen real painting.' Whereas in Mexico, you just wouldn't get that kind of a question." "Perhaps the Mexican masses were more harmonious to me," she speculated to Huxley.[34] Art-saturated Mexican life, she thought, gave the average person greater appreciation. Marion hoped easel painting would prove less taxing and more lucrative.

Married to Charles and enraptured by Julian Huxley, Marion kept writing to Josie. "In spite of the fact that you've evidently forgotten that I exist, that your last letter was as icy as the north wind," Marion wrote, "I'll forgive you because I love you very much."[35] Marion wanted to visit Josie at her Pennsylvania farmhouse, but the murals left her too spent to travel. She also needed to guard funds to help Grace and Musy, who were both sick.

A third reason would prove more troublesome. Marion admitted to Josie that she didn't want to leave Charles alone even for a weekend. This seemed to contradict their openness to other lovers. Charles did not see Marion's relationship with Huxley as a threat. Yet infidelity hovered as a problem for Marion, along with other tensions. She'd hoped marriage would promise escape from her financial burdens. She hated dealing with bill-paying and life's "trifles" that kept her from painting. Charles, ever practical, saw that goal as irrational in the throes of the Depression.

Despite their differences, they were still in love. In an earlier letter from Woodstock, Marion had anticipated Charles's upcoming visit. "I miss my Poodgy but am quite happy in the new warm and honest feeling that seems to have developed between us."[36] The letter ended with a drawing of her naked body, which surely presaged a happy reunion. Before too long, however, her fear of leaving Charles alone and her planned departure from WPA murals would both prove prescient.

CHAPTER 16

Art for Every Home

In June 1940, a return invitation to Yaddo arrived in Marion's mailbox. The retreat shimmered like an oasis in the desert. Marion soon forgot her fears that Josie had disclosed their relationship to Elizabeth Ames. At Yaddo, she could "gather my thoughts and my scattered self and be in the country. After years of constant disciplined production, I feel like a machine that's running down." She needed a "spiritual hauling over, and the motto will be 'less quantity and physical labor, more quality and searching thought.'"[1]

Marion arrived at the colony on August 3 and stayed through most of September. Ames invited Charles to dinner on that initial night but declined to have him stay. Yaddo parties could be raucous, but Ames prided herself on protecting the artists' time and space. Residents were especially serious during the summer she called "the most terrible of all civilization." "I have never known a year in which people have so quickly settled into complete absorption in their work," Ames wrote. "They seem to be carrying out the philosophy I hoped they would, that if some men of their ages must die, then those who are free to do the works of peace must not squander time."[2]

Marion affirmed Ames's feelings: "The world is a frightful mess, isn't it, God knows what the future will bring."[3] The Depression stoked long-simmering discord into global crises throughout the 1930s. Among them were conflicts between China and Japan, the Italian invasion of Ethiopia, the Spanish Civil War, and the outbreak of World War II. Although the United States had not yet formally entered the war, its specter hung over the country.

If the world was a frightful mess, Marion's personal life wasn't far behind. Her relatives besieged her with their problems. She and Charles had almost split up in the spring of 1940. They remained together, but Marion told Ames that a temporary separation would do them both good.

It did and didn't. Their letters during her Yaddo stay shifted from affection to acrimony. On the affection side, Marion applauded Charles's gradual movement from textile salesman to photographer. After some of his photos were published, she celebrated that he had at last found his career. Soon he would be able to "thumb your nose at the cotton business world."[4]

The acrimony circled their respective marriage roles. Charles focused on his career change; Marion wanted a helpmate. He had promised to send photos of her work for a planned Yaddo exhibit. Where were they? "Dear Babykins" often turned to "darling please send." In today's parlance, Marion needed a wife, not a role Charles embraced. Marion's absence allowed him freedom and productivity. He didn't urge her quick return, which left her wounded.

The couple's differences had been evident from the start. Charles was straightforward, sometimes brutally honest. He was surprised when his words hurt Marion. She reported from Yaddo that she was the most attractive woman there and received lots of compliments: "It has brought back a lot of my old self-confidence . . . because you have criticized me so through the years that it was bad for me but I still love you and there's no one here that interests me that way."[5] Beauty is a shaky foundation for a solid sense of self, but Marion knew how to use her looks. The message to Charles was clear: had there been someone at Yaddo who interested her "that way," husband beware.

Marion relished her time alone but also made important connections at the colony. It's like being on a ship, she said, coming to know people in unexpected ways. Spanish surrealist Federico Castellón, whose productivity she envied, was a great companion. Marion and the poet Harry Roskolenko haunted the Saratoga Springs dive bars where she sketched jockeys from the nearby racetrack.[6] Novelist and *New Masses* contributor Rebecca Pitts became a close friend. Marion described her as a "fine rare person," "very lovely and has marvelous brains besides."

Marion and Rebecca were among the "well-seasoned Yaddonians" Ames invited back to help mold "the Yaddo manner."[7] Perhaps they were too "well-seasoned." They hosted a party in Marion's studio that prompted an apology letter from Rebecca to Ames. She took responsibility for borrowing blankets from a Yaddo sitting room for the sleep-over guests. Marion's only misdeed was her impulsive offer to host the party. Rebecca swore to Ames that there was no "bohemianism" involved.[8]

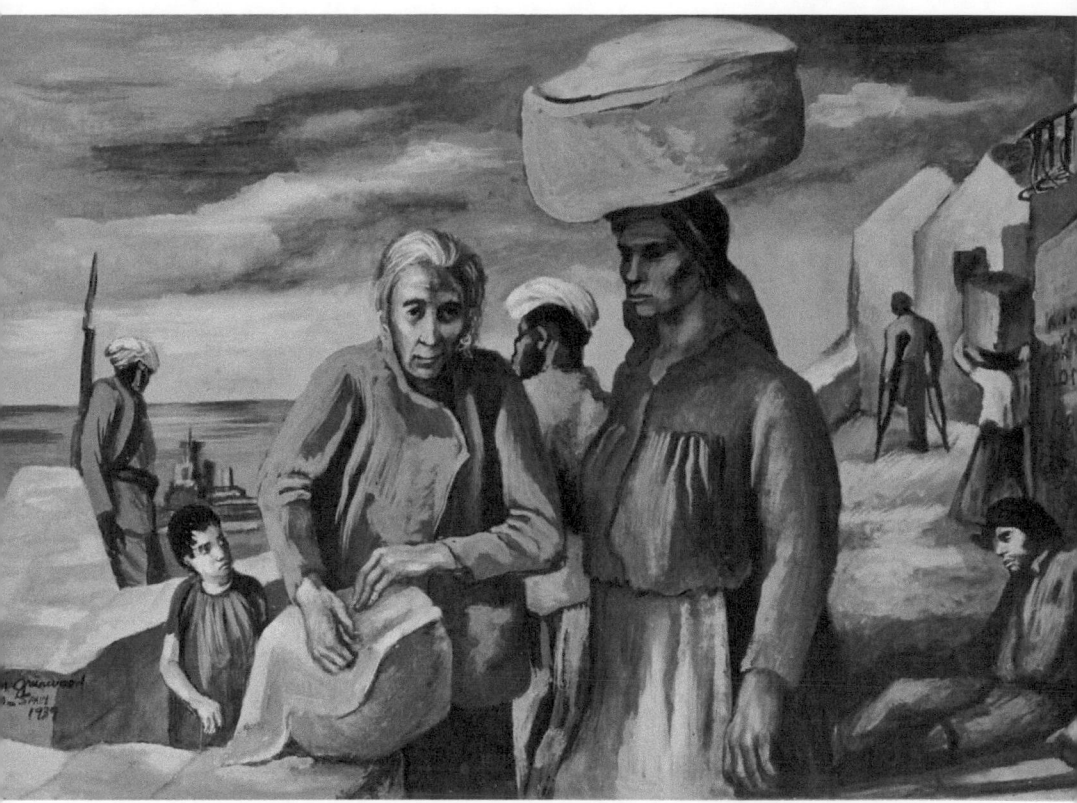

FIGURE 16.1. *Vigo, Spain,* by Marion Greenwood, circa 1939. (Photograph © and courtesy of the estate of Marion Greenwood.)

In late fall, Marion was the only artist left in a cold, dreary Yaddo, but she was determined to keep painting: "I'm in a quandary again about my work, each picture is in a different style completely but I'll keep on until I find myself."[9] "Keeping on" led Marion to endlessly rework her paintings, ruining some canvases. When she sought Charles's advice, he admonished her to leave her oils alone. He would repeat this plea ad nauseum during their years together.

Marion was productive at Yaddo. *The Jockey: Portrait of Eddie Arcaro* depicts a man in knee-high boots and brimmed cap leaning against a horse stable. She mined earlier travels for an oil painting of a Mexican woman and a gouache of a Tunis subject that she ultimately rejected as similar to a travel poster.

Marion, like many artists, was anguished over the Spanish Civil War. She knew artists as well as writers, intellectuals, and workers who enlisted in the

Abraham Lincoln Brigade. The international group formed by the Communist International (Comintern) to fight Francisco Franco's regime served as foot soldiers, medics, and technicians. Several gouaches express her angst. *Night in Spain* depicts a woman on the ground, head back, hands clenched, knees separated under her skirt. Her position suggests rape, death, or both. Roskolenko, whom Marion greatly admired, wrote a poem based on the painting.

Another gouache likely inspired by Marion's 1939 trip to Europe with Charles features the seaside town of Vigo, Spain. In the background, a turbaned man with a gun stands sentinel, while an amputee ascends a narrow road. Another one-legged companion rests on the ground behind two women, one balancing a jug on her head. "Bomba" is scrawled on an adjacent wall. The horrific effects of war saturate the image.

Marion often included sketches in her letters to Charles. One must have finally prompted him to visit. The couple appears naked, legs intertwined. The title "Mrs. Fenn" rests on a line drawn around Marion's neck like a string of pearls. "Mr. Fenn" adorns his. In the background sits an easel with a palette and paintbrush next to a camera on a tripod. A vision of Marion's utopia: lots of sex and each partner pursuing their craft.[10]

It's unclear how long Charles stayed at Yaddo or where he slept, but Marion cried when he left. She met up with fellow resident Newton Arvin on the road: "We walked around the lake and in his dry professional manner, he told me his troubles and I told him mine and I felt better."[11]

Marion and Charles shared a passionate bond. Both loved travel, adventure, art, and literature. Those interests, combined with an ineffable something that attracts opposites, kept them together. But given their opposing temperaments, how long would those suffice? Marion was emotional, all Sturm und Drang. In letters from Yaddo, she wept onto the page, complaining she'd had to drag "I love you" out of him on the phone. She had known from the beginning that he was not the type to give her the warmth, affection, and kindness that she needed and could return. Charles viewed her behavior as overly emotional and childish. She called him "erratic, temperamental, peculiar, and difficult to live with."[12]

Yet they endured. Even when growing apart, they slept together. In one alliterative tour de force, Marion wrote that she could say anything to Charles because "after all we've fought and fucked and frowned and fretted and fumed together for so long, it's fine." She parodied his expected response: "Don't be so vulgar, Marion, please." To his formality, she responded simply, "Yes, Charles." It's easy to imagine her glee in composing that missive.[13]

Then there was the infidelity. Charles often reported on his affairs. He thought that because he loved Marion far more than other women, what did it matter? Marion was hardly innocent. In one letter, she teased, "Did I tell you about the boy on the pine needles? . . . I just couldn't help myself. It was too tooooo . . ." She mimicked his feigned indifference, "My dear, will you please stop bothering me? Why did I have to get married to a sex-crazed woman?" She felt compelled to warn "any females who happen to be sniffing around you, let them have your big toe and a lock of hair (from where?) but tell them that the rest belongs to Daddy—that's me!"[14] Little wonder she'd told Josie she feared leaving him alone in New York.

Did Marion feel threatened by Charles's affairs? In a philosophical mood, she said "human relationships are impermanent, transient shadows." Many of her past lovers were now "enchained by their wives and lives and hives and chives." Not Marion and Charles. They were professed bohemians, free from the prison of convention. At thirty-one, despite professed insecurities, Marion was at the height of her power as an artist and a woman. She could easily match his infidelities. Yet she feared that women's sexual power faded with age. When she went into Woodstock to get her mail, people constantly remarked on her beauty. "It will be awful when I'm old and I won't hear it anymore," she wrote to Charles, "I've gotten so used to it."[15]

Poverty further strained the marriage in the early 1940s. Marion's resignation from government programs left her scrambling. She claimed her departure from the Federal Art Project would open a spot for Grace. The drive to discover her own vision, coupled with her family's needs, haunted every decision Marion made. Now she worried over whether easel paintings would sell.

Marion was finished with murals, but she took advantage of the promotion of her Red Hook painting during "Buy American Art Week," November 25 to December 1, 1940. The Metropolitan Museum of Art, MoMA, and *Life* magazine joined the Federal Art Project's sale of art at reasonable prices. This collaboration signaled a shift of support for the arts from the government to individual buyers, collectors, and private museums.

The 1939–1940 World's Fair at New York's Flushing Meadows Fairgrounds in Queens offers a striking illustration. Nodding to the past, the fair celebrated public art like Marion's as she demonstrated fresco technique in the Contemporary Arts Building. On the other side, the organizers used the fair's utopian theme, "The World of Tomorrow," to push consumerism. Technology, science, and industry dominated. Visitors lined up to see streamlined trains, toasters, and utilitarian objects. Notably, these new aesthetically sophisticated objects were for sale. For all its professed idealism, the fair was a paean to commerce. The Federal Art Project held on until June 1943. But the message of empowering the masses as creators faded with the New Deal. Average Americans would now be consumers rather than producers. Even Roosevelt, pushing recovery from the economic downturn of 1937–38, lauded consumption as key to the nation's vitality. "All power to the sponsors [of the fair]," he declared.[16]

An ambitious entrepreneur had anticipated this shifting of cultural tectonic plates. In 1934, Reeves Lewenthal created Associated American Artists (AAA) to generate art consumption. He was "an enthusiastic, restless, practically sleepless businessman" as well as a former reporter and art dealer. Believing the gallery system doomed, he reached out to an untapped market of middle-class consumers. Before the Depression, few Americans could afford fine art. But the AAA price of five dollars a print was reasonable even in those lean years. The business was not a cooperative. Artists had little say about how things worked. Lewenthal paid $200 for rights to print editions of 200–250.

Many, including Marion, were desperate to sell work. Lewenthal approached 750 artists with his idea. Forty answered the call. Among them were Thomas Hart Benton, John Steuart Curry, and Grant Wood, artists whose images of the rural Midwest sold consistently. The AAA also took on unknown artists, launching some of their careers.

The AAA prints mixed romanticism, social critique, and much-needed levity amid the Depression. American Regionalism, part of the American Scene movement, included rural and urban images. Benton's farmers, Yasuo Kuniyoshi's circus performers, and Isabel Bishop and Peggy Bacon's working women exemplified Regionalism's range. All worked to create a distinctly American identity.

Prints reached new buyers through exhibits in department stores and Sears Roebuck–type catalogues that went out to homes all over the country. Hotels, schools, social clubs, and other public spaces hosted traveling exhibits. In 1936, AAA opened a gallery on Madison Avenue, which later moved to a larger space on Fifth Avenue. Additional galleries eventually appeared in Chicago and Beverly Hills.

The AAA's roster of artists ballooned over its sixty-six year history (1934–2000). For nearly thirty of those years, Marion created and sold prints through their gallery and catalogs. She enthusiastically resumed the lithography she'd learned years before in Woodstock. When she joined AAA in the early 1940s,

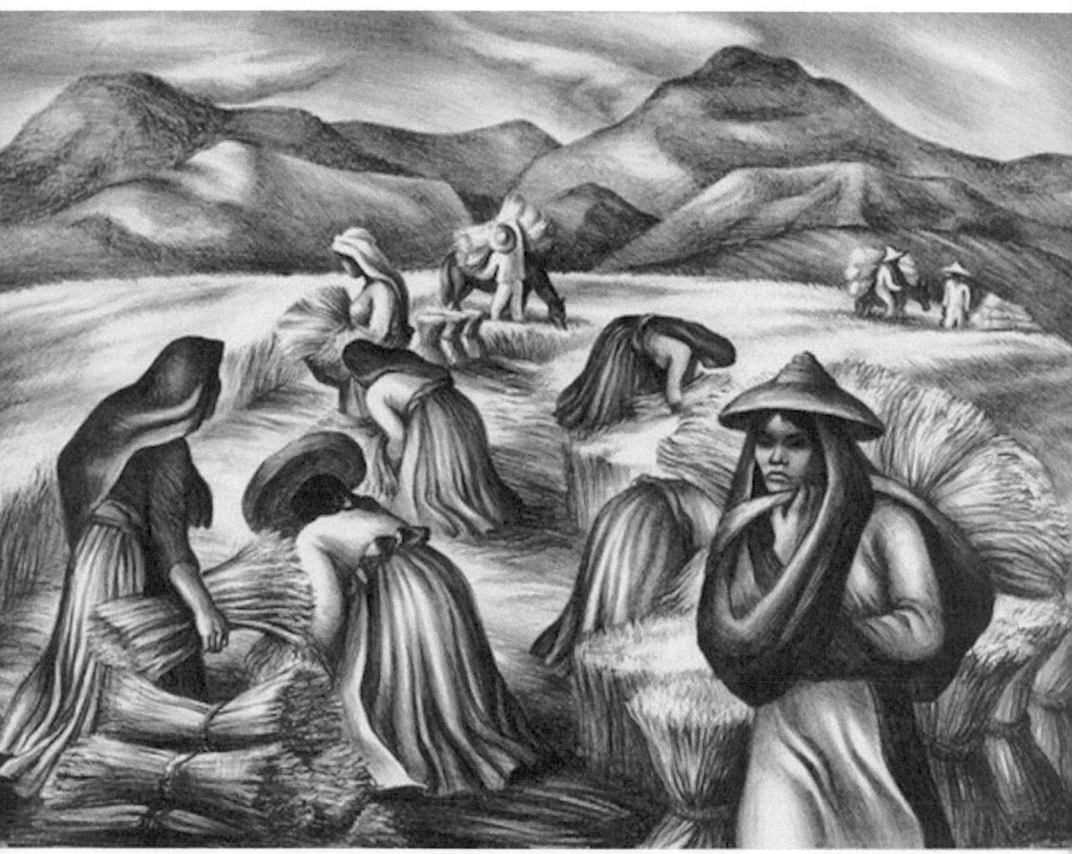

FIGURE 16.2. *Mexican Harvest*, by Marion Greenwood, circa 1940. (Photograph © and courtesy of the estate of Marion Greenwood.)

many of her friends were already members. They came for the camaraderie as well as income, making it a "concentrated group of talented people as strong as any America has known," said artist Aaron Bohrod. Marion concurred. She also praised the gallery's openness to "the American masses" who would pore over her sketches and portfolio. Marion had quit the scaffold, disillusioned with "the masses." Now she welcomed them back as consumers.[17]

Prints freed Marion from her tendency to overwork oil paintings. Once etched onto the litho stone, the image stayed. Her first AAA print, *Mexican Harvest* (1941), reproduced some of her fresco images. As in her Morelia mural, she foregrounds women workers, who bend over bundled wheat. The diminutive figures of three men fade into undulating hills in the background. Shadows dominate the image and the only visible face is unsmiling, yet the print has a haunting beauty.

In the lithograph *Mountain Family*, a careworn mother on the porch of a ramshackle wooden house holds a naked baby. Four other children hover in the background. The crowded space leads to a narrow back door whose frame fills with swirling darkness. The expressionistic elements mix with classic 1930s social realism to portray the suffering of the rural poor. Marion experimented with other styles in the nearly forty prints to follow. Her work sold so well that a later AAA director, Sylvan Cole, urged his mother to collect her art.

The Federal Art Project (FAP) and AAA offered a lifeline to artists. Many, including Marion, worked for both programs. The FAP employed a few African American artists; AAA employed none. The AAA was less inclined toward experimentation and highly charged social issues, with some exceptions. Harry Sternberg's *Enough (Boundman)* (1947), an image of a monumental muscular man with his wrists tied, critiques the exploitation of workers.

Neither program dictated a choice of subjects, yet the market exercised its own censorship. Many middle-class American buyers rejected images of suffering for their living rooms, even at the bargain rate of five dollars. A more overt ban forbade mail-order sales of Grant Wood's *Sultry Night*. A farmhand bathing nude was deemed "obscene."[18] Anthony Comstock was long dead, but his effect on the US Post Office lingered.

Both programs hired women, with a higher percentage at the FAP. Marion, Peggy Bacon, and Doris Lee served on the AAA Board of Governors. Lily Harmon joined later. A photo of a board meeting at the Gotham Hotel in New York shows a smiling Marion amid friends, including former lover and Woodstock artist Adolf Dehn.

The war boosted this emerging alliance between business and government. A 1937–38 recession halted the gradual recovery from the Depression, leaving millions unemployed. Exports of steel, arms, and ships to the Allies offered financial relief. After a decade of clashes, the government encouraged labor leaders to work with industry. Artists responded with prints celebrating workers' contributions to the war effort. Images of strikes and horrific working conditions receded.

The Spanish Civil War and the rise of fascism pushed some normally pacifist artists to support the war. As early as 1934, Marion had responded through illustrations for *New Masses*. *Civil War in Austria* focused on the Hitler-directed chaos unleashed by Austrian Nazis. A man hangs, hands tied behind his back, while a group of soldiers linger beneath the scaffold.[19] As the war edged closer, *New Masses* published numerous anti-fascist cartoons and illustrations. Siqueiros's *Untitled Worker* features a man stomping on a swastika.

Marion and Charles had been in Europe on August 23, 1939, when Germany and the Soviet Union signed a nonaggression pact. This left Stalin free to build his military and the Nazis to pursue expansion. To understand how this pact split the Left, we have to go back to the heady optimism of earlier decades. John Reed's 1919 *Ten Days That Shook the World* ignited hope for radical change with the story of Russia's transformation. Artists often journeyed from the United States to Mexico, then to Russia to witness the new egalitarian order. Even though Stalin's show trials were already evident, hope lingered.

On September 1, 1939, hope shifted toward despair. Germany's invasion of Poland shattered many artists and intellectuals. On that day, Arshile Gorky and other artists met at Isamu Noguchi's studio on Twelfth Street to sketch together. Working until dawn, "they drew as if they were afraid to stop."[20]

Over a year later, while Marion was still at Yaddo, Congress passed the Burke-Wadsworth Act, the first peacetime draft in US history. A month later, in October 1940, Charles registered. Just how sympathetic he felt toward his adopted country is open to question. He was a sharp observer of US culture, puzzling over unhappy citizens in one of the most affluent nations in the world. Charles blamed a fixation on material success among those who "strive, worry, interfere and domineer."[21] Yet he appreciated the openness of American society.

Charles's attitudes were socialist, internationalist, and pacifist, as were those of the couple's friends. Yet he supported the war, one in which he had a personal stake. While Marion was at Yaddo, he awakened to headlines such as "Nazis again raid London by Night." His father and friends lived in terror, especially after the bombing of the British Museum and Home Office.[22]

Whatever Charles's feelings about military service, he itched for an overseas assignment to launch a photography and writing career. He hadn't yet escaped his job at Cannon Mills, a form of "slavery that made me come home savage every evening."[23] On days when Marion agonized over painting and Charles chafed under the salesman role, tensions escalated. They were broke and looking for new opportunities.

Charles's chance soon arrived. Marion's connections often led to party invitations with influential people. At a fundraiser for Chinese victims of the war, the Chinese Counsel invited Charles to document his country's resistance to the Japanese. The offer included letters of introduction but no payment. Charles declined. However, a few weeks later at an art opening, he met *Friday* magazine editor Dan Gillmore. The publication, which Josie wrote for, had a small but devoted left-leaning readership. Charles convinced Gillmore to hire him as the Asia news photographer, then obtained the Chinese Counsel's introductory letters. He was soon on his way.

Marion mourned when Charles left in March 1941, but she supported this opportunity. China could launch a new phase for him as Mexico had for her. Both could pursue their passions. "We can both do big things alone and bigger ones together," she wrote. "So young man, get to work and do wonderful things and take care of yourself in every way." Her bravado hid anguish over a memory that would haunt her: his face through the window as the train pulled away. "Parting is a little death, as the French say."[24]

As Charles took leave of Marion, he was shocked to see her eyes fill with tears. He claimed he had never seen her cry. He wrote, "It was only then I realised how much we cared for one another despite our clashing temperaments."[25] Both hoped that their mutual respect and affection would sustain them in coming years.

CHAPTER 17

War, Departures, and Returns

WHEN CHARLES LEFT FOR CHINA IN 1941, THE UNITED STATES HAD NOT formally joined the war. However, the US Lend-Lease Act authorized sending supplies to nations vital to American defense. Support for American involvement grew steadily. Marion panicked. If war erupted, when would Charles return? Amid the buzz of New York City, with friends and family nearby, she felt isolated. "New York is a place," said writer and *New Yorker* fiction editor William Maxwell, "where one can weep on the sidewalk in perfect privacy."[1]

Financial problems intensified her worries. How would she pay for their E. Thirty-Fourth Street apartment? Her Yaddo friend, Rebecca ("Becky") Pitts, moved in to help with rent and cooking. It wasn't enough. In April, Marion put her belongings and Charles's darkroom into storage and moved into the Hotel Albert. She set up her easel and hoped for commissions.

The next month brought work—the "raft in a flood," as Josie had termed it. Marion's independent spirit resurfaced. She assured Charles that he need no longer worry about her, "not that you ever did."[2] *Time* magazine commissioned a May 26 cover, a portrait of French Admiral François Darlan. Soldiers fill the background behind Darlan's half-turned face. To the left are the words "Travail," "Famille," and "Patrie"—ironic as Darlan had joined the Nazi-controlled Vichy government. Marion might have winced at his politics, but she was surely heartened by seeing her signature in the lower left corner.

From the hotel, she made her seasonal move north into a Woodstock spring bright with apple blossoms, frogs singing in vernal pools, and owls haunting the night. Marion loved country life and being close to animals. She rented an airy studio once home to John Carroll, an artist who taught at the Art Students

League. She gloried in the season by day but needed companions at night. Grace and her husband, Rollin Crampton, sometimes stayed with her.

More financial success followed the *Time* cover. Reeves Lewenthal of AAA sold some of her paintings. He now realized, she said, "that a woman painter is not such a bad gamble."[3] She spoke at the Women's Century Club in Scranton, Pennsylvania, for fifty dollars and created portraits and prints inspired by the working poor. The oil painting *Simple Confession* shows two men sharing drinks in a bar. One man slings an arm around the other's shoulder in brotherly fashion.[4] The vibrant red sweater of one figure stands out; if she overworked some paintings, this was not among them. The loose brushstrokes resurrect those of Marion's newsvendor from her 1928 stay in Paris. She also created a stunning portrait of Charles around this time.

Marion proudly announced that she earned this money through "my own little fingers and paintbrush." She celebrated with the purchase of a $200 "swanky" 1936 Chevrolet. Like many New Yorkers, she didn't know how to drive, so friends gave her lessons.[5] Hills daunted her, and she failed the test the first time. She kept going until she passed.

In June, Marion finally received a letter from Charles posted from Hong Kong three months earlier. That delay was minimal compared with later years when mail delivery further deteriorated. Letters, often opened by censors, sometimes took seven months.

Charles's base was the wartime capital of Chungking (Chongqing) in south central China. His return address was the Chinese Industrial Co-ops in Paochi, Shensi (Baoji, Shaanxi), a landlocked area of North China. His letter was filled with news from so many places that Marion was often confused about his location.

How well did Charles understand the complexity of China-Japan relations before he left? Given his diligent self-education, he likely knew something of their tangled history. Both countries had fought on the Allied side during World War I. After the war, China expected that the 1919 Treaty of Versailles would return Chinese territories held by Germany. Instead, the Allies awarded the German-occupied Shandong and other areas to Japan. Indignant Chinese diplomats in Paris walked out in protest. Angry Chinese students launched a boycott of Japanese goods.

President Woodrow Wilson supported the treaty terms. However, he expected that after throwing China under the bus, the League of Nations would compensate their loss. That never happened. Instead, Japan's territorial

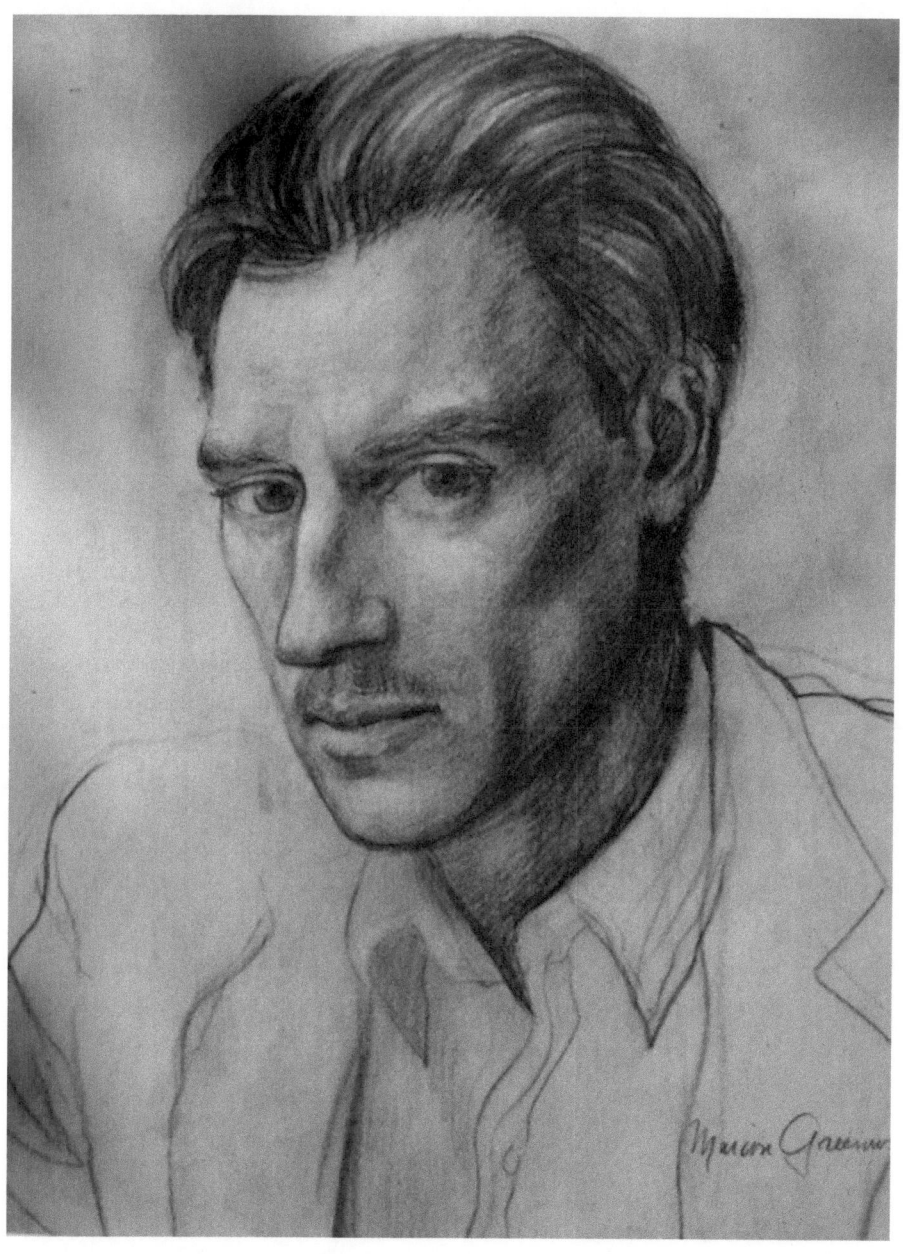

FIGURE 17.1. Portrait of Charles Fenn, by Marion Greenwood, circa 1940. (Photograph © and courtesy of the estate of Marion Greenwood.)

expansion continued. A violent assault on Nanking mushroomed into the Sino-Japanese war of 1937–1939. In 1940, Japan joined the Italy-Germany Axis. International alarm escalated. American sympathy for China blossomed, a striking contrast to the anti-Chinese nineteenth-century exclusion laws. The embrace of China grew alongside anti-Japanese sentiment that culminated in the 1942 internment camps. "Jap" became standard usage, showing how quickly racism flips its target.

Charles shared the pro-China fervor, launching a lifelong love affair with the country and its "gloriously colorful" people. He was willing to overlook the tenuous nature of his job with *Friday* magazine, which had not promised to accept his photos. He alerted Marion that he would stay for at least a year. Why didn't she join him? She would love China, especially a cuisine so fabulous that she would "die of overeating." No one, Charles claimed, could be an epicurean without a trip to China.[6]

Charles had assumed his Asian travels would be no more challenging than immigrating to the United States. He scoffed when a China expert advised him to create a bed by taking a door off its hinges. Otherwise he would face misery sleeping on dank earthen floors. Charles found this ridiculous, but the door-as-bed ritual soon became regular practice. Add to that fourteen-hour days in "bone-shaking lorries" bumping over bad roads to Loyang, where he would document the Japanese advance. For Charles, these were trifles. His real worry was getting to the front and producing photos. Perhaps "I've bitten off more than I can chew," he wrote. "It isn't so easy to start a new career at halfway through life."[7]

Charles's temporary home in Loyang was a large room with the unbelievable luxury of electric lights. When his letters dryly reported on troop movements, Marion asked for affection. "Please be nicer to me, Sweetie. I'm so lonely and I've worked so damn hard." In her spacious apartment in the country outside Woodstock, she and the cat longed for Charles. Still, "we both think you're a rascal, a bastard, and a self-centered cold, cruel thing but we can't help but love you and miss you, damnit! And admire your skill and daring and talent and good looks."[8]

A loving letter finally arrived. "Dearest Popsy," Charles wrote, "I am always thinking about you and of how much we can make of our lives now that those hard, hard years from '36 to '40 are behind us." Marion joyfully affirmed that when he returned, a new phase would begin. She, too, attributed the turmoil in their relationship to years when their careers stalled. Now he would advance as a photographer-writer while she would earn the esteem that they both thought she deserved. Throughout their years of conflict, Charles never stopped believing in Marion's talent. He signed off with love to her and the cat.[9]

Throughout her life, Marion fantasized about a life devoted to art, unburdened by niggling details. This was not her fate. After supporting Charles's professional move, she realized that his opportunities thwarted hers. She lost focus in the myriad details of life, bill payment, and house upkeep. Charles sent money to help with household expenses, but he suspected Marion funneled money to her family. She denied the accusation and speculated that his purchase of photography equipment was straining their budget.

Marion also worried over his fate as Asia grew more dangerous. The daily headlines reported bombings in the Pacific. President Roosevelt sent a personal plea to Emperor Hirohito "to stay Japan's hand" after an attack on Thailand.[10] Despite professed neutrality, the US government deemed national interest imperiled. Japan and the United States froze funds in their respective countries. The Japanese military rolled into Indochina, and the Russo-German war veered into its sixth week. Newspapers and radio broadcasts built war momentum. In newsreels before movies, declarations of America as the "Hope for Democracy" mixed dramatic background music with rhetoric about duty and obligations beyond our borders. United States involvement seemed inevitable.

Then the shock of December 7, 1941.

Marion might have heard about Pearl Harbor in her new place in the Fifth Avenue Playhouse Building above an art house movie theater. She'd gotten the eighty-five-dollar-a-month apartment for fifty dollars. The bargain rate included a caveat that she had to exit at a moment's notice if someone else wanted it. She could have been at the AAA gallery at 711 Fifth Avenue, which she used as a return address. Either way, Roosevelt's famous broadcast about "a date which will live in infamy" shook her to the core. The *New York Times* headlines the next day featured a map of the Pacific theater of war. She could trace the lines from Hawaii to China.

Marion had not heard from Charles for months. She wrote into the void, panic bleeding onto the page: "God knows when this will reach you now that the war is on. . . . I knew it would come. That's why it was so ridiculous that you kept writing suggesting I should think seriously about coming to China!"[11]

As Marion mailed her letter, Charles was traveling via public bus and army truck to Chungking. He knew nothing of the war. As he enjoyed a five-cent meal of rice and the promise of a real bed, someone shared the news. He also learned that his employer *Friday* had folded. Subscribers canceled to protest the editors' support for the Soviet party line, a schism dating back to the Nazi-Soviet non-aggression pact. Charles now had no income as a global war escalated.

Ever resourceful, he contacted the American Military Mission. Their representatives had arrived a few months earlier in 1941 to help Chiang Kai-shek, leader of the Chinese Nationalist Party. Charles got a job in the pay department, which he described as "insufferable boredom." After three weeks, he quit. That he lasted that long was due to the patience "my close association with Chinese people had impressed into my basically fretful nature."[12]

Charles soon glimpsed another option. When the Japanese invaded Burma in January 1942, he dashed over to see a friend at the Associated Press (AP) office. He convinced the agency to send him to Burma, the corridor for Allied supplies to China. They would pay expenses but no salary, no insurance, and they might or might not accept his photos. These dismal conditions sounded fine to him.

Charles spent two extremely dangerous months in Burma. He faced mountainous terrain, famine, and conflicting priorities among the Allied forces. At one point, he raced across a jungle past blazing vehicles set on fire by the Japanese. The Australian correspondent driving was intent on getting the story. Charles could hardly let fear leave him behind. He could have ended up in a camp or beheaded as a spy. "Where ignorance is bliss, 'tis folly to be wise," he later wrote. He felt little affinity for the Burmese, whom he saw as ground down to subservience after a century of colonization. In contrast, the Chinese were never "subservient, boastful or two-faced," even if sometimes "irrational" or "incomprehensible."[13]

Charles continued working for the AP, sending back material from China, Burma, and eventually Africa. In Ceylon, now Sri Lanka, a Royal Air Force pilot invited him for a flying adventure to an atoll where he could alight for a swim. The pilot would return for him later. Charles swam back to the atoll and waited. But the plane had disappeared, never to be found. A fisherman called in a request, and a week later, Charles was rescued. He was shaken but only temporarily. His next flight landed him in Abyssinia, now Ethiopia, to interview the newly restored emperor Haile Selassie, whose throne was guarded by two growling Great Danes.[14]

Marion knew nothing of these near catastrophes, yet she anguished over his whereabouts. She had written the State Department, the Red Cross, and Charles's father in London, who was equally in the dark. After seven months with no word, a friend, Louis Fischer, reported having seen Charles. Otherwise, she wouldn't have known he was alive.

While Marion scrambled for work, she negotiated with potential publishers of Charles's photos. Many were lost in transit or arrived too late to be used. Marion's efforts kept him alive. Unable to be her own agent, she got tough as his. Before *Friday* folded, she'd hounded the editor to use Charles's photos. She reported, "I'll go anytime and make him send you money, and damn quick! I'm Irish and he better treat you right or I'll bash his teeth in!"[15] She pressured the AP to pay him $125 for photos from Ceylon. She sent his novel manuscript to Doubleday. They rejected the book, perhaps because of Charles's prominent leftist sympathies.[16] Marion's responsibility for the business details of both their lives would linger far longer than she knew.

In December 1942, a year and a week after the outbreak of war, she received a packet of jewelry from Charles. His attached note had no return address or news. It was nothing "but a description of the jewelry as if you were around the corner instead of the other end of the earth! What is wrong with you!" Was he in prison, sick, broke? Could he not give her a single clue? Did he have a heart of stone? "I wouldn't treat a worm the way you've treated me."[17] Her worry over Charles left her unable to paint. Lewenthal had promised her a one-person show at the AAA gallery. Now she postponed it for lack of art. If Charles returned, she could be productive again.

Before the United States entered the war, Marion had repeatedly rejected Charles's suggestion that she come to China. She cited the cost, danger, and visa problems. Perhaps more important was Marion's need for stability. She, too, loved travel and adventure, but there were limits. War, economic deprivation, and loneliness shaped a yearning for home life. She began to sound more middle-class than bohemian: "I want an ordinary good life—a husband—a house in the country—and work."[18]

Marion didn't want children when she met Charles; she often worried when "the curse" was late. Still, it's hard to know whether she wanted a family. In 1941, she picked up some photographs at the home of abstract artist Konrad Cramer and his wife, Florence. According to Florence, Marion said, "I'm just getting to the point where I'd like to have a house and settle down. I might even enjoy having a baby (or isn't it safe at 32?) but my husband doesn't care to have children and he likes to wander!"[19]

Despite her anger at Charles, Marion felt they were meant for one another and could make the marriage work. In frustration, she covered the top of her next letter with "Come home come home come home."[20]

Charles probably never received that correspondence. In February 1943, he headed to Algeria to cover the war but was held up by red tape. From there, he heard of an opening on a Consolidated B-24 Liberator, an American heavy bomber. He later wrote, "Liberator by name and liberator by deed! Ten days later (on the South Atlantic route to avoid U-boats, flights took that long), I was back home: what joy!"[21]

Furious as Marion had been, she quickly forgave him. She never forgot the day he walked in the door: March 3, 1943. Charles found Marion at home, "still young and beautiful," entertaining a few friends. One of them was Buckminster Fuller. He immediately wanted to know more about Charles's activities in China. They met the next morning to discuss a possible role for Charles in the Office of Strategic Services (OSS).

Roosevelt established the OSS, precursor to the CIA, in 1942. Before the war, the United States had no intelligence agency. Top military brass initially balked at creating one, but they backed down. Under the control of the Joint Chiefs of Staff, the OSS had multiple subdivisions and drew experienced men and women into clandestine work. Among them were future US Supreme Court Justice Arthur Goldberg, historian Arthur Schlesinger Jr., and chef Julia Child. She began as a clerk and then joined a team of scientists to develop shark repellent. Her last appointment was in Chungking, the Chinese headquarters where Charles had been based. Other specialists included adventurous writers and artists, missionaries with established in-country connections, inventors like Fuller, and linguists.

It may seem odd that the OSS would attract iconoclasts like Fuller and Charles. But the young agency's nickname, "the cloak and dagger boys," likely appealed to both. Charles was also opportunistic. Nearly two years trekking around Asia had not extinguished his appetite for adventure.

The OSS director was a fellow iconoclast. William Donovan's nickname, "Wild Bill," might seem incongruous for an Irish Catholic Republican Wall Street lawyer. But Donovan welcomed the unconventional. One former CIA operative wrote, "Every eccentric schemer with a harebrained plan for secret operations (from phosphorescent foxes to incendiary bats) would find a sympathetic ear in Donovan's office." "Wild Bill" often bypassed military protocol. He said, "I'd rather have a young lieutenant with guts enough to disobey an order than a colonel too regimented to think and act for himself."[22]

The OSS was awash in officers. Many came via Donovan's connections to elite business and legal worlds. Rank was supposed to correspond with qualifications. The agency overlooked Charles's less-than-highbrow credentials, recruiting him to the officers corps. His code name, selected from the OSS Shakespearean roster, was "Hamlet." The agency also ignored his work with the leftist *Friday* magazine. Had he been a member of the Communist Party, this might not have been an impediment.

Donovan was conservative and would turn anti-communist later in life. He was also practical and determined to enlist allies to defeat the Axis powers. On his watch, communists, garden-variety liberals, and conservatives collaborated. The FBI, who repeatedly attempted to thwart the OSS, once produced evidence that three employees had communist affiliations. Donovan considered leftists to be the most effective field officers. He responded, "I know they're communists; that's why I hired them." He recruited members of the Abraham Lincoln Brigade who had fought for the Spanish Republicans. Workers from labor unions joined, including some from the IWW, the "Wobblies," a group the government had brutally suppressed. One group of leftist intellectuals worked under the vice-president of the decidedly capitalist International Railways of Central America.[23]

Charles got the OK to proceed to basic training.

When he left for boot camp, Marion wrote, "How little I knew what leave takings and separations I would go through in these last seven years! Perhaps it is well we do not see what the future holds for us," she wrote. "I'm trying to face the fact that I'll be lonely, whatever I do."[24] That would prove true for more years to come.

CHAPTER 18

Lost Time and Jealousy's "Revolving Fire"

"AT THE AGE OF THIRTY-SIX A MAN IS WELL PAST HIS PRIME."[1] SO DECLARED Charles during his grueling training with the US Marines. To join the OSS, he had to choose one military branch. The marines seemed to be the most prestigious. Later he discovered that army or navy training would have been less rigorous. After a few weeks at boot camp, he may have regretted accepting Buckminster Fuller's recruitment.

Charles surprised himself by earning a medal for special competence with a Colt .45. His next stop was the OSS Training School, where he joined the Morale Operations (MO) division. Some field officers described the group as "rear-echelon insanity."[2] The branch attracted other creative types, progressive writers and filmmakers charged with generating "black propaganda." They circulated rumors and reproduced enemy newspapers with subtle, misleading changes. The goal was to demoralize their opponents, spread chaos, and incite division. Charles warmed to the task. He later noted that MO training diluted his upbringing as a strictly law-abiding citizen. "Not all the wounds of war are caused by missiles."[3]

With Charles in training, Marion packed up the New York studio and headed to Woodstock. She disliked storing furniture, art equipment, and other possessions, but she loved moving with the seasons, especially to embrace autumn in the country. Fall also triggered a deep melancholy. "The awareness of the passing of time and beauty and the transient quality of all things. Is it just the Irish melancholy of my ancestors?"[4]

Marion might have added, "Or is it our reading of Marcel Proust's *In Search of Lost Time*?" At Yaddo in 1932, she and Josie traded volume two, *Within a Budding Grove*. Her earlier reading of volume one, *Swann's Way*, left an indelible impression. When Marion met Charles, she gloried in their shared love of Proust. The English translation of the seven volumes of *In Search of Lost Time* had arrived sequentially between 1922 and 1931. Critics on both sides of the Atlantic celebrated the book's modernist style and exploration of inner consciousness. On reading it, Virginia Woolf reportedly cried out, "Oh, if I could write like that!" Proust delved into territory where few dared to tread: homosexuality, antisemitism, jealousy twinned to love, social mores that he both mocked and celebrated. Many of these themes turned up in Marion and Charles's letters.

The motif of time dominated Marion's Proustian references. "I was born remembering," she once wrote to Josie about a painful experience that lingered like a "burnt hole" in her chest. Marion longed to shed such recollections; she labored to resurrect others and find meaning in the past. Proust spoke to this need in the novel's most famous scene. When the narrator, also called Marcel, mixes crumbs of his petite madeleine with his tea, involuntary memory renders him "attentive to the extraordinary thing that was happening inside me. A delicious pleasure had invaded me." He searches for the source of his ecstasy until a childhood memory appears: his Aunt Léonie offering him cake dipped in her tea. Taste, like smell, carried what had seemed lost, "like souls, remembering, waiting, hoping, upon the ruins of all the rest, bearing without giving way, on their almost impalpable droplet, the immense edifice of memory."[5]

Angst over time and memory bled into Marion's realization that Charles would soon be gone indefinitely. Uncertainty sometimes paralyzed her. Should she attend a dinner party at the home of Russian-born painter Anton Refregier and his wife, Lila, without him? Should she find a permanent place in New York or Woodstock where they could settle down? How long could she wait for his return from Asia?

At every juncture where she felt defeated, Marion went to work. As she couldn't escape to Europe or Mexico, she found subjects to "arouse empathy" closer to home. From Woodstock, she drove to Kripplebush, a rural community about twenty miles away. Inspiration came from the daily life of local people.

Marion harbored a fantasy about moving to a farm to paint animals. If only she could gain an intimate view of their lives! But to paint them, she would have to live with them and know their reality. She longed to "get the essence of a horse or a bull like I get an expression on a face. It's because I *know* faces and not the other."

She stuck with human portraits. She met a Kripplebush couple in their eighties who were still in love. Merry pranksters, they hung out at the local cemetery to scare people with practical jokes. She also sketched a solitary old woman. Marion found the idea of aging alone "ghastly." "I certainly wouldn't want to live if I found myself in that situation," she wrote to Charles.[6]

Another painting, *Carnival (Festival) at Kripplebush*, a gouache and lithograph, illuminates Marion's expressionist impulse. A group of revelers perch on the porch of an old clapboard house. Under strings of lights, the figures' boundaries blur, blending the blues and reds of their clothing into the background. Splashes of white illuminate a night sky. The festive air of a community event permeates the image. It was one of the rare paintings that Marion finished feeling satisfied.

When the weather turned cold, she headed back to New York and reconnected with AAA. The gallery sold one of her earlier lithographs, *New Year's Eve*. An African American man wraps an arm around his beautiful young partner. In a strapless party dress, she holds a cigarette in the hand resting under her chin. They gaze into the distance, unsmiling. The New Year's balloons and noisemakers cannot hide the ennui holidays trigger, especially during war. The couple's ethereal beauty and somber expressions link them to artistic renderings of melancholia begun during the Renaissance.[7] When the *New York Times* Sunday arts page reproduced the print, the critic stated that "Miss Greenwood is now invading Harlem," a fact she proudly reported to Charles.[8]

Since her days in Winold Reiss's studio, Marion had socialized with both African and African American artists and actors. She often joined friends at Café Society, one of the first racially integrated nightclubs in the country. Barney Josephson founded the club in 1938 to feature Black performers and ensure equal treatment for all their patrons. At a party, she met Canada Lee, who played Bigger Thomas in a Broadway production of Richard Wright's novel *Native Son* and pioneered roles for Black actors. He later came to pose for her. Marion's friend Mura Dehn, whose portrait she painted, introduced her to other Black artists.

The Russian-born dancer Mura had lived in Paris in the 1920s. Josephine Baker's performances, which electrified Parisians, inspired Mura to document African and African American dance. Paris also introduced her to her husband, artist and lithographer Adolf Dehn. After they immigrated to the United

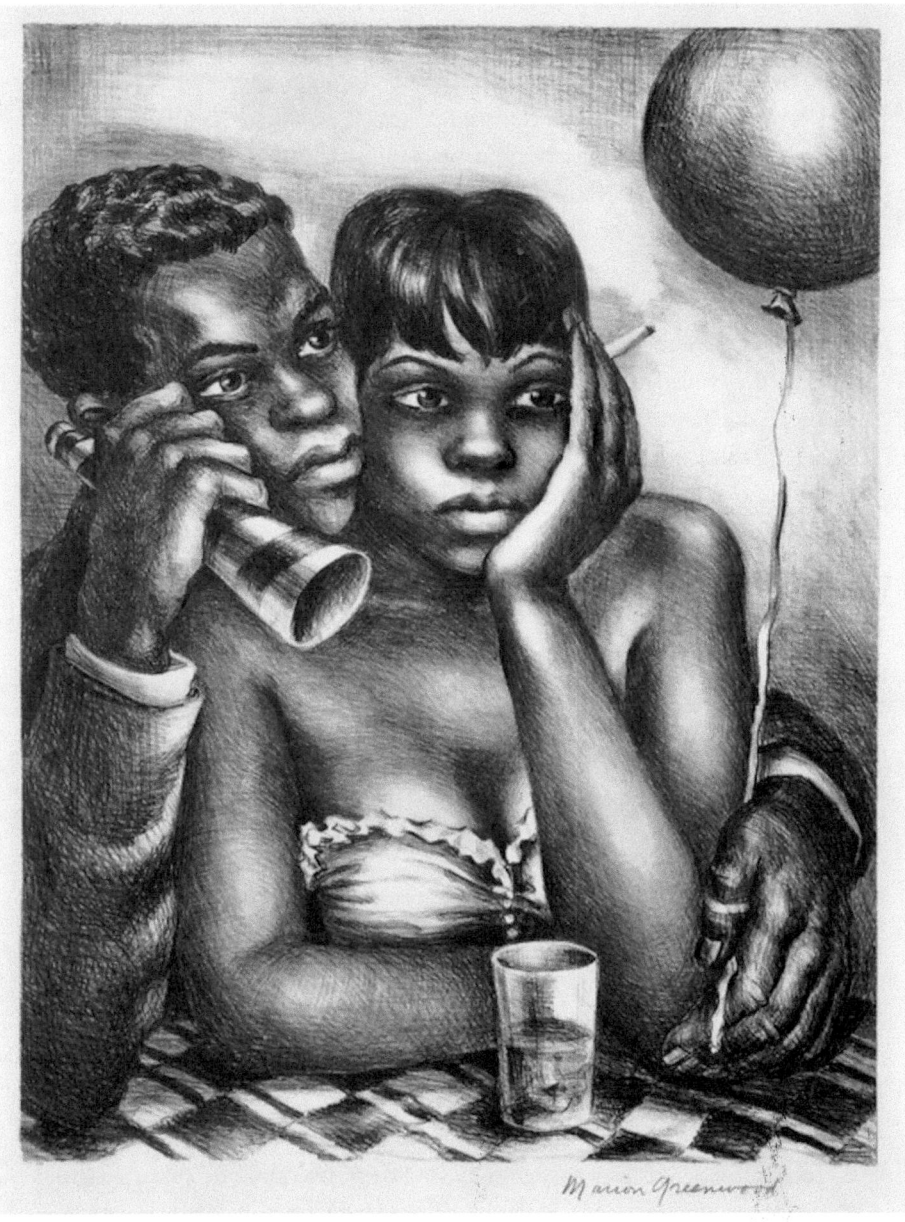

FIGURE 18.1. *New Year's Eve,* by Marion Greenwood, 1942. (Photograph © and courtesy of the estate of Marion Greenwood.)

States, they divorced, but their friendship endured. Marion and Adolf had once been lovers, and he would remain an important part of her circle.

Marion often dropped by Mura's studio and other venues to watch Sierra Leonean dancer and musician Asadata Dafora.[9] He introduced African drumming to American audiences and performed in the "Negro Units" of the Federal Art Project. These theater companies created new dramas of Black life and pushed American audiences beyond racist minstrel shows.

Dafora performed in Orson Welles's all-Black Broadway production of *Macbeth*, which toured nationally. He highlighted the sophistication of African arts, a goal that aligned him with Alain Locke and other Harlem Renaissance luminaries. His 1934 musical drama, *Kykunkor* (The Witch Woman), generated such enthusiasm that it had to be moved to a larger theater. Still, some critics ignored the cultural import of Dafora's work and focused on the "primitive" nature of the dance.

After witnessing a studio session of Dafora and his dancers, Marion stayed up late reworking her sketches for a painting. She found his work "thrilling." *Rehearsal for African Ballet* depicts a circular group of dancers and musicians. A drummer, probably Dafora, bends over his instrument, cigarette hanging from his mouth. Two women singers sit behind him, open-mouthed, song books in hand. Across the room, a young woman leans on a drummer's shoulder. A central spotlight illuminates the dark, smoky background. Marion later said that she wanted to show "the interplay of line and light and shadow masses, spatial and color relationships, and the mood and expression of the scene as I felt it." Critics celebrated the painting as "an example of her unique style of composition and theme."[10]

Charles applauded Marion's success from his hospital room, where he had landed with a leg injury from basic training. Marion half-joked that he'd better stay away from the military nurses. Charles would soon be thousands of miles away, his return uncertain. Her earlier fear of leaving him alone in the city when she was in Woodstock returned. Confessing to jealousy and fear of loss went against the bohemian code. How could she talk about her anxiety?

If there were a third partner in Charles and Marion's sexual adventures, it was Proust. *The Captive*, Volume Five of *In Search of Lost Time*, offered a code for discussing infidelity. The story brims with affairs, jealousy, and thwarted love. The narrator convinces one of the novel's key love interests, Albertine, to live with him. He then keeps her imprisoned in his Paris apartment. He spies on Albertine's every move, while she repeatedly denies his accusations of affairs with men and other women. This only convinces him of her deceptions. Proust describes jealousy as a "revolving fire," "a demon that cannot be exorcized and constantly reappears in new incarnations."[11]

Marion devoured the jealousy sections of *The Captive*, spellbound by how zealously Marcel guards Albertine. When other themes dominated, she lost interest. Charles had an opposite response, bored by jealousy. Their different readings should have been a sign.

Charles was straightforward and unabashed in confessing his affairs, at least some of them. In retaliation, Marion sent tales of late nights, morning hang-overs, and men she met in the art world. She recalled one boozy dinner with a man who knew Charles, claiming she had dazzled him with her explanation of Proust. He claimed no college graduate he knew understood the novel, and here was Marion, high school dropout, full of insight.

She shared a wine-soaked dinner with a wealthy French industrialist and former diplomat, Mr. Schwartz, an "old widower and looking for something" in their encounter. Did he find it? Marion was all tease and in "good form" that night: "I had my new John Fred hat and had just knocked them all over at the [AAA] gallery."[12] The message was clear: two could play this game.

Sometimes Marion reported that Josie had spent the night. Were they still lovers? Josie eased Marion's loneliness despite lingering tensions over their fraught past. Charles's view of their relationship is hard to pin down. In Proust's novel, lesbian and gay relationships are both portrayed, though sometimes in veiled fashion. Charles described Proust's homosexuality as a "sexual inversion," a term common in psychology at the time. He shared the dominant view of "normal" sexuality but didn't see himself as prejudiced. That, he said, was "like accusing the snake of being a reptile." The majority of humans are "driven like sheep along that straight and narrow path leading to our heterosexual mating grounds."[13] This view doesn't mean that he condemned Marion and Josie.

Proust also enters Marion's correspondence in the figure of her favorite cat, Albertine, named for the central character of *The Captive*. This queen feline and sexual adventuress caroused at night looking for action and demanding food that depleted Marion's ration coupons. The cat so dominated Marion's letters that it's easy to confuse the identity of the sexual adventurer.

Contradictions abound. Marion would confess to a fling, then turn around and claim she'd been so angelic that she would soon sprout wings. Amid this confusion of saints and sinners, animals and humans, it's little wonder that Marion and Charles turned to Proust for a way to communicate.

Marion's bravado about lovers revealed both her freewheeling self and its inverse, her emotional need for a stable companion. She eased her loneliness with family, often eating and sleeping at Musy's. Her usually absent father turned up to help her stretch canvases. They got along better on the rare occasions when they were alone. Grace stayed with her off and on as well. Marion appreciated her sister's painting advice, her sense of color and ability to visualize images. But the family's dark side always surfaced. Wally showed up at one point with two fingers smashed from work in the wartime shipyards. He was "his usual black haunted unhappy self." That Lester was in Bellevue to dry out was meant to be a secret. Marion lamented in a letter to Charles, "What a family!"[14]

Renewed passion alternated with fraught confessions the winter of 1943–1944. Marion waited for Charles's release from training, delayed by days that he'd missed while hospitalized. They spent his November furlough in New York. A month later, Marion traveled to Washington to see Charles off for Asia. At the Roger Smith Hotel, he confessed to a crush on a woman he'd met. Hurt by this confession, Marion retreated from her laissez-faire bohemian attitudes. "Maybe you just like to see me cry," she later wrote. "You used to even before we were married."[15]

On January 17, 1944, Marion watched Charles depart from Washington, DC. Heavy-hearted, she took the train back to New York. Perhaps she surveyed other women alone, wondering about their partners or fathers. Marion had tamped down fears about the war during Charles's training, but the bloodshed at Tarawa Atoll in the Gilbert Islands haunted her. The fierce November 1943 battle between the United States and Japan left 6,400 Japanese, Koreans, and Americans dead. She hoped Charles would never face such brutality. Yet similar savagery was everywhere and would only accelerate. The German siege of Leningrad was still underway. D-Day, the invasion of Normandy, was six months in the future. In the Asian theater where Charles headed, one of the "flying tigers," Pappy Boyington, had been shot down and would spend twenty months in a Japanese POW camp. Marion didn't want to ponder possible fates. For distraction, she began reading *War and Peace*.[16]

When Marion returned to her Manhattan apartment, a man awaited her in the vestibule. He identified himself as a naval officer and friend of Charles. Since he knew her husband's whereabouts, Marion figured he was legitimate. She accepted his offer to carry her heavy suitcase up the five flights to her apartment. Once inside, the man claimed he was really looking for another Charles Fenn. Alarmed, Marion forced him to leave. At midnight, the mysterious visitor called to ask whether he could return some evening. "Did you ever see such cheek!" she wrote to Charles, unsure whether the man was a "wolf" or a spy.

A few days later, Marion was dining in Chinatown with artist Julio de Diego and a group of friends when she looked up to see the same man at an adjacent table. "Like a Hollywood movie," she told Charles, "You and I are certainly being looked for by God knows what." Concerns about this surveillance compounded her worries about his safety. Someone knew about his OSS work and had access to her contact information.[17] Marion never mentioned the outcome of this incident, but their letters would be opened on both ends during the war. Charles was now one of the "cloak and dagger" boys.

How troubled was Marion as the partner left behind? Perhaps she exaggerated her loneliness to Charles. After all, in Manhattan and Woodstock, she often dined with artist friends. Still, local outings couldn't compete with Charles's adventure-filled missives. His initial journey took eight days via Miami, Trinidad, Brazil, and Karachi en route to Delhi. In an undisclosed location, he passed the time swimming, learning Chinese, reading, writing, and playing poker and dominos. Not a bad life. His sign off, "Fondest always," was not the passionate message Marion awaited.[18]

From India, the OSS crew flew to Ceylon to start work with Admiral Louis Mountbatten in Kandy. Charles reveled in a return to the lush hillside town where he'd reported for *Friday*. He remembered photographing Mountbatten in China for the magazine. At that meeting, he had alerted the admiral that his tie was crooked, something he thought the impeccable dresser would want to know. Mountbatten said, "Was it Beau Brummel who said that a well-tied tie is the first serious step in life?" "Actually, sir," Charles replied, "It was Oscar Wilde." Mountbatten might have been miffed. Instead he smiled broadly. First Lieutenant Fenn could match his artist wife in the charm arena.[19]

Charles next wrote from the Burmese border, where he stirred up rumors and circulated pamphlets to create hostility against the Japanese. He found time to offer Marion strict career advice. Give up taking jobs. "Be polite but firm" in saying no. Stick to painting for yourself. He threatened never to return if she took work strictly for money. "No," he wrote, "repeat no, repeat no, repeat no, NO NO Oh-oh-oh commercial stuff or I shall put the FBI on your tail."[20] Charles might sound domineering, but he wanted to keep Marion focused on her professed goal of artistic exploration.

Back in New York, Marion sometimes ignored Charles's advice and said yes to jobs. Prompted by her commitment to "ethnic types," she illustrated one of her own—an Irish American man to accompany an article by Louis Adamic, a Slovenian immigrant who wrote about US ethnic diversity. Marion took other jobs through AAA. The organization had branched out from mail-order catalogs and gallery sales to businesses collaborations. She painted Mexican scenes for a health care brochure on disease prevention in Latin America—$500 for her—good money during the war years. She reasoned that the gallery's portion of the profits could fund the upcoming solo show that Reeves Lewenthal had promised her.

Marion's long-standing relationship with Lewenthal ranged from friendly to antagonistic. On the positive side, he often invited her to his family home for dinner while Charles was away. He respected her work, offering that ultimate compliment for the era: she was a woman who "paints like a man," to which she added, "true enough."[21]

In the negative column, Lewenthal kept artists on a tight rein, expecting them to consult AAA before any independent moves. He exploded when he discovered Marion had secretly contributed a piece to "Masterpieces of Tomorrow," a department store art sale. Worse, she'd accepted the store's demand for a 40 percent commission, while AAA took 33.3 percent. Marion wrote a conciliatory letter, arguing that she had wanted to increase art awareness among the public. She offered to give AAA the higher percentage if her "unimportant piece" sold. She had her eyes on the prize, her first solo show at AAA. Until then, "I don't care how I grovel."[22]

Lewenthal came through. On Monday March 20, 1944, a huge crowd of artists, friends, and Marion's family trekked through rain and sleet to the AAA gallery at 711 Fifth Avenue. They wandered the exhibit sipping sherry and eating hors d'oeuvres. Not normally extravagant about clothes, Marion splurged for the event. She arrived in a new beige hat with a strap under the chin, gardenias that a friend sent, and "my new slim figure." Always a hearty eater, Marion worried about her weight. Before the show, pills and injections thinned her from 152 to 145 lbs. She described the "treatments" as something for thyroid problems that she combined with vitamins. They may have been amphetamines since they made her heart race and increased her nervousness.[23]

The exhibit's press release emphasized Marion's focus on human struggles and aspirations, citing *Rehearsal for an African Ballet* and *Exile*, an image of a Polish refugee. Three paintings sold. One of them was *Rendezvous*. A woman with a melancholy expression sits alone at a bar table nursing a drink. One hand holds a cigarette, the other is gloved. The image evokes a universal longing but also the specific lives of women with partners at war. At the opening, women clustered around her portrait of Charles exclaiming over his good looks. The exhibit generated recognition, sales, and a much-needed boost to her confidence.

Positive reviews followed in the *Herald Tribune*, *Art Digest*, and the *New York Times*. Art critic Howard Devree declared that Marion "had arrived," achieving an individual style that was "direct and unsensational" in portraits that "probe sympathetically for the underlying character of the subject."[24] She riffed on his praise, signing a letter to Charles as his "loving faithful beautiful successful 'arrived' wife, Popsy."[25]

Even "arrived," Marion feared her reputation would fade amid changes in the art world. Every era spurs artistic rebellion, but the first half of the twentieth century stimulated enormous tumult. Artists in flight from Europe swelled the avant-garde ranks in the United States. The New York–based Dadaists flourished between 1915 and 1921, claiming absurdity, anarchism, and irreverence as logical responses to World War I. From the 1930 into the 1950s, surrealists created a legacy that similarly rejected war-torn landscapes but mined dreams and the subconscious for inspiration. Paintings of Salvador Dalí's melting clocks and André Breton's dreams made more sense than humans slaughtering one another in trenches.

Prominent surrealists in New York included Man Ray, Salvador Dalí, Max Ernst, and many others. At a party at the home of German Dada artist Hans Richter, Marion ran into Max Ernst and his "new girl," Dorothea Tanning, an accomplished surrealist artist. Ernst was still married to Peggy Guggenheim but they would soon divorce. Marion liked Tanning but found her to be "affected," a quality she chalked up to the surrealist world, "a smart fashionable racket, as is much of the abstract."[26] Despite Marion's connections to Theosophy, she did not share her contemporaries' goal of reaching for an unseen reality through dream images or abstract geometric shapes on a canvas. Those styles could not achieve her artistic purpose: to portray the depth of feeling other people evoked in her. Yet those "fashionable rackets" would soon dominate the New York scene.

Marion worried that her beauty fueled positive reactions to the AAA show. One reviewer praised her painting, adding, "Nature has been lavish with Miss Greenwood. It seems almost unfair that a girl with such talent should be as comely as a sheath of wheat in autumn sunlight."[27] Art critic Devree, who had heralded Marion as "arrived," was known to gravitate to beautiful women. Did he want something? If she lost her looks, what then for her career? Why did this thirty-four-year-old accomplished artist predict a downfall if her beauty passed?

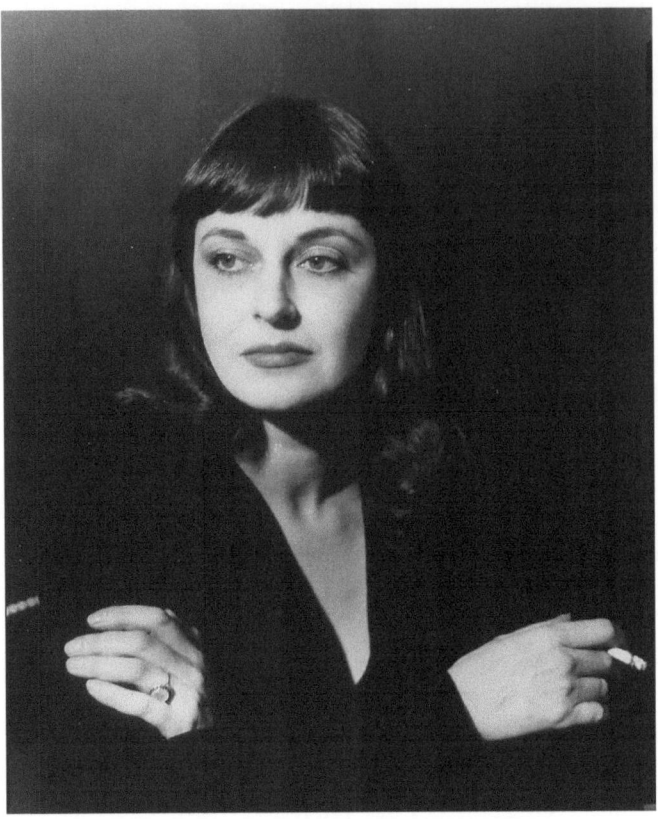

FIGURE 18.2. Marion Greenwood, 1944. (Photograph © Peter A. Juley and Son Collection, Smithsonian American Art Museum.)

At the launch of Marion's career, a *Vogue Magazine* interviewer had noted that she seemed oblivious to her beauty. If that were ever true, it didn't last. The press fixated on her face and body in ways she could not ignore. "Why do people insist on calling me beautiful—you know I really don't think I am—but I have to live up to this legend which makes it doubly sad as one grows older."[28] Would Charles love her when she was old? She told him that the exhibit photos made her look awful, likely due to the "treatment" pills. She claimed she was finished with doctors and would lose weight on her own.

Marion had read the last, mortality-haunted volume of Proust. The fate of older and formerly famous characters exposes the shallowness of society's concerns. An aging character based on actress Sarah Bernhardt finds herself sidelined. Proust exposed how we deny the reality of aging, fixated on superficialities that change and die as surely as human bodies.

While Marion waited for word from Charles, she kept Proust's novel close by. *In Search of Lost Time* offered a way to talk about their disconnected tempo as well as their varied love affairs. They were always slipping in and out of time, of love, of the grounded life Marion had hoped marriage would bring.

Most compelling for Marion was the truth Proust's narrator finally discovers: only through art can we see the world anew, banishing the force of habit that deadens us to both past and present. Thus did Proust's novel resonate with the Greenwood family credo that art trumps life. After all, Marion had "arrived" as an artist. Her work was thriving and she would persevere.

CHAPTER 19

The War Art Program

ON A SWELTERING DAY IN THE SUMMER OF 1944, MARION HELD A RED-drenched paintbrush to a canvas in the operating room of Atlantic City's Thomas England Hospital. *Neurosurgery* depicts a scalpel-wielding surgeon and his assistants bent over a wounded soldier. The eerie green of their medical scrubs forms a nimbus around the painting's bloody center. Marion fought nausea by focusing on her task. How she found herself in Atlantic City is a story of dashed hope but also opportunity.[1]

Soon after Charles left, Marion attended a dinner at the home of artist Joseph Hirsch. He regaled the group with stories about his time in Italy as a war artist-correspondent. Like Marion, Hirsch was committed to social realism and progressive causes. He was a founding member of Artists Equity, a group that would be denounced as communist during the Red Scare. Given his politics, the group gathered that night might have seemed an odd combination. There were other left-leaning artists, AAA director Reeves Lewenthal, and Colonel Baer, an official from the army medical purchasing department.

The mix was not contradictory. Many progressive artists accepted wartime roles. Some served as soldiers, others like Hirsch as artist-correspondents. Making art transcended Rosie the Riveter's "We can do it" patriotism. As Hitler devastated Europe, he sold off or destroyed "degenerate" modernist works by Picasso, Klee, Miró, Ernst, and countless others. Artists fought fascism by reclaiming creative freedom and, with it, the very fabric of civilization.

One of Hirsch's most reproduced images, *High Visibility Wrap*, features a private in a combat helmet. One eye is visible in his bandaged face. Drawn lips support a dangling cigarette. He is damaged but defiant. Like much of the work produced by twentieth-century war artists, Hirsch's met the program's goal of documenting war's true horror. War art in the United States has a long history going back to John Trumbull, but heroic figures of the Revolutionary War are generally blood-free. Only during World War I did a shift toward more honest representation begin.

The US Army launched the World War II art program in 1943, joining those created by the navy and the marines. Frances Brennan of the Office of War Information argued that this was the time "to find out if another Goya is still farming in Iowa." Artists would inspire Americans to signal "their anger, their grief, their greatness, and their justice."[2]

George Biddle, an artist who had worked his connections to help create the Federal Art Project, did so again. He was a former classmate of President Roosevelt, brother to the US secretary general, and soon-to-be chairman of War Department Art Advisory Committee. His letter of invitation to selected artists encouraged freedom in style and subject matter. They might choose "the front line; battle landscapes; the dying and the dead; prisoners of war; field hospitals . . . the nobility, courage, cowardice, cruelty, boredom of war." Omit nothing, he said, except official, sanitized portraits. Biddle added that artists might be "guided by Blake's mysticism, by Goya's cynicism and savagery, by Delacroix's romanticism" in following their "own inevitable star."[3]

The call resonated for Marion. The year before Charles left, she had applied for an overseas assignment. She hoped to join him in China, but she was willing to face combat anywhere. For her one-person show at AAA earlier that year, the gallery's announcement read: "Young woman artist asks [for] war front assignment." Her quote followed: "American women are no different than those of Russia or China. In this war, they have learned the fight is theirs, too. I, as an artist, cannot see why being a woman should prevent me from going to the front to use my particular talents to help."[4]

Awaiting news of her application, Marion worried that her Mexican political activity had nixed her chances. The House Un-American Activities Committee (HUAC), formed in 1938, was hunting "subversives." Josie had already been targeted. In an extraordinary act of betrayal, Katherine Anne Porter had turned on her during a 1942 FBI investigation. Josie had been escorted from her job in the Office of the Coordination of Information with no explanation. She had never joined the Communist Party and the charge strayed so far from the facts that her biographer, Elinor Langer, struggled to find an explanation. Tensions between the two friends had erupted over the years. More telling, perhaps, was

Katherine Anne's tendency to fabricate stories and sometimes believe them.[5] Malice could not be ruled out. The fallout would linger and plague Josie in the 1950s, when she again came under investigation.

Politics probably didn't account for the government's slow response to Marion's application. Many of her leftist artist friends, including Hirsch, represented the program in Europe and elsewhere. Pure sexism was the more likely culprit.

When the government program offered Marion the Atlantic City job documenting soldiers' recovery, she thought she had to accept. She still hoped it might lead to an overseas assignment but also feared that the program could disappear. As with the New Deal, Congress wavered on support. In 1943, Congressman Joe Starnes called the war art program a "piece of foolishness."[6] He rallied enough support to have funds cut, leaving artists stranded. *Life* magazine editor Daniel Longwell immediately hired many of them. In 1944, Congress reinstated funds for the Army program while *Life* continued to play a pivotal role.

The AAA was a key war art program partner. After Pearl Harbor, Reeves Lewenthal went into high gear to get commissions for artists, starting with Thomas Hart Benton. On the day of Roosevelt's war declaration, Benton was partway through a lecture. He stopped, left the lectern, and headed to his studio to produce *The Year of Peril*—or so goes the story about the origins of his provocative paintings on the violence of war.[7] Lewenthal convinced another pivotal player, Abbott Laboratories, to buy the paintings, which AAA exhibited in their New York gallery. The images, now critiqued as ethnically stereotyped, helped rally the United States to the cause of war.

Earlier, Marion had created eight paintings for an Abbott medical folder. The company, begun in 1888, played a role in both world wars. They created alternatives to German anesthesia, then sent penicillin to the front.[8] Their glossy magazine, *What's New?* went out to physicians and pharmacists all over the United States. Work by artists like Hirsch appeared in every issue, often sandwiched between ads for Pentothal and other drugs.

Marion's formal letter of appointment as a war artist came on June 26, 1944. She grumbled about being sent to a hospital. However, her twelve-day stay in Atlantic City proved more interesting and productive than she'd expected. From the late 1880s, the city had drawn tourists to lounge on its beaches, see previews of Broadway plays, and hear jazz at Club Harlem on Kentucky Avenue. During the war, the city transformed into what Marion called the "great impersonal machine" of the military, including her hospital base. The scene initially depressed her. The nurses she lived with were cold and unwelcoming. The

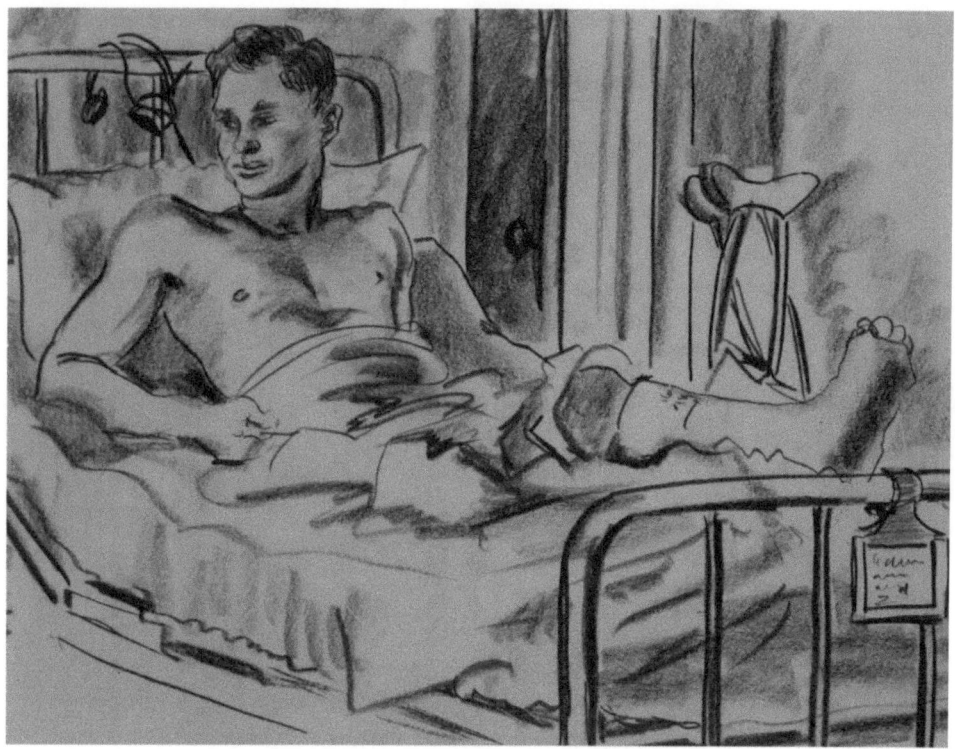

FIGURE 19.1. *Wounded Boy*, by Marion Greenwood, 1944. (Photograph © estate of Marion Greenwood; courtesy of the Army Museum Enterprise Art Collection.)

officers were "stuffed shirts," her most damning description. She came to appreciate the medical staff, even some of the officers. Still, she preferred the enlisted men, joking to Charles that she was "a hit with the boys." Alas, she wrote, their wounds dampened any romantic possibilities. She saw "tragic hopeless cases," men who were "ugly, vulgar, and tough," others, "sensitive, beautiful, intelligent."[9]

Never shy about stating her opinions, Marion alienated the psychiatrists. She remained deeply suspicious of Freud, even though earlier radicals whom she admired had embraced him. Emma Goldman made a pilgrimage to Clark University in 1909 to hear him lecture.[10] By the time of the war, intellectuals discussed superegos, Oedipal complexes, and repressed memories. Not Marion. She had struggled against "the male in one form or another in my career, trying to be masculine in a male's world when there was never anyone more feminine than myself. But the Freudians would cast away my noble lifetime sacrifices for painting with the mere words 'penis envy.'" She denounced psychoanalysts as "narrow, undisciplined, ill-mannered jerks." She advised one therapist to simply talk to his patients as she did. He would discover that "the so-called psycho-neurotics" were "simply shell-shocked and war weary . . . and completely sensible."[11] For psychological insight she turned to Proust.

At the hospital, Marion documented varied sites and stages of soldiers' rehabilitation. She welcomed inspiration from the real world rather than "the hell" of making up images.[12] The white casts against military-issue red bathrobes offered natural compositions. She painted multiple surgeries and physical therapies with elaborate pulley devices and macrame weaving. In *Speeding Recovery*, a nurse attends a man on crutches. A medieval-looking apparatus encases another soldier's torso. Wounded men in wheelchairs, arms in slings, await dental treatment. Vacant faces and downcast eyes dominate some images; others show muscles growing taut as they gain strength. The experience brought near the reality of war and Charles's life.

Marion came to love Atlantic City, "seething with amazing types" over the July 4th weekend. There were "acrobats, fortune tellers, Salvation Army, and rows of old people with their backs to the sea, watching the crowds on the boardwalk, all looking like Grant Woods." She longed to paint those wild city scenes but was too worn out by long days at the hospital. In the end, she was pleased with the seventeen paintings and drawings that appeared a year later in the book *Men Without Guns*. Exhibitions of war art also included her work, bringing additional recognition.[13]

Marion's art endures as testament to war's trauma. It's therefore curious that she's received little recognition as an artist-correspondent. In 2000, a book and PBS film, *They Drew Fire: Combat Artists of World War II*, brought overdue attention to this group. Yet the authors failed to mention Marion or the only other woman artist-correspondent, Anne Poor. While Marion painted in the operating room, Poor sketched bandaged men being lifted into planes on a Pacific airfield.[14]

Poor was an equally intrepid if more privileged young artist. Her stepfather was well-known painter and sculptor Henry Varnum Poor. She enlisted in the Women's Army Corps in part to escape her "rather cloistered life." Poor haunted the Pentagon clamoring for an overseas assignment. She was finally approved to join a B-29 bombing mission over Tokyo. She arrived at LaGuardia Field on the appointed morning only to be told that the ship had no toilet facilities for women. Instead it was "Fort Totten [on Long Island] for me," Poor wrote. There, she met incoming planes to sketch the wounded onboard. The stench from the amputees nearly overpowered her. Poor persisted in her overseas quest; she was finally sent to the Pacific to record medical evacuations in the Philippines, Guam, and China.[15]

These two artists likely never met, despite parallel paths through the Art Students League, stints in Paris, the Federal Art Project, and the war art program. Marion would have celebrated a sister war artist. She repeatedly lobbied to include more women. She wrote to George Biddle to recommend twenty women artists, including her sister Grace, Peggy Bacon, Doris Lee, Minna Citron, and Louise Nevelson. She further argued to Mrs. Henry Morgenthau Jr. that "considering the tremendous scope of war activities and the large number of women artists available, we feel that their employment should be greatly expanded."[16] Not only was her suggestion ignored, but the program cut two other artists, Lucia Wiley and Doris Rosenthal, who were initially included.

Why did the authors of *They Drew Fire* neglect Marion and Anne Poor? Perhaps they reasoned that women didn't literally "draw fire," although Poor might have while stationed in Pacific airfields. This narrow focus on the battlefield obscures women's contributions. Male dominance of art history furthers this neglect, argue art historians Paula E. Calvin and Deborah A. Deacon. Men's portrayals of war "lionize the winners, trivialize the losers, and largely ignore the women from both sides of a conflict." Art historian Catherine Speck offers another way to recognize women's work: expand the "geography of what constitutes the war-torn landscape."[17]

If Marion was discouraged by the lack of response to her lobbying efforts, she got over it. Her career was flourishing. In May, the AAA gallery sold *Mississippi Girl*, a stunning image of a young African American woman. The buyer, art collector, and investment banker Maurice Wertheim invited Marion to dinner at his house. Ecstatic, she couldn't take her eyes off her painting hung between a Picasso and a Matisse. Finally, she exclaimed to Charles, she was "in a real collection!"[18]

More recognition followed. In 1944, *Mississippi Girl* garnered second prize in the national Carnegie Institute competition. The official review described the painting's vitality and human sympathy. Her use of color in the green blouse, pink slip, and flowered skirt earned special praise, while the "head is perfectly poised on the lithe, graceful body, and beautifully painted." A critic for *Art News* echoed praise for Marion's ability with color but saw the work as lacking emotional content.[19] That didn't dampen her elation at the $700 prize.

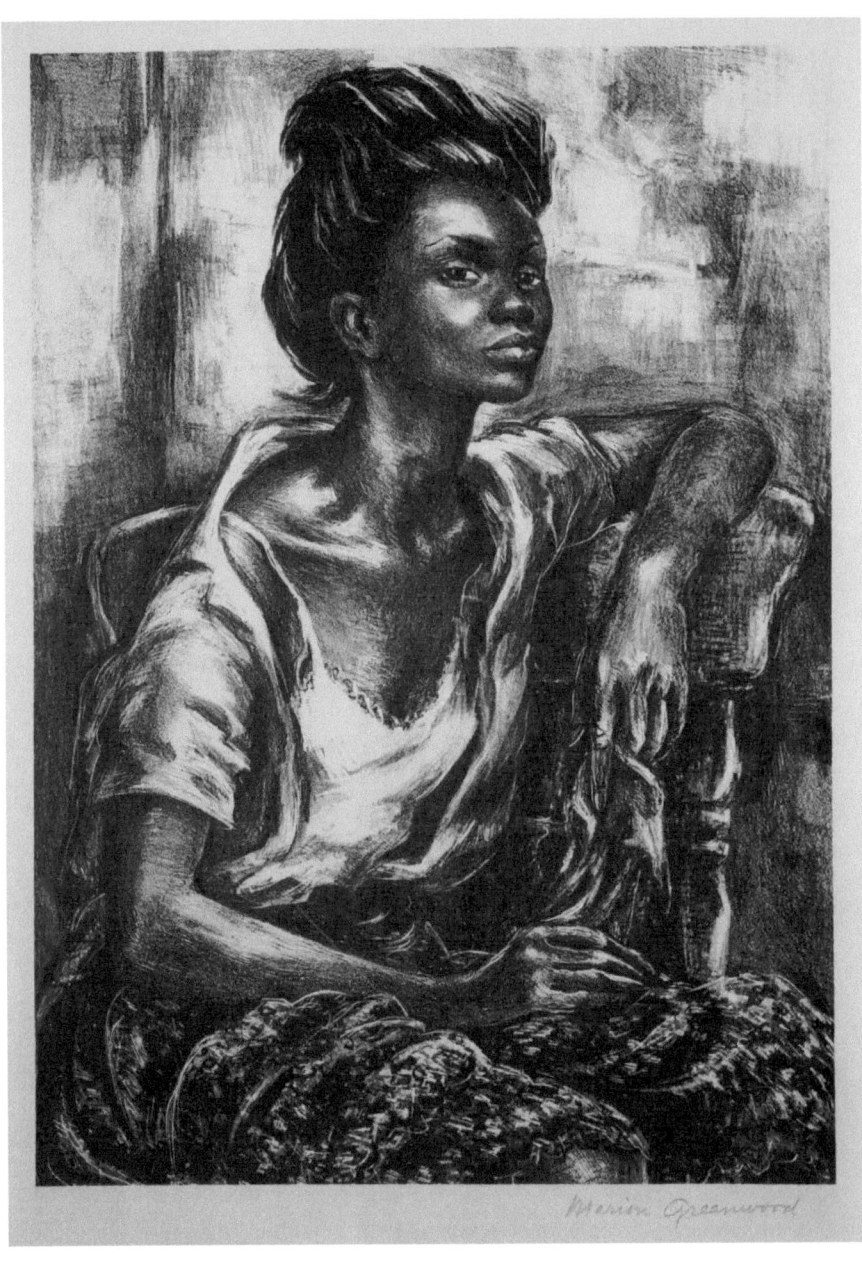

FIGURE 19.2. *Mississippi Girl*, by Marion Greenwood, 1945. (Collection of the Madison Museum of Contemporary Art. Bequest of Rudolph and Louise Langer. Courtesy of the Madison Museum of Contemporary Art, photograph by Paige Holzbauer. Photograph © the estate of Marion Greenwood.)

Marion was grateful that museum professionals had judged the Carnegie competition. She saw other artists as unsympathetic to realism. In fact, the prizes went to a range of styles: Doris Lee's third place *Siesta* was in the "so-called primitive manner," while first prize went to Yasuo Kuniyoshi for an expressionistic still life. One review described the jury as "not prejudiced by the Japanese birth of the artist as it indicates that the value of art goes beyond the bitterness of temporary feeling. Kuniyoshi has established himself as a loyal American who has worked ardently for the war effort."[20]

The critic failed to note that after Pearl Harbor, the US government labeled Kuniyoshi an "enemy alien," impounded his bank account, and restricted his travel. Despite those actions, Kuniyoshi emphatically affirmed his support for the Allies.

Isamu Noguchi also tried to express his patriotism. In 1941, he was living in California, driving from Los Angeles to San Diego for art supplies when the radio announced the news about Pearl Harbor. He turned back, seized by fear. "I was not just American but Nisei. A Japanese American." His terror was justified. All around him in California, anti-Japanese fervor grew. In March, 1942, Roosevelt issued the order to create internment camps.

Against the swell of racism, Noguchi strove to display loyalty. He went to Washington, DC, to meet with John Collier, the progressive head of the Office of Indian Affairs. Collier suggested that Noguchi volunteer at a camp in Poston, Arizona. He could design and help residents build a park and recreation center but would not be incarcerated.

Noguchi embraced the idea. Once there, his initial enchantment with the vast Arizona desert soured. He encountered oppressive heat and dust storms, little common ground with the younger Nisei, and a lack of funding for the proposed recreation center. Husbands of the married internees resented that Noguchi's fame and good looks magnetized their wives. All this deepened an intense loneliness that had marked Noguchi's life. Worst of all, although not formally imprisoned, he could not leave without permission. In July, the government blocked his attendance at an exhibition of his work at the San Francisco Museum of Art. He finally wrote to Collier to secure his release but he remained under intense FBI scrutiny until late 1945.[21]

Marion had to weigh her disappointment about not being sent overseas against what Noguchi and others endured. In fact, 1944 was a banner year for her: the war art job, seeing *Mississippi Girl* hung between a Picasso and a Matisse, then garnering the Carnegie prize. Still, she wanted a partner to share her success and comfort her in failure. "Charles Fenn," she commanded in one letter, "You've got to stop roaming—*or else*! Also, if I knew that you would stop roaming, we could have a child, concentrate on it this time. But I realize that war or no war, you have a wanderlust that is something to contend with. If you think for one minute that when you come home I'm going to ever let you go again, you're very much mistaken. So with this warning you'd better start preparing now for a good, settled bourgeois life—pattering feet, the New York Sunday Times, and as a concession to your Chinese past, several pretty Chinese maids to wait on us—mostly you, of course, knowing your needs are many."[22]

Charles intended to keep roaming. He flourished amid the novelty of new places and people, even during the brutality of war. He admonished Marion to quit her complaints. After all, he could do nothing to help her from China. Their contrasting hopes, dreams, and visions of the good life would intensify into 1945.

CHAPTER 20

Hsu Lost and Found

DURING CHARLES'S FIRST STINT IN CHINA FOR *FRIDAY* MAGAZINE, MARION rarely knew his whereabouts. Now with the OSS, his return address hid under acronyms like CBI for "China-Burma-India" theater as he moved between those countries. He finally landed in Kunming, a Chinese military and US air base close to Indochina.

Charles shared a room there with Captain Toman, a research and development specialist who loved destruction and chicanery. He experimented with exploding pencils and poison-laced chocolates. Those deterred the rats that devoured their Palmolive soap. Bats dropped in on their poker games, especially when they played deuces wild.[1] Charles's stories were meant to amuse Marion and keep worries at bay. If he sounded carefree, it was because his initial days were less fraught than those to come.

Charles also resumed a habit from his AP reporting years: refuge in "bathhouses, tea houses, opium dens, and sing-song girls parlors." Sex, he claimed, was secondary to foot massages, gambling, and smoking opium. Marion was surely unhappy that Charles was frequently caught in these off-limits places.

One OSS superior named him "Fearless Fenn" for his willingness to risk opprobrium. Others thought the name celebrated courage in the field. He later earned a US Soldier's Medal for Valor, the Bronze Star, and a citation from OSS Director William Donovan. Charles's bravery also triggered the name "Lawrence of China." Finally, there was "Troublesome Fenn" for his tendency to vex his superiors. He found all these titles absurd.[2]

As an AP correspondent, Charles had met General Claire Lee Chennault, the legendary air force commander of the "Flying Tigers" in China. He

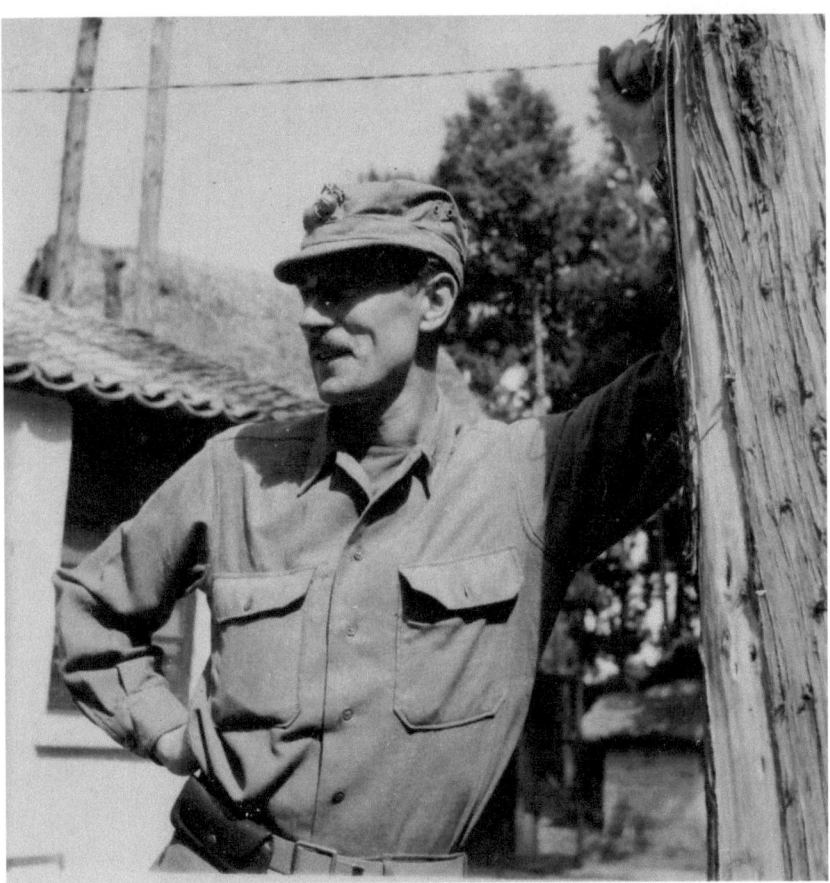

FIGURE 20.1. "Fearless Fenn" in uniform, circa 1944. (Photograph © and courtesy of the estate of Marion Greenwood.)

celebrated Chennault's joie de vivre, or at least his ability to "live life to the full if you are not too weighed down by convention, high principles, and who your friends are."[3] But Charles's jovial attitude might have shifted when Chennault sent him across the mountains to Kweilin on a truck transport. Goodbye to the halcyon days of poker and bathhouses. Enter fourteen-hour treks over rutted roads, alert to possible enemy fire. Even this new reality didn't dampen Charles's enthusiasm for China.

The American public shared that enthusiasm, at least for the version presented by the Kuomintang, the Chinese Nationalist Party. When Madame Chiang Kai-shek and the Generalissimo graced a 1937 *Time* magazine cover, support swelled. Madame followed with a lengthy 1943 visit that wowed Americans. Her US education from age ten to nineteen rendered her "like us" yet representative of China. As she traversed the country by train, fans sent hundreds of letters, money, and even homemade cookies from the station master's wife in one Midwestern town.[4]

The nationalist Kuomintang burnished a false image of China under their control to keep the communists at bay. For years, the nationalists censored local and foreign correspondents' reports on the real situation. In fact, the Chinese economy grew stagnant, workers and soldiers suffered from malnourishment, mines and other production sites closed, and corruption ran rampant. The US government, fearful of civil war, condoned news suppression. When reporters finally accessed communist-controlled regions, they praised the organized troops, workers' cooperatives, abundant food supplies, and vital communities—descriptions that matched those Charles sent back.[5]

Curiously, despite still-virulent anti-communism among Americans and fear of the "Sovietization" of Asia, the military viewed the Chinese version as benign. General Joseph Stilwell, the US commander on the Asian front, reasoned that "communism" was the wrong label. "Their leaders," Stilwell wrote, "adopted the methods and slogans of communism but what they were really after was land ownership under reasonable conditions. It is not in the nature of Chinese to be communists."[6]

This sentiment might seem laughable today but Stilwell saw Chinese communism as local and admired their organization and resolve. The Chinese were seen as hapless victims of historical events and the menacing Japanese. The long history of American missionaries in China aided this vision of a "protégé, an image which carries an accompanying sense of obligation toward the object of one's own beneficence."[7]

Letters between Marion and Charles through 1944 and 1945 were filled with both affection and frustration. As Marion awaited their unpredictable arrival, she was hardly idle. She finalized her Atlantic City paintings and produced new work to keep food on the table, preferably the kind she didn't have to cook. Mainly she ate out, along with other women with partners at war. Her letters filled with quotidian details: sublets, dirty floors, income taxes, standing in ration lines, and sending Charles's photos to possible publishers. She insisted she was "biologically, chemically, and psychologically not made to be efficient." "Oh God, I need a secretary, a cook, a maid, and a nurse—and most of all my own husband."[8]

Her social life in Woodstock picked up when she rented a fabulous studio near a swimming hole and waterfall. Friends flocked to the idyllic spot. Doris Lee and her painter husband, Arnold Blanch, visited. Anton and Lila Refregier lifted her spirits. Artist and sculptor Alexander Archipenko, once Marion's teacher, joined the scene. She kept so busy that only at night did "the moon and the crickets and soft night air" fill her with "an unspeakable sadness."[9] Her letters vacillated between a public image of the independent, undaunted artist and a woman lonely for her partner. Both versions compete for the True Marion of the war years.

One day, a huge box arrived with a gift from Charles that sent Marion swooning—a piano. She had always turned to music for inspiration, especially Brahms's concertos with "the deep piano notes that seem to fall down and down." She began lessons, vowing to master Chopin and Beethoven before Charles returned. He was, she declared, "the most wondrous husband on earth."[10]

And she read. Marion always gravitated to long, heady novels. Along with Proust and Dostoevsky, she dove into *Jean-Christophe,* a ten-volume novel whose author, Romain Rolland, won the Nobel Prize for literature in 1915. The hero is a suffering, spiritually tormented genius musician and composer. One insomnia-wracked night, Marion picked up *Jean-Christophe* and found solace in his "ghastly life": "I understood it so damn well."[11]

Charles winced at Marion's comparison of her life to the musician's tortured existence. His tolerance for what he saw as Marion's whining deteriorated. When she described being sick, he mocked her as claiming she was near death. Charles was a pragmatist. Since he could do nothing about her illnesses from China, he suggested she report back when better. His gripes about her "self-centeredness" reached a boiling point. He refused to "consider your last note a letter. It is merely a burst of indignation at the inherent dishonesty of everybody except Marion Greenwood."[12]

Marion threatened to strip emotion from her letters, calling this formerly "wondrous husband" unspeakably selfish and patronizing. She would henceforth only report surface trivialities. That effort was short-lived, and she soon returned to emotional outpouring. Marion regarded Charles's war reports as self-aggrandizing. She accused him of "falling in love with yourself." When he described Chinese soldiers and civilians willing to risk their lives for him, she insisted their sacrifice was strictly for their country. She wrote, "For God's sake don't get the traditional Colonial English feeling of superiority and delusions of grandeur which is why the English can go native so easily . . . . You should be above all that."[13] What he needed, she declared, was a furlough to get back in touch with the realities of daily life.

In fact, the misery of daily life in China soon filled Charles's letters. He recorded a boat trip where a sick Chinese child died as the military men played poker; the story of a boat keeper's daughter whose hand was blown off by a detonator; a place with so many rats that a fellow officer sat up all night, grabbing them by the tail and dashing them to death. There was an old Chinese man named "Pop" who saved the life of an American pilot. An Allied plane whisked the pilot to safety but failed to thank his Chinese rescuer, which infuriated Charles. Another story haunted him. A captain had discovered one of his gunners pinned in a plane's wreckage, shrieking in agony. Two shots in the man's temple ended his torture but nearly earned the captain a court-martial. Charles increasingly felt the weight and trauma of war.[14]

One can easily imagine their mutual outrage: Charles aghast at Marion's belief that standing in ration lines and loneliness were true hardships, Marion outraged that Charles saw himself as a war hero.

Yet hope for their marriage remained. Charles carried a beautiful photo of Marion everywhere he moved, writing that it kept him sane. In the same letter where Charles denounced Marion's self-centered "burst of indignation," he raved about China as a future home for them and possible children: "How you would love this place! What with the river boats, the craggy rocks, the pavilions, the distant sugar-loaf mountains, the lotus pond, the bombed ruins." He ended with "Oh god, nobody to share it with."[15] Marion must have rejoiced. Finally, both emotion and future plans!

In one letter, Charles recalled a Thanksgiving dinner where he'd been "quite disagreeable. What staggers me now is, why did I stay at CM Inc [Cannon Mills, the textile sales job] when all I had to do was walk out?" Marion in turn wondered why they had tortured one another in the early years of their marriage. "Were we *crazy* to have misunderstood each other and made our lives miserable?" For all his faults, Charles continued to fascinate her. "You have never bored me," she wrote, "That's a lot to say." With Charles, she appreciated how "the 'unexpected' is always around the corner."[16]

Their intertwined work deeply connected Marion and Charles. He pored over the glowing reviews of Marion's solo show. "This success makes up for not only all your own hard times," he wrote, "but mine too: because the canvases reflect me as well as you, just as there is so much of you in what I write."[17]

Infidelity kept showing up in letters but Marion's responses varied. Years before, she had feared leaving Charles alone in New York. Now, after he reported his adventures with concubines, Marion read the letters aloud at a party. "Several of the stuffed shirts who call themselves artists here were probably shocked," she said, "but I wanted to show them the honest and at the same time sophisticated intelligent understanding that can exist between two wonderful, rare creatures like ourselves!"[18] She read *The Way of All Flesh*, a novel by Samuel Butler that attacked Victorian hypocrisy. She seemed to need continued affirmation of their open-mindedness about sex with others.

Also on her nightstand was Marcel Proust, "which alas brings me close to you," she told Charles. She dreamed that the character of Albertine came to life but Marion killed her. "She must be a symbol of possessing and loving in my life." If only she weren't starved for love, Marion said, she wouldn't dream such things.[19]

Cracks emerged in Marion's shield of independence and willingness to live on the edge. She wrote, "Poor Greenwood still looks for solidity, honesty, and truth. You call it bourgeois, I call it maturity." She cursed her need to paint. Why would the average American businessman want a "gal who has one eye cocked for her canvas or typewriter at the other end of the room, even in the middle of an orgasm?" Women like her, driven by their art, ended up alone. If Marion were a man, she would stick to call girls.[20]

Charles was silent on Marion's musings about bourgeois life, immersed in war's chaos. He had earned his "Troublesome Fenn" title through an independent streak that led to clashes with superiors. However, that quality made him perfect for an assignment at Lungchow, about a hundred miles from the China-Indochina border. There, a complicated mix of players jockeyed for position on the espionage board. The Japanese occupied parts of Indochina, whose control they ceded to the Vichy French. The Free French infiltrated as well, controlled from abroad by Charles de Gaulle. As Europe edged toward victory, both sides of the French political spectrum suddenly united with the British to guard their colonial enterprises.

There was another, independent espionage network that supplied information to the OSS and the French: the GBT. The acronym came from the names of three men who formed the group: two former Texaco employees, Canadian Lawrence L. Gordon and American Harry Bernard, and Frank Tan, a Chinese American businessman.[21]

The OSS needed one of their own to join the GBT at Lungchow. Charles eagerly agreed. He had met Gordon and Tan earlier, an unlikely pair but both projecting "quality, intellect, and purpose." He felt an immediate connection he named as *hsu*, a Confucian concept "inadequately translated as 'reciprocity,'" which "denotes that the heart is always sending out waves, and if you meet someone on your own wavelength you find immediate 'reciprocity.'"[22]

After a flight to Nanning, Charles and Gordon spent the first night eating a delectable meal of river trout while two girls sang and played zithers. Next, they met up with Tam and Harry Bernard to set up intelligence operations near the Indochinese border. Their work was slowly progressing until the news flash of March 1945. The Japanese had seized posts throughout Indochina, interning the French administrators. All contacts went dead. Charles, his GBT cohort, and the French were desperate for information about weather and troop movements. They needed someone to carry a radio and generator into Indochina. Charles remembered the story of a brave Annamite, the term for the people of Annam, now part of Vietnam. This intrepid fellow had rescued a pilot shot down inside the jungle and delivered him to safety.

That Annamite, Nguyen Ai Quoc, was a thin, bearded, and deceptively frail figure whose devotion to Indochinese independence was already legendary. Then over fifty, he had risen from poverty and traveled the world, living in Britain, France, the United States, and Russia before he returned to Asia. The Chinese nationalists imprisoned him in 1942, threatened by his success as leader of the communist Viet Minh. In a turn worthy of a spy novel, a Chinese warlord bent on exploiting the communist network for his own ends maneuvered Quoc's release a year later. To hide his identity, Quoc emerged from prison as Ho Chi Minh.

Charles and the GBT considered Ho an excellent prospect to scout inside Indochina. The US government initially rejected the idea, wary of triggering the Chinese nationalists' hatred of the communists. Ho's struggle for independence also made him anathema to the French. Yet he was clearly unique. After rescuing the pilot, he had refused a reward. He had but one request: he wanted to meet General Chennault to express his admiration. Chennault and his Flying Tigers were so celebrated that contact with him would add to Ho's leadership cachet. Charles, who knew Chennault from his days reporting for the AP, thought he could make a connection. First he had to meet Ho. A contact arranged a rendezvous at the historic Dragon's Gate.

Ho turned up with Pham Van-Dong, who would later become prime minister of Vietnam. The trio spoke French for Pham's sake. Ho had mastered

Russian, English, Siamese, some German, and several Chinese dialects. His simple cotton high-necked jacket was missing a button. Most striking to Charles was Ho's alert face, "enhanced by the brightest eyes I ever saw. I have heard much the same comment from people who have met either Lenin or Picasso, and it is said that such eyes are an indication of genius, intelligence, determination, and purpose." Charles believed that he and Ho "had *hsu* from the start." Once, describing his communication with OSS headquarters, Charles quoted Baudelaire, "Today I had a strange warning: I felt the wings of insanity brush my mind." After meeting Ho, Charles wrote, "Baudelaire felt the wings of insanity touch his mind, but that morning I felt the wings of genius touch mine."[23]

The US military finally approved Ho to carry a radio set into Indochina. His intelligence code name was "Lucius" to Charles's "Hamlet." In return for Ho's service, Charles set up the meeting with Chennault. There were rules: no favors asked and no discussion of politics. Charles feared that Ho really might bring up the independence movement. He revered the US origin story and kept alive hope for Indochina's freedom. Charles supported Ho's dream but was anxious to keep it out of the meeting's discussion.

Chennault appeared in his heavily medaled uniform and held out a chair for Ho. Ho had replaced the missing button on his faded cotton jacket. From behind his gigantic desk, Chennault thanked Ho for aiding the Allied cause. When their discussion neared an end, the general looked directly at Ho. "Is there anything you'd like to ask about?" There was one thing, Ho said. Fenn held his breath. "May I have your photograph?" Chennault seemed delighted to present one of his glossies, signing it, "Your sincerely, Claire L. Chennault." "Sincerely" seems like a pat response in English, but it carried greater weight in Ho's language.[24]

Ho returned to Indochina, bringing the photo along with six Colt .45s he'd gotten from Charles. He gathered a group of leaders from diverse political factions, produced Chennault's photo, and gave each person a pistol. They were equally dazzled by the marvelous weapons and Ho's brilliance in obtaining them. His network produced critical intelligence until the end of the war.

Ho impressed a number of US officials. One OSS lieutenant recalled that Ho knew more about the Declaration of Independence than he did: "As a matter of fact, he knew more about almost everything than I did but when I thought his demands were too stiff, I told him anyway. Strange thing was he listened. He was an awfully sweet guy." Though Ho was sometimes ruthless in pursuit of independence, it was his gentle nature that many remarked upon.[25]

When the war ended, Ho's final letter to Charles expressed his regard for Americans. He wrote that "we small and subject countries have no share, or very small share, in the victory of freedom and democracy. . . . I believe that your sympaty and the sympaty of the great American people will always be with us."[26]

Americans still live with the tragic consequences of that failed hope. Throughout his life, Charles reproached the Allies for supporting Kai-shek and the nationalists. The European colonial powers, including the French, retained their colonies. Even Roosevelt, known for his anti-colonial stance, failed to intervene. Decades of war would follow before Vietnam finally achieved independence.

Charles's critics saw his collaboration with Ho as a disaster, while supporters mourned the lost opportunity to aid the independence movement. One historian affirmed that Charles had been instrumental to Ho's rise to power, an achievement "out of proportion" to his otherwise modest role in the OSS.[27]

While the United States and other allies abandoned Ho Chi Minh, Charles did not. In 1973, he published a well-regarded biography of Ho. He celebrated his friend's ability to work from the heart and his essential belief in humankind. Why, Charles asked, had Maoism, Marxism, and other ideologies endured while "we have no Hoism?" "Perhaps Ho does not go with 'isms.' What he represents is less a political cult than a philosophical concept. For want of a better word let us call his contribution Hochiminity."[28]

Marion learned Ho's story only later, but she would have applauded Charles's collaboration with him. She shared her husband's faith in an egalitarian society whose realization had been distorted by totalitarian regimes. Her letters to Charles often responded to the global news. When the story of the death camps broke, she described repugnance and despair. She mourned Roosevelt's death and lamented the resulting lack of leadership.

Marion joined the rest of the country in yearning for the news that finally arrived on May 8, 1945. When Germany surrendered, the streets of New York City exploded with jubilant, flag-waving crowds. Marion's emotions ranged from relief to panic. Where was Charles? Had he not written or had the mail and/or censors obstructed his letters? She'd heard nothing.

Marion's final release from worry should have come on August 14 when President Harry S. Truman announced Japan's surrender. Instead, she wrote to Charles that she was "grief-stricken in a deadly quiet way which frightens me. I've been warding off a nervous breakdown by sheer will power." The victory celebrations broke open the realization that "I have a husband that doesn't want me, doesn't want to come home to me. Don't you see?"[29]

Through the years of Charles's absence, Marion suffered from stress, eye strain, and skin eruptions that were probably psoriasis. Dieting worsened her health conditions, but she wanted to look good for Charles's return. The young woman in overalls on the scaffold, unconcerned about clothing, now wanted to dress up and garner compliments. In one letter, she described a new sequined hat, ankle strap shoes, and a black cocktail dress purchased under the "bourgeois influence" of a friend: "Everyone says I look well, I know you'd think me too fat though. I'm doing my damnedest to diet."[30] Mid-century ideals for women didn't mandate thinness as much as the next decades would. Still, Marion frequently complained about being fat. Those fears worsened in Charles's absence.

He railed against injections to lose weight: "For Christ's sake, stop fooling around with this sort of thing. You are fat simply because you eat too god damn much."[31] That was Charles, brutally honest. He added that beauty had a much fuller meaning than just being pretty, though that didn't likely lessen the sting.

Proust on her nightstand, Marion obsessed about time. While a neighbor pecked away on a typewriter, she closed her eyes to fantasize that it was Charles. She sent him a Thomas Hardy poem, "A Broken Appointment": "You did not come / And marching Time drew on, and wore me numb . . . Grieved I, when, as the hope-hour stroked its sum / You did not come."[32] In September, Frank Tan, the Chinese American partner in the GBT network, returned to the United States. He brought Marion tea, a paintbrush, and the news that Charles would be home in mid-November.

As of November 21, there was no sign of Charles. He was in Hong Kong, where he received a message that day via the US Naval command: "Doctor Neugarten states wife critical neurotic condition J Phoguosis serious wife anxious officer's presence discuss situation by correspondence husband overseas."[33] Was "phoguosis" a misspelling of "phlogosis," an inflammatory condition? How had Neugarten, Marion's general practitioner, arrived at "critical neurotic condition"? She was fond of the doctor, but was he equipped to judge her mental health?

The medical world of the 1940s labeled a host of women's afflictions as neuroses, psychosis, or the old standby, hysteria. During the war, many suffered, as Marion did, from loneliness and relentless financial pressure. Perhaps Marion's statement about the soldiers she painted in Atlantic City applied to her: they were not the neurotics the doctors declared them to be but simply suffering natural reactions to war.

Marion's saw Charles's retreat as inevitable, abetted by his silence as well as his words. She beseeched him to reclaim his possessions and relieve her of peddling his photos and writing: "Ever since you asked me to try and give you up, I knew it was the end. I accept it but for god's sake come and get me out of this mess." She insisted that he afford her the respect "you'd give to a dog if you kicked him out."[34]

Marion's grief stymied her work. She feared an end to her meteoric ascent to the Art Students League, Yaddo, Mexico, and beyond. Where was the confidence of adolescence? Reflecting on her monumental mural in Morelia, she said that in those years, "I could have muraled the Tri-Borough Bridge. Now, I don't know."[35]

Perhaps Marion's faltering confidence was a reaction to age or only temporary. Regardless, Charles could not offer the affirmation she needed to recover. Letters that crawled across oceans strained many marriages, but other factors complicated theirs. Marion often wrote at whim, propped up in bed with insomnia or a bottle of Four Roses when she had "the curse." Charles grew annoyed at how often she forgot his queries and advice from previous letters. She only wanted affirmation of his love; he believed his advice proved his affection: "Don't forget that I only go on like [this] because I love you enough to want to do everything I can."[36]

The *hsu*, heart songs that once flowed between them, seemed blocked. That impasse made the next part of their story highly improbable.

CHAPTER 21

The "China" Experience

ON THE STREETS OF HONG KONG, MILITARY TRUCKS AND MOTORCYCLES
hurtled past hand-pulled rickshaws. Old men in tea shops gazed out at Allied
soldiers in dusty uniforms on the streets. Students milled about while women
and children hawked dried fish to a malnourished population. Laundry hung
from balconies of apartments stacked like beehives, and huge ships in the harbor towered over wooden sampans rigged for sailing. The scenes were by now
familiar to Charles. He'd been transferred to Hong Kong as the war ended. For
Marion, the setting was new and exotic.

The couple's journey to the British colony had been fraught with missed
communication. In October 1945, Charles had written to Marion with fantasies
about their new life in Hong Kong. His postwar job with a Chinese publisher
entailed contacting American counterparts. He'd found Marion a perfect studio
with a magnificent harbor view. Hong Kong was far less expensive than New
York. Adventure and travel, with occasional visits to New York, awaited them.
He promised to be home by Christmas or early 1946 to prepare for their move.

His letters languished in postal purgatory. Hearing nothing, Marion feared
he was dead or had deserted her. Only when Charles made it back to New York
later that winter did Marion learn of the plans that he'd sketched out in letters.[1]

Charles declared the worst behind them: the war, the uncertainty, and their
constant bickering via star-crossed mail. He grieved postwar injustice, especially the Allied failure to aid Ho Chi Minh. Yet he'd found a happiness that he
credited to a "further dose of Confucianism." "Let the past be dead and let's
think about the future," he wrote.[2] He inserted a cautionary note: this picture
of bliss rested on trust and tolerance for one another's differences. The fury

of their letters would endure if they weren't willing to move past the hard war years. The *hsu* seemed to flow once more.

From New York, Marion and Charles left for Hong Kong in spring 1946. They stopped in London to visit Charles's father and see Julian Huxley. April found them in Paris just as French negotiations over Indochina began. Ho Chi Minh hadn't yet arrived. Charles met with Pham Van Dong, whom he'd encountered at his initial meeting with Ho and who was now a government minister.[3]

Charles's publishing job left him time to write plays. Marion could simply paint, a longed-for life of creative freedom. There was just one wrinkle in this scheme: Marion's fear of losing her New York art connections. She had just won the John Herron Art Institute lithography prize, but she knew how quickly artistic reputation could fade. From London's Mayfair Hotel, she'd written to Emanuel Redfield, an art collector and civil liberties lawyer who had recently purchased an oil painting. She assured him that she'd be back in a year or so, adding her Hong Kong address, 18 Kennedy Terrace. To Musy, she bemoaned being "separated from you—my friends—the *gallery*." Her greatest fear was that she'd be forgotten "after working so hard for a little niche in the art world."[4] Hope that a new exotic environment would awaken her painting helped calm her fears.

After passing through Europe, Marion and Charles stopped in Calcutta and Darjeeling for a month awaiting transport to China. Marion described the living conditions and poverty as "unspeakable" for everyone "except of course for the rich Indian merchants and feudal lords."[5] The couple traveled to the border with Tibet, then to Indochina and China, and finally to their new home. Marion sketched throughout the journey, but most new work would come from war-ravaged Hong Kong. The Japanese occupation had stretched from December 1941 to the war's end. Repair of the natural environment, fishing fleet, and essential infrastructure would take years.[6] The human suffering was incalculable.

Charles celebrated his return but mourned friends who had died, been imprisoned, or were physically and emotionally disfigured. Two noteworthy examples were Sir Percy Selwyn-Clarke, Hong Kong director of medical services, and his wife, Hilda, a social activist and writer. Charles had met them before the war so immediately sought them out when he returned to Hong Kong. The auburn hair of the vivacious Hilda had turned white while living in an internment camp with their daughter. Percy walked with a cane, bent and aged by ten months of imprisonment. Under Japanese occupation, he'd continued to direct medical treatment, even aiding the wounded enemy. Charles viewed his own hardships during the war as paltry by comparison. Marion grew fond of "this wonderful old doctor Selwyne Clark who lives near us [and] is a fine person. . . . I like him, he likes me, and we see him occasionally but he's very busy directing the medical health department."[7]

Charles connected Marion to a wide range of people in Hong Kong. Refugees, nationalist as well as communist, streamed into the colony to escape China's now full-blown civil war. Despite myriad problems, rapid population growth fueled the economy. The ever entrepreneurial Charles developed several businesses. In addition to his publishing job, he established a toy company and the Cosmos Club, a gathering place for locals and expats.

Soon, Marion was dancing and dining at the Cosmos with international artists and intellectuals. One important circle was Renjian Huahui (The Human Studio). This group of scholars, writers, cartoonists, and artists from the mainland was broadly anti-Nationalist, some more aligned with the communists than others. Marion was drawn to the traditional Chinese painters whose work she celebrated in a talk she gave at the Sino-British Club titled "The Indelible and Fatal Brushwork of Chinese Art." She marveled that even advertising signs on the streets showed the "rhythm and vitality" of Chinese art and calligraphy. She may have been introduced to these forms earlier by Isamu Noguchi, who had studied in Peking in 1930.[8]

Marion often took Charles's car to get to the deep green rice fields surrounding Hong Kong. She carried a bamboo stick, ink, and a piece of silk to create rapid sketches. Sometimes Chinese artists accompanied her. Compelling images came from people standing in ration lines, workers crushing rocks, and the teeming life in waterfront sampans and junks. Her portraits included a Japanese soldier on trial for war crimes, and several members of the Cosmos Club.

One Renjian Huahui member, Pauline Chen, modeled for the oil painting *Hong Kong Girl*, which collector Marc Sandler later bought and renamed *Fan Girl*. Chen holds a fan, dazzling in a red *qipao*, the slim-fitting, high-collared traditional Chinese dress.

Compelling as Hong Kong was, Marion longed to get to the "real China." Charles was too busy to travel apart from a weekend they spent in the nearby Portuguese colony of Macao. Finally in April, a friend, Susan Chang, accompanied Marion to Canton (now Guangzhou) for several days. Charles used his military connections to procure a letter of introduction to Marshal Chang Fa-Kwei that described Marion as "one of America's foremost painters." She welcomed a shift from the "colony" atmosphere in Hong Kong to booming

Canton. In the rural village of nearby Fatshan she sketched sampans "rowed by strong young Chinese girls as thick and as strong as truck drivers" and locals "making lanterns, weaving, welding in front of their little homes." Four days sufficed. Marion admitted she couldn't tolerate a steady diet of "primitive life & filth that goes with it."[9]

Canton sharply contrasted with the newfound luxury of Marion and Charles's home. Maids cleaned the house and cooked three meals a day so the couple could pursue their work. Charles swam and ate well, encouraging similar habits in Marion. They shared sumptuous food with locals like Mr. Soo Shih Teh, who sent a formal paper invitation to a multicourse meal at the Fu Lu Su Restaurant in late May 1947.[10] Marion reported feeling better than she had in years.

Marion had journeyed far from the shared bedroom with Musy in Sheepshead Bay to the halcyon days in Hong Kong. She even had the reliable companionship of a beloved cat. Yet something in her being or artistic process or the setting triggered her deepest fear: that the art world would forget her.

Marion and Charles stayed in touch with Reeves Lewenthal at AAA to keep her on the gallery's radar. In fall 1946, Charles had proposed an exchange between Hong Kong artists and the AAA gallery. The plan hit numerous snags. The AAA artists wanted a rental fee or guaranteed sales since their work would be off the floor for six months. But more telling: they simply didn't want foreign artists in the gallery. Thomas Hart Benton had already resigned over a disputed European exhibit. Marion's worries about keeping the toehold she'd established before leaving for Hong Kong may have been warranted. Foreign images were suspect.

Throughout the war, Marion had yearned to be settled with Charles. She now did an about-face. In June 1947, she boarded the *Castleville*, a new Norwegian ship bound for New York. Her needs as an artist trumped their comfortable new life. As she often told Musy, life must be sacrificed for art.

On the ship, Marion loved her private room and bath with a porthole on one side. Her letters fill with the marvels she witnessed: flying fish, nine whales, and an Albatross-like bird that followed them. Her favorite spot was at the prow: "I lie there for hours with my head hanging over like a figurehead. It's thrilling and frightening because it projects way out over the sea." But there were no movies, games, or interesting companions. Her shipmates were a lackluster group: "three old couples (English), a young couple, dumb and silent (American), two old maids."[11] She hated the pervasive smell of copra, the dried coconut palm kernel the cargo ship carried. Marion always preferred working people to fat cats but the crew was too busy to socialize. Still, she could read and work on her sketches. The rest of her art was safe in the ship's hold.

At night in her comfortable cabin, misgivings crept in. Was she crazy to have left? Charles had slipped a sweet note into her room that calmed her worries. He'd been so loving before her departure, supporting hope that they would soon reunite. Charles had encouraged her to pursue her "mission in life." In response, she wrote, "Why can't we work out our mission together? We will, won't we Charles. . . . We will always have each other no matter what happens. Then one can face what happens more bravely. Remember even the stars aren't alone in space, as you showed me in the telescope. They're two, not one. We can do more *together* than separately."[12]

Given Charles's loving send-off, what are we to make of his version of events? The day after Marion left, he wrote to Grace. He had maintained good relations with Marion's sister. Now he unloaded his frustration and anguish. "It is damnable," he wrote, "but she seems unable to be without me for a single moment. She went up to Canton and came rushing back almost by the next train. As you can well imagine, this sort of dependence is trying to me. It is exactly the reason for my not getting married prior to meeting Marion. I thought she was the one person who would be independent."[13] Charles called Marion's treatment of him "mental torture" and accused her of berating him and the two servants. He was a wreck, in a state of nervous exhaustion from what he described as her Jekyll and Hyde reversals. She'd grown so jealous of other women, he said, that he stopped going out.

If Marion were jealous, a witness to their shared life affirmed that she had plenty of reasons. She and Charles esteemed their maid and cook, Ah Sung. Charles described her as a "special person—dignified, hard-working, efficient, honest and loyal." That honesty spurred her reproach to Charles for his twice-weekly "business meetings" that Marion rightly suspected were trysts with other women. "You are bad man, Mister Fenn," she said. "You go off to your paid women, and while you gone, your wife cry and cry." It was the worst rebuke he'd ever received. Charles would later reflect that his impatience, selfishness, and "the male craving to always be right" had played a role in their parting.[14]

Charles also claimed that Marion's art had suffered in Hong Kong. While she produced beautiful bamboo stick and wash ink sketches, the paintings were a disaster. She "slaved from morning to night" on oils begun with confidence and skill. "She would not leave them alone and tortured them and ruined them (just as she has tortured and ruined our love)." Perhaps Marion did overwork, if not destroy, some oil paintings, an impulse she fought her entire life. Certainly she was emotionally volatile compared with the more restrained Charles. But if she could not live without her husband, would she have left when she did?

Charles affirmed Marion's need to return to the New York art world. Doing so clearly met his own needs, yet he anguished over their lost *hsu*. "I feel so sorry for Marion, sometimes my heart could burst. . . . In fact, I literally weep for her. To face facts: I think she's going to be desolate without me and I hope you will all try to be considerate," he told Grace. Marion was fond of her sister, he added, and was always thinking about her welfare "(altho in that strange Greenwood way she wont [*sic*] show it.)" Charles asked Grace to subtly alert Musy and perhaps Irwin about Marion's state and to destroy this letter lest Marion find it.[15]

What are we to believe? Marion later said Hong Kong had been one of the best periods of her life.[16] Did she sugarcoat her experience in hindsight? Did Charles justify his desire to be rid of Marion by describing her as unhinged? Herein a dilemma: how to balance retrospective views with letters from the time, how to envision the Janus face of public presentation and private life, and how to hold in place two radically divergent versions of reality?

Marion sailed into New York Harbor on June 30, 1947. A family welcoming committee of Irwin, his wife, Jessie, Lester, and Grace awaited. "They couldn't get over how well I looked," Marion wrote to Charles. She worried about Grace, who seemed "quite a nervous wreck from her life of narrow drudgery. I don't know what could possibly help her, except money and confidence. She's so talented."[17] Was her family's positive reaction to Marion genuine or were they humoring her? Had Grace received Charles's letter?

To face her worries about the art world, Marion reconnected with Lewenthal right away to plan a "comeback" exhibit at AAA. She fretted that realism and representation were seen as old-fashioned—a rational worry. In 1947, Jackson Pollack began dripping paint onto canvases and Clement Greenberg ruled the art criticism world. There were of course, other artists committed to realism, but they weren't garnering the critical attention now devoted to abstract work. Money worries filled her letters to Charles. He returned a mix of admonition and guidance.

From Hong Kong, Charles offered directives. Do not complain. Don't work for pay, just prepare for your show. Sell the diamond ring (a gift from him) rather than take paid jobs in order to buy things. "It is a sin to prostitute one's art for them [material comforts]." Stop drinking. Do not tolerate boors, clean the apartment, overeat, or bow down to Reeves Lewenthal. Get some sex if you find someone you like. Above all, avoid family: "That you should sacrifice your art for the sake of your worthless family is even a greater sin. I say worthless only from the point of view of permanent contributions to our society, that is to say they take, but give nothing, except of course Grace, who could give quite a lot if only she was strong enough to stand alone. All this is what has made me so sad in regard to your life."[18]

Charles also sent instructions for the AAA exhibit. Get friends to stage a party, he proposed, but don't try to be too fashionable. It doesn't work. Wear something simple, your long-sleeved black dress and gold bracelet. Act both superior and humble. Your work obviously eclipses those lesser artists but you don't need to point that out. One letter mimicked a telegram: "NEVER NEVER NEVER LET YOURSELF BE TAKEN UP WITH FADS STOP." Charles likely meant abstraction. But he also admonished her to ignore other AAA artists, especially "DORIS LEE GLADYS ROCKMORE DAVIS PHONY MASTERPIECES TO SAY NOTHING OF FAD ART." He had long urged Marion to concentrate on the Old Masters, "classical Chinese art, color relationships, and use of space." Charles also suggested that Julian Huxley, head of UNESCO and "still one of the great hopes of the intellectuals," would be the best person to write an exhibit catalog statement.[19] Marion in turn advised him to turn from plays to novels. Maybe their *hsu* wasn't dead but had turned from personal to professional.

The exhibit opened on December 1, 1947. Did Marion wear the black dress and gold bracelet? Refute Charles's advice and indulge in something new? The ample news coverage suggests the event was well attended. Marion must have been hugely relieved to see the fruits of her Hong Kong year grace the gallery walls.

The show displayed sixteen works on paper and ten oil paintings. The oils that Charles had described as ruined were either reworked or created from the sketches Marion considered to be her best work. She'd focused on rice farmers, street vendors, a rock breaker, a water carrier, and a "sampan girl." *The Toilers* captures the muscular exertion of a man pulling a cart with huge wooden wheels, while four thick-legged companions push from behind. *China Granite Quarry* features a group of laborers wielding picks. Their bodies bend toward towering rocks in geometric shapes somewhere between figuration and abstraction—a sign that Marion was still open to experimentation.

Many of the works, especially The Rice Line series in ink, oil and gouache,

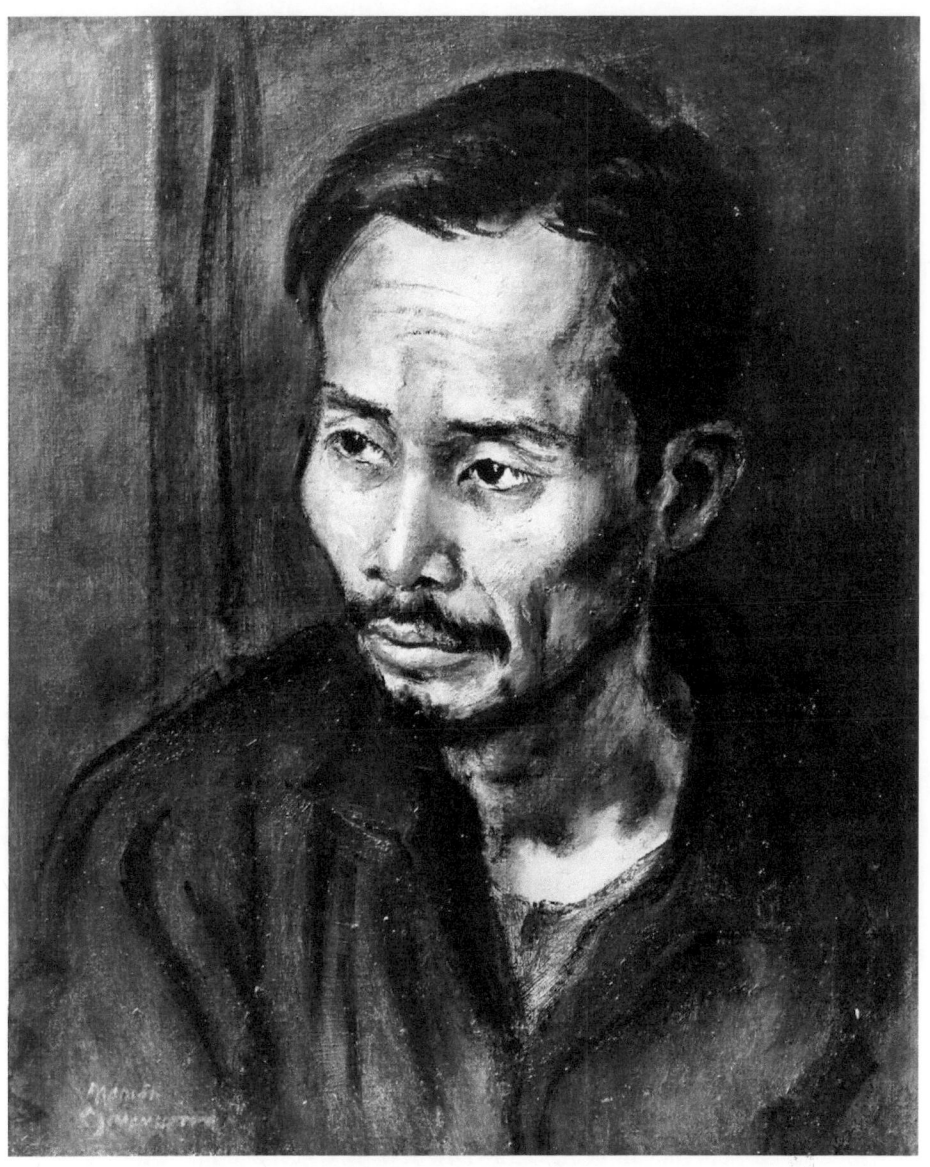

FIGURE 21.1. Portrait of Fu Luofei, by Marion Greenwood, 1947. (Photograph © and courtesy of the estate of Marion Greenwood.)

portray the poverty and despair of postwar Hong Kong. Other works capture joy in everyday life. In a marvelous harbor scene, Chinese lanterns illuminate a couple lifting chopsticks as they savor a wedding meal. More urban and sophisticated subjects included a student, an ink grinder, a Buddhist priest, a calligrapher, and the artist Fu Luofei.[20]

In the exhibit catalog, Pegeen Sullivan, the AAA gallery director, celebrated Marion's "strong Celtic sensitivity." She was able to capture "the salient features of Chinese life" in "pictures that won immediate recognition from the Chinese themselves for their penetrating insight and sympathy."

Charles's advice to ask Julian Huxley for a catalog statement proved useful. He wrote, "Marion Greenwood is one of those original artists whose depth and maturity of vision can reveal new aspects of reality. Already in her early Mexican frescos, acute perception of a fine people created enthusiastic response. Since then in her murals and easel painting in the U.S.A., her own people have seen themselves translated into aesthetically new yet humanly familiar aspects. At the present exhibition, Marion Greenwood offers further exciting proof of her capacity to expand expressive power under the stimulus of new experience. Universal human sympathy underlies all her work."[21]

Before the exhibit, the *New York Post* featured a story about Marion, "An Artist Views the Smiling Poor of China." The accompanying photos feature a laughing, expressive Marion waving one hand, a cigarette in the other. She does not look like the woman in crisis Charles depicted. The author describes her as "green-eyed, bang-haired, and bold-souled," "a big woman with long, strong hands" whose "large eyes under the bangs seemed to have a slightly hypnotic power." Perhaps her "hypnotic power" helped the author imagine the scenes he described: Marion tagging along as the police raided opium dens and urban dives. Given her adventuresome spirit, those exploits might have happened yet remain curiously absent from her letters or any other documentation.[22]

The reviews were mainly positive. One glowing article stated, "*Water Carrier* or *Ink Grinder* might be cited as outstanding examples of distinctive calligraphic patterns in which as much is suggested as recorded." The show's images of people revealed "a warmth of sympathetic understanding that makes them not so much types, but human beings." The *New York Times* echoed praise for Marion's ability to enter "lives with insight, profound sympathy and conviction."[23]

Harry Salpeter's long review in *American Artist* celebrated Marion's embrace of other cultures. He noted her derring-do in trekking about the world and the range of her "curiosity about ordinary human beings of all lands: Indians,

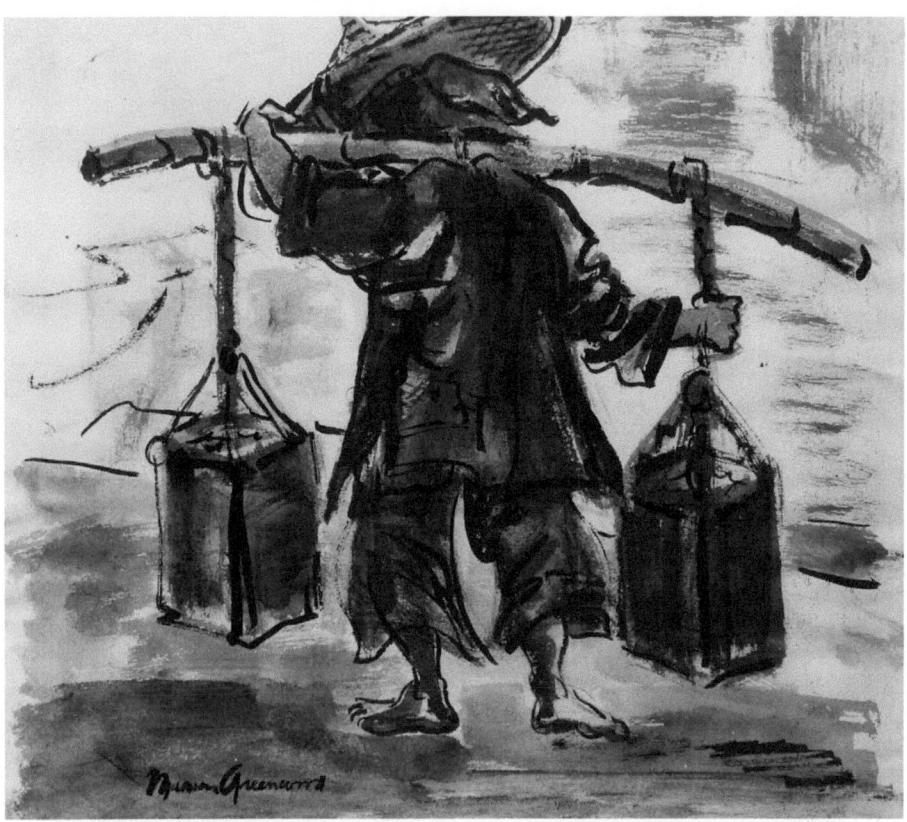

FIGURE 21.2. *Water Carrier*, by Marion Greenwood, 1947. (Photograph © and courtesy of the estate of Marion Greenwood.)

Negroes, and Mexicans, as well as Chinese. She is American to her core in her optimism, humor, and gaiety, in her hopeful looking and striving outward, and in that positive quality of ambition which cuts through difficulties and achieves its objectives." It's rare enough to see ambition celebrated in a woman of that era, but Salpeter also cited Marion's political commitment to "outcasts and peasants, workers and farmers united against imperialism." Marion was moderately pleased, noting that the magazine was mainly read by students but "better than nothing."[24]

A *New York Sun* review offered a contradictory vision. First, Marion is misidentified as "Charlotte." The reviewer praised *The Toilers* as the work of "a trained draftsman" who "composes well, knows character, and looked as understandingly upon the Chinese as she formerly did upon the Mexicans." In a surprising turn, he added, "Miss Greenwood draws the Chinese the way they look to Americans but plunged no deeper into the subject than that. How could she? She is not native and could not tap the hidden springs. The Chinese, who are a polite people, were astonished that she came as near them as she did, but they must have been equally astonished at what she left out."[25] The critique sounds surprisingly like our current discussion of cultural identity and representation. Yet it likely stung Marion. Her respect for diverse cultures were the very qualities Huxley's catalog statement celebrated. Further, criticism of what was left out could apply to almost any work of art.

One curious aspect of the gallery catalog, news stories, and art reviews compels our attention. Why did all describe China as the site of Marion's experience? Hong Kong is rarely mentioned. Pegeen Sullivan's catalog copy cited Marion's two years in South China when in fact she'd only briefly visited. Ignoring the differences between a British colony in recovery and a country engulfed in civil war had a political dimension. Art historian Catherine MacKenzie offers a detailed analysis of how this erasure served the US government's support for the Chinese Nationalists.

The press coverage on Marion's "Chinese" experience highlighted the country's suffering. One critic noted images of "sad mothers and children and laboring little people in their misery."[26] In contrast, Marion celebrated the Chinese as a diverse, wonderful, active people rather than stereotyped passive folk or "Fu Manchus created in Hollywood." They were not hapless victims. Instead, they found joy despite poverty, chaos, and exploitation by the merchant class. The critics' focus on the poor and downtrodden also bypassed Marion's paintings of the joyful harbor wedding and sophisticated subjects like students, artists, and professionals.

In ignoring Hong Kong, the range of diverse subjects, and other possible interpretations of the work, critics reinforced the political views of US conservatives who supported Chiang Kai-shek's nationalists. One influential figure was a US press scion, *Time* and *Life* publisher Henry Luce. Born to American missionaries in China, he pushed the storyline of the struggling Chinese in need of aid—a Christianized, anti-communist vision.

Marion's politics veered toward sympathy for the communists or at least for nonintervention. She told the liberal magazine *PM* that members of Renjian Huahui opposed US government support for the Nationalists but respected Americans as people.[27] In her interview with the *New York Post*, she relayed a message from the Chinese to Americans: please stay out of our affairs and let us decide our fate.

How aware was Marion that her exhibit became fuel for a conservative vision? Hindsight affords a view not necessarily clear at the time. Perhaps Marion simply saw references to the Chinese as natural because she strove to represent people rather than particular places. Hong Kong, after all, was "just an island, a British colony off the coast of China." But if she had objected to the China label, was she in a position to argue? She had left Charles to resume her career. Americans wanted to buy art that fed a long-standing passion for aid to the "smiling poor" of a "needy" country.[28]

The obsession with a single, suffering Chinese "type" echoed reactions to the Native American and Black portraits done by Marion's teacher Winold Reiss. Critics often ignored his representations of African Americans in professional roles or Native people in western dress. Consumers wanted "primitive" and ethnic images.

Marion suffered at critical slights, which surprised Charles, who wrote, "In all matters that don't relate to your work, you are indifferent to world opinion (particularly socially)." In contrast, he thought he could fairly judge the merits and flaws of his work. Social matters were a different story. Trained in British decorum, he winced at such stings. Charles told her to ignore the philistines ill-equipped to judge—among them, he might have added, one who couldn't get her first name right. But he agreed with the *New York Times* critic Howard Devree that "your oil technique lacks knowledge." Focus on "texture (Klee), soft browns and greys (Braque), outlines (Chinese)."[29] Despite that judgment, he remained his wife's most devoted fan.

Overall, the "comeback" exhibit was the success Marion needed. Her Hong Kong experience would fuel her art for many years. Her style changed and "loosened up" while there. "After the sieve of time takes place, you really know more about what you want to say personally," she told an interviewer. "The memory thing comes . . . when you're painting from sketches of a far off time and place. You have to paint from memory." In a Proustian turn she added, "Poetry, you know, is remembered experiences."[30]

Marion had urged Charles to return for her show and rebuild their life together. Excuses for his delay piled up. He had to shift ownership of the Cosmos Club, deal with their flat, give away the cat, and send back a trunk of goods. He'd head to London if a new theater decided to stage his play, *School for Scamps*.[31] Did Marion not wonder why he had sought production in London and not New York? Perhaps she chose to ignore those implications.

Charles left Hong Kong in December 1947 for Egypt. From Cairo, he happily reported that he had ignored Christmas, eaten heartily, and visited the pyramids under starlight. During the trip, he found inspiration in a book about Near East and Indo-European art. "That is what keeps me traveling," Charles wrote. "Seeing the places is the best stimulant for finding out about them."[32]

Marion's Hong Kong art had launched a new phase of her career, yet Charles's "keeps me traveling" added a bitter note. She described a Chinese poem Charles sent her as a fitting description of her life with him: "Amid diamond clusters of happiness glow rubies of sorrow."[33] The latter brightened as the diamond's sparkle dimmed.

PART IV

Rupture and Renaissance
(1948–1970)

CHAPTER 22

"I Treasure What You Gave"

JANUARY 1948, NEW YORK. MUSY NURSED HER AILING DAUGHTER, JUST out of the hospital after a severe case of mumps. As Marion recovered, she pondered who would care for her when she grew too old to paint. "I desperately need a husband, one who wants to plough life together, come what may," she wrote to Charles. "Will you be that? For eleven years I've asked that question."[1]

Marion laid out a plan to save their marriage. New York held endless opportunities for a playwright. Charles could access progressive theater groups, literary magazines, and art world friends. Together they could economize, work in separate studios, and support one another's creative efforts. Britain, she argued, might not welcome a native son turned American. She jokingly promised to wait on him in the manner of Ah Sung, their Hong Kong housekeeper: coffee for breakfast, the *New York Times* on the table, Mozart playing in the background.[2]

If she could not entice him, surely a flourishing New York would. Rising skyscrapers signaled the city's aspirations. Plans were underway for the Manhattan United Nations headquarters. Workers swelled factories built during the war's manufacturing boom. Tons of freight passed each day through the city's thriving ports. Cultural flowering matched the economic boom. Leonard Bernstein headed the New York Philharmonic and Charlie Parker bedazzled an uptown crowd. The city was now a visual art capital. British writer Beverly Nichols described this "great international city to which all the ends of the world had come. London used to be like that, but somehow one had forgotten it. . . . Coming from that sort of London to America in the old days, New York had seemed just—American. . . . Now it was the centre of the world."[3]

Charles, however, found his center back in London. As Marion recovered from mumps, he walked the streets in search of a cheap apartment. The city was rebuilding from the war's devastation. Iconic double-decker buses again breezed past buildings shattered by the Luftwaffe bombings, especially the Blitz of 1940–1941. The unrelenting campaign destroyed a million houses and killed more than forty thousand people. When Charles returned in 1948, bread, petrol, and clothing were still rationed.

Despite hardships, Charles glimpsed literary opportunity. At night, he strolled to the theater and savored a recovering cultural scene. His brother Bob, a literary agent, regaled him with tales of screenwriters making piles of money. Marion had sent Charles's plays and novels to New York publishers in his absence. He'd had little luck but remained determined to make his way as a writer.

Did he ever intend to return to Marion? Into 1949, old dilemmas and debates filled their letters: infidelity, Marion's need for companionship, Charles's demand for independence. To his dream of travel, Marion wrote, "There is nothing more empty than aimless wandering." She hadn't given up exploring other cultures, but she needed time depth and purpose in order to paint. Just flitting about the world was "for people who have nothing to say." She briefly considered, then rejected Josie's offer to return to Mexico together. Despite their estrangement, Josie knew Marion was desperate for change.[4]

Marion grew increasingly furious about the years she'd waited for Charles. She could not tame her emotions and need for affirmation; Charles could not dampen his passion for travel and other women. Blame their oil and water temperaments. Blame their upbringings. Blame history and the war.

Marion's letters mention suicide. Was she was serious or being dramatic to wound Charles? She wrote to him, "I can of course always get out of the whole mess, someday I probably will. [Arshile] Gorky, my old abstractionist friend, just hung himself last week. I'll do it in a more comfortable fashion." Her friend Amy Charak paid for an initial appointment with an analyst. Even with her deep mistrust of therapy, Marion was willing to grasp "any straw for a drowning man and I'm drowning."[5] Charles offered to pay for continued treatment, but the therapist insisted that both partners participate. In the end, she rejected therapy.

Despite fury and frustration, Marion kept up a good front with friends. She maintained the ruse that her handsome British husband would return any day. Soon doubt eclipsed hope. At a Whitney exhibit that included one of Marion's Chinese ink drawings, she ran into old friends and acquaintances. To Charles, she described those encounters as "like the last chapters of Proust—everyone seemed to be covered with a hazy film of frosty age." She imagined them searching her face for something familiar.[6] Later, a stranger at a dinner party said, "Marion looks tonight as if someone has hurt her terribly and she can't quite take it." She unburdened herself to Josie and Musy: "Everyone thinks I'm so strong and gay and independent and talented and still beautiful etc. etc. look what it's brought me—nothing!"[7] Her mother's increasing dementia led to childlike complaints, shaky hands, and sudden bursts of tears or laughter. Marion deplored the cruelty of aging.

Charles's financial support for Marion in Hong Kong was anomalous. She had always supported herself. Now her notebooks filled with columns of expenditures and income, the former always dominant. Options seemed limited. Even famous male artists, she argued, marry someone with money, teach, or write books. After a brief stint teaching fresco at Columbia University, Marion applied unsuccessfully for work at the Art Students League, Cooper Union, and other places. She finally gave up. The men had all those jobs, she declared; many had gone to art school on the GI Bill. Gladys Brodsky confirmed gender bias in art departments. When she applied to teach art at SUNY New Paltz, "They actually said to me, 'We don't hire women for studio teaching classes' . . . I just walked out in shock. I had no recourse whatsoever. I'd had shows and prizes."[8] The greatest compliment, Gladys added, was one Marion heard repeatedly: "You paint like a man."

Charles offered to share cash from a US account, but the bank refused release. Women could not open their own bank accounts or access their husband's without his signature until the 1960s. Even then, some banks complied only when forced by the 1974 Equal Credit Opportunity Act.

Marion scrambled to sell work. She wrote to her onetime lover, photographer Nickolas Muray, asking to borrow money or sell work via his connections. He sent back a note with condolences that he hadn't placed the art. He signed off "love and kisses," which didn't seem to bother his fourth wife, Peggy, who added an invitation to an upcoming party.[9] Muray had married her in 1942 after his long affair with Frida Kahlo ended.

When Marion scrounged up a bit of cash, she ordered two dozen eggs and two pounds of bacon sent air express to London. Charles appreciated such luxuries, even as he sighed over her extravagant, impractical nature. Linked to her emotionality was generosity.

Underlying Marion's money worries was fear that she could not reclaim her previous artistic glory. The emotional toll of Charles's long absence kept her from the studio. Her work wasn't selling. She condemned the "abstractionists and phony primitives making thousands, being acquired by the Whitney and Modern museums while my work gets lost in the great anonymous bourgeois public who buys once in a while for their front parlor in Arkansas or their Bronx flat." "What I haven't sacrificed for this art of mine," she wrote.[10]

Charles shared her frustration. He considered Reeves Lewenthal a friend, but that didn't temper his angry letter berating AAA's treatment of his wife. The gallery's handling of her art was "at best a joke and at worst, a disgrace." The AAA should push major museums to buy Marion's work and feature it prominently in art publications. He bemoaned the "desert of American art today with its dried up camel droppings, fly blown offal, its twisted cacti with their poisonous flowers." It's hard to know whose "camel droppings" he had in mind. Marion was overly emotional and worked slowly, he said. Those faults did not negate the fact that no one in the AAA roster could match her talent. He reported to Marion that he "told Reeves off proper. That bunch of philistines. What do they know about artists like you."[11]

In fact, AAA continued to support Marion's work. The exhibition of her China paintings, gouaches, and drawings moved from their New York gallery to its Chicago counterpart in April 1948. However, the reviews left Marion in despair at the critics' description of the work as "strongly realistic and reportorial." One critic called *Coolie*, a highlight of the exhibit, "essentially an illustration." This description echoed earlier views of the New York China show as having a "certain vivid, documentary quality that make them more valuable than photographs."[12] Marion considered "illustration," "documentary," and "reportage" to be dismissive.

What led to this view of her Hong Kong art? Was it her style or the subjects or the dominant trends? She and Charles blamed the rise of abstraction in the 1940s and 1950s. Realism was sometimes seen as simply mimesis, reproduction without creative merit. But another force seems evident: the hard-to-uproot notion of "others" as anthropological/ethnic curiosities whose images were "documentary." A parallel issue was the museum practice of labeling objects from "other" cultures as artifacts rather than art, a trend only recently addressed.

Dismissal of realism as reportage met sexism in reviews. The critics' focus on Marion's beauty is impossible to ignore. A party following the Chicago exhibit featured a special cake decorated by artist Aaron Bohrod. Marion surely knew him from shared experience in AAA, the Federal Art Project, and the war art program. Yet rather than explore their artistic connections, the article detailed the image of Marion atop the cake. "The enormous eyes, bangs and curves he gave her were no exaggeration. Unfortunately, the guests ate it." The author added, "Painting Miss Greenwood, even with a pastry tube, is a pleasure many would envy artist Bohrod."[13]

Another artist, one very different from Marion, also suffered critical neglect during her time. Mainstream critics ignored the now-celebrated Alice Neel until near the end her life. She, too, painted diverse people, including her Cuban husband and East Harlem neighbors, before such images were commonly exhibited. Style and substance contributed to her sidelined status. Other figurative artists kept working despite suffering from similar indifference among art critics. Neel would join many of them in the Alliance of Figurative Artists founded two decades after Marion's China exhibits.[14]

Although the reviews disappointed Marion, the range of guests at the Chicago exhibit must have heartened her: the mayor of Chinatown, several friends from her Hong Kong sojourn, and Clinton King, an artist she'd known in Mexico. Three black-and-white sketches sold, but that hardly alleviated her financial worries or vexation over being labeled "documentary."

In November 1948, the China art traveled to Bloomington, Indiana, where Marion gave a talk to an enthusiastic art association. The local paper celebrated the mythic life of "Mrs. Charles Fenn" as a bohemian New Yorker with a summer home in Woodstock. No reader of that description could have pictured Marion's frantic sublets of her Greenwich Village fifth-floor walk-up or known that her "summer home" involved a seasonal, frenzied search for a rental where she would not face her insomnia alone. To readers of the Bloomington paper, she seemed to have it all.[15]

Marion's self-portraits from the late 1940s offer a different vision of the glamorous beauty atop the party cake. One charcoal sketch she described as "small and gloomy" depicts an unsmiling Marion. Her large, usually expressive eyes look vacant. A 1948 self-portrait purchased three years later by New York's Metropolitan Museum of Art shows Marion in profile, half-turned, her eyes pensive. That portrait sits on an easel in the background of a photo of Marion. She gazes at the viewer, unsmiling. The dual images ask us to consider different Marions and how they depart from public perception.

Despite gloomy self-portraits and her angst over Charles, the feisty Marion did not roll over and fade away. Her charm was front and center at her Chicago show as she greeted Swedish businessman and art collector Marc Sandler. He

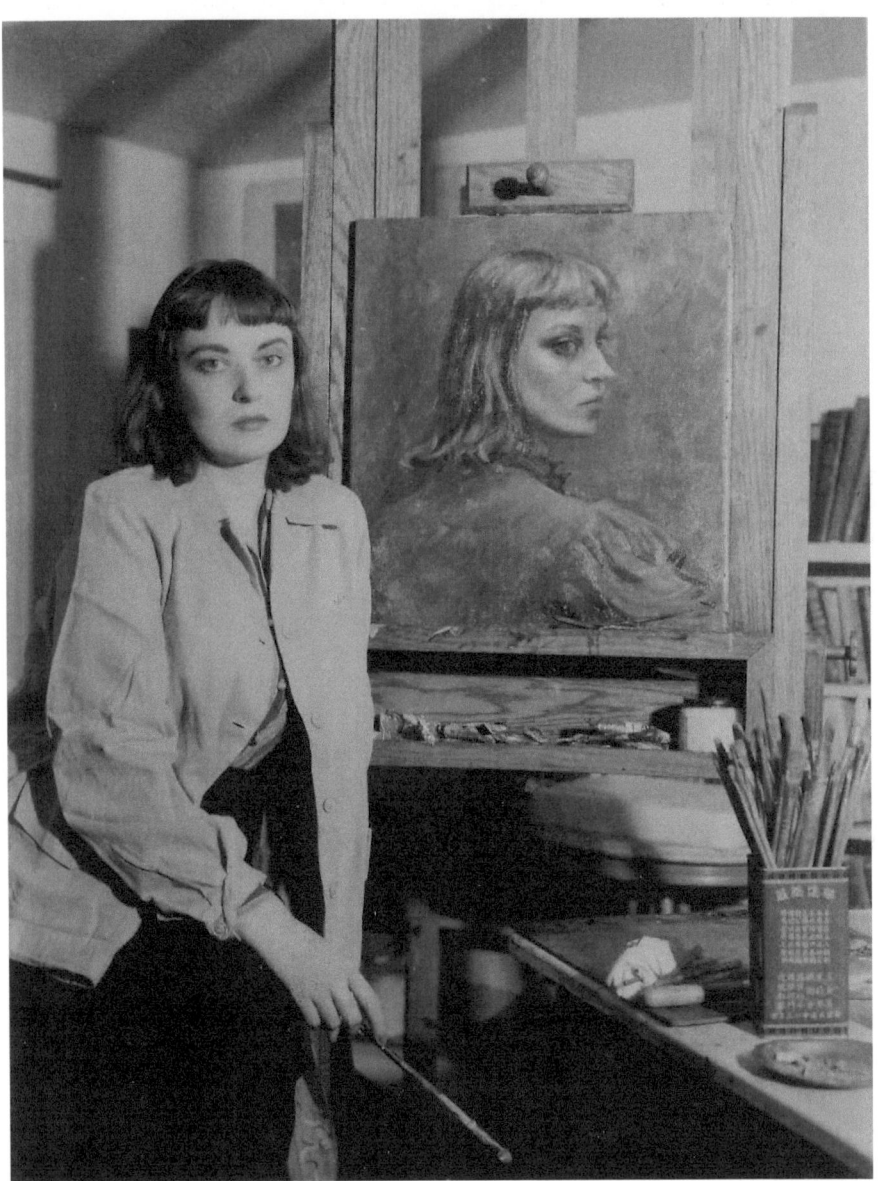

FIGURE 22.1. Marion Greenwood with *Self-Portrait*, 1948. (Photograph © and courtesy of the estate of Marion Greenwood)

sought work by American artists who had created a path outside European traditions. After he bought Marion's *Fan Girl* Hong Kong portrait in 1947, she wrote to thank him, signing off "Sincerely, Marion." By winter 1948, her letters shifted to "Love, Marion." She was clearly open to a tryst with the married Sandler. She had sent him her itinerary, anticipating his phone call to the Drake Hotel. "Don't disappoint me or I will be miserable!"[16]

Sandler, like many men who pursued Marion, struggled to separate the woman from her work. "The devil knows what relationship will eventually develop between us," he wrote. "You believe in destiny so we will leave it up to destiny to decide. But if I can bring to the woman Marion now and then hours of happiness and some inner contentment, I will be happy and if this will in any way further the artist Miss Greenwood, it will make me even happier."[17] He declared her to have become "part of my blood."

Sandler was not inclined to leave his wife. Marion wanted her own "wife" like male artists had, one to cook and cater to her needs. Her love affair with Sandler lapsed, but they remained friends for years. There were plenty of other admirers waiting in the wings. Some, like Sandler, wanted an affair. Others were more serious. Eugene O'Neill Jr., the son of the playwright and a professor of Greek literature, pursued her with marriage proposals. He quit only when she stopped answering his letters.

After her 1948 shows in the Midwest, Marion returned to Woodstock. During a cool rainy June, she made fires in her rented studio woodstove and listened to the afternoon birdcalls. The sounds triggered memories of Charles's whistling—"three questioning notes that tear my heart out, for it makes me miss you and painfully recall things past."[18] Marion's friends and family urged her to give up on Charles. Even her favorite brother, Lester, who had stopped drinking and become a great help, joined that chorus. Marion was furious to discover that Charles had sought Josie's advice on how to end the marriage. He had also contacted Musy and their accountant, Mr. Goldberg. Marion wrote, "You have made it quite clear to him [Goldberg], to Mama, to Josie, and at last to me that you are finished. . . . I understand and resign and accept it."[19]

The practical Marion went into survival mode. She demanded that Charles come to help her settle in Woodstock. As the town's population swelled, economic growth accelerated and rents rose. Marion knew what she needed: Virginia Woolf's proverbial room—and studio—of her own. She wrote, "I now ask you again and please don't keep me begging (as it is humiliating) to see that I am supplied with something to help me. I stand alone in these awful times."[20]

Marion's letters to Charles, he later wrote, "pierced my heart."[21] Despite his affairs and determination to end the marriage, he still loved her. With conflicted emotions, he finally returned to New York on October 2, 1948, on the ship *Parthia* from Liverpool. Travel papers list his occupation at age forty-one as "executive."

Since neither party had much money, they might have lived together between the New York studio and Woodstock rentals. Did they share a bed? Did Marion play Beethoven on the piano Charles had bought for her, the gift that made her declare him the most perfect husband? It's tempting to imagine that they reveled, at least briefly, in a snow-blanketed New York during the record snowfall of December 1948. But it's not likely. For part of that winter, Charles rented a "shack" in Woodstock to supervise the construction of a home-studio for Marion. He had heard her pleas and wanted to make amends.

Regardless of how those months unfolded, on February 21, 1949, Marion and Charles sat in the Kingston New York Savings and Loan Association. Still a married couple in the eyes of the bank and the law, they signed papers for a loan of $5,500. At 4 percent interest, $33.33 a month, the loan would not be paid off until July 1, 1968.[22]

The money transformed Marion's dream into 1.76 acres of land on the north side of Shady-Woodstock Road on which her "little house" would reside. The design of an architect friend, Abel Sorensen, included a big, open living room cum studio. It was the heart of the house, with a drafting table and large windows with views of Overlook Mountain. The tiny galley kitchen reflected Marion's priorities. Who wanted to cook when you could paint? The planning kindled excitement. Under the surface hovered the bittersweet awareness that when the building was complete, Charles would be gone. Before he left, he planted a lilac and a willow tree, which became poignant symbols of memory and loss for Marion.

On May 28, 1949, Charles boarded the *RMS Queen Elizabeth* bound for Southampton, England. Marion saw him off from the dock. When the ship pulled out, she collapsed. Blinded by tears, she drove the car into a concrete pillar. Her brother Lester, who had accompanied her for emotional support, took the wheel. He had started drinking again, and she didn't realize how drunk he was. After getting lost in Chinatown, they stayed overnight at the Sorensen's place before driving back to Woodstock.[23]

The day after Charles's departure, Marion sent a radiogram to the ship: "I treasure what you gave . . . May you find what you want Love Marion."[24] She hoped to remain friends but the failed union haunted her. Charles would carry the weight of how he had hurt her for many years.

Marion returned to Woodstock alone, where friends kept asking after the "charming Charles"—salt to the wound. She told herself stories about how and why Charles turned against her. It was Josie and her conniving ways. It was another woman. It was his family. She poured out her pain, then turned around and thanked him for their happiness in Hong Kong. She loved her little house, then complained about it. The contradictions drove Charles crazy. He accused her of shattering his happiness with her "destructive darts." She was gleeful at the fantasy of herself as a "stormy Greek goddess with lightning bolts at my disposal—Boy I wish I could."[25]

Amid the slings and arrows, they continued to advise one another on their work. But soon, acrimony outweighed affection. Charles had been sending money but wrote to say that was over. "You have your life and I have mine." Marion reminded him of how she had aided his career during painful years of waiting. Charles admitted as much but insisted that he was "horribly miserable most of the time, of course, you were not wholly to blame, there was Cannon Mills and New York and other things, but it was your selfish tentacles that reduced me to the real depths of misery." He repeated the description of her Jekyll and Hyde persona, her "loving bright intelligent nature" ruined by her "ignoble" upbringing. He would not bear another letter of complaints and requests. "Because I am being brutally frank, don't think that I didn't love you." He understood that Marion could not control her response, and "neither can I help writing this. Please, please, let this be the end." He affirmed his great belief in her talent, signing off with good luck and "love of its kind."[26]

In April 1949, Charles was served notice of an adultery charge. Due cause was a legal necessity. Marion likely agonized between April and January 1950 when the divorce was finalized. Emanuel Redfield, the civil rights lawyer who owned some of Marion's paintings, acted as her attorney. She did not ask for alimony. Though she complained about lack of recognition, she was too well known to escape public announcements. "Brushes Hubby" read one headline. Another article described the March 23, 1949, "raiding party" that "entered a room in the Tudor Hotel, 304 E. 42nd St, and allegedly found Fenn with an unnamed woman."[27] That it was likely a trumped-up event didn't lessen Marion's distress.

Marion longed for a companion who would stand by her and accept her. It had been clear for years that Charles would not be that person. She wrote to Julian Huxley after she was "all divorced," admitting that she'd known since Hong Kong that Charles would not come back.[28] Yet Marion continued to believe they were meant to be together despite the stubborn fact that neither of them would change.

In one letter to Charles, she included an excerpt from Algernon Charles Swinburne's poem "When the Hounds of Spring Are on Winter's Traces":

> And time remembered is grief forgotten
> And frosts are slain and flowers begotten
> And in green underwood and cover
> Blossom by blossom the spring begins.[29]

Marion would cling, in Proustian fashion, to "time remembered" and hope for renewal in "flowers begotten." Spring would blossom again for Marion but not with Charles.

CHAPTER 23

The Caribbean and "That Nice Young Man"

Marion wanted a partner who was cultured, intelligent, and attractive—someone like Charles minus the troublesome traits. Someone who could cook and attend to daily chores. Even with a new stove in her galley kitchen, she mainly ate out of cans.

Before her divorce, Marion's friend Dane Rudhyar, the modernist composer, astrologer, and Theosophist whom she had met in Taos years before, sent an alert: Marion's marriage was ending—hardly news at that point. He also predicted possible happiness in 1952 or 1953 with a new partner who had a "strong personality."[1]

Rudhyar's prediction came to pass, although his timing was off. Before the end of 1950, Marion reported that "a young man" had fallen in love with her. Initially, the age difference of nearly ten years loomed as a problem. "Like Sappho said, it's sad to be loved by youth if one is a woman not young."[2] Her relationship with Robert (Bob) Plate evolved slowly as the wounds from her divorce healed.

Bob's virtues eventually overcame her apprehension about love with a younger man. Here was someone with qualities she sought and then some. He was handsome, with sandy hair, bright eyes, and an athletic build honed through tennis, swimming, and other sports. He was a "strong personality" in the sense of rock-like steadiness rather than an overpowering presence. Topping the list of his stellar qualities, Bob could cook.

Marion met Bob not long after he moved to Woodstock with his brother

Bud in 1950. Before long, she reported to Charles that Bob was "a great help, a fine person, quite studious." She saw him as a one-woman type, a striking contrast to Charles. "Sweet and kind," he entered her life like the song, "God, how I need someone to watch over me."[3]

Bob had assumed responsibility for others early in life. His father, Oscar, worked as an auditor to support his six children. Oscar Jr., who went by Jeffrey or Buster, was the eldest child, followed by Bob and Muriel. A set of triplets followed. Their mother, Loretta, always had big babies, so she never suspected the outcome of her fifteen-pound pregnancy. Local papers celebrated the identically dressed triplets in feature articles. When Bob was about fourteen, Loretta died during an abortion, shattering family life. His father divided the children among extended family until he could establish a home on Long Island. Despite that fracture, one of the triplets, Betty, found wonder in her childhood. "I had these two handsome brothers. We had a lot of the same friends and were very close."[4] The family's hardships made each child resilient. Bob became the kind of person others relied on, "a rock" in Betty's words—exactly what Marion needed.

While Bob might not have shared Charles and Marion's Proust obsession, he was intelligent, educated, and philosophically inclined. He studied at Duke University and New York University before turning to writing in his twenties. His historical biographies, what we now call young adult literature, were based on noteworthy US figures, including artists Charles Wilson Peale and John Singleton Copley. He also wrote detective fiction, journal articles, television scripts, comic strips such as Captain Midnight, and short stories for the *Alfred Hitchcock's Mystery Magazine*.

Like Marion and Charles, Bob was politically progressive. All three resisted adamant ideologies but stayed true to socialist principles. Bob was also a committed pacifist. He chose conscientious objector status during World War II, a wildly unpopular position for which many were reviled. He spent the war years with the Dorothy Day Catholic Workers fighting forest fires. A letter Bob later sent to Marion while she was overseas is telling. He described a 1951 grand parade for General Douglas MacArthur in New York. On a sunny day, laborers climbed atop pile drivers. Restless children and secretaries on work breaks clamored for a view of the man many celebrated as a war hero. Not Bob. It was "not my idea of patriotism" to stir bitter feelings rather than work toward reconciliation.[5] Here was a person with backbone.

Marion now had the security of her own house, a growing relationship with

Bob, and a mainly amicable epistolary friendship with Charles. They compared notes on books. She applauded when his plays were produced in London; he returned praise for her artistic success. They debated the state of the postwar world as people on both sides of the Atlantic sought stability. That quest exacted a price as 1950s international politics took a dark turn.

Rudhyar had prophesized that the world would be in a terrible state by the time Marion met her new partner—another not so startling revelation. Fear pervaded American society. After Hiroshima and the first successful Soviet bomb launch in 1949, McCarthy and his henchmen exploited American anxiety about nuclear war and communism. Daily papers offered advice on preparation for an atomic bomb. "What an age to live in," Marion wrote. "Fear, confusion, and anxiety is in the air we breathe."[6] With postwar suspicion growing on both sides, alliances from World War II faded. June saw the start of the Korean War. Marion worried that Charles would be called to service despite being outside the country.

Charles was not likely to return stateside even if called. He was thriving in London. His play *School for Scoundrels* was soon to be produced. Had he chosen to come back, his options would have been limited. In a curious twist to the era's politics, he had lost his US citizenship, rendering him stateless. Earlier, at the urging of Vietnamese students he met in England, he'd planned a return to Vietnam to see Ho Chi Minh. When he tried to renew his passport, he found it stamped "for return to US only." A 1941 law decreed that naturalized US citizens would lose their citizenship if they returned for more than three years to their country of birth. For the next eighteen years, Charles would fight for permission to travel. This law was the supposed justification, but he wondered if his leftist, internationalist beliefs had come back to bite him. Marion was dismayed. "What does it mean to be a citizen of the world?"[7]

The House Un-American Activities Committee (HUAC) had a long reach. Charles feared that the committee had followed his activities postwar. In London, he often saw his old friend, writer and activist Agnes Smedley. Earlier, Charles had tried to connect her and Marion. It's unclear if they met, but if so, they would have hit it off. Smedley was an outspoken feminist, freewheeling radical, and author of the classic semiautobiographical novel, *Daughter of Earth*. She'd been embroiled in a scandal during a long-term residency at Yaddo and returned to London in 1949. She now lived with Hilda Selwyn-Clarke, the wife of the doctor Charles and Marion so admired in Hong Kong. On a May night in 1950, Agnes was at the theater with Charles when she suddenly complained of pain. Soon after leaving, she was dead. Charles asked Marion whether she'd read "the dirt." Smedley had ostensibly spied for the Chinese Communists before she crossed Mao, was expelled, and went to work for Soviet military intelligence. Charles also heard via the US Consulate in London that Marion had "admitted" something about him, presuming she had been questioned by the HUAC. Had she revealed Charles's socialist if not communist leanings? She was enraged: "I never did! I was never investigated so how could I?"

Marion remained sympathetic to the poor and workers, still clamored for social change, and was no fan of capitalism. But Stalin's purges shifted her convictions to anti-Soviet, anti-Marxist, and "anti-everything except my own desperate 'ivory foxhole.'" She stopped working with Artists Equity because she feared the group's Communist Party members would use her for their purposes. The anti-communist legions invoked even greater scorn. Her friend, artist Adolf Dehn, "a good old American and lukewarm liberal," couldn't get a passport to Europe with his Guggenheim award because of the sketches he'd done for *New Masses*.[8]

Marion and Charles hoped the Chinese communists would triumph while avoiding Soviet totalitarianism. Yet Marion decided against seeing Kung Peng and her husband, old Hong Kong friends, when they came to New York as delegates to the newly formed United Nations. Marion wanted to protect herself as well as her friends. She had long suspected that her Mexican murals triggered US government suspicion. Charles concurred that Marion should avoid their Chinese visitors.

Amid political turmoil, Marion's personal life blossomed. She and Bob divided their workspace—one in New York, the other in Woodstock. Studio and living spaces were cramped and both were more productive alone. Yet their letters filled with terms of endearment and longing. She was "Green Eyes," while he was "Babykins" or "fatty orchid lids." Half-joking questions appeared: "Does ya love me? Ya doesn't!!" was soon abbreviated to "Ya doesn't!!" randomly scattered in letters. Her old humor was back but her question was half serious. Charles had left her. Would Bob as well? Would he see other women? He was free, she reminded him, ever faithful to the bohemian ethos. She insisted she had no interest in sleeping around. Still, sex was among the remaining pleasures after her family doctor advised her to stop smoking. Alcohol remained a constant, as it did for most of her crowd. She shared gossip from parties and openings in New York, noting when she drank too much and when she held back. The art scene met the cocktail culture of the 1950s to form clouds that would become a perfect storm.

Marion's old energy for work was back, fueled by Bob's support and Dexedrine her doctor prescribed. Success followed. In 1952, she found herself at the majestic National Academy of Design on Fifth Avenue overlooking Central Park. Her painting *Lament* had won the Academy's Benjamin Altman (figure) Prize in the organization's 127th annual exhibition. The gallery was housed in a sumptuous mansion once owned by railroad heir Archer Huntington. Like Yaddo, the Academy offered award recipients a sense of belonging to the elite. For that beautiful spring night in the city, Marion could fantasize about how to use her $1,200 prize. The daily tallying of expenditures disappeared. Friends called to offer praise and congratulations. Many believed that "I'm painting well and getting prizes just because of you," she wrote to Bob. "Which is true."[9]

Lament is one of three paintings from the 1950s that Marion considered her best work. A woman with a harrowed expression holds a child who appears to be sick or recently deceased. The woman is Asian, either a composite or someone Marion met in Hong Kong amid postwar turmoil. *Elegy* is similar to *Lament* in its subject's sorrowful eyes and long elegant hands. In November, the Metropolitan Museum selected *Elegy* for an exhibit, boosting Marion's morale. The painting would garner the Second Purchase Prize at the Butler Institute of Art in 1956.

Invocation is another "suffering kind of mystic image."[10] A Black woman in a full-skirted dress and simple blouse leans back, eyes closed, lips slightly parted, perhaps in trance. Her hands are upstretched in supplication. In 1951, the Pennsylvania Academy of the Fine Arts awarded *Invocation* the Walter Lippincott award for figure painting. Marion took the train to Philadelphia and stayed with a friend, luxuriating in a day to wander the museum. As with the Carnegie prize she'd won seven years before, museum professionals judged the competition. Other artists, Marion thought, were too willing to follow trends, while museum directors had to appeal to a broad public with more traditional work.

Finally, money coming in! The *New York Times Book Review* used some Chinese sketches. Add to that the $300 from the Academy prize and Marion felt flush with cash. More important, *Invocation* marked a breakthrough. Marion had destroyed the original image, then painted the prize-winning version in four days. The deadline forced a rare show of restraint that paid off.

All three paintings depart from strict realism toward the expressionistic style Marion wanted to cultivate. "Unless I think emotionally about a subject," she said, "I still fall into the old literalness." She added, "My best things rely on mood . . . symbolic things like my *Elegy*, *Invocation*, two of the most important

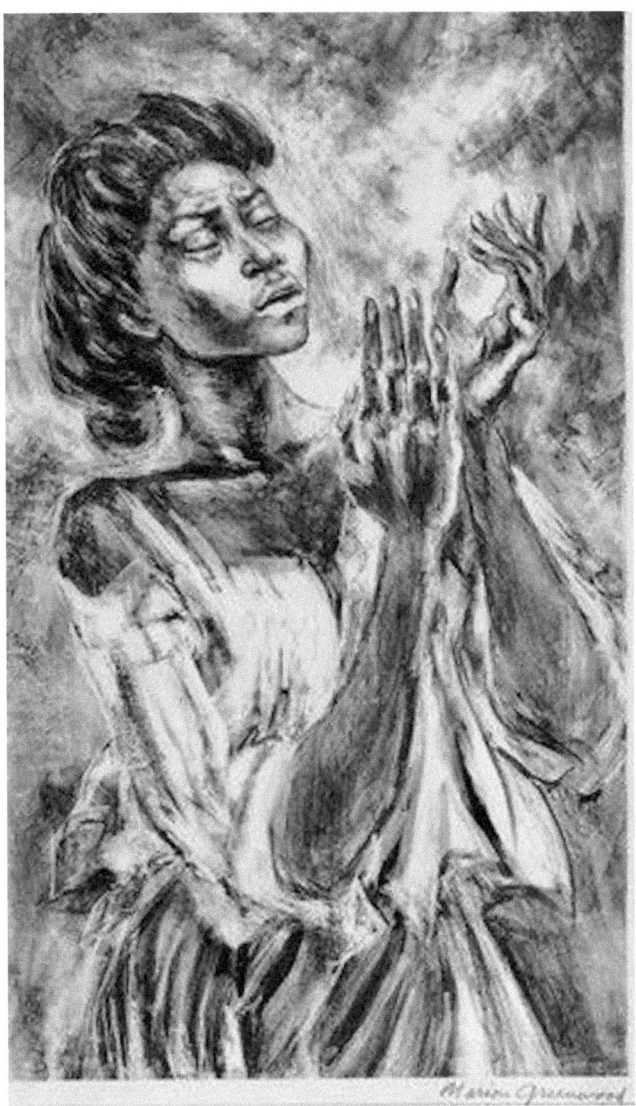

FIGURE 23.1. *Elegy*, by Marion Greenwood, 1950. (Photograph ©
and courtesy of the estate of Marion Greenwood.)

paintings, which stand for that whole period. One can't always reach that level."
Marion stuck with realism when she feared losing sales. "This sort of expressionistic work I'm doing might help my rep but [I'm] afraid it won't sell to the
type of Bronx housewife that buys my old stuff."[11]

This stretch of success rested on Marion's Hong Kong paintings. Now she needed new subjects. In April 1951, she launched a month-long solo trip to Haiti. She budgeted $550—$300 from the award plus some extra from recent portraits. Adolf Dehn sent her contact names. Reeves Lewenthal of AAA wrote a letter of introduction that described Marion as exceptionally talented at depicting diverse cultures. He stressed she would need access to "certain native material" to create work for a 1952 exhibit.[12] However, AAA didn't seem to offer financial support. She was on her own and nervous about this leap into the unknown.

The cramped plane trip left Marion achy, exhausted, and outraged when the customs official asked to come visit her that night. She settled into a modest pension, the Hotel San Michele in Pétion-ville, just outside Port-au-Prince. A local woman, Madame Maval, squired her about town where the lively scene of dancing, racing cars, and general "babble" delighted her. Even the roosters that woke her at five each day didn't dampen her spirits. She simply indulged in the one to three o'clock siesta. Andre Roosevelt, a seventy-six-year-old expat and distant relative of Theodore's, drove her to villages to sketch. The smells and sounds reminded her of Mexico.

Marion's letters to Charles during her trip were long on cultural detail, while those to Bob veered emotional. She missed "darling" Bob and had wept as the plane departed. He teased her about getting too chummy with Jean Evan Chenet, an important Haitian artist whose work she knew. Affiliated with the Centre d'Art in Port-au-Prince, Chenet had received a Rockefeller Foundation Fellowship. He later created a jewelry business in the capital with his artist wife, Winifred Mason Chenet.

Haiti has a long and varied art tradition, but the 1940s brought international attention to indigenist painting, much of it inspired by Vodou. The work of visionary Hector Hyppolite so impressed André Breton that he arranged shows throughout Europe. The surrealist declared Hyppolite's work capable of changing the entire course of French painting.[13] American art curator René d'Harnoncourt made several trips to Haiti. In 1942, he visited as general manager of the Indian Arts and Crafts Board of the US Department of the Interior, then returned twice during his tenure as director of the Museum of Modern Art.

Haiti inspired Marion to depict her favorite subjects: workers, women, dancers, and musicians. Some of her best work featured Martha Graham's dancers, Asadata Dafora's drummers, and a stunning 1948 portrait of African American dancer and anthropologist Pearl Primus. Haiti offered something with even greater appeal: Vodou rituals. The complex system of belief, music, trance, dance, and visual art left the deepest impression from her journey. She left anxious to return.

Her chance came in 1952. The Standard Oil Company hired her to document their production facilities and employees. Marion swallowed her disdain for capitalism and big business. She needed contacts and funding. Her images would appear in the "Changing World of the Caribbean" issue of the *Lamp*, a publication that went to Standard Oil's subscribers, employees, and stockholders. Like Abbott Laboratories' *What's New*, the magazine intended to burnish an image of industry as beneficial to the nation and the world.

This time, Marion's letter of introduction came from Edward. R. Sammis, editor of the *Lamp*. She hid the contract and planned trip from AAA. She was always at odds with Lewenthal over loyalty to the gallery. He fumed when Marion sold reproduction rights of *Mississippi Girl* to Bantam for the book jacket of *Rock Bottom*, the story of a Black woman's journey from Mississippi to Harlem.[14]

Marion traveled from New York to Florida and into a dizzying schedule of "If it's Tuesday, this must be . . ." From Cuba, where she stayed from March 6 to March 11, she moved on to sketch in the Dominican Republic, Haiti, and Trinidad between March 12 and April 1. The final stretch sent her back to Key West and then to Cuba for a television show. Puerto Rico was on the original itinerary but she dropped that country when the whirlwind zapped her energies.

Imagine the American romance with 1950s Cuba, Marion's first stop. Nights filled with dancing and rum cocktails. Beautiful couples watched the sunset on the Malecón as Buicks and Cadillacs glided along Havana's streets. Pull back that veil and a darker reality hovered. Cuba's economic inequality was deeply integrated with US business interests. The 1898 explosion of the battleship USS *Maine* in Havana Harbor prompted the Spanish-American war, ending with Cuba's independence that year. The *Maine* was there to protect already established US investment in sugar, tobacco, and other industries. The Cuba Company, based in Jersey City, New Jersey, was among the influential businesses that dominated Cuban development in the early twentieth century. By the 1950s, Americans owned parts of key manufacturing plants, supermarkets, public railway, telephone, and power industries. Land grabs went both ways. Wealthy Cubans bought real estate in Florida and New York, while American tourists flocked to romantic "old Cuba." Marion wanted to get below that surface to glimpse working people's lives.

Throughout the trip, she reserved her greatest disgust for plutocrats, corporate flunkeys, and dictators. She had entered a hotbed of all three. In Cuba, she visited a petroleum refinery to sketch, then attended company lunches, dinners, and nightclubs with her guides. The settings were alluring, the company less so. Drawn to the sexy rumba and mamba dances, Marion tried to enliven her stodgy escorts. On March 10, after a day sketching in the sugarcane fields and a yuca factory, Marion staggered hot and tired back to the hotel. The place was abuzz with the news: former president Fulgencio Bautista had ousted the current leader, Carlos Prío Socarrás. Bautista planned to run again but facing certain defeat, he launched a coup. Socarrás was generally anti-communist, but he had instituted public work projects and other reforms. Now the coup upended the relative stability of those years. Since Batista supported business interests, the US government quickly affirmed his takeover. A year later in 1953, Fidel Castro sent the first volley that culminated in the 1959 revolution.

Marion was alarmed by the coup but so caught up with her frenzied schedule that she had trouble getting details. She suspected Bob knew more about the political scene from US news. The Standard Oil representatives continued business as usual, ferrying Marion to her flight to the provincial city of Camagüey. From there, she traveled to the Dominican Republic on Hispaniola, the island shared with Haiti. President Rafael Leónidas Trujillo Molina had launched one of the most brutal regimes in the Western Hemisphere, including a 1937 slaughter of the country's Haitian residents. Marion noted the lingering antagonism and differences between the now independent countries.

In the Dominican Republic, she did a wash, rinse, and repeat cycle with the "Esso men": into the country to sketch cattle ranches, coffee and cocoa production, and water systems, back to the monstruous, commercial hotel she hated. She preferred the small pension where she had stayed in Haiti the year before for five dollars a day. Standard Oil's local guides were courteous enough but "hopelessly narrow minded." They espoused great love for Trujillo, which either speaks to the class of people the company engaged or their fear of political retaliation. Perhaps both. Marion got a tour of the "private kingdom (and that it is!) of the dictator," noting that every move she made was watched by soldiers. "You can imagine what a time I've had trying to take a leak."[15]

Marion added Trujillo to her list of most reviled, headed by Stalin. The Dominican Republic created a veneer of a clean, prosperous nation, except of course "for the starving natives and 'slave labor.'" She found the atmosphere "spiritless" and was relieved to go back to Haiti. Though people were poor, Haiti was "at least running itself and trying to be proud of being black."[16]

That pride was hard won. After a revolt against the slave-holding French,

Saint-Domingue became the independent nation of Haiti in 1804. The price of freedom from France was the outrageous demand that Haitians pay compensation. Unable to sustain such crushing debt, Haiti fell into economic and political instability. US businesses had invested heavily in the country, in part to ensure dominance over another occupier, Germany. In 1914, officials from the National City Bank of New York arrived on a navy destroyer. The ostensible reason, to ensure stability, masked the real goal of guarding their assets amid turmoil the bank had in fact created. The Marines followed the next year, establishing the US occupation that endured until 1934.

Considering that history, Marion viewed ordinary Haitians as particularly heroic. An article in the *Haiti Sun* extolled her ability to "transfer onto canvas the emotional vigor of these people." Marion's scorn for big shots and colonial leaders echoed as she moved to other countries. "The colonial British and Scotch are frightful in Jamaica—hating the negroes," she wrote to Charles, who shared her anti-colonialism. The exception was Trinidad, the only country she hoped to revisit, especially since she'd missed their carnival celebration. Though a British colony, it had a cosmopolitan, less colonial feel with its mix of "Negroes, English, French."[17]

Throughout the trip, Marion sketched people or made mental notes on images for the *Lamp*. She juggled her goals with Standard Oil's requirements. When they sent word that she should sketch transportation and industry leaders in Trinidad, she rebelled by filling the foreground with working people. She had learned from Winold Reiss to balance the artist's desires with the commercial concerns of a sponsor, in his case, the Great Northern Railroad.

One cover for the *Lamp* shows her double agenda. Bright green hills contrast with the deep blues and crimson dress of workers harvesting sugarcane. Black women balance baskets of produce and other wares on their heads; men carry sugarcane from the hills while a car edges up the road. The Esso gas pump in the foreground seems like an afterthought Marion would happily have cut. She disdained the *Lamp*'s obsession with their corporate image, relating the story of a photographer who "dared to have a cow pass in front of a service station." When she forgot to sketch details the oil company wanted, she decided to "fake it later."[18]

Marion's most striking work came from her two trips to Haiti. Paintings and prints of markets, musicians, and Vodou practitioners echo the emotional energy of *Elegy* and *Invocation*. The brushstrokes are rough, the lines sometimes jagged. *Haitian Market Women* depicts vendors in a crowded space backed by

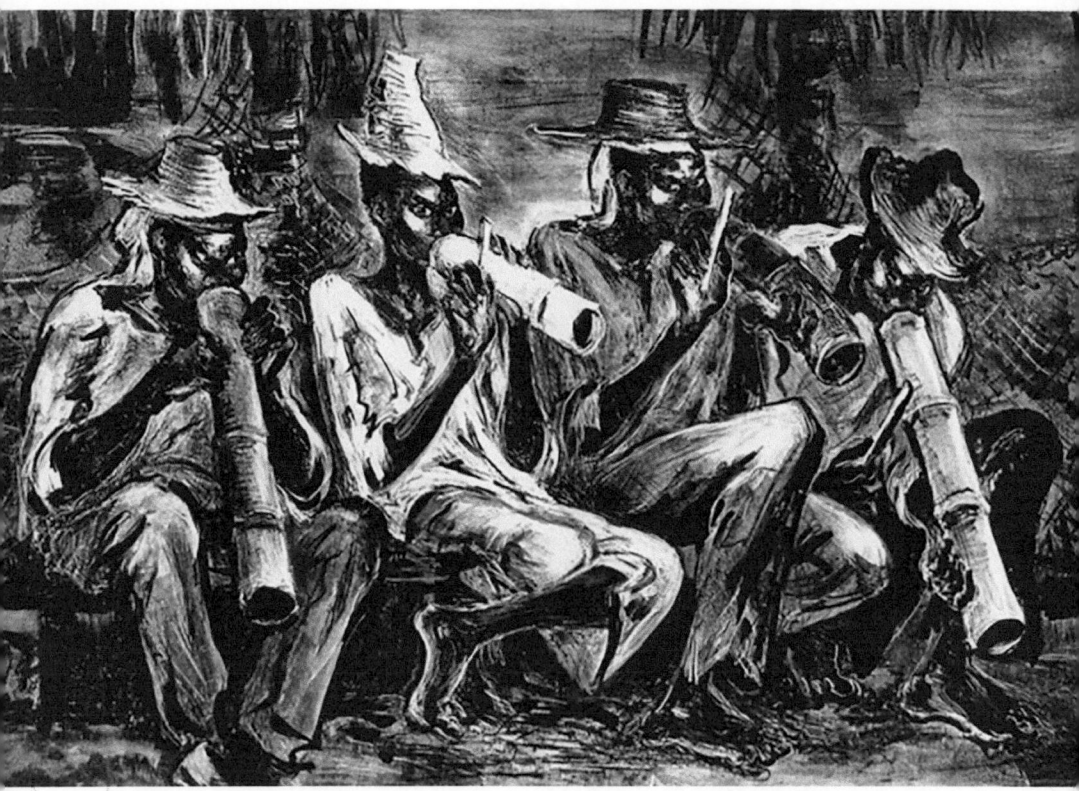

FIGURE 23.2. *Haitian Musicians*, by Marion Greenwood, 1953. (Photograph © and courtesy of the estate of Marion Greenwood.)

a palm tree. Vibrant reds and purples dominate and sometimes blur in *Haitian Dancers*. Women fill the foreground with elastic movement, while two male drummers occupy the background. *Voodoo Ritual* features a man in ecstatic trance near a fire's edge. Dancing women and a man, possibly a priest (*oungan*) with a rattle-like instrument surround him. The conical hats, loose clothing, and cylindrical instruments in *Haitian Musicians* portray important ethnographic details and the centrality of music to ritual.

Vodou married Marion's spiritual quest to her pursuit of cultural difference. Yet to understand the rituals' meaning, she confronted an onslaught of misinformation about this complex tradition and its West African roots. "Haitian Vodou," writes anthropologist Karen McCarthy Brown, "is not only one of the most misunderstood religions in the world; it is also one of the most maligned."[19] This remains the case today, and it was surely true in Marion's time.

The United States justified occupation of Haiti in part by creating and circulating ideas about Vodou as a bizarre cult linked to the savage "Cacos." In fact, this peasant resistance movement emerged in reaction to debilitating taxes on agricultural production.[20] A rash of pop culture lore perpetuated a racist vision of Vodou. The horror film *White Zombie* (1932) introduced fear that the dead could return to a semiconscious state. Based on a popular book by William Seabrook, *The Magic Island* (1929), this film powerfully reinforced an obsession with Haiti's "exotic" but frightening culture. A complex way of life and Haiti's dominant religion were reduced to the hysteria of savages. US Marines were trained to counter spells and sorcery.[21] One wonders why the military felt compelled to teach anti-sorcery techniques if they regarded Vodou as poppycock.

Anthropologists, folklorists, and writers fought this racist vision of Haiti. Many explored Vodou's merger of Catholicism and traditional African beliefs and rituals. Given Marion's connection to the Black community in Harlem, she may have read the work of celebrated writer Langston Hughes, who had traveled to Haiti in the 1930s. He was among a pantheon of Harlem Renaissance figures inspired by the country, along with writer, folklorist, and anthropologist Zora Neale Hurston. Winold Reiss had painted portraits of both. Hurston's fieldwork in the American South showed the endurance of African culture in the diaspora, and a 1937 Guggenheim fellowship brought her to Haiti. Even if Marion never encountered writing about Vodou, she took the religion seriously.

The Caribbean trip fed Marion's work and pocketbook, but she swore an end to corporate jobs, hotel hopping, and brief dips into culture. She complained, "One only gets glimpses and no reality."[22] The constant cycle of movement and airports confused her memories of the sketches she frantically created. What had sounded like an artist's dream was, if not a nightmare, somewhere between the two.

In 1952, the forty-three-year-old Marion in the Caribbean had different concerns from the twenty-six-year-old Marion in 1935 Mexico City. Even though she preferred the five dollar pension in Haiti to luxury hotels, middle age made certain demands. At home, she needed a basic income, creative freedom, and a companion. Amid the blitz of planes and Esso men, Marion's letters filled with longing for Bob.

Bob's "orchid lids" may have been heavy, but his eyes were open. Even in early stages of their relationship, he recognized Marion's flaws as well as her many gifts. He witnessed her contradictory relationship with paid work—griping when there wasn't any, panicked when there was. He accepted her distaste for practical matters, and he took over cooking and house-related problems. On the night before she left for Haiti, Bob recorded her frenetic preparations. "With her usual genius for making the simple complex, she has been in the past week the center of a cyclone of activity and confusion. . . . Marion is perpetually looking for efficient people who will counterbalance her own admitted inefficiency, her amazing inability to cope with the simplest facts of daily existence." Yet her fumbling through life's necessary tasks didn't deter him. He celebrated her joie de vivre in his reaction to Josie's 1947 novel, *Somewhere the Tempest Fell*. The character of Anna Gates—a tempestuous, gifted, outspoken, passionate but unhappy artist—was ostensibly modeled on Marion. Bob pointed out that much as Josie tried to present an unfavorable picture, the Anna/Marion character's "great vitality carries right through the book."[23]

In 1952, the summer after Marion's return from the Caribbean, she told Charles that Bob was the only redeeming feature of her life: "He is very unusual in his quality of innocent goodness. I wouldn't have been mature enough to appreciate it years ago."[24] Someone, finally, to watch over her.

CHAPTER 24

The Singing Mural

IF ANYTHING THREATENED MARION'S RELATIONSHIP WITH BOB IN THEIR early years together, it was her family's mounting demands. In 1951, Papa suffered a stroke. Marion searched for a place to manage his care and Musy's increasing dementia. She considered Grace and Wally hopeless in terms of potential aid. Lester, despite his drinking, offered emotional support. Irwin came through with funds. Even together, the family couldn't afford the fifty dollars a week for the least expensive nursing home or residence. Marion struggled as Papa's health disintegrated. When he died in August 1952, she considered it a blessing for all involved.

Lester took in his mother, but drinking soon ended that option. He had been in a house fire where two women died, and his hands and feet were terribly burned. "Alcohol, of course," Marion rued.[1] Musy ended up in the Hotel Earle on Washington Square while Lester went to an institution to dry out. Irwin

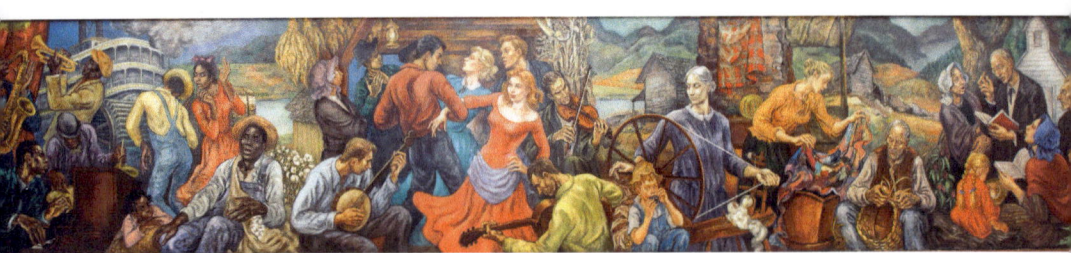

FIGURE 24.1. *The History of Tennessee (The Singing Mural)*, by Marion Greenwood, 1955. (Photograph © the estate of Marion Greenwood; courtesy of University of Tennessee Knoxville, UT Downtown Gallery.)

and his wife, Jessie, promised to bring Musy to the larger apartment they were about to rent on Second Avenue at Fiftieth. That offered Marion temporary relief but not a long-term solution.[2]

Bob shared Marion's exasperation with her family, especially their explosions of "fury, frustration, self-pity, and righteous anger." He groused that Marion, too, fell prey to what passed for normal Greenwood communication. Bob echoed years of Charles's and Josie's concerns. All thought that Marion bore the brunt of family responsibility. Now she had reached a breaking point. Bob was not far behind. He was most scathing about Musy. Like Charles, he lacked sympathy for her Irish sense of tragedy. Bob abhorred her attempt to instill in Marion a dark sensibility—"this to a girl bursting with the love of life on every level."[3]

If Bob seems overly critical of the Greenwoods, he was equally hard on himself. After visiting a painter who was also a productive writer and musician, Bob chastised himself for doing little beyond scattered writing along with movie and theatergoing: "Strictly passive. Before it's too late, I must grip time and circumstance in my hands, and try to shape something. I should have learned to play the piano this winter, had a part-time job, learned something about business, written three times as much."[4] Bob, like Marion, lived on freelance income. He had yet to find success with his historical biographies of John Singleton Copley and other figures in American history. In the 1950s, he haunted employment agencies seeking writing-related work in New York. "Good luck" was the most common response. He finally landed a job reading scripts for a literary agency for sixty dollars a week.

Lack of funds plagued Bob and Marion. She tried to produce work for another one-person show but kept procrastinating to take paid jobs. That thwarted her pursuit of a signature painting style. Commissioned portraits created tension when the patron was unhappy. Marion learned a trick she later shared with artist friends. She would paint an oil portrait, adding one exaggerated feature in erasable acrylic that she knew the sitter would hate. When the person invariably balked at their oversized ears or crooked eyes, Marion would acquiesce to changing it. Contentment prevailed. Still, anxiety could impede her creative process.

The combination of tensions rendered Marion unable to paint or sleep. She fell in the house, sprained her ankle, and tore ligaments. At the end of 1953, Bob wrote to Irwin, "Far be it from me to intrude on the problems of the Greenwood family" but Marion was "cracking up" and had to get far away from Lester and Musy. He argued that Irwin and Wally should sell the Greenwood's family house and put Musy in a nursing home. Bob acknowledged Irwin's assistance in the past and apologized again for butting in: "All I'm interested in is saving Marion, and I intend to do so."[5]

Marion had her own plan for salvation. She would stockpile funds by renting out her Woodstock house and taking short-term jobs. An invitation to exhibit at the White Mountain Festival of the Arts in New Hampshire boosted her morale. Her illustrious companions included Governor Hugh Gregg, Eva Gabor, Arthur Miller, Louis Untermeyer, and her good friend Adolf Dehn.[6] Once she sold some work, she'd go to a Mexican pension where she could live on five dollars a day.

So much of Marion's life depended on serendipity. Before she could head to Mexico, a different escape hatch opened. In July, she received a letter from C. Kermit "Buck" Ewing, head of the Department of Fine Arts at the University of Tennessee-Knoxville. He proposed an appointment as a visiting professor of art for the 1954–1955 academic year. The job would entail six hours of classes in painting and six in drawing or design each week. She would also be charged with painting a mural in the Carolyn P. Brown Memorial Student Center, a recommendation of the university's architect, Malcolm Rice. Marion was a logical choice. Her murals in Mexico and for the WPA, including one for the Crossville, Tennessee, post office, had established her reputation and expertise. But it was two relative strangers who put her name forward— the well-connected director of the Birmingham (Alabama) Museum of Art, Richard Howard, and his wife, Helen Boswell. Her brother, Peyton, had been editor of the *Art Digest*. Before Charles left for China, he'd joined this couple for dinner so he could promote Marion's work. Who knew such a casual encounter would bear fruit?[7]

A university committee had final say on the artist. "I will undoubtedly be asked about your educational background," wrote Ewing.[8] Roadblocks might have emerged: Marion's quixotic exit from high school at fifteen, her well-known ties to the Left in Mexico and the United States, and her Yankee status. Perhaps Ewing urged the committee to ignore potential objections. Marion got the job. The salary of $7,500 was the most money she had ever made.

The contract ran from September 20, 1954, to June 3, 1955. Marion arrived in fall's lingering heat, which she described as "worse than Calcutta's." She stayed in a hotel to prepare classes while she looked for housing. Under the surface of her excitement were "fears of teaching and fears of speaking in groups, and fears of almost everything." A big university intimidated her. She missed Bob. To Charles, she wrote that she "almost had a nervous breakdown at first."[9]

Was this Marion's tendency toward drama or the ghosts of Morelia haunting her? Here she faced "the horrors" that she'd reported to Josie in 1933: living in a hotel, about to ascend the scaffold at a university, lonely and unsure of the mural's theme. The twenty-four-year-old Marion lived inside her forty-five-year-old self, but the elder won out. She had more than twenty years of experience and acclaim as an artist, and that $7,500 check motivated movement. She reverted to her lifelong strategy when faced with fear: she got to work.

Knoxville in 1954 seemed a world apart from Woodstock and New York City—this despite the moniker "Sin City" for a thriving pornography and sex work scene. When Marion arrived, fin-tailed Buicks, art deco storefronts, and bars serving 3.2 beer filled Gay Street downtown. The nearby university spread out around a bend in the Tennessee River. The campus featured stately checkerboard brick buildings with turreted bell towers alongside refurbished old homes. Marion eventually rented an apartment in a house at 1830 White Avenue in the student neighborhood of Fort Sanders. That Knoxville was dry—3.2 beer hardly counts—was a problem. She quickly found a bootlegger.

Marion settled into the short daily walk from Fort Sanders to the university. Once she discovered the informality of the art department, her nervousness about teaching abated. She made short work of one professor who "bossed me around until I told him off." She found academia to be like the army—"top brass and protocol and everyone afraid of their own next top boss."[10] Her outsider status delivered her from university politics and rules. She couldn't, however, overstep the prohibition of nude models in class. This likely came as a shock to an artist who at fifteen had painted nudes at the Art Students League.

The students liked Marion. She was a "real" artist. One news clip began, "Sit down. Close your eyes. Draw a mental picture of what a woman artist should look like. Now look at the accompanying picture of Miss Greenwood." The photo shows Marion gazing up, her hair in a short bob with bangs, paintbrush in hand. Marion also acted like an artist. The evidence? "For one thing, she lives in Greenwich Village."[11] Enough said. News coverage contrasted her to other women of the time, "still wrestling with sorority problems." The legend of the artist unconcerned with social mores took hold. When art is paramount, why worry about niceties? A later description affirms the image of nonchalant Marion as a "serious beauty that would not brook the nonsense of curlers." She was a "middle-aged Cyd Charisse" with an undramatic pageboy hairstyle. Here was "a woman who doesn't have time to deal with haircuts. She wore simple clothes, fit to be spattered."[12] The fact that she had been everywhere added to the allure.

Marion took to the students, too, especially those committed to art beyond a course credit. She overcame loneliness by socializing with other faculty. One member of the English department, Martha Lee Osborne, was fond of the "very charming" Marion. As an academic in a male-dominated era, she shared her friend's intrepid nature. Martha described how they "ran around" together. She added, "My husband was an amateur painter and once he did a scene from New Orleans. When Marion saw it, she said, 'It looks like those two chairs are making love to one another.' She was like that.'"[13] Marion was also close to art instructor Robert W. Schlageter.

Between classes, she pondered the ballroom of the university center. The space she had to fill, 5.9 × 28.10 feet, resurrected her earlier struggles with mural design. She had sworn off painting walls after her final WPA project in the Red Hook Houses. Perhaps she circled the site like one of her beloved cats, prowling for ideas. University administrators suggested themes, including sports and Revolutionary War battles. It's easy to imagine Marion's response to those. She reportedly "tolerated the proposals gracefully."[14]

Marion scoured books on Tennessee for ideas on how to depict the state's diversity and folklore. Always drawn to indigenous people, she considered Cherokee traditions, particularly the Green Corn Ceremony. She made field trips to the Smokey Mountains and visited moonshine suppliers, dockworkers, and small clapboard churches. Despite her complaints that Tennessee was Bible Belt country, the mural's images came from the rural, sometimes conservative countryside.

One central theme quickly emerged. Simmering under 1950s conformity was the cauldron of music, a reflection and driver of social change. Tennessee was a paradise for rhythm and blues, jazz, country, and other genres. A young singer named Elvis Presley had just recorded his first 78, which was selling like mad in a record store on Market Square.[15] However, the music that would animate and unite the mural leaned traditional. The painting's formal title was *The History of Tennessee* but it would be known informally as *The Singing Mural*.

Marion had a packed schedule. She taught classes, created and then discarded designs, worked on the cartoons, and attended events in her honor. The nearby city of Oak Ridge displayed her preliminary mural drawings with lithographs from Haiti and Hong Kong. From October 1 to 17, the university sponsored an exhibit of work in the building soon to be graced by the mural.

Prices ranged from five dollars for sketches to several thousand for oils. She sold enough to stockpile some cash. At multiple receptions she was dined, if not "wined." A Southern city might lack New York's ready alcohol and cultural stimulation, but in Tennessee, she reclaimed the kind of celebrity she'd known in Mexico.

Locals, including other faculty with their children, gathered to watch Marion on the scaffold. Few of them had witnessed the painstaking mural process. First she sketched the designs onto the canvas in charcoal, followed by an earth-green wash, then applied white paint on lighter sections, finished with thin color glazes. She found the familiar experience of being on display affirming but distracting. Perhaps that's why she often worked at night. Students sometimes assisted her until 4:00 a.m., while she reputedly drank gin and chain-smoked as she painted. Faculty members posed as key figures. History professor LeRoy Graf appeared as an East Tennessee preacher, art instructor Robert Schlageter as a banjo player.[16]

Marion worked furiously toward the June 5 unveiling scheduled as part of commencement. Press announcements promoted the event. Roughly one hundred people were expected; three hundred attended. When the curtain covering the mural parted, "there was a spontaneous acknowledgement of awe."[17]

On the mural's left side, Marion depicted western Tennessee. Two African American jazz musicians bend over a piano on a red-curtained stage. Saxophone and trumpet players and two dancers shimmy beside them. In the foreground, a Black farmworker in a straw hat, a little girl at his side, holds a sack of cotton. He leans toward the musicians, mouth open, possibly in song. A steamboat tops the frame, either a showboat or one awaiting cotton for transport to New Orleans. In a shift to central Tennessee at the mural's middle, country square dancers hook arms to the rhythms of a string band. A boy with a harmonica kneels beneath a weaver spinning cotton, while a younger woman lays a quilt over a baby's crib. Finally, eastern Tennessee is represented on the right. A denim-clad man weaves a basket, his long fingers carefully grasping the oak strips. Bonnet-clad women and long-faced men behind him sing in the sacred "shape-note" tradition in front of a steepled white church. The mountains, the Tennessee and Mississippi Rivers, mountain laurel and rhododendron, ears of corn and hanging tobacco—all frame the vibrantly colored, larger-than-life figures. The separate sections reflect the reality of geographic and racial division, but each flows seamlessly into the next. Everything is there: human toil and celebration, diverse traditions and communities, the fruits of the state's creativity.

Marion repeated features of her easel portraits, notably the large hands and long fingers of the jazz musicians and basket weaver. These resemble those of women in her award-winning paintings *Lament* and *Invocation*. Art historian Fred Moffatt points out the parallel to hands in Thomas Hart Benton's work. Both echo the original source, the sixteenth-century master El Greco.[18]

At the opening, Robert Schlageter celebrated Marion's depth of human feeling and her ability to deftly link figures into rhythmic harmony. University administrators, faculty, students, and the public exalted the work as a progressive gem. The press office promoted the mural to *Art Digest*, *Art News*, and other publications. Friends and strangers wrote to express gratitude and report on the ongoing positive response to her "wonderfully alive" painting. Marion called *The Singing Mural* her best work in the United States, a triumphant return to murals after frustrating years on WPA projects. She confessed to feeling empty after the herculean drive toward completion.[19]

Marion packed up her suitcases, paints, and other supplies and headed north after the mural's unveiling. She left behind friends and at least one former lover. Rumors abounded that she'd had "a thing" with an art student. Her Woodstock friend Gladys Brodsky later confirmed a relationship with a handsome assistant on the mural. Marion confessed to Charles that she'd had an affair with someone "way too young for permanence."[20] Despite sadness at leaving her lover and friends, Marion surely celebrated a return to New York, land of plentiful alcohol, museums, and theater. She departed satisfied that *The Singing Mural* was a fine legacy. Neither Marion nor her companions anticipated the complications ahead.

In 1955, Knoxville's movie theaters, restaurants, schools, and buses remained segregated. On May 17, 1954, a few months before Marion's arrival in Tennessee, the Supreme Court had ruled on *Brown vs. Board of Education*. "Separate but equal" was dead but integration happened slowly. The Knoxville undergraduate campus would stay segregated until 1961. Marion's letters don't illuminate her feelings about the racial issues she encountered. However, the mural offers evidence of her beliefs. On a campus with no Black undergraduates, she chose to depict eight of the mural's twenty-seven figures as African American. At the time, no one in Knoxville noted that decision.

The mural's journey offers a case study in shifting attitudes toward an artwork. For fifteen years after the mural's completion, the only grumbles came from visiting speakers or musicians who thought the powerful images distracted the audience. Then on May 1, 1970, a student protest against the Vietnam War erupted on campus, echoing those at other universities and beyond. On May 4, the Ohio National Guard fired into a crowd of unarmed Kent State student protesters, leaving four dead and nine injured. Fury over racial injustice further ignited unrest. On the Knoxville campus, the ROTC center was firebombed. Broken windows and other vandalism followed. Amid the destruction, someone dumped white paint over the mural's square dancers, followed by an attack with a knife or razor. The university officials blamed anti-war protesters, but the culprits or possible motives never emerged.

Students, faculty, and staff contributed money to repair the damage. New critiques followed. "Under scrutiny," reported a local paper, "the painting was soon getting new criticism that it was racist."[21] The controversy focused on the Black man with bales of cotton. Critics described him as smiling, perpetuating the myth of contented servility, possibly slavery. No evidence emerged to link racism to the vandalism, but threats to the mural continued. In 1972, university officials covered the painting with wood paneling.

Few visitors to the ballroom knew about the hidden mural until 2006, when student Eric Harkness spearheaded a drive to display and discuss the mural. He later said, "There were wounds on our campus, especially when you consider UT's history as a white institution (which it was when the mural was painted). Given that history and the history of the mural, storytelling about it can be a force for healing." What was needed was "an honest, civil, and loving dialogue."[22]

The university convened a multiracial panel of five experts representing history, art history, race relations, and ethnic studies. Local press and a student publication highlighted the public event well in advance. Stories and debates about the mural swirled in bars and classrooms. The panel drew three hundred people, equal to the number who'd attended the 1955 unveiling.

About one-third of the crowd was Black. A spirited and wide-ranging discussion followed. Master of Ceremonies Anton Reece, the African American UT director of student activities, praised Marion's work. P. Eric Abercrumbie, a senior African American scholar from the University of Cincinnati, condemned the painting as a racist depiction of segregation and plantation life. Among audience members, some considered Marion a pioneering woman muralist; others, including some Black attendees, applauded her inclusion of people of color when white people dominated American murals. The cotton worker didn't appear to be a slave, negating rumors that he was shackled. He was not in fact smiling. A few people saw the portrayal of women as subservient; others objected that the only whites were hillbillies. Amid the flurry of perspectives, a decision: the mural should be saved but covered again, this time with plexiglass and a curtain.

Leap forward to 2013. The university center was slated for demolition. What to do with the mural? A committee ultimately hired a restoration company to painstakingly remove the canvas and store it in a warehouse. The director of the university's downtown gallery, Sam Yates, was determined that it should not languish there indefinitely. He decided to stage the mural as part of a public exhibit of Marion's work the following summer. Mike Berry, the gallery's manager, and his team got busy with research and securing loans of art owned by local people. Berry recalled the earlier hope that a new generation could one day see Marion's work in historical context: "I think that time is now."[23]

The exhibit opened on June 5, 2014. A mixed-race crowd of locals mingled with the university community, including international students. Marion's friend from the English Department, Martha Lee Osborne, sat at the gallery's center with bearded journalist and local historian Jack Neely. Martha's abundant white hair was pulled up in a barrette. Her earrings matched her royal-blue jacket, her wide glasses the latest style. She looked as hip as some of the students. She had lived through each stage of the mural controversy and pronounced it beautiful. Others agreed, including an African American administrator who had been charged with safeguarding the mural when she arrived at UT. Ted Williams, an eighty-four-year-old artist and model for the square dancer at the mural's center, related fond memories of Marion. Her cosmopolitan life had impressed everyone, even a well-traveled GI like him who had just returned from the Korean War in 1954.

The Crossville, Tennessee, post office transported Marion's WPA mural on canvas, *The Partnership of Man and Nature*, to Knoxville to hang across from *The Singing Mural*. In an address to the assembled group, retired professor of art history Fred Moffatt compared the two paintings as examples of how humans transform nature to culture. The 1940 Crossville painting reflects the era's celebration of the Tennessee Valley Authority, while *The Singing Mural* stresses farming. The African American man with his bales of cotton represents the importance of agricultural workers and the land's productivity. He "humanizes the harvest," said Moffat. If anyone objected to the mural or Moffat's interpretations, they stayed silent. The UT student paper summed up the general reaction with the headline, "Controversial Mural Seen in New Light."[24]

Moffat had previously glimpsed the painting only in the dark ballroom. Now the gallery's lighting revealed a mix of orange, yellow, bits of pink, and red as "an impressionistic carpet."[25] From June 6 to August 9, Marion's mural sketches and lithographs from Hong Kong and Haiti hung alongside the larger paintings. The reactions of hundreds of visitors over that time were overwhelmingly positive. That enthusiasm prompted the university to loan the mural long-term to the Knoxville Museum of Art. The text detailed the controversy, allowing visitors to judge for themselves.

Images and symbols don't belong to their creators. Our interpretations vary with every era. When Marion painted murals and portraits of diverse people—her New York immigrant neighbors, the Navajo, workers in Mexico, Hong Kong, India, Haiti, and other parts of the globe—she wanted to display the beauty of the human form in all its manifestations. Today, humanism can appear to erase difference. This was precisely what Marion, along with Winold Reiss, anthropologist Franz Boas, and many others, struggled to avoid. What did her quest mean in Knoxville in 1955? In the 1970s, when students challenged her representations? What did it mean in 2006 and in 2014 when the work was reassessed and then embraced? What does it mean today?

Marion did not live to respond to those questions. However, we can be sure she would not have stayed silent. Bob Plate said that if she'd known of the vandalism, "the bellow of her strong voice would reach from here to Knoxville."[26]

There are as many shifting perspectives on Marion's "strong voice" as there are on *The Singing Mural*. To Bob, much as he loved Marion, her willingness to say what she thought was socially "clumsy." She brought up issues that others preferred to ignore. Charles was similarly puzzled by Marion's disregard for social slings and arrows. In contrast, critiques of her work sent her spinning. Of course they did! She had a more important agenda: her "raft in a flood," as Josie once described creative work. She was an artist too busy to worry over sorority trifles, carefully coifed hair, and public protocol. The Knoxville press was right on that score. They recognized what others, even her intimate partners, did not.

The vision of the two men Marion loved, thoughtful and intelligent as they were, reflect their histories and the era's norms. Charles admitted that his British upbringing made him more attuned to social rules. Bob stepped outside gender roles in his life with Marion, yet he also seemed to expect that women should be sensitive, discreet, and diplomatic. Marion neither believed nor acted according to 1950s dictates. If clumsiness meant saying what she thought, she was indeed clumsy.

Her female friends celebrated that trait. Artist Gladys Brodsky described her as "forthright": "She said what was on her mind, very directly. If I looked good, she told me how beautiful I looked. If she didn't like something, she would tell somebody."[27] Marion was the kind of woman who, when she saw two chairs making love, would say so. She was, with a quirkiness Martha Osborne celebrated, "like that."

Marion was, in short, a woman artist determined to defy the demands of a conformist time. She stayed true to her artistic impulses as the art world exercised its own orthodoxy. Back from Tennessee, she once again faced being out of step with larger trends in New York City and Woodstock. Before long, she'd be searching again for her distinctive style and subjects "to arouse empathy."

CHAPTER 25

In and Out of Tune

JUNE 1955. MARION ALIGHTED FROM THE TRAIN INTO THE FADING GLORY of New York's Penn Station where Bob awaited her with open arms—a tempting but perhaps unlikely scenario. Marion, saddled with luggage and painting supplies, might not have taken a train from Tennessee. The route was complicated. Bob might not have been there. There were signs that Marion was ambivalent about the relationship.

One clue is a letter she sent to Charles from Knoxville with "a desperate call for a working partnership with somebody mature and close." He thought she'd proposed a romantic reunion, which roused her fury. "I thought by now you'd have grown up," she fired back. Charles asked whether Bob was still in the picture. For Marion, the ten-year age gap had reemerged as a problem. "There's no future in it. Again, he's too young or maybe I'm just old-fashioned," she said.[1]

Bob had supported Marion's temporary move to Knoxville to generate income and flee her family. His writing flourished in their New York apartment with his alluring but distracting partner away. Bob also knew about the affair with the young mural assistant. That was no problem; according to a close friend, Bob was no angel. Despite Marion's lingering concerns, before long the two reunited.

In Tennessee, Marion suppressed fears of being out of touch with the art world. Locals in Knoxville celebrated that "she wasn't one of those Abstract Expressionists."[2] She was a famous "real artist" who lived in Greenwich Village. Now back in that very Village, Marion had to reestablish herself amid the changing art scene. Where did realism and portraiture fit? She felt "completely out of tune with my age (always have been except it's worse now)."[3]

Marion never departed from a core belief: "To know what counts vitally in his [the artist's] experience—inner experience—and try to express it." "The spiritual and esthetic," she wrote, "must be fused with technique simultaneously." She saw contemporary art as obsessed with the "how" of technique rather than the "why" of painting itself. Paradoxically, she said, this "actually negates the vital development of new art forms."[4]

She felt most "out of tune" with Abstract Expressionism, also called the New York School. Geography tells the story. Standing outside Marion's New York apartment-studio at 60 W. Ninth Street, one can shoot an arrow straight to the mirror image address of 60 E. Ninth Street—site of the iconic studio that launched the Abstract Expressionists. It was an eight-minute walk but, for Marion, an incalculable art distance.

In 1951, the Ninth Street Art Exhibition of Paintings and Sculpture shook New York. To the surprise of participating artists, the show attracted elites. Among them were Alfred Barr Jr., the first director of MoMA, and critic Clement Greenberg, whose writing shaped the movement. The seventy-two featured artists included soon-to-be household names, among them Willam de Kooning, Jackson Pollock, and Robert Motherwell. Only later did the featured women generate equal enthusiasm: Helen Frankenthaler, Grace Hartigan, Elaine de Kooning, Lee Krasner, Joan Mitchell, among others.

Marion and Charles had long disdained "AbEx," which they called "bunk" and a "press stunt," not enduring art.[5] Some viewers agreed as they stood bewildered before a Jackson Pollock drip painting. In this "press stunt," Marion saw no trace of her humanistic goal of creating empathy. She wanted to depict the feelings evoked by her search for something that revealed a person's character. That vacillation between realism and expressionism plagued her. She wanted more of the latter but felt stuck in the former, the "old literalness" that would sell to the "bourgeois public."

Yet Abstract Expressionists were not disconnected from society. Many, like Marion, had been social realists creating politically engaged art during the 1930s. They, too, recoiled from fascism, the Holocaust, and war's trauma. Believing that such horror lay beyond literal representation, they exploded traditional forms. Some looked inward for meaning; others used gestures and the act of painting itself to evoke emotional response.

In her groundbreaking work on women Abstract Expressionists, Mary Gabriel notes, "Art serves a social function not unlike religion. For those who are open to it, it speaks directly to that aspect of man that is not beast-like, his soul."[6] Like Marion, AbEx artists were seekers. Some embraced spiritual influences, including Theosophy; a youthful Jackson Pollock had attended Krishnamurti's camp in Ojai, California. Whether or not Abstract Expressionists voiced Theosophical or similar beliefs, they shared the notion that a purified art, reduced to essentials, created meaning beyond realistic representation.

Feeling out of tune with New York City's E. Ninth Street crowd, Marion might have found Woodstock more welcoming. The town's 1950s visuals made it less of a departure from Knoxville. Fin-tailed Buicks parked along Tinker Street and American flags hung from village center storefronts. From her earliest days, Marion had also witnessed the colony support for multiple art styles. The Woodstock Artists Association promoted realistic portraits, landscapes, abstract work, and a full roster of prominent artists. An embrace of the natural world bound many of them. One critic described the "the so-called 'Woodstock school'" as more rooted in geography and a sense of place than in style.[7]

Still, the avant-garde scene kept growing. After 1955, Greenwich Village artists could make the summer pilgrimage north in a record two hours via the New York Thruway's newly completed stretch. Abstract Expressionists included Bradley Walker Tomlin and Philip Guston, both featured in the Ninth Street show. In the 1960s, Guston would return to figuration with a unique and sometimes controversial style. Marion's friend, Anton Refregier ("Ref"), and Edward Millman promoted international brotherhood and social justice through their art.[8] Arnold Blanch, known unofficially as the "Mayor of Woodstock," migrated from landscapes, portraits, and cubist images into Abstract Expressionism.

The town's art history was not entirely tension-free. Back in 1913, Robert Winthrop Chanler reacted to the Armory show with "Parody of the Fauve Painters." In a dense forest, an ape instructs a group of five human painters. Reproductions of Matisse and Gauguin litter the ground in a lampoon of artists who "aped" the modernist Europeans.[9] During the 1930s, bitter struggles erupted as artists competed for New Deal jobs and mural commissions. However, a willingness to adapt was more common than long-standing grudges, argues art historian Bruce Weber.[10]

Some artists only socialized with their stylistic brethren. However, Marion befriended a range of abstract painters: Grace's husband, Rollin Crampton, Bob's younger brother, Bud Plate, and his wife, Gladys Brodsky, among others. She stayed friends with Arshile Gorky, whose work skimmed Surrealism and Abstract Expressionism. His 1948 suicide left her bereft.

Marion's women friends included artists from varied backgrounds. She sometimes joined Doris Lee, Cecile Forman, and others in a dance class led by Yasuo Kuniyoshi's wife, Sarah. Bob, sitting by the quarry pond reading *War and Peace*, recorded their "squeals and laughter, girlish, the beat of the tom-tom, and occasionally an extra loud grunt."[11]

Bob and Marion made the Woodstock social scene with Bud and Gladys. Bud had been painting for years before he rose to prominence as an Abstract Expressionist. As a Marine in 1943, he was assigned to depict pin-up girls on the sides of planes. The work tempered his other, trauma-inducing role as a bombardier. After the war, he made his way to the Paris atelier of Fernand Léger. There he befriended abstract artist and poet Herman Cherry, who became a strong influence. Bob had initially visited Woodstock in the summer of 1949; the following year, he and Bud returned together. Always drawn to water, they found a local swimming hole with two naked women splashing about. This was the place for them.

By 1950, Bud was studying with Yasuo Kuniyoshi at the Art Students League. The teacher declared his student "too good to be taught," so Bud struck out on his own. He soon earned acclaim for masterful use of color.[12] For years, he pondered moving to East Hampton, then a center of Abstract Expressionism. However, he had met Gladys in Kuniyoshi's class. Once settled in Woodstock, they stayed. She established her career as a painter and sculptor while raising two sons, teaching art in the public schools, and showing work in New York City as well as Woodstock.

Gladys was still married to her first husband, Robbie Robinson, when she met Marion. The shop that she and Robinson owned often framed Marion's work, sometimes pulling canvases off the easel so she wouldn't keep repainting. Gladys was sure that Robbie was sleeping with Marion, who often called him for superfluous reasons like cat rescue. Gladys bore no hard feelings. The town's laissez-faire attitude toward sex was part of life.[13]

When Marion, Bob, Gladys, and Bud weren't hanging out at the Seahorse Bar, they were assembling a party crowd. Gladys recalled, "In those days, everybody got together—cartoonists, illustrators, you didn't care who it was. . . . You needed enough people to make a party. You couldn't be discriminating— carpenters, plumbers, whoever could drink and smoke. Come to the party!" When Gladys and Bud married, Marion and Bob hosted the wedding reception. That way, Marion could invite all the people to whom she owed a dinner.[14]

Bob skewered the social arena in his diary. At a party at artist Federico Castellón's, one guest was a "mustached talkative artist . . . whose brain was not quite as large as his intellectual pretensions." Only good friends like Adolf and Virginia Dehn escaped Bob's sharp wit. Like all scenes, Woodstock's was sometimes problematic. Alcohol took a toll on partners and families. Other times, tedium prevailed. Bob recorded one art opening that featured "the usual crowd, usual mysterious opening punch, usual emphatically cordial hypocrisy."[15] Despite occasional duds, these parties were a riotous good time for Bob, Marion, Bud, and Gladys.

Marion and Bud got on well. They would go into the kitchen to talk and toss back a drink before heading out for the night. Occasionally, artistic differences arose. Marion believed abstract artists lacked basic drawing skills. When she challenged Bud to a sketching duel, she likely felt confident she could beat him. They pulled out their pencils like sabers from sheaths. Marion produced a good drawing, then Bud did an equally fine one. He dared her to create an abstract image. Marion faltered, unable to produce art without a model in the world to whom she could connect emotionally.

Other members of Bob's family embraced Marion. Betty, one of the triplets that included Bud, admired Marion's fun-loving nature as well as her art. Bob's siblings also accepted her quirks. Another sister, Muriel, had married Barney Walker, head of the American Tobacco Company. He was known for inventing the slogan "Us Tareyton smokers would rather fight than switch." Visitors to their home knew they were supposed to smoke his brands. Not Marion. A lifelong smoker, she brought along her own pack. As she lit up one night, she pronounced, "I'd walk a mile for a Camel."[16]

While Bob's family welcomed Marion, her own continued to plague her. To escape the Greenwoods, she returned to Mexico in 1956. She was in high spirits as she packed her bags. A windfall had arrived—a prize from the Butler Institute of Art for her 1950 painting *Elegy*. Marion was grateful for the cash but even more for the recognition. Clearly not every institution saw her as out of step. She planned a one-person show when she returned.

Adding to her excitement was an invitation to a new exhibit space. Adolf Dehn had recommended her to the Milch Gallery, then at 55 E. Fifty-Seventh St. Marion enthused about having her art in a real gallery, "not a department store."[17] That barb referenced Associated American Artists' extension into greeting cards, ceramics, and fabric design under Reeves Lewenthal. Her relationship with the gallery only improved when Sylvan Cole took over in 1958.

Marion anticipated spending a month between Oaxaca, Mexico City, and San Cristóbal de Las Casas in Chiapas, where she'd never been. She contacted

Pablo O'Higgins and Jaime Plenn, who booked her into Mexico City's Maria Cristina Hotel. Plenn and his wife had offered their couch, but she likely wanted her own space. The flight to Mexico on July 11 was a radical departure from the long boat trips of the 1930s. The journey held great hope for renewal.

When she arrived in Oaxaca, a Mexican paper noted her presence as a "well known American painter from the University of Tennessee."[18] Despite the inaccurate label, she would have been pleased if positive press had smoothed her path. Instead, she hit obstacles as soon as she ventured out from the Hotel Francia to sketch. In the market, Marion promised a local seller five pesos to draw her image. A Mexican woman witnessed the scene and offered the potential subject two pesos to refuse. Marion's higher bid lost. She ran into a Russian artist from New York who'd been visiting Mexico for years. He confirmed that outsiders were increasingly less welcome. This was not the first time Marion had trouble convincing people to pose. In other settings, she had initially encountered suspicion but always won her subjects' trust. By the 1950s, attitudes had changed, at least in Oaxaca. Marion captured quick sketches on the street, then reworked them in her hotel room.

It's logical that Marion would have celebrated greater autonomy for her subjects. From Pátzcuaro in 1933, she'd told Josie that Indians should have the chance to paint their own walls. Three years later, she wrote to Willard W. Beatty at the Office of Indian Affairs to suggest ways for indigenous artists to join the US mural program. He wrote back, receptive to the idea of hiring "our more talented Indians."[19] Now, however, she faced one consequence of those politics.

Marion kept changing plans. Should she go to Cuernavaca? Spend more time in Mexico City? Where was the inspiration Mexico once offered? She also faced travel's less savory side effects: digestive problems and flare-ups of skin outbreaks, likely psoriasis. Distance from family did not erase her worries. She asked Bob to check on Musy and ensure that Wally had deposited the rent on Ninth Street. The darkest demon was loneliness. She missed Bob terribly and felt lost when she didn't hear from him. She sent frequent letters, signing off, "Your Green eyes" or when fatigued, "Iguana lids." Mired as we are in today's immediate communication, it's hard to remember the traveler's sense of displacement. Aloneness can foster resilience, but Marion sought stability as much as new challenges.

Marion's Tennessee experience had resurrected her glory years as a muralist, but in Mexico, she again felt "out of tune." Mexican art trends shifted after 1940 with the end of the Lázaro Cárdenas administration. Artist José Luis

Cuevas was one of the Generación de la Ruptura (Breakaway Generation) who rebelled against the social realism of the first half of the century. Another key figure whom Marion admired, Rufino Tamayo, had returned to acclaim after living in New York. He mixed figuration and abstraction but had been rejected by the 1930s muralists because of artistic differences with Rivera.

Rivera remained a compelling presence, but Marion failed to contact him. In a bizarrely worded 1949 note, he wrote, "My Very Darling Marion, This is my first letter, naturally of love, but impersonal love, including my very personal for you. The impersonal is for permanent peace in the effort you are already sponsoring, but now as many years ago, no love realization is possible without money. So send some for the Peace Congress, which is, let us say, born broken and we have to make him rich." She likely never responded and certainly didn't send funds. In 1956, artist Philip Reisman would contact her to say that Anton Refregier suggested she might sign Rivera's seventieth-birthday telegram. Her response: "absolute no."[20]

Marion's attitude toward Rivera reflected a broader shift in her thinking. Even before she left Mexico in 1936, she glimpsed how ideologies and artistic freedom could clash. Reassessing her earlier enthusiasm for communism, she later said everyone was "very, very socially conscious. It was all over the world at that time, and we were terribly sincere and very eager to make it very clear, if we had anybody suffering in our murals, why they were suffering. . . . I no longer believe in the kind of thing I believed in then. It imposed a kind of stiff formula thinking in, let's face it, this group of what you call Stalinists at that time. The stiff, almost rigid idea of propaganda which I think was very bad for all of art at that time."[21] As Stalin's totalitarianism splintered the Left, she parted ways with the party faithful. She couldn't fathom how old friends justified support for the Soviet regime. Exceptions were Mexican friends like Pablo O'Higgins, mentor and champion of her work. She overlooked his commitment to communism.

Marion may have unfairly conflated Mexican communists with Soviet henchmen, damning Leftists of all stripes. She railed to Charles, "For the record, I decided long ago that Freud and Marx completely ruined the creative art of this century, especially Marx. I despise communism. I wish I'd never heard of it. It ruined my youthful life and talent and warped my whole approach to everything. No room here for a list of long regrets."[22]

Did she believe that? Had she abandoned hope for a socially transformative art? Marion's statement conflicts with her celebration of the heady days of hiding Communist Party papers in her Mexico City apartment. Throughout her life, she waxed nostalgic about the artistic freedom that she'd had in Mexico. Her role in one of the most exciting art developments of the twentieth century remained a source of pride.

Perhaps we all contradict ourselves in revising our histories. Maybe Marion publicly acquiesced to the story art critics and news reports created. She helped promote that persona: the gutsy, intrepid adventurer willing to climb rickety scaffolds and risk censure for her overalls. Maybe her feelings about art and communism conflated with sorrow over her unlucky marriage, retrospectively merging all that had gone wrong. In any case, she was no longer enamored of politically polemic art. Maybe she never had been. Orozco, with his rejection of mixing art and politics, had long been her hero.

On this trip to Mexico, Marion neglected to bring attention to her murals. Her friends artist Philip Reisman and his wife, Louise, traveled to Taxco in August 1956 while Marion was in Oaxaca. They reported on the mural in the Hotel Taxqueño that had catapulted her to fame. It looked wonderful but needed repair and her signature. The current hotel owner was excited and surprised to discover that the artist was a gringa. Louise wrote, "We told him to tell people you were a prominent, talented, beautiful gringa!"[23] But instead of returning to Taxco to fix the problems, Marion headed home.

Mexico didn't deliver what Marion hoped for, but Bob buoyed her through. When she had problems getting subjects to pose, he encouraged her to keep going. He wrote almost daily to his "sweetheart green eyes" at her shifting addresses. When she didn't hear from him, she sent frantic notes to her family. Calls from Grace and Wally soon flooded Bob. Why hadn't he written? For all the Greenwoods' faults, the clan rallied for one of their own.

Dealing with the family tortured Bob. He'd been to Lester's place on Library Lane in Woodstock, which he suggested renaming "Gin Lane." Musy looked ancient but "could moan on for another ten years."[24] The house problems, including contaminated well water, multiplied. Bob enlisted Wally to help with the family in order to guard time for his writing.

Bob often berated himself for idleness, but he was a disciplined writer. Marion applauded his two thousand words a day that her absence made possible. He sketched out ideas for novels, including one on his life as a conscientious objector. He regularly sent plays and stories to magazines including the *New Yorker*. During the 1950s, he wrote synopses for the Fawcett Publication magazine *Gabby Hayes Western* (1948–1957). The stories paid homage to character actor George Francis "Gabby" Hayes, sidekick to cowboy star Hopalong

Cassidy. Bob feared running out of ideas for "Gabby" but kept digging for new angles. His greatest success would arrive with his 1960s young adult biographies. In the meantime, he read work for aspiring authors.

Bob and Marion struggled with inadequate workspace. Their Ninth Street New York apartment and the Woodstock house were simply too small. She disturbed his work, while he acknowledged that he also interrupted hers: "You were just too sweet not to complain enough about it. Imagine my Marion not complaining enough about something!"[25] Her grumbling did not diminish his love.

Soon, the couple faced greater financial strain. In 1959, Marion broke her hip in an auto accident. The repercussions would later haunt her. Bob's loving attentions, provided despite his bum knee from the accident, sped her recovery. He'd helped her face health problems before, cooking a salt-free diet for her high blood pressure. "If it wasn't for Bob, I'd never be able to eat right," she told Charles.[26] Bob did house repairs and stabilized her life. He was, as she'd once said, "someone to watch over me." Any anxiety over their age difference disappeared.

By the mid-1950s, Marion and Charles reached a truce after years of postdivorce tension. They traded stories about mutual friends like Julian and Juliette Huxley and the art crowd Charles had enjoyed. She congratulated him on his theater success and asked about Mair Lewis, Charles's Welsh-born new wife. Marion wrote about the willow tree that he'd planted outside the Woodstock house. In earlier letters, the tree had represented bittersweet longing for what might have been. The balm of her relationship with Bob soothed that yearning and her anger.

Despite greater peace in her personal life, Marion still agonized over her art. One night, she stayed up until one o'clock devouring a novel, *The Horse's Mouth* (1944), by Anglo-Irish writer Joyce Cary. The story follows an artist, Gulley Jimson, whose popularity plummets when Impressionism displaces his realistic style. He never stops painting, stealing so he can eat. At the novel's end, he ponders his lack of regret about his sacrifice of family and stability to pursue art. The story called to Marion, but at least she hadn't been driven to theft.

By 1959, despite feeling out of step artistically, she was hardly in Jimson's position. The spring brought more recognition. In May, the National Association of Women Artists granted her an "Award of Merit for Outstanding Contribution to the Arts." The acknowledgment focused on her oil paintings, which thrilled Marion, having long struggled to stop overworking them.

Even more exciting, Marion was elected to the National Academy of Design.

She was not the first woman to join that world of august men. Eliza Great-orex garnered that initial spot in 1869, but men still dominated. The academy asked chosen artists to donate one of their works. Marion's was a self-portrait. Against a green-brown background, her right upper torso turns. A smudge of red-orange under her lower eyelid draws the viewer to the mischievous look in her large eyes. Ochre edges one prominent cheekbone. Elongated fingers hold a cigarette to slightly pursed lips. Her expression and arched eyebrows offer a dare.

This was the painting that stopped sculptor Judith Shea in her tracks. In 2012, she curated for *Her Own Style: An Artist's Eye,* one of the academy's member-organized shows. Combing the archives' vast possibilities, she fixed on women's self-portraits. "Women were so honored to be elected in those early years. This was their shot at being remembered," she said. "The more independent and flaunting they were—that was what interested me." For Shea, the way Marion held a cigarette showed her unconventionality. She imagined Marion "portraying herself like a Hollywood head shot, there's both defiance and humor in it. She's not unaware of the effect. It's a wonderfully outrageous stance."[27]

That outrageous stance characterized much of Marion's life. The cigarette in her self-portrait was likely the Camel that she lit up in defiance of Bob's brother-in-law's dictate that she smoke his brand. That stance reappeared at the 1959 Guggenheim Museum opening when Marion dripped her cocktail onto connoisseurs below to protest the art world's obsession with abstract (male) art. We're back to the appreciative comment by Marion's Knoxville friend Martha Osborne. Marion saw two chairs in a painting as making love because she was just "like that." Being "like that" drove success in ways not always measured by critics' responses or astronomical sales.

If Marion was "out of tune" with art trends, she kept time with an internal rhythm. Early on, she had learned to trust her own judgment. When an interviewer confessed that she didn't understand art, Marion replied, "Who does? Art is only communication. If you like a work you like it. If you don't, it's not 'good art' for you. Who's going to tell you you're wrong? Certainly not the person who painted it."[28] Marion's stubborn belief in her own definition of "good art" sustained her amid the art world's many upheavals.

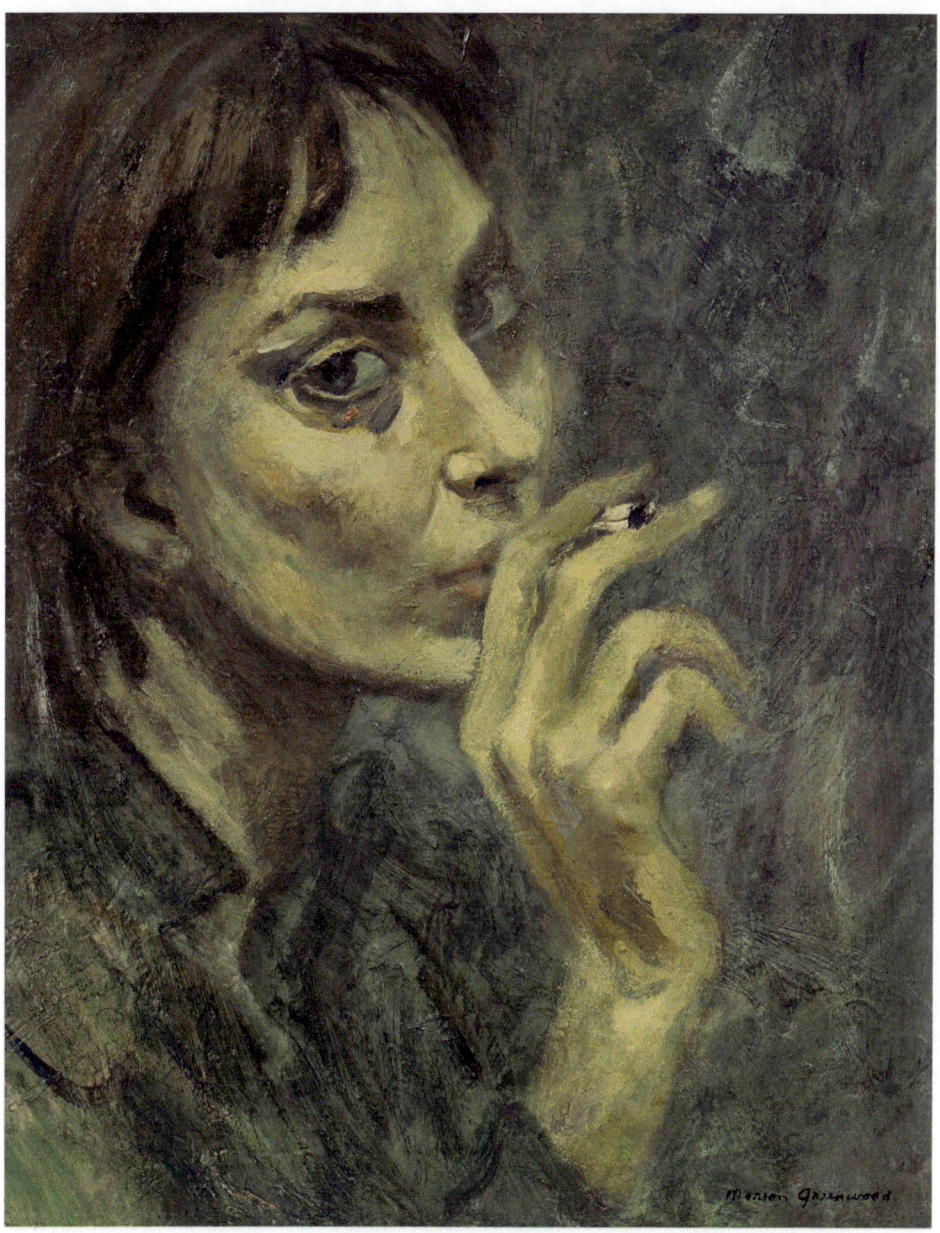

FIGURE 25.1. *Self-Portrait*, by Marion Greenwood, 1954. (Photograph © the estate of Marion Greenwood; courtesy of the National Academy of Design, New York/Bridgeman Images.)

CHAPTER 26

Tributes to Women

ON A MOONLIT NIGHT IN JUNE 1962, MARION RELAXED IN AN IBIZA PEN-
sion perched above Roman ruins. Turquoise waters, bougainvillea dripping
over white walls, dinners with wine, and a view of fishing boats headed out
to sea—Ibiza was the heavenly final leg of a seven-week stay on the Iberian
Peninsula.

After a visit to Nazaré, a fishing village on Portugal's Atlantic coast, Marion
spent two days in Lisbon. In Madrid, she visited the Prado and Goya's tomb
while staying with artist Federico Castellón. He and his wife lived in New York
but were back in his natal country when Marion arrived. She'd remained friends
with the surrealist painter since their 1940 Yaddo residency. The trio planned a
sketching trip around the country, but when it fell through, she headed for Ibiza.[1]

The shimmering island off the coast of Spain was a global hot spot. In 1955,
Spain joined the United Nations, ending their postwar isolation. Economic reforms boosted development and tourism. Hippies, that new class of bohemians,
flocked to Ibiza from all over Europe. Long-haired, sandaled figures draped in
beads walked alongside Spanish women in long black dresses, lingering symbols of Franco's oppressive regime.

Marion reveled in the sun-drenched setting. Two English girls and their boy-
friends escorted her to the beach. She ran into young Germans and Americans,
free-spirited couples darting about the island in old cars and scooters, babies
in tow. Amid the novelty, some unwelcome familiarity: "Awful Washington
Square types," a variant on Marion's usual objection to the Greenwich Villager
hangers-on. Some of the creative types were equally unimpressive, especially
one writer "who thinks he's James Joyce."[2] She charmed him, as she did so many

others, and he paid for dinner. When Marion was lonely, she simply headed to an outdoor café or one of the popular bars with her sketchbook.

Like Mexico in the 1930s, Spain was cheap. Marion fantasized about returning with Bob. They could rent a house for twelve dollars a month and hire help for fifteen cents an hour. Sharing the experience would have changed Marion's usual travel pattern: initial ecstasy turned to loneliness, sometimes accompanied by danger. She fought off a man who attacked her one night as she returned to her hotel a little drunk.

Marion sometimes skipped scheduled stops when travel reality didn't match expectations. She headed from Ibiza to Madrid but cut her Paris visit. Money was short and she missed Bob. Arranging to meet him in New York on July 10, she wrote, "What would I do without my darling to come home to. All I see are happy couples, even the beatniks."[3]

Even truncated, the Iberian trip spurred productivity. Her new paintings and sketches refocused attention on women and children. The blue-gray wash of *Fish Market, Nazaré* depicts two women buying and selling, a child wedged between them. *Lisbon Woman* features a melancholy beauty in a dark coat and hood with wounded eyes. *Woman of Nazaré* (also called *Iberian Motif*) captures a figure straining to pull a twisted net into a boat. The turquoise tones blend her into the sea beyond. In *Night Song*, a young singer with flowing dark hair strums a guitar, eyes closed and mouth open. Her doleful expression suggests Fado, Portugal's mournful music that evokes the sea, the struggles of the poor, and nostalgia for lost time. Marion would have loved Fado. So Proustian! In her Iberian paintings, nearly all the women are unsmiling. Was this a sign of postwar hardships or an undercurrent in Marion's life?

The year before she headed to Europe had been cataclysmic. On August 7, 1961, Musy died. Marion had groused about caring for her mother through a ten-year slide into dementia, but Musy emotionally anchored her baby. Marion and Bob had last seen her at the Hadler Nursing Home in Kingston a few hours before her death. When Irwin called with the news, Marion fell apart. In keeping with the Greenwood tradition of confusing love with combat, fights erupted between Marion, Irwin, and Grace. Bob witnessed the fallout, interpreting Marion's anger as protection against grief. Irwin's ever-practical wife, Jessica, organized the funeral, which Wally seems to have skipped. Bob summed up the view of many who loved Marion: Musy, this "daft, interesting and terrible character" was now gone, but "her dismal effects will go marching on for a number of years."[4]

The same year as Musy's death, Marion painted a dark self-portrait. Cavernous cheeks frame a set mouth and unfocused eyes. How much did that image reflect the loss of Musy? What did family mean to Marion? She cursed them; she couldn't escape them. They were bound at the root, especially Marion and Musy. She once sent her mother a Christmas card that read, "Merry Xmas and 10,000 Happy New Years—Yours for eternity and then some, Just a few thousand years, then we shall once more be together!" She signed off, "Your Golden Heart."[5]

Given her family, it's unsurprising that Marion had mixed feelings about having children. Her youthful "no" turned to a middle-aged "maybe," then to an occasionally proffered "yes." At least she claimed to be open. Did she fully consider the financial and emotional cost of having a child? Perhaps the disappearance of that possibility joined her divorce in regret's shadow.

Marion's correspondence with Verna Carleton, who married Mexican physician Ignacio Millan and moved to Mexico, chart the friends' conflicted emotions about art and family. After Marion left Mexico City in 1936, Verna acknowledged the sacrifices that women make to be artists. "No one realizes better than I do," she wrote, "the tragedy of your life, your aloneness, your terrific struggle to maintain your integrity as an artist." She added, "the only thing I ask is that you realize, for once, that other people suffer and face terrifying tragedies also."[6]

Verna described the sacrifice of her career and US citizenship when she married Millan. She would later succeed as a writer, particularly with *Mexico Reborn* (1939), which mixed personal stories with analysis of Mexican politics. But no crystal ball predicted that achievement. At the time of her letter, Verna envied what Marion had: devotion to her art.

Verna next reported that another friend, Sylvia, now had a baby. "Of all the dirty tricks to play on anyone. I feel just the way you did about Grace MacFarland. Something has gone forever that cannot be replaced." Grace, "Mac" to Marion's "Zaddo" during their Taos adventure, had moved to California and had children. The friends stayed connected, but Verna clearly knew of some change in their relationship. In a surprise turn, Verna's next missive confesses that she, too, is pregnant. "Please do not faint . . . nor bawl me out," she wrote, promising she would never bore Marion with her child's cute sayings. Marion's papers contain no response to Verna's announcement.

The topic of children came up with Charles as well. Until the 1960s, he held off sending photos of his wife, Mair, their daughter, Alyn, and son, Robert Kerry. Charles feared his newly created family might trigger pain for Marion.

Instead, she expressed interest in Mair, the children, and their imminent move to Ireland. She asked about Mair's children's books and their shared interest in spiritual matters—Mair's transcendental meditation to Marion's Theosophy. Charles inquired about Bob's writing. His *Palette and Tomahawk: The Story of George Caitlin*, a biography for young adults, came out in 1962. *Kirkus Reviews* starred the book, setting Bob on a path of publication success. Three more would follow, including one about rival paleontologists, *The Dinosaur Hunters: Othniel C. Marsh and Edward D. Cope.*

Marion and Charles's letters were lively and caring, seeming to banish years of conflict. Bob's stable and nurturing presence surely prompted that change. Perhaps Marion also realized that Mair, with a steadier temperament and higher tolerance for upheaval and discomfort—they were living in a caravan—was a better match for Charles.

Some demons lingered. The funny, charming artist who magnetized people on Ibiza competed with Marion's dark 1961 self-portrait. Bob's diary is replete with reports on Marion's increased drinking, often in the context of the general zaniness of Woodstock social life.

Among the legendary party givers were investment banker Belmont Towbin and his artist wife, Phoebe. Generous supporters of the arts, their names now grace a wing of the Woodstock Artists Association and Museum. One August gathering after Marion's return from Ibiza began innocently enough. For the first hour, food and drink for sixty people flowed and the pool stayed empty. Then Ed Gilligan, a "granite domed Irish Boston writer," gave way to temptation and pushed the fully clothed artist Fletcher Martin into the pool. "Martin clambered out of the pool with his clenched cigar still clamped in his mouth, his suit clinging to him like a wet silk on Sophia Loren."[7] Martin returned the favor by sending Gilligan into the water. He emerged naked but for his tight jockey shorts, feet thrust up in the air like a cat.

Amid the drunken hilarity, it's easy to overlook the casualties. Among them were Bob and Marion's tolerance and patience with one another. Marion spent the party lounging poolside, drinking and listening to the music. An ankle injury in Spain kept her from dancing. She urged Bob to do the twist in her stead. He refused. His knee still smarted from their auto accident a few years before. Marion kept goading him. Bob's temper flared as he denounced her "bulldozer touch" and, generally, their life together. His worry about Marion's accelerating drinking vied with his deep love. Marion was equally annoyed, her joie de vivre cramped by his lack of fun.

Did Bob voice his feelings to Marion? Many people dump angst into journals, unbeknownst to partners. Whether or not they discussed squabbles, their relationship endured. Bob diffused tension with jokes. He invited their friends Adolf and Virginia Dehn to a complaint fest with "that peerless, untiring queen of complainers, M.G. and her star pupil, me."[8] Marion adeptly repeated the same complaints, whereas Bob diluted his with too much variety. Her strong voice could also bellow over his.

One legitimate source for both complainers was lack of workspace. Tensions eased when one person worked in New York City, the other in Woodstock. The light in Marion's studio was never adequate but she still went to the easel daily. During the first half of the 1960s, several group shows featured her lithographs and oils. The Milch Gallery still represented her, and her relationship with AAA blossomed when Reeves Lewenthal left in 1958. Sylvan Cole, who had run AAA's mail-order business in the 1940s, returned as director of print publication and the gallery.

Like Lewenthal, Cole was a big personality, but he and Marion were simpatico. He "reestablished AAA with great originality and farsightedness," according to print specialist Susan Teller, who worked with him for ten years. "Sylvan loved women," in a gallant, old-fashioned sort of way, she said. "He also loved artists."[9] When an aging Isabel Bishop came to the gallery, he escorted her around in courtly fashion. His attitude showed in his relationship with Marion. He admitted to being "madly in love" with her, but he also respected her and her work. At the annual AAA Christmas party, Cole assigned his shipping manager, Murray Kaplan, to keep an eye on Marion and get her into a cab when she drank too much.[10]

Cole heavily promoted Marion's prints. In 1965, he arranged for her inclusion in a show at the University of Maine in Orono. This was her first print retrospective, with work from 1929 to 1965. Cole called her lithographs "vigorous yet sensitive and play one great theme capable of infinite variations—the diversity of humanity."[11] Images begun as paintings often transferred to prints, making them more accessible.

Marion described her creative process as a response to particular settings and people. Whether working with wet plaster, a bamboo stick on rice paper, oil on canvas, or a lithography stone, the artist's "ingenuity is excited by the very limitation of the medium. At the same time, my strongest motivation seems to be deeply involved with the human element."[12]

Marion stayed in the public eye through the 1960s. For an exhibit at Bard

College in 1963–1964, Anton Refregier praised her commitment to realism despite prevailing trends. In 1964, she won the Lillian Cotton Award from Audubon Artists for *Gazing Children*. The portrait, exhibited at the National Academy of Design, featured three children of mixed ages and ethnicities. She would soon repeat that mix in her major work of the decade. In the spring of 1965, Syracuse University offered her a visiting appointment in their mural program for the following summer.

Dean Lawrence Schmeckebier of the Art Department announced the decision: "Without question, Marion Greenwood is the most distinguished woman mural painter in America today."[13] She was the program's sixth artist but first woman. Refregier, among others, had preceded her. The Orono print show was the closest to a retrospective exhibit she'd had. Now her choice of the mural's theme and name, *Tribute to Woman*, offered a different review of her career.

Marion embraced working with three student apprentices. She hoped to infuse their practice with understanding of how form and content fused. The obsession with being avant-garde, she believed, had soured their passion for finding their true voices. Students shared her enjoyment and appreciation. One young mother about to complete her degree said that her weeks "with Miss Greenwood were among the most valuable of her college career."[14] Another apprentice was a graduate student who'd painted murals at a local high school. The third, studying art education, sketched Marion as she painted. She listened attentively to the students' ideas as she chain-smoked and played with the gold chain on her glasses. Bob came from Woodstock to assist.

Marion worked on the cartoons for months, then painted daily and on weekends through July and into August. The oil-on-canvas mural filled a square approximately twelve-by-thirteen feet. The theme seemed perfect for the setting of Slocum Hall, which also housed the home economics program. *Tribute to Woman* pulled images from more than thirty years of global treks. Disconsolate faces of women suffering from war and famine are absent. This group stands side by side in solidarity.

Marion stated that she celebrated a "variety of women here, so different in age, race, occupation, privilege, and hence the indication both in a symbolic central figure and elsewhere of the eternal role of woman as the bearer of life."[15] To the left, a Chinese water carrier rises above a blonde teenager with a guitar at her feet. On the lower right, a Portuguese woman reels in fish. Black and Mexican mothers cradle children. Two figures tower above the others: A white woman with flowing hair holding a baby—the model provided by one

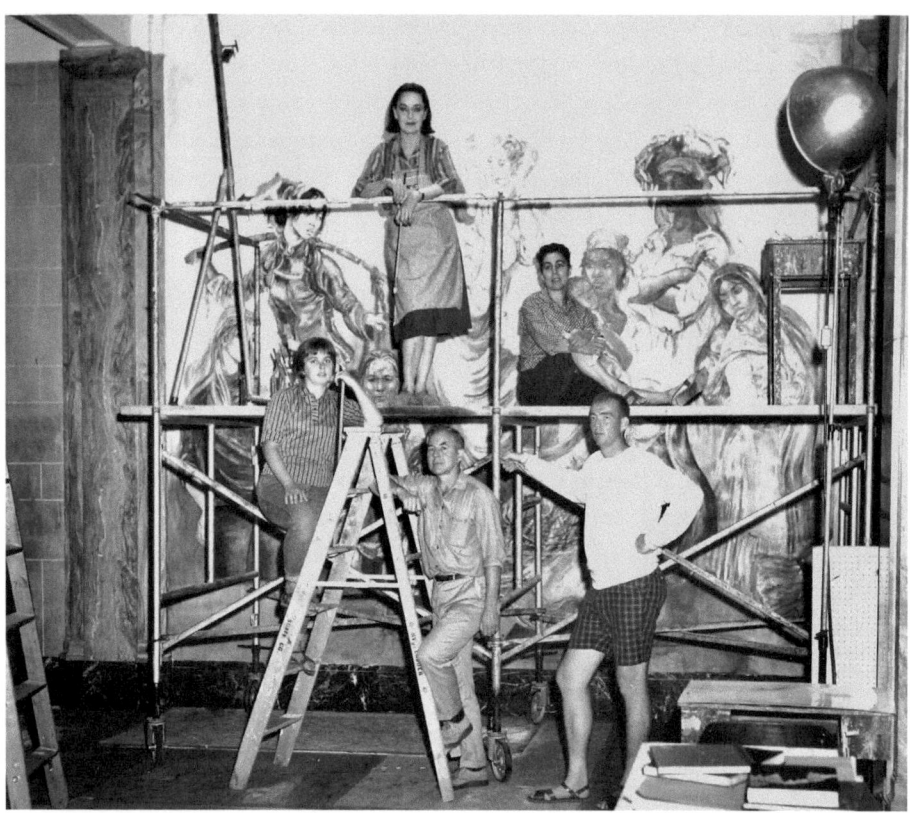

FIGURE 26.1. Marion Greenwood with assistants and Robert Plate at Syracuse University, 1965. (Photograph © and courtesy of the estate of Marion Greenwood.)

of Marion's student assistants. Of equal height is a Caribbean caryatid, the draped female figures that function as building supports in Greek-style architecture. The figures glow under green and brown earth tones on a burnt sienna background.

The university held a formal dedication in November. *Tribute to Woman,* said the dean, was the mural that created the most widespread interest among other artists and among the students, faculty, and friends of the university. At the ceremony, Marion expressed gratitude for her freedom to choose the theme. She hoped viewers would create their own interpretations.

What was hers? How did Marion conceive of "bearing life"? Some figures hold children. She may have intended artistic creation as a kind of birth, yet only the teenager with a guitar at her feet suggests that vision. Given her correspondence with Verna Carleton, Charles, and others over the question of children, what did she want to convey?

The second wave of feminism was ascendant. Betty Friedan's *The Feminist Mystique* (1963) had sold more than a million copies. The 1965 Supreme Court ruling in *Griswold vs. Connecticut* guaranteed married couples the right to contraception; unmarried women would wait until 1972. The *Griswold* repudiation of Comstock came too late for Marion but changed many women's lives. Lawsuits challenged gender inequality in the workplace. This was especially important for longtime workers, especially women of color. Yet Marion, too, had faced discrimination as the teaching jobs she sought went to men.

Whether or not she embraced the label, Marion embodied feminist principles. At fifty-six, she had fought from the age of fifteen to be taken seriously as a woman artist. Throughout her life, she mourned Musy's limited opportunities. En route to the Art Students League, she watched women on the streets demanding birth control and the vote. She traveled the world alone, fighting fear, loneliness, and attempted assaults. Women's enormous strength as well as their suffering deeply affected her work.

In an interview, Marion said, "A mural is a public endeavor. It doesn't belong to you. It's not like doing a painting in your studio—it's a communal thing."[16] Her statement would prove true in ways she did not foresee. *Tribute to Woman*, like her Tennessee mural, ignited controversy. In a student publication, a graduate student railed against the "'lovely' romanticized white 'lady'" at the center. "Her Madonna-like pose employs all of the trite techniques and cliches of middle class public media from comic books to 'The Ladies Home Journal.'"[17] Another woman, Mrs. Lillian Homen Mohr, retaliated. She found the white woman with her baby "innocuously beautiful and seemingly capable of little more than pride in showing off her offspring." The other figures, in contrast, looked as though "their reproductive function is just one facet of a continual struggle with life." The mural, she wrote, "excites the imagination more than the blots and drips, the pop and op, of much modern art."[18] Marion must have loved the takedown of abstraction as well as the recognition of her intent.

The controversy would reignite. In December 1982, the mural was vandalized and then removed. The paintings of three other muralists, including Anton Refregier, were also put into storage or covered over.[19] Marion would never learn of the destruction. She left campus satisfied but determined that she was finished with murals.

Had Marion wanted to climb another scaffold, it soon became impossible.

On June 6, 1967, she was driving home from a laundromat in Woodstock. Leaning over to rearrange the laundry on the passenger seat, she plowed into a tree. She fractured her ankle, knee, and hip, the same one she'd broken nearly a decade before. Her right leg was in traction for weeks, and her hip required a lengthy and expensive surgery. Infection set in. "I've been through agony," she wrote to Charles, "but most of all, I feel guilty about ruining Bob's life. He's got no writing done and of course, I've done nothing but a few sketches now and then." That she produced anything while recovering seems extraordinary. So, too, does Bob's steady support. "There is nothing to do but endure," he told his brother Bill. "He has compassion," Marion wrote of Bob, "the only noble emotion of humanity as far as I can see."[20]

Marion gave up the Ninth Street studio in New York City. Ascending four flights of stairs was out of the question, as was paying rent. Back taxes and hospital bills accrued. News of the accident spread quickly to art world friends and colleagues. The National Academy of Design bought an additional painting for their collection. The Art Students League raised about $2,000. Sylvan Cole of Associated American Artists sent a letter with a check: "Tell Marion she still looks beautiful, and we all still love her." The Artists' Fellowship sent $500.[21]

Crises reveal true friends. Grace MacFarland, "Mac," had stayed close to Marion despite their divergent life paths. She called immediately when she heard about the accident. Marion's voice, which Gladys Brodsky once compared with Tallulah Bankhead's, "was the same as ever—strong and positive and full of warmth and affection. It is in truth the mark of a great soul." She commiserated about the hardships in Marion's life. "I am baffled why more suffering was due you who have already had so much."[22] In a bittersweet nod to adulthood, Grace asked whether she should use "Marion" instead of "Zaddo." Their nicknames embodied youthful willingness to risk all for art and adventure.

Artist Georges Schreiber and his wife, Lilly, sent joking but loving notes. In a Christmas greeting, Georges recounted a dream where Marion was running after him. "You were griping, griping, griping! 'My God, Marion,' I said, 'You are your real self again, walking and running and swearing.'"[23] Adolf and Virginia Dehn suggested a special surgeon and a place to stay in the city. Artist Fletcher Martin framed one of Marion's paintings from the Woodstock house for a show in upstate New York. Support flowed in for months.

Bob's family members wrote and called. Gladys and Bud loaned Bob a car to visit Marion in the hospital. There are few records of her family's reactions. Lester had moved to California. Wally was living in a retirement center. The once dapper Broadway dancer occasionally performed for other residents. "I made a decided hit singing 'In Old New York,'" he wrote to Lester. In a possibly delusional addition, he claimed that another resident, Caroline, "crafty, cunning like a female fox," was pursuing him. He ended with his signature formality, "W. J. Greenwood."[24]

Grace apologized for a delayed response due to vexing house problems. Her advice mixed Musy's esoteric beliefs with Norman Vincent Peale's still popular *The Power of Positive Thinking* (1952): "Try to keep a constructive and cheerful state of mind as this, too, is more important than you may think." Grace added a quote from a book on healing: "Do not hold before your mind's eye an image of yourself as weak, ill, or helpless. Identify yourself *with yourself* as a strong, well, perfect man or woman."[25]

By the winter of 1968, Marion could hobble around on crutches. She and Bob vacationed in Florida. By summer, she had resumed making lithographs in Woodstock. As the year ended, she could bathe and dress herself in a triumphant return to independence.

The following winter, she and Bob drove to Mexico. They chased better weather, but Marion always pursued something deeper in Mexico. She loved witnessing indigenous life in rural communities, as she had on her first trip in 1933. The cities were another story. The assault of cars had so polluted Mexico City that Marion and Bob couldn't see beyond a few blocks from their hotel.

After three days, they decamped to Cuernavaca for a planned extended stay. "It was hatred at first sight," Bob wrote to Bud and Gladys. "I have never so quickly, completely, and thoroughly despised a place."[26] He condemned the rich gringos and Mexican businessmen as hypocrites. They espoused communist beliefs from behind high walls, protected from the town's squalor. Bob was grateful to finally see Marion's murals in Mexico City, Morelia, and Taxco. The Hotel Taxqueño had become a convent school, but the mural was intact.

Marion and Bob spent the final three weeks at Lake Chapala near Guadalajara, a popular enclave for foreigners. In a big, light-filled room, Marion sketched and Bob wrote. She abandoned one crutch during long walks in the sun.

The Mexico sojourn didn't revitalize Marion in ways she'd hoped. She didn't share Bob's enthusiasm for the murals. A decade of painting walls, she believed, had delayed her command of easel portraits and entry to galleries. She might have simply regretted loss of her earlier confidence. A return to places central to one's youth often disappoints. Marion's disenchantment reflected age and inevitable loss. Several of her Mexican companions were gone, including José

Gutierrez, the plasterer on her murals. In 1968, she lost her lifelong friend Adolf Dehn. Others followed, among them Josie. She died in January as Bob and Marion were leaving for Mexico. She told Charles, "The news left me quite cold, as you can imagine."[27]

After Mexico, Marion's travel urge subsided, partly due to her sustained injuries. Changes in Woodstock also uncovered subjects in her own backyard. Classical music had always been central to the town's identity, but in the 1960s, a new crop of musicians and visual artists arrived. In 1963, Suze Rotolo, then Bob Dylan's girlfriend, studied with artist Arnold Blanch. Dylan had visited earlier, but he moved to Woodstock in 1966 for two and a half years. The Band, Janis Joplin, Jimi Hendrix, and their attendant groupies followed. Another student of Blanch, Bruce Dorfman, taught Dylan painting. The two collaborated on a red, white, and blue image of a young hippie to promote the 1969 Woodstock Music and Art Fair. Despite the misnomer—the festival happened in nearby Bethel— the now iconic event put one of the country's oldest art colonies on the map. Later that summer, Bob and Marion sat in the Woodstock Green watching an array of colorful characters with wild hair and clothing float by. Marion said, "My God, I've traveled all over the world—and here it is, at last, right at home."[28]

Marion and Bob began a house remodel to create more workspace. Even with physical limitations, she was producing lithographs and paintings. When the work bedeviled her, she'd switch from painting to prints or put away the canvas temporarily. Pop art, minimalism, and other trends now vied with Abstract Expressionism amid the 1960s explosive cultural shifts. Marion went regularly to galleries in Woodstock and New York City. "I'd come back very stimulated," she said in a 1969 interview. Yet she always returned to portraits. "I'm just myself again. I can't help it!" She bemoaned the destruction of "the human thing in art. I think it's all very decadent. But I think of art in a long-term basis which is why I've never been concerned about being in fashion."[29]

A student once asked Bob how Marion worked. "Hard," he said. "Every day." She could no longer maintain eight-to-ten-hour workdays, but nothing kept Marion from the studio. There, sitting before her easel, she became "just myself again."

CHAPTER 27

"The Most Alive Person I've Ever Known"

THREE YEARS AFTER HER ACCIDENT, MARION AND BOB WERE POISED TO enter a new era. Westbeth Artists Housing in Greenwich Village offered them a spacious apartment in the soon-to-open complex—an exciting base for reentering the city's art scene. They had finally resolved problems with water and heat in their Woodstock house. Their remodel created huge windows in Marion's studio, achieving the balance of light she'd wanted for years. She began experimenting with a looser, more expressive painting style. Bob was working on a novel based on his experience as a conscientious objector during World War II. At a Labor Day party, everyone exclaimed over Marion's recovery and enduring beauty. "Not bad for a woman of sixty," Bob wrote to friends.[1]

On September 2, 1969, Marion was at work in her studio, bent over a lithograph of African American dancer and anthropologist Pearl Primus. She suddenly complained to Bob of a terrible headache. The world went dark. An ambulance rushed her in a coma to the Kingston Hospital where doctors diagnosed a cerebral hemorrhage. A few days later, she was transferred to the Albany Medical Center. Bob moved there to be close to her during a three-month stay. As the days ticked by, costs skyrocketed. Marion's Blue Cross insurance through Artists Equity was due to run out in a few months. Bob tamped down emotional and financial panic.

He sent the first of numerous eloquent requests for help to Raymond Kinstler at the Artists Fellowship. A check for $900 soon arrived, with the promise of $150 of monthly support until April 1, 1970.[2] Bob ranged between hope that such need was wildly improbable and a sinking feeling that it would not be enough.

By late September, Bob leaned toward the wildly improbable. Marion's disorientation and passivity began to lift. Bob tested her mental state by declaring her work superior to German expressionist Käthe Kollwitz, an artist Marion esteemed. She found inspiration in Kollwitz's depictions of human suffering and the effects of war, especially on women and children. Bob's comment stirred Marion to declare, "That's because I have more emotion to dispense." Her lifelong goal was to suffuse art with her own emotions and to evoke a response in viewers. Perhaps her subconscious finally recognized this attempt to connect as her contribution, rather than a single, defining style. Gladys visited with Bud, who told Marion he was stealing all her brushes. "She said 'whoa,'" Gladys recalled. "He knew what would get to her."[3] The doctors predicted Marion could move to a nursing facility, then home.

Optimism proved short-lived. The next day, the aneurysm leaked blood. Two more hemorrhages followed. Bob searched in vain for a nursing home. The wait for a bed was several months to a year. A hospital administrator finally wrote to the Ulster County Department of Social Services calling for help with "this desperate situation." He strengthened the case for assistance by adding, "Miss Greenwood has no known relatives."[4] Marion and Bob had never married, and her siblings clearly could not offer help. In December, Bob moved Marion to a nursing home in Kingston. It was dismal but the best option.

Bud and Gladys loaned Bob their car so he could visit Marion daily. He maneuvered around feeding tubes to massage her hands and exercise her limbs, interrupted when the nurses came every two hours to turn her in bed. Her hair was beginning to gray against her pale, beautiful face.

At home in his solitude, Bob replayed loving phone messages Marion had sent after her 1967 accident. His journal chronicled a growing anguish. On New Year's Day, 1970, when he got her to smile, he nearly burst into tears. "The smile was so pitiful, mouth open and slack."[5] Still, it was forward movement. He went to a party that night at Bud's studio to cautiously celebrate.

Reasons for jubilance dimmed. Throughout January 1970, Bob recorded Marion's demise. "M weak and drowsy. Threw up her jello water again this morning." "My darling Marion/My green eyes/My beloved pest," he wrote, tortured by seeing her "bruised brain, numbed tongue . . . pinioned like a butterfly between your life and death." "Oh my darling Marion, I anoint you with lotion, seek to contact your mysterious mind . . . but I know it is over."[6] He began to pray that she would slip away. If she didn't, he pondered how to enact a promise to her: that he would not let her live in mindless dependence. She had feared the senility that claimed both her parents well before their deaths. If necessary, Bob would write to Charles Fenn for help. Marion sometimes mentioned methods he'd picked up in the OSS.

In late January, Marion was moved to the Ulster County Infirmary. Another horrific setting with awful roommates: a plump grandmother who scolded her companions in Norwegian and a woman who howled, "Mama! I want my Mama!"[7] Bob alternated between compassion for these trapped women, longing for Marion, and flight from the "bureaucratic bastards" who pursued him for medical payments.

Friends and supporters, the National Institute of Arts and Letters, and the Artists' Fellowship kept Bob and Marion from financial ruin. On February 11, Bob wrote to Raymond Kinstler for more help. He listed the meagre income from sales of Marion's existing prints and paintings. These paled against current bills: the cost of ambulances, a dizzying array of medical specialists and facilities, dues to Artists Equity, and overdue taxes. Bob held back money for the burial, which he guessed was not far off. A worst fate would be Marion's lingering in what he regarded "as the ultimate in wartime horror—a basket case." He concluded the letter with, "And so, downhearted at this tragic and premature closing scene of a beautiful woman and splendid artist, I labor—somewhat muddle-headedly I fear—to present the accounts herewith. In Marion's name, I assure you of deepest gratitude."[8]

On February 19, Marion's temperature rose to 104. Bob expected he would be prepared, even grateful, for her death. Yet as her breathing grew labored, he raced to the car to collapse in sobs, then drove "foolishly fast." The next day, he arrived at two in the afternoon to find her gasping "like a poor, stranded fish, open-mouthed. . . . God, what a fighter! As she fought in life, she fought for it." Bob watched her struggle for nearly three hours, panting and exhausted. "At 4:45, my darling Marion was gone."[9]

Bob's world collapsed. Some days he could hardly get out of bed. "If you were here—you might be cooing to me, 'come to bedsie,' ever hungry for affection, ever ready for sex. Or dying for coffee, toast, egg, orange juice. How you loved to eat! Much more than I."[10] Once when Marion fretted to Charles that she was fat, he chastised her for eating too much. Bob envied her appetites. Awakening to a beautiful spring day made him miss Marion more intensely. For anyone, the death of an intimate partner creates a "frightful emptiness."

Losing a person as vibrant and exuberant as Marion left Bob feeling half alive. He struggled to fathom that she did not exist: "The most alive person I've ever known, dead."[11]

Bob ignored that Marion had sometimes driven him crazy. The liberation from anxiety and uncertainty that he expected never arrived. He chastised himself for "sloth," for not earning more, for not beating back the wolf that had long hovered at their door. At fifty-one, he faced that Marion had been "the central fact and influence and even meaning of my life, and now she, and they are gone."[12] He gave away armloads of her clothes, unable to bear the lingering scent of her body, powder, and perfume.

Bob pored over Marion's old letters, especially moved by those from Mexico—"touching, youthful letters so often to her mother, full of love and concern for that dizzy old bitch, and of excitement about Taxco and her first mural there." He found missives from scores of besotted men. There were wannabe lovers, "a mixed bunch—artists, writers, musicians, businessmen—of course they were all dying to get in bed with her or even just to be with her. Some capitulated without shame, like hungry spaniels, squirmed like worms, literally groveled. Others poured out passionate poetry." He made lists of former paramours to contact: "her first *real* lover," Chilean writer Armando Zegri, Isamu Noguchi, and Joe Pollet, among others.[13]

When he felt brave, Bob scaled the mountain of paperwork. He made lists of Marion's prints that might sell to offset medical bills. Death notices went to old friends like Grace MacFarland ("Mac"), Pablo O'Higgins, and Jamie Plenn in Mexico. To Charles Fenn, he detailed the six-month ordeal, summing up with, "Bitter ending—but despite tragedies, a wonderful life."[14] That anodyne sign-off belied the depth of his despair.

The supportive letters that had streamed in after Marion's accident three years before now turned to a sea of condolence. June Sandler, who had collected Marion's paintings and prints with her deceased husband, Marc, wrote to Bob, "We shared a great love and admiration for her. She was the most beautiful woman I have ever known."[15] She sent the cache of publicity they'd saved about Marion and her work.

Then there was Marion's family. Lester was in California. Perhaps he'd stopped drinking and turned his life around. If so, Marion would have celebrated. Irwin had died two months before Marion's hemorrhage, leaving Jessie a widow. Bob had to deal with the remaining siblings, Wally and Grace. Marion had not seen them much in recent years. Bob assured Grace that her sister had dearly loved her; she especially treasured their youthful adventures. To keep Grace from feeling sidelined and jealous, Marion always downplayed her accomplishments in letters to her sister. Bob wrote, "Only somebody who knew the Greenwoods and their ferocious emotional needs and relationships, could understand M's letters."[16]

Grace's husband, Rollin Crampton, had died a month before Marion. Doris Lee and other friends tried to help Grace with the will, but she seemed too manic to focus. According to Bob, she believed Rollin had been in tune with the occult. She wanted to keep him on ice for three days to prepare him for the next life.[17]

During stable periods, Grace would remain a productive artist. But in the immediate aftermath of Rollin's and Marion's deaths, her grief took tragic form. Bob might have seen it coming. Irwin's widow, Jessie, had warned him. Based on a conversation with Grace, she wrote, "She is very reasonable at times but watch out for fangs." Those soon appeared in Grace's verbal public assaults on Bob. At Deanie's Restaurant in Woodstock one night, her mudslinging was so vicious that Bob's friends refused to repeat her comments. Jessie, a stabilizing force in the family, relayed tentative plans to travel somewhere with Grace the following year. Mexico was one option. "I'd be happy if it worked out," Bob wrote to Jessie. "Still—remember the fangs."[18]

Grace staged a standoff on the will, stalling Bob's efforts to have her and Wally, who was living in Croton-on-Hudson, sign off before probate. The will clearly stipulated that Bob would inherit Marion's few possessions. Marion had cautioned Bob that if she died first, beware of her sister. Grace tried to further punish Bob with detailed memories of Marion's affairs—all of which Bob knew about in even greater detail.[19] Both siblings eventually cooperated on the will.

After Marion died, numerous women pursued Bob. Every encounter left him conflicted: "Marion, there is no competition for you in my heart. There can be none. I can fall in love again, yes, and honor and love another woman but it would be a woman of another species. You were a species unto yourself." He vowed to keep Marion alive through writing about her. On what would have been her sixty-first birthday on April 6, he wrote, "My extraordinary darling, I will strive to make you live again and even 10% success will be a *superb* achievement."[20]

Bob's resolve was in part redress for the paltry *New York Times* obituary of February 21. Before Marion's death, he had pulled together details of her life and work. He wanted her 1961 self-portrait included. He sent the material to Sylvan Cole of Associated American Artists, perhaps thinking an art world expert could better summarize her achievements. It's unclear who was responsible for the mix-up, but the obituary didn't make the deadline. The final text was a scant 164 words, noting a few museums that owned Marion's art, several prizes from her long list, and brief mention of her Mexican murals. Bob was furious. He wrote to Charles, "She was brushed off, inaccurately, in a few inches, less space than many a hobbyist painter gets."[21]

Bob immediately composed a letter to Emily Genauer, an art critic who had praised Marion's work: "Anton Refregier suggested that I send some material about Marion Greenwood, in the hopes that you would be able to write something about her—and rectify to some degree the appalling skimpy obituary that appeared in the *New York Times*." He added that he'd lived among artists for twenty years. None could equal Marion's "range of endeavor or commitment to art." In a three-page draft, he detailed Marion's life, her travels, and the importance of her work. Genauer may have ignored his letter or perhaps Bob never sent it.[22]

Jaime Plenn, a longtime Mexico City expat and friend to Marion and Grace, wrote an extensive and glowing obituary for the *News*, a Mexican English-language paper. The piece filled with photos of Marion and her paintings, including one with Diego Rivera and the self-portrait missing from the *New York Times*. "Everywhere she looked she saw beauty," Plenn wrote. "She enjoyed a fabulous endowment of physical attraction and superior talent. But she was not a delicate or fragile type. Her appetites—physical and esthetic—were lusty and earthy. She was a natural born Bohemian in the sense that she drove incisively to discover the essence of people, whether as painting subjects or friends. Their position, power or wealth, or lack of any of these things, were not of primary concern."[23] The two-page spread covered her personal life, global travels, and artistic philosophy; Plenn included seventeen of the many museums that owned her work. Local Hudson Valley papers also offered greater praise and more coverage than the *New York Times*. All noted her beauty as well as her achievements. In death as in life.

If Bob abandoned the letter to Genauer, it may have been due to his broader agenda of writing a novel based on her life. He made several attempts. "Where it all began" opens one sketch. Barking dogs, tile-roofed houses, narrow streets, black-eyed children, braying burros, and smoky skies from charcoal fires— these set the scene for Marion's emergence as a muralist in Mexico. Sounds "filter into the delicate perfect ear of the girl with the flawless complexion, La Gringa . . . her full-breasted chest rising and falling slowly as the sounds of

Taxco spoke to her in the night."[24] This biographical novel was intended to be the crowning achievement of Bob's life. He would get to it, he swore, once he finished his book about his conscientious objector experience during World War II. The specter of both projects hovered over him for years. He never completed either one.

On September 17, 1970, Bob and a group of friends and family made their way to the Artists Cemetery in Woodstock. In accordance with Marion's wishes, they simply toasted her at the grave site. Bob's journal is spare, describing the "small circular tin can with all that remains of my vital, green-eyed beauty" thrown into a hole in the ground.[25] He circled the entry, then moved on to quotidian matters.

Perhaps Bob went home that day to realize another of Marion's requests. She once asked him to think of her when he heard Bach pieces or Richard Strauss's "Death and Transfiguration." Strauss wrote this tone poem in 1889 to explore death and a possible life beyond. In the late nineteenth century, music offered spiritual sustenance to balance rising scientific rationalism. "Death and Transfiguration" tells the story of a dying man who devoted his life to reaching "the highest idealistic aims, maybe indeed those of an artist."[26] The haunting music reaches a crescendo as pain wracks his body and death nears. He recognizes that he hasn't realized his longing for artistic achievement. A gong's strike signals the soul's departure. Transfiguration awaits as we leave this broken world of suffering and human imperfection.

How fitting that Marion, the spiritual seeker, loved Strauss's piece. She once described to Josie her ideal state seated on a peak in the Himalayas, "having become incapable of tears, and killed out all desire, having triumphed over the painful wheel of re-birth—being and becoming."[27] How fitting that the Greenwood family gospel that art will triumph over life proved true. The elusive perfection the artist seeks arrives only with death, yet the quest forms the very definition of existence.

If there was solace to be had, perhaps Bob found it in imagining such transcendence for Marion, on a path bathed in the golden light that now, finally, flooded her studio.

CHAPTER 28

Marion Greenwood's Legacy

MARION GREENWOOD'S STAR BLAZED THROUGH THE TWENTIETH CEN-
tury. She came of age in a world on fire with revolution and creativity. The last
words of International Workers of the World "Wobbly" hero Joe Hill captured
the zeitgeist: "I have lived like an artist, and I shall die like an artist."[1] The bohemian ethos fused art, labor, and politics, igniting social transformation.

Had Marion not been an artist, her adventuresome life would still compel
our attention. She charted a path that traversed the globe, crossing cultural,
class, and racial boundaries to explore diverse people and societies. Her in-
tention as an artist was to "arouse empathy" for a range of human experience.
Some subjects were luminaries, among them anthropologist and dancer Primus Pearl, multidisciplinary musician Asadata Dafora, and dancer and chore-
ographer Martha Graham. Many were lesser-known people whom she deemed
equally important: Haitians performing Vodou rituals, Chinese workers in rice
fields and wedding celebrants on a river boat, a Portuguese woman hauling fish,
and American workers in factories and slaughterhouses. Her stunning paintings and prints garnered awards from the Carnegie Institute, the Pennsylvania
Academy of Fine Arts, the National Association of Women Artists, the National
Academy of Design, among many other honors. More than thirty international
museums own her work.

Everywhere she went, people were in thrall to her charisma and daring. Yet
loneliness and a profound sense of dislocation often accompanied her. Despite
feeling that she didn't belong, she kept searching. When she lost faith in ideologies, she held firm to the belief that something fundamental connects us across
differences. In her friend Jaime Plenn's words, "she saw beauty everywhere" but

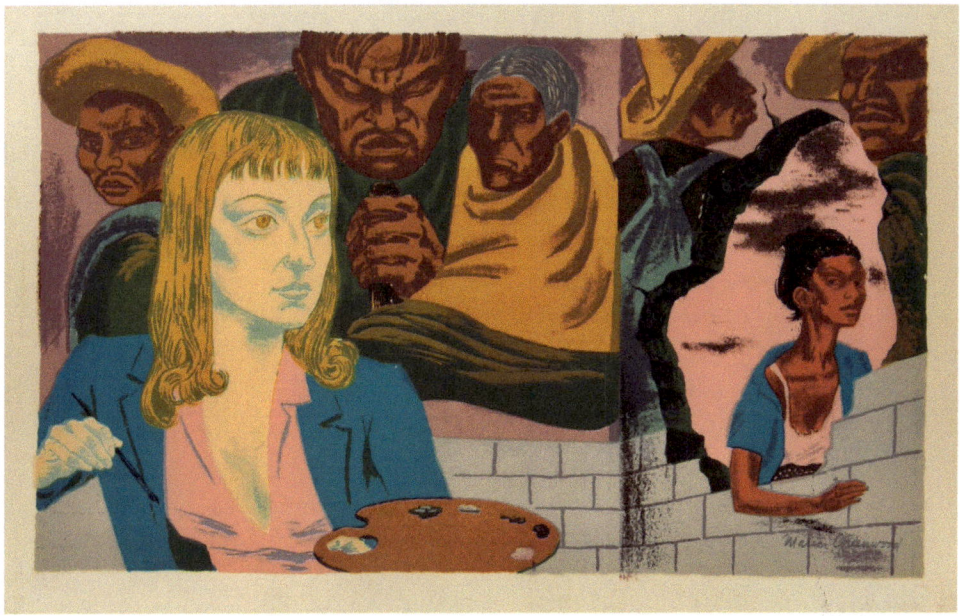

FIGURE 28.1. Harry Sternberg portrait of Marion Greenwood, 1944. (Photograph courtesy of the Estate of Harry Sternberg and the Susan Teller Gallery, New York, New York.)

also witnessed the suffering wrought by inequality, political repression, and war. She portrayed both extremes.

Today we ask different questions about cultural representation than viewers in Marion's time posed. Her Mexican murals reflect the "romantic primitivism" of the era, as did the work of other American and Mexican artists. Marion admitted to being romantic about indigenous people, but she also advocated for their inclusion in WPA mural programs. She departed from the status quo, showing Mexican women as active agents in daily labor. For her mural at the University of Tennessee-Knoxville, she included eight African American figures on an undergraduate campus with no Black students.

Today, some members of those diverse communities might reject Marion's images while others will embrace them. Although her portrayals don't always reflect the sensitivity she felt or that audiences now seek, she fought the entrenched racism of her time.

Artistic inclination and financial need both drove Marion's realist style. She longed to experiment but feared losing her art world niche. Portraits paid the rent and helped support her troubled family. They also won praise during the

1930s and 1940s. Critics applauded her ability to capture a subject's inner spirit, one "excavated from beneath surface fact."[2] When realism fell from grace, her work was deemed "documentary" or "reportorial," a mere reproduction of reality. But Marion's portraits are imbued with her subjects' emotional life and the social, often political context of the places she explored.

Marion feared being "out of tune," especially when Abstract Expressionism and Pop Art swept the art world from the 1940s into the 1960s. However, portraiture, among the oldest and most enduring forms of art, kept her "in tune" with history. People still flock to see Leonardo da Vinci's *Mona Lisa* and Diego Velázquez's *Las Meninas*. We might attribute their appeal to art tourism. The fame of "must see" paintings begets more fame. Yet portraits hold a deeply human appeal. Alison Smith, chief curator at London's National Portrait Gallery, says, "Portraiture stands apart from other genres of art as it marks the intersection between portrait, biography and history. They are more than artworks; when people look at portraits, they think they are encountering that person."[3] We forget the artifice and sense, however fleetingly, a flesh and blood personage. Something compels us to probe the story behind the image, the context of another time and place.

Encountering those stories is the basis for human connection. If we don't see people represented, how can we imagine their experience? Traditional European and American portraiture depicted men, most often white and prominent—the better to adorn the landing of a manor house staircase. Elite women were generally shown at home, sometimes with children. People of color, when present, were often in servile positions. The nineteenth century shifted toward images of the middle-class, while the social convulsions of the early twentieth century brought workers and ordinary people to center stage.

Portrait painters did not disappear in eras dominated by other movements. Throughout history, these artists represented themselves and their communities. Yet their work, especially when created by women and people of color, was not exhibited or valued. Curators now reach back to find and display such early portraiture. Highlighting this work, argues art historian and curator Kelli Morgan, could expand our understanding of how diverse people saw themselves.[4]

Winold Reiss continued to paint lesser-known people as well as prominent figures of the Harlem Renaissance despite the refusal of galleries to exhibit the work. Alice Neel produced remarkable portraits celebrated by her community but only recently recognized by the mainstream art world. Marion kept painting people long after realism and portraiture lost the limelight. Regardless of trends, she said, you have to follow your passion "if you have any guts or feeling."[5]

Had Marion lived past age sixty, she might have come back "into tune." Figuration and portraiture returned to the American scene in the late twentieth and early twenty-first centuries. Marion would have applauded the movement and its pioneers, African American and other artists of color. However, to explain neglect of her work as an "out of tune" portrait painter has inherent limits. The opposition of figuration to abstraction was never as firm as some argue. Artists have always mixed figures with abstract design. Art critic Peter Schjeldahl quotes Picasso's statement, "All things appear to us in the form of figures."[6]

What keeps certain stars shining while others fade? Some artists earn applause in their time; others garner attention decades or centuries later. Jason Farago describes the "reputational caprice" endured even by stars like Johannes Vermeer. His work sold during his lifetime, then met lukewarm reception or none at all for two centuries. Now, "Vermeeromania" has turned *Girl with a Pearl Earring* into a meme.[7] Realists and portrait artists, including Marion, suffered neglect in part because the art world narrowly fixed the modernist canon of twentieth-century art on postwar abstraction.

Critics, galleries, museums, and collectors anoint the art worth remembering. One can argue that this is the nature of the fickle art world. Yet how is that slippery category decided? Which reviewers, gallerists, and others dictate the stream of dominant criticism?

Consider a 1976 review of Marion's work by renowned art critic Lucy Lippard. A Vassar College show, *7 American Women: The Depression Decade* displayed Marion's prints, sketches, and paintings, some of which the gallery later purchased. Lippard declared her "the star of the show" whose "immensely powerful fresco studies and powerful *and* sensitive conté portraits of workers and peasants combine the strength that was the greatest virtue of the Mexican mural movement with a sympathetic view of humankind."[8] Why, Lippard asked six years after Marion's death, was her work not better known?

Lippard added an intriguing note. Marion's sensitivity, she "unashamedly" declared, rested on "the artist's experience as a woman."[9] A view of women as inherently more sensitive? Perhaps. But Lippard's words also suggest that the plight of women artists birthed that awareness. Painting "like a man" was the highest praise granted women in early to mid-twentieth-century America. Marion declared her breasts and hips an inconvenience when she ascended an often dangerous scaffold in men's overalls. She kept her name, made a living as an artist, and refused to sign her paintings with gender ambiguous initials. She fought, although unsuccessfully, to bring more women into the war art program.

Some male reviewers praised her for ignoring gender boundaries. In a 1947 review, Harry Salpeter wrote, "She is a woman but is not a member of the weaker sex. In her femininity there is a drive that sweeps her over great distances and across barriers from which even truly masculine artists would turn away in frustration. The story of her career and her conquests makes the average male artist seem like a repetitious doodler and stay-at-home knit-by-the fire body." He added, "It remains to be seen how deeply in the chronicles of time her name will have been etched."[10]

Given her achievements, the depth of etching seems shallow. However, the art world is now shining a brighter light on women artists. Some, like the abstract expressionists Grace Hartigan and Lee Krasner, were previously acknowledged but overshadowed by their male counterparts. Others have been rescued from obscurity. The 2018–2019 Guggenheim Museum exhibit of Swedish artist and mystic Hilma af Klint broke all attendance records. The frenzy around Frida Kahlo now surpasses mere fame, but she wasn't always an icon.

Amid this flurry of attention to women, Marion remains better known today via images *of* her than by her. Mexican photographers Manuel and Lola Alvarez Bravo captured a glamorous Marion. Winold Reiss portrayed her youthful promise in his art deco portrait. Harry Sternberg pictured her holding a color palette against a backdrop of *Mississippi Girl* and portraits of indigenous Mexicans (above). Max Beckmann's charcoal sketch highlights her prominent eyes and nose. Isamu Noguchi's bust of her head accentuates her firm, set mouth.

Each emphasized the beauty Gladys Brodsky called "almost a handicap." Marion could not escape it. She'd earned early acclaim, wrote one critic, while "in the bloom of pulchritude." Another review compared her to "a sheaf of ripe wheat."[11] Recall that a party after her Chicago show of Hong Kong art featured a cake with Marion's image on top. "The enormous eyes, bangs and curves he gave her were no exaggeration," wrote a reviewer. "Unfortunately, the guests ate it." "Painting Miss Greenwood, even with a pastry tube, is a pleasure many would envy artist [Aaron] Bohrod."[12]

We're left with a deeper truth: Marion was not only a woman but an outspoken, staggeringly beautiful, sexually adventuresome individual who thumbed her nose at convention. Her freewheeling sexuality fit the bohemian ethos of every place she lived, yet she was scrutinized and critiqued in ways men were not. Gladys Brodksy tells an oft-repeated story. Marion went to a Woodstock party one night, surveyed the crowd and said, "I've had every man here and there isn't one I'd want again."[13] The story's truth matters less than its repetition.

The stories we tell reveal what we value and what we condemn; they also point to an in-between, ambiguous realm. Do we celebrate or castigate the Marion Greenwood who resisted gender boundaries? She was hardworking and tough, said Gladys, making her way in a closed world: "Women were supposed to wear a lot of beads, long skirts, and show up. That was really the rule and Marion broke it. Marion would be up there with the guys ... drinking with them, telling them where to go, and not following the usual course."[14]

Did Marion's strength and unconventionality trigger the femme fatale moniker? Perhaps so for Alexander Calder in creating a wire sculpture of Marion.[15] Her mouth is open, revealing crooked teeth. Many of Calder's wire creations are playful and often caricature the subject. Yet his image of Marion is startling. In traditional portraiture, only "the poor, the lewd, the drunk" smiled with visible teeth."[16] Smiling suggested lust, licentiousness, and sexual availability. In photographs and her self-portraits, Marion's mouth stays closed.

We're back to the siren leading men to ruin. One art historian offered me another way to ponder the femme fatale label. When he suggested that some of Marion's images of other women fit this category, I balked. Then I reconsidered. In a discussion of Francis Bacon's portraits, Richard Brilliant writes, "To the degree in which they can be distinguished from one another, each portrait retains its own integrity; to the degree that they resemble one another, they implicate the artist in each image as if he mirrored his own anxious appearance in their faces."[17]

Marion feared her reputation would fade with her looks and sexual allure. Did her images of women sometimes carry her anxiety about the double-edged nature of beauty? Janet Malcolm, writing about photographer Margrethe Mather, one of Edward Weston's beautiful subjects, argues that we cannot break free "of the idea that exceptional beauty in youth is a defining characteristic, whose loss is a diminishment of the inner as well as the outer person."[18] This message lurked as Marion aged.

Here's another view: Marion's "femme fatale" portraits may be layered with irony and rebellion. Recall that at age nine, she chose Cleopatra, that ultimate femme fatale, as the subject of her first portrait. Ponder the lithograph *Mary in Black* (1961, also called *Dancer*). A beautiful young woman, hair cascading over her black leotard, turns away from the viewer. The figure exudes self-confidence, but her unsmiling face suggests something else as well. She glances back and her dark eyes dare us to look—a defiance perhaps born of Marion's years of being obsessively viewed. Some of her portraits of women reveal this ambivalence about beauty, the ways it serves and hinders. If we can't escape the gaze, we can at least resist its power.

Marion resented commissioned portraits when she felt compelled to meet her subject's needs. Representing herself offered freedom. When one of her former lovers, art collector Marc Sandler, wanted a self-portrait, he rejected one possibility as "too sad." "I'm not painting pictures to please Sandler," Marion grumbled. "It should go to a museum."[19]

Self-portraits also illuminate the history of women artists. The form blossomed in the fifteenth century when flat mirrors appeared and religious strictures against self-aggrandizement loosened. By the sixteenth century, women, excluded from art schools and access to models, found the perfect subjects: themselves.

One of the first women to paint self-portraits was Sofonisba Anguissola, whose talent was considered freakish by sixteenth-century standards. How could a woman, seen as passive and vastly inferior, productively wield that most phallic instrument, the paintbrush? Yet wield it she did in ways that astonished patrons who bought the paintings promoted by her aristocratic but cash-strapped father.[20]

Art historian Jennifer Higgie writes, "The act of female self-portraiture—a woman declaring that her existence is something worth recording—is one of radical defiance: 'Look at me,' she is saying. 'I exist. I have something to say.'"[21]

What did Marion Greenwood want to say? How did she see herself? Her self-portraits are not glamorous. In a 1948–1949 painting now in the Metropolitan Museum of Art, her figure half turns from the viewer. She looks back, chin thrust slightly forward—a woman who wants to be taken seriously. She is unsmiling but not "gloomy," as Marion once described her later self-portraits. Those reflected the strain of supporting a troubled family, yearning for an absent husband, and recovering from a failed marriage.

Musy tried to instill in her daughter an Irish sense of tragedy, yet Marion's resilient spirit always triumphed. That side emerges in the self-portrait discovered by sculptor Judith Shea at the National Academy. Here is a mischievous Marion puffing on a cigarette, gleefully rebellious, full of the fun-loving spirit her friends treasured. Each of her self-portraits offer a revolving sense of self: pensive and serious, sometimes brooding, occasionally "gloomy," other times joyful. Each challenges the world to accept her as she was—the "most alive person" Bob Plate had ever known.

Bob never wrote Marion's biography, but before he died in 2005, he labored to bring attention to her achievements. He collaborated with Vassar College's art gallery on the exhibit that Lucy Lippard reviewed. A later Vassar show, *For the People: American Mural Drawings of the 1930s and 1940s* (2007), also featured work by Marion. The Woodstock Artists Association held a memorial exhibit in September 1972. In 2020, the Whitney Museum of Art included her Mexico City murals in *Vida Mexicana: Mexican Muralists Remake American Art, 1925–1945* (2020). Yet a focus on Marion's 1930s work doesn't capture her artistic range.

Marion constantly sold art to survive. To locate paintings and prints after she died, Bob joined forces with Charles Fenn. They continued to correspond as Charles, his wife, Mair, and their children settled in Ireland. Through shared love for Marion, they tried to ensure her reputation, a goal I fervently share.

I sometimes feel the shadow of Bob Plate's ghost, wondering what he would have written. The tension between objectivity and passion can paralyze those closest to a deeply loved person. Being an outsider poses other challenges. Our subjects retain their mystery. Like portrait painters, biographers select colors and shapes while yoked to the evidence before us. The fear remains: what we leave out might be the part that reveals the whole.

How can we assess Marion Greenwood's art and life? She produced thousands of paintings, drawings, and lithographs. All prolific artists falter at times. Her oils sometimes lack the depth and the expressive quality of the award-winning *Mississippi Girl*, *Lament*, and *Elegy*. Yet she offered us something we need now more than ever: art that reaches for a shared human experience yet never accepts the systems that elevate some individuals and cultures and denigrate others.

Peter Schjeldahl argued that "the proof of any art's lasting value is a comprehensive emotional necessity: it's something that a person needed to do and which awakens and satisfies corresponding needs in us."[22] Marion's murals and portraits aroused a kindred need in me. Something seized me standing before her Morelia mural in 2013. After a five-year journey through Mexican bureaucracy, I was able to have a plaque made. The black metal plate simply states her name and the mural dates, 1933–1934. I'm left wondering what else she might have wanted inscribed.

About one thing, I feel certain: Marion Greenwood would insist on being remembered as an accomplished and pioneering artist driven by a passion to create. We need her model of an intrepid woman who lived unfettered by society's rules. That Marion Greenwood was outspoken, sensuous, oblivious to social critique, and utterly devoted to her work remains deeply inspiring.

Marion would applaud the societal changes wrought by feminism since her death in 1970. She had hoped women artists could escape the stark choices she felt forced to make. During a 1969 interview with Woodstock artist Karl Fortess, Marion said, "It's pretty difficult to be a woman and a painter because you have to sacrifice one thing for the other. And I've always sacrificed, I guess, the woman part." "But you're still a woman," Fortess said. Marion laughed, "Still very much a woman, alas."[23] Given those alternatives, she chose artist.

Acknowledgments

THE SPARK FOR THIS BOOK WAS LIT IN MORELIA, MEXICO, IN 2013 WHILE I was teaching through a fellowship from Fulbright-García Robles. I'm deeply grateful to those who made that year at La Universidad Latina de América transformative: Marivel Ortega Arreola, the late Victor Vargas Anguiano, and my extraordinary students. Thanks to Maureen Rosenthal and Catherine Ettinger for responses to chapters and fantastic lunches; Catherine also facilitated the plaque for Marion Greenwood's mural. A salute to other friends in Mexico for enlivening discussions of art and culture: Krista and James Botsford, Kathleen Collins, Ann Decker, Jerry Engelbach, the late Brenda Hancock, Joel Hancock, Susan Knowles, Jeff Love, Patty McBratney, Teo and Margarete Merlino, Victoria Ryan, Andrew Saftel, Marlene Swartz, and Oriana Wickenkamp. Susan provided photo assistance, as did Florence Leyret. Jed Horne and Jane Wholey offered unwavering enthusiasm and a diamond tiara to mark the book's completion.

James Oles shared archival materials at a critical juncture. I'm indebted to his writing about the Greenwood sisters and to the publications of other scholars. Among them are Aída Castilleja's articles about Purépecha life, Dina Comisarenco Mirkin's book on women muralists in Mexico, and Susan Vogel's biography of Pablo O'Higgins. Thanks to Michael Schuessler for his support and for collaboration on a *Nexus* article that spurred interest in this book.

Fundamental information about Marion's relationship with Diego Rivera in Mexico came via Will Maynez, steward of Rivera's work in San Francisco. Will connected me to L. D. Kirshenbaum, who generously provided photos and film footage of Marion and Diego. Thanks to her and Norman Goldwyn for this visual treasure trove.

North of the border, I owe thanks to a multitude of friends. This book would not have happened without Elinor Langer's alert about the Morelia mural, followed by her encouragement through many spirited dinner conversations. Her biography of Josephine Herbst was an essential foundation. I owe much to my long friendship with Holly Sylvester and to her discerning responses to selected chapters. Michael McGregor's insights about writing and life inspired me during our loops around Laurelhurst Park. A huge thanks to Andrea Carlisle, who took time from writing her book of essays to listen to my dilemmas and respond in meticulous detail to my work. Melissa Madenski put aside her poetry to help hone my thinking and my prose. Both writers are part of a Portland community of friends who have sustained me for decades: Judith Barrington, Leigh Coffey, Ruth Gundle, Perrin Kerns, Scott Lyons, Diane McDevitt, Kim Stafford, and Judy Teufel.

A big abrazo to Sully Taylor for deepening my understanding of Mexico. She and Bob Amundson offered unending support. Richard Adams, the late Martha Banyas, Michael Hoeye, and Wendy Rankin urged me on with regular queries. A loving thanks to all.

I'm endlessly grateful to Judy Blankenship for our walks and talks, her thoughtful response to chapters, and expert photo advice. Crucially, Judy connected me to the amazing Wendi Schnaufer at the University of Alabama Press. No writer I know gets same-day responses and such unending encouragement from an editor. Working with her has been a gift. UAP's project editor Jennifer Blanchard Manley and copy editor Penelope Cray expertly guided the book to completion.

Wendi chose excellent readers whose suggestions made this a far better book. Bridget Quinn offered creative revision ideas and critical insight into Theosophy, modernism, and other subjects. Jennifer Jolly proposed additional sources and edits on a host of topics, including Haitian culture and Mexican art, history, and politics.

Woodstock and New York City were central to Marion Greenwood's story. A timely grant from the Barbara Deming Memorial Fund funded a visit to both places. My profound thanks to Marc Plate, executor of Marion Greenwood's estate. From the day he opened up his Woodstock storage unit of papers and photos, he has patiently supported this project. His mother, artist Gladys Brodsky, gave me a pivotal first interview and proved a vital fount of Marion tales. Marc also introduced me to Mary V. Donohue, whose commitment to Marion's story inspired me.

Two Woodstock art historians helped me grasp the colony's place in American art history. Bruce Weber offered his expertise via phone conversations, email exchanges, and insightful reading of the Woodstock chapters. I'm grateful for Tom Wolf's research, the interview in Chinatown, and for connecting me to Renate Reiss. I can't thank her enough for encouragement, photo reproductions, and prompt response to my queries about her late father-in-law, artist Winold Reiss.

Emily Jones at the Woodstock Artists Association and Museum answered my first request in 2013 and kept answers coming for more than a decade. JoAnn Margolis at the Historical Society of Woodstock was equally welcoming and furnished a CD of the Karl Fortess interview with Marion. Hearing someone's voice triggers a deep sense of connection. Thanks to Eric Caren for access to some of his collected papers and photos.

Several New York City–based art experts supplied invaluable material and perspectives. Sculptor Judith Shea offered a novel vision of one of Marion's self-portraits. I'm grateful to Stephanie Cassidy at the Art Students League for ASL documents and the invitation to publish in the journal, *LINEA*. Many thanks to Amy Wolf for illuminating Isamu Noguchi's relationship with "his women" and for sharing Robert Plate's short biographical sketch. Without that document, my knowledge of Marion's family would have been limited.

Much of biography research depends on serendipity. A footnote in James Oles's dissertation led to another invaluable New York connection. My deepest thanks to Carol and Irene Sirugo for sharing photos, letters, and news clips from the Grace Greenwood archives. That material and our phone interviews radically revised my perception of Marion's gifted and troubled sister. An interview with print specialist Susan Teller enriched my understanding of Associated American Artists (AAA). My knowledge of AAA expanded through work with the Portland Art Museum's Mary Weaver Chapin and her assistant, Chyna Bounds. Thanks as well to Nancy Kelly, the daughter of AAA director Sylvan Cole, for the lovely afternoon in her downtown Portland home.

The sheer luck of timing led me to Knoxville, Tennessee. When I began research, Marion's 1955 mural was still covered over. In 2014, the university's Downtown Gallery unveiled the painting for a retrospective exhibit. Gallery director and artist Mike Berry graciously hosted my visit and cheered me on for a decade. An interview with art historian Fred Moffatt yielded new insight into Marion's work. Local historian and journalist Jack Neely imparted critical knowledge and perspectives. Thanks to Eric Harkness for our interview and his courage in provoking discussion of the mural controversy. The Ewing Gallery of Art's Sarah McFalls facilitated complicated permissions, and the University of Tennessee library archivist Alexandra Sabau searched for relevant information among papers that had not yet been accessioned.

At every turn, I met similarly generous archivists and librarians. Among them are the staff members of the Smithsonian Institution's Archives of American Art, the Smithsonian American Art Museum, the Beinecke Rare Book and Manuscript Library at Yale University, the New York Public Library's Brooke Russell Reading Room and the Lionel Pincus and Princess Firyal Map Division, and Syracuse University Library. Individuals who deserve special recognition include Adam Ryan at the Center for Photography at Woodstock, Lewis and Clark College Watzek Library's Erica Jensen and Jenny Bornstein, Norie Guthrie of the Fondren Library at Rice University, and Sarah Forgey and Carrie Gabarée at the US Army Center of Military History. Their work is the invisible foundation of this book.

My global treks couldn't match Marion's, but one memorable trip led me to the late artist Alyn Fenn in the beautiful windswept village of Schull, Ireland. She entrusted me with her father Charles Fenn's stories and unpublished memoir. Her generosity made this book possible. In Montreal, art historian Catherine MacKenzie produced a brilliant interpretation of Marion's work in Hong Kong that altered my understanding.

Other feminist interpretations expanded my vision. An interview with art historian Deborah Deacon elucidated war art for my article in the journal *Hyperallergic*. Thanks to Anna Poor for sharing stories, diary entries, and photos of her aunt, war artist Anne Poor. I'm grateful to Karen Chernick for the initial connection to Elisa Wouk Amino and the other *Hyperallergic* editors who polished my work.

One boon of the pandemic was virtual connection. Through Biographers International, I joined a group of women biographers who provide abundant support and writerly wisdom. Its members are Susan Bailey, Marcia Biederman, Heidi Feldman, Sara Fitzgerald, Jacqueline Jones, Theresa Kaminski, Rebecca Lallier, Shelley Puhak, Bridget Quinn, and Andrea Friederici Ross. Thanks also to Bio's Cathy Curtis, whose revision ideas strengthened my book proposal. An interview with Megan Marshall enriched my understanding of biography. Martha Graham's biographer Neil Baldwin extended insights about Marion's connection to Graham.

I'm grateful to my late parents for encouraging their children to find our own paths. My always supportive sister Pat, editor and writer, responded to sections of the book with astute suggestions. My siblings Matt, Nick, and Christine never lost hope that I would, in Chris's words, bring my "BFF Marion" to life.

I owe the most to Bob Hazen—brilliant and patient reader of multiple drafts, eagle-eyed typo catcher, and unfailingly loving and supportive husband. He has lived with Marion Greenwood for almost one-third of our lives together. My gratitude and love for him are boundless.

Notes

PROLOGUE

1. Gladys Brodsky thought there were no women in the inaugural exhibit, but the wall lists include two: Maria Helena Vieira da Silva, a Portuguese abstract painter (1908–1992), and Natalia Goncharova, a Russian painter, writer, and set and costume designer (1881–1962).

2. Interview with Gladys Brodsky, Woodstock, October 14, 2013.

3. Quote from writer and actor Emlyn Williams in Robert Gottlieb, "'Dah-ling': The Strange Case of Tallulah Bankhead," *New Yorker*, May 8, 2005.

CHAPTER 1

1. James Oles, "Walls to Paint On: American Muralists in Mexico, 1933–1936," PhD diss. (Yale University, 1995), 248.

2. The initial group included O'Higgins, the Greenwood sisters, and Mexican artists Ángel Bracho, Ramón Alva Guadarrama, Antonio Pujol, and Miguel Tzab Trejo. Raúl Gamboa, Pedro Rendón, and Isamu Noguchi, Marion's friend and sometimes lover, joined later in the process. O'Higgins is sometimes included in lists of the Mexican group.

3. The Woodstock Group interviewed by Dorothy Seckler, Woodstock, NY (September 26, 1964), 2. Transcript in the Archives of American Art, Smithsonian Institution, Washington, DC. Quoted in Oles, "Walls to Paint On," 26.

4. Leonard Folgarait, *Mural Painting and Social Revolution in Mexico, 1920–1940: Art of the New Order* (Cambridge: Cambridge University Press, 1998), 5.

5. Jennifer Jolly, "Animating Internationalism: David Alfaro Siqueiros and Antifascist Art in the 1930s," *Art History* 45, no. 4 (2022): 806. For a discussion of the political divisions, see Esther Acevedo, "Young Muralists at the Abelardo L. Rodríguez Market," in *Mexican Muralism: A Critical History*, ed. Alejandro Anreus, Robin Adèle Greeley, and Leonard Folgarait (Berkeley: University of California Press, 2012), 125–31.

6. Anita Brenner, *Idols Behind Altars: Modern Mexican Art and Its Cultural Roots* (Mineola, NY: Dover Publications, 2002), 279.

7. Marion Greenwood (MG) to (JH) Josephine Herbst, December 15, 1934, Yale University, Beinecke Rare Book and Manuscript Library, Elinor Langer Collection of Josephine Herbst, MSS 475, Box 2, p. 111. All of their correspondence is from this collection. Marion was a lively writer, but she often misspelled words. I've corrected most of the errors in her letters but kept some to impart her colorful use of language, as in the example above.

8. "like a hungry woman," "very 'sweet' to me," MG to JH, December 26, 1934.

9. L.D. Kirshenbaum provided information about the Guggenheim letter. A draft letter of Marion's grant proposal is in the MGA.

10. Film courtesy of L.D. Kirshenbaum and Norman Goldwyn, who also provided this footage of Marion and Diego to director Carla Gutierrez for her 2024 documentary Frida. In the original sixteen-minute film, shot in 1935 or 1936 by art collector Alfred Honigbaum, a statuesque blonde appears next to the pair, holding a camera and with a cigarette dangling from her mouth. She may have taken the still photos of Marion and Diego included in this chapter.

11. Irene Sirugo, phone interview with the author, Tuesday, July 28, 2020. Reference to women on scaffolds from Jennifer Higgie, *The Mirror and the Palette: Rebellion, Revolution, and Resilience: Five Hundred Years of Women's Self-Portraits* (New York: Pegasus Books, 2021), 15.

12. Chapter 13 examines Marion's mural and the politics of the Rodríguez Market in greater detail.

13. See Oles, "Walls to Paint On," 268–88, for a full description of Marion's mural. See also Acevedo in *Mexican Muralism: A Critical History*, 136–39.

14. "Marion Greenwood Applauded for Steady Rise to Mural Fame," *Washington Post*, April 12, 1936, MGA.

15. Oles, "Walls to Paint On," 28.

16. Marion Greenwood, oral history interview with Dorothy Seckler, January 31, 1964, Archives of American Art, Smithsonian Institution, 10.

17. MG to JH, October 26, 1935.

18. Seckler, 9.

19. MG to JH, December 28, 1935.

20. Josephine Herbst, "The Artist's Progress," *Mexican Life* 11, no. 3 (March 1935): 25.

21. JH to MG, n.d.

CHAPTER 2

1. Robert (Bob) Plate diary, June 27, 1952, Marion Greenwood Archives (MGA), courtesy of Marc Plate.

2. Mary Gabriel, *Ninth Street Women: Lee Krasner, Elaine de Kooning, Grace Hartigan, Joan Mitchell, and Helen Frankenthaler; Five Painters and the Movement That Changed Modern Art* (New York: Little Brown and Co., 2018), 63.

3. Elliott Wellensky, *When Brooklyn Was the World: 1920–1957* (New York: Harmony Books, 1986), 21.

4. Catherine H. Greenwood was listed in the 1892 New York state census an artist. A letter from Sculptor Michael Lantz to Grace states that he paid $200 to borrow one

of her paintings, a sign that other artists knew her work. ML to GG, September 17, 1954. Grace Greenwood Archives (GGA). Grace's correspondence cited in this book is from GGA.

5. Marion Greenwood to Josephine Herbst (MG, JH), December 5, 1932.

6. New York state and federal census data vary between "Boylen" and "Boylan" and include the following names and birthdates: 1892 NY state census: "Catherine C. Greenwood" born "about 1873," age 19; 1900 federal census, "Catharine" born February 1874, no age listed; 1905 NY state census, "Kathrin" born 1875, age 30; 1910 federal census, "Catherine" born 1876, age 34; 1915, "Catharine C." born 1877, age 38; 1920 federal census, "Kathryn" born 1879, age 41. Some census data list both parents as born in Ireland, some her father born in Ireland and her mother in Pennsylvania.

7. MG to Musy, November 28, 1933.

8. Ann Douglas, *Terrible Honesty: Mongrel Manhattan in the 1920s* (New York: Farrar, Straus and Giroux, 1995), 32. Emily Midorikawa creates a vivid portrait of spiritualism in *Out of the Shadows: Six Visionary Victorian Women in Search of a Public Voice* (Berkeley, CA: Counterpoint Press, 2021).

9. Unpublished collection of Musy's poems, MGA. Marion mentions her mother's membership in the Writer's Club in a letter to Yaddo. MG to Elizabeth Ames, April 15, 1927.

10. Photos, GGA.

11. Robert (Bob) Plate unpublished biographical sketch of Marion Greenwood, 1, MGA.

12. Plate, biographical sketch, 2.

13. Plate, biographical sketch, 3.

14. Musy's poems, May 30, 1916, MGA.

15. Plate, biographical sketch, 3.

16. Interview with Irene Sirugo, July 28, 2020.

17. Musy to GG 1935.

18. [8] Marion's school drawings are referenced in the publication M. Fernand Huré, "Ambassades et Consultats, Revue Mondiale Illustrée" (Paris: Diplomatie Mondanites Actualites, 1928), 2.

19. Brodsky interview with the author, Woodstock, New York, October 14, 2013.

20. Marion Greenwood interview with Louise Rago, *School Arts* magazine, June 1961.

21. Jiddu Krishnamurti, *International Star Bulletin* Star Bulletin, 1931.

22. Plate, biographical sketch, 15.

23. Elizabeth Wilson, *Bohemians: The Glamorous Outcasts* (New Brunswick, NJ: Rutgers University Press, 2000), 1.

24. "Art, hedonism," Christine Stansell, *American Moderns: Bohemian New York and the Creation of a New Century* (New York: Holt and Co., 2000), 17. "Bohemian plot," 248.

CHAPTER 3

1. Judd Tully, "The Art Students League of New York," *American Artist*, August 1984, 53. Avis Berman cites the 1906 fall catalog in *Rebels on Eighth Street: Juliana Force and the Whitney Museum of American Art* (New York: Atheneum, 1990), 66.

2. Tully, "The Art Students League of New York," 52.

3. Emma Goldman, "Love and Marriage," in *Anarchism and Other Essays*, 3rd rev. ed. (New York: Mother Earth Publishing and London: A.C. Fifield, 1917), 234.

4. Verna Carleton Millan, "Montparnasse to Mexico," *Brooklyn Daily Eagle*, March 1, 1936, F8-F9, Grace Greenwood archives (GGA).

5. Stansell, *American Moderns*, 238.

6. Karal Ann Marling deals with shifts that brought women artists greater prominence in the 1930s; Karal Ann Marling, *7 American Women: The Depression Decade* (Poughkeepsie, NY: Vassar College Art Gallery, 1976), 8.

7. In the first decade of the twentieth century, there were forty-two artists on the League roster, but only four were women: Lucia Fairchild Fuller, Alice Beckington, Rhoda Holmes Nicholls, and Hilda Belcher.

8. Catalog of the Art Students League, season of 1924–25.

9. Described in Deborah Solomon's *American Mirror: The Life and Art of Norman Rockwell* (New York: Farrar, Strauss, and Giroux, 2013), 40–41.

10. Berman, *Rebels on Eighth Street*, 5.

11. Robert Hughes, "The Wave from the Atlantic," American Visions, Episode 5, BBC, February 5, 2002.

12. Marion Greenwood interview by Karl Fortess, June 1969, Woodstock, New York.

13. Linda Nochlin, "The Realist Criminal and the Abstract Law," *Art in America*, September 1, 1973.

14. Helen Langa, *Radical Art: Printmaking and the Left in 1930s New York* (Berkeley: University of California Press, 2004), 133. Regarding terms for people of color, my references reflect the historical context of Marion's era as well as current use. I alternate between "African American" and "Black" except when an institution or entity used "Negro." For example, the "Negro Theater Project" was an important subsection of the WPA.

15. "Talented Woman Artist Changes Technique Often," *Waterloo (Iowa) Daily Courier*, December 20, 1950.

16. Frank A. Gallt, *Picturesque Catskills Official Guide* (Catskill, NY: Catskill Mountain Resort Co., 1922), 25.

17. Alf Evers, *Woodstock: History of an American Town* (Woodstock, NY: Overlook Press, 1987), 413. For more on how Byrdcliffe developed, 398–432.

18. Bruce Weber, "In Quest of Harmony: The Founding and Early Years of the Woodstock Artists Association," *Hudson River Valley Review* 36, no. 1 (Autumn 2019): 35–54. The WAA is now WAAM after adding "Museum" to its name.

19. The story of fourteen-year-old Marion joining the Woodstock Art Association, Plate, biographical sketch, 5. The WAAM has no record of an enrollment date.

20. MG Fortess interview, 1969.

21. Anita M. Smith, *Woodstock: History and Hearsay* (Arkville, NY: Catskill Mountains Publishing Corporation, 1959), 60.

22. The statement from Marion's mother was related by artist Claude Howell, part of the oral histories and photos included in the Maverick Festival archives in the Center for Photography at Woodstock.

CHAPTER 4

1. George Bridgman to Elizabeth Ames (EA), March 31, 1927. Marion Greenwood guest file, Yaddo records, Manuscripts and Archives Division, New York Public Library, Astor, Lenox, and Tilden Foundations. All Yaddo letters referenced throughout the book are from that collection (boxes 211, 212, 220, and 225).

2. MG to EA, April 2, 1927.

3. MG to EA, April 15, 1927.

4. Quoted in Davis S. Ferriero and Elaina Richardson, "Forward," *Yaddo: Making American Culture*, ed. Micki McGee (New York: Columbia University Press, 2008), no page number.

5. Plate, biographical sketch, 6.

6. Plate, biographical sketch, 7. "Erwin" Edman should be "Irwin."

7. MG to Yaddo, no date but likely August 1927. She thanked Ames, George Peabody, and "Miss Pardee," Allena Gilbert Pardee, honorary president of the Corporation of Yaddo.

8. MG to JH, December 28, 1935.

9. The figure of $1,000 appears in "Marion Greenwood," by M. Fernand Huré, "Ambassades et Consulats, Revue Mondiale Illustrée" (Paris: Diplomatie Mondanites Actualites, 1928), English translation, 3. Plate's biographical sketch states that Marion received either "$500 or $1000, probably the former," 8. But $1,000 is possible.

10. MG to EA, April 14, 1928.

11. Mark Braude, *Kiki Man Ray: Art, Love, and Rivalry in 1920s Paris* (New York: W. W. Norton, 2022).

12. Photo and poem, MGA.

13. Wanda Corn, *The Great American Thing: Modern Art and National Identity, 1915–1935* (Berkeley: University of California Press, 1999), 91–21.

14. Description of the street, Grace Greenwood Archives (GGA). The reference to Max Steinbook in Oles, "Walls to Paint On," 75.

15. Tom Wolf, "Introduction" to *Woodstock Portraits* exhibition, May 8 through June 28, Woodstock Artists Association, 1999: 3–5.

16. MG to Musy, February 24, 1933.

17. Huré, *Ambassades et Consulats*, 1.

18. Huré, *Ambassades et Consulats*, 5.

19. Dan Franck, *Bohemian Paris: Picasso, Modigliani, Matisse, and the Birth of Modern Art* (New York: Grove Press, 2003), 281.

20. MG interview with Karl Fortess, 1969.

21. Fondation Richard Walker, Première exposition annuelle d'un nouveau groupe internationale de peinture moderne, du 30 septembre au 14 octubre inclus, A La Galerie René Zivy, 57, Avenue Montaigne, Paris.

22. Hayden Herrera, *Listening to Stone: The Art and Life of Isamu Noguchi* (New York: Farrar, Straus and Giroux, 2015), 82.

23. Herrera, *Listening to Stone*, 101.

24. Plate, biographical sketch, 15.

25. Plate, biographical sketch, 10A.

CHAPTER 5

1. Musy to GG, January 14, 1935, GGA.

2. Plate diary, 11.

3. Julie Levin Caro points out that these combined functions were unusual. "The Winold Reiss Studio and Art School as a Hub of Transcultural Modernism," in *The Multicultural Modernism of Winold Reiss, 1886–1953: Transnational Approaches to His Work*, ed. Frank Mehring (Berlin: Deutscher Kunstverlag, 2022), 195.

4. Plate, biographical sketch, 5.

5. Jeffrey C. Stewart, *To Color America: Portraits by Winold Reiss* (Washington, DC: Smithsonian Institution Press for the National Portrait Gallery, 1989), 93.

6. Renate Reiss interview with Joanne Mulcahy, Hudson, New York, September 21, 2015. Renate married Reiss's son, Tjark, after Winold's death.

7. Terms for indigenous people in the United States and Mexico vary with time periods and locations. During the early to mid-twentieth century, "Indian" was part of everyday language and government institutions. Today, indigenous people use a range of designations. The Smithsonian Institution's National Museum of the American Indian recommends using specific names for tribes and other groups whenever possible.

8. Stewart, "Winold Reiss as a Portraitist," *Journal of the Cincinnati Historical Society* 51 (Summer–Fall 1993), 3.

9. P. W. Sampson, "A Modern Cellini—Winold Reiss," Du Pont Magazine 25, no. 3 (March 1931): 8.

10. Receipt for payment in the Reiss Archives, courtesy of Renate Reiss. The check is dated February 6, 1929. It's either a late payment or could be for a different portrait. Plate's biographical sketch states that Marion's portrait hung in the Longchamps restaurant.

11. Stewart, *To Color America*, 34. The Blackfeet include separate tribes living in Canada and on the reserve near Glacier National Park: The Siksika, the Kainai or Blood, and two sections of Piegan or Piikani.

12. Stewart, "Winold Reiss as a Portraitist," 4.

13. Stewart, *To Color America*, 33. For an overview of Curtis's photographs, see Jill D. Sweet and Ian Berry, *Staging the Indian: The Politics of Representation* (The Tang Teaching Museum and Art Gallery at Skidmore College, 2001).

14. The railway's founder, Canadian Louis Hill, was an entrepreneur who hired only full-blooded members of the Blackfeet tribe to perform for his tourist hotels. Some Blackfeet welcomed the chance for income; others objected to the railway's policies. William (Billy) Big Spring, who posed for Reiss, reported that his father refused to work with the railway: "He felt it was very degrading." See Stewart, *To Color America*, 73.

15. Stewart, "Winold Reiss as a Portraitist," 1.

16. Sydelle Rubin-Dienstfrey, "Transcultural Readings of Winold Reiss, Franz Boas, and Miguel Covarrubias: Art and Ethnography of the Harlem Renaissance," *Multicultural Modernism of Winold Reiss*, 108. For an excellent overview of Boas and other anthropologists, see Charles King, *Gods of the Upper Air: How a Circle of Renegade Anthropologists Reinvented Race, Sex, and Gender in the Twentieth Century* (New York: Doubleday, 2019).

17. Jochen Wierich, "Painting the Old West New: Winold Reiss' Blackfeet Portraits," *Multicultural Modernism of Winold Reiss*, 102.

18. Unpublished poems, MGA.

19. Poem, MGA; description of the trip, Plate's biographical sketch , 12–13.

20. Jens Barnieck, "Sonata for Winold Reiss," *Multicultural Modernism of Winold Reiss*, 210.

21. Notice of the G.R.D. exhibition and news clip n.d., MGA. The gallery initials stood for Gladys Roosevelt Dick. The show included one of Reiss's students, Edith Bry, and Virginia Snedeker. From January 25 to February 6, 1931, at 58 W. Fifty-Fifth Street.

22. News clip, n.d. Photo of Marion captioned by "Evening Journal staff photographer." The Hearst paper was published between 1895 and 1937 and merged with the *New York American* to form the *New York Journal-American*.

23. Oles, "Walls to Paint On," 77.

24. Barbara Babcock, "'A New Mexican Rebecca': Imaging Pueblo Women," *Journal of the Southwest* 32, no. 4, *Inventing the Southwest* (Winter 1990): 400–37.

CHAPTER 6

1. Both letters cited in Plate's biographical sketch, 13. Biberman's letter was posted from Goulding's Trading Post, Kayenta, Arizona, September 4, 1931; the other, from a woman named Merriam, March 26, 1932. The reference to "Art School Bisttraus" misspells Emil Bisttram (born Bistran) in Merriam's letter or in Plate's reproduction.

2. Frank Mehring, ed., *The Mexico Diary: Winold Reiss Between Vogue Mexico and Harlem Renaissance* (Tempe, AZ: Bilingual Press, 2016), 17.

3. Author's email correspondence with Renate Reiss, November 13, 2022.

4. Mehring, *The Mexico Diary*, 41 and 42.

5. Aaron Douglas came to New York in 1925 and quickly joined the group at Reiss's studio. Charles H. Alston appears on the October 1926 evening class page in the school ledger. Another African American student in the studio was Cecil H. Gaylord. A March 30, 1925, *New York Evening Journal* article about Reiss's exhibition of Harlem portraits at the 135th St. New York Public Library states, "Cecil H. Gaylord, a colored student in the art class conducted by Winold Reiss, is in charge of the exhibition room." Email from Renate Reiss.

6. Stewart, *To Color America*, 148.

7. Stewart, *To Color America*, 49.

8. Stewart, *To Color America*, 50.

9. Quoted in Frank Mehring, "How Silhouettes Became 'Black': Winold Reiss and the Visual Rhetoric of the Harlem Renaissance," Multicultural Modernism of Winold Reiss, 148.

10. "A pretty good likeness," in Jeffrey C. Stewart, "Winold Reiss's American Studies," in *The Art of Winold Reiss: An Immigrant Modernist* (New York: New York Historical Society, 2021), 54. See page 52 for Stewart's analysis of Reiss's portraits of women. Quote from Tjark Reiss, 53.

11. The 1920 Blackfeet portraits were shown at the Hanfstaengl Gallery, 153 West

Fifty-Seventh Street/Opposite Carnegie Hall. From email correspondence with Renate Reiss, November 13, 2022.

12. *Creative Art*, 1932, news clip from the MGA.

13. Plate, biographical sketch, 14, for description of the *New York Times* drawings, 11-A for quote about Mondrian.

14. Neil Baldwin, *Martha Graham: When Dance Became Modern* (New York: Alfred A. Knopf, 2022), 136–37.

15. Exhibit announcement in the *New York Times*, April 3, 1932.

16. Plate, biographical sketch, 14.

17. "Cooler headed third man," Plate biographical sketch, 11-A. Grace Greenwood recalled the same story in an interview, stressing that Gorky was with Marion and instigated the fight when someone (Pollet according to Plate) flirted with her. *Woodstock Times*, August 2, 1979.

18. Robert Plate writes, "Joe Pollet—do I really have this straight? I'm sure that's what she told me"; Plate, biographical sketch , 15. Plate admits that since Marion was "definitely going out," his speculation may have been wrong.

19. Paul S. Boyer, ed., *The Oxford Companion to United States History* (Oxford: Oxford University Press, 2006), 3.

20. Sylvan Cole interview with Avis Berman, Smithsonian Archives of American Art, June–October 2000, 35.

21. "Dear lady," MG to EA, April 11, 32; "Wings to my recovery," May 7, 1932.

CHAPTER 7

1. nypl.digitalcollections.510d47e4-6e02-a3d9-e040-e00a18064a99.001.w.

2. Philip Stevenson (PS) to EA, April 15, 1932. Philip and Gladys's situation is described in a recommendation letter from writer Evelyn Scott Metcalfe to EA, January 30, 1932.

3. Elinor Langer, *Josephine Herbst: The Story She Could Never Tell* (Boston: Little, Brown and Company, 1983), 73–74. Chapter 15, "The Music Comes on Strong" recounts Marion and Josie's relationship, 126–42.

4. EA to JH and John Hermann, February 9, 1932.

5. Langer, *Josephine Herbst*, 127.

6. Langer, *Josephine Herbst*, 65.

7. Langer, *Josephine Herbst*, 127.

8. Langer, *Josephine Herbst*, 129.

9. MG to Adolf Dehn (AD), May 25, 1931, from Adolf Dehn papers, 1912-198, Box 2, folder 5, Archives of American Art, Smithsonian Institution.

10. MG to AD, Smithsonian Archives of American Art, 1931 (month and day illegible).

11. In Bob Plate's diary, he cites Marion's later relationship with "the lesbian Helen Fisher," but there is no other mention in Marion's papers. March 3, 1970.

12. See Lillian Faderman's *The Gay Revolution: The Story of the Struggle* (New York: Simon & Schuster, 2015), for a history of the movement including the shifting terminology around sexual identity.

13. Barry Werth, "Refuge and Crucible: Newton Arvin's Yaddo," in McGee, *Yaddo: Making American Culture*, 17–30.

14. Langer, *Josephine Herbst*, 131.

15. JH to MG, Sunday morning, n.d.

16. JH to MG, September 17, 1932.

17. MG to JH, n.d.

18. MG to JH, October 19, 1932.

19. MG to JH, October 19, 1932.

20. MG to JH, October 19, 1932. James Oles mentions the fall 1932 abortion in "Walls to Paint On," 79n90. The earlier abortion in spring 1932 appears only in Plate's biographical sketch. The Yaddo letters confirm that Marion arrived in the summer of 1932 still recovering from the spring operation.

21. MG to JH, n.d.

22. MG to JH, n.d.

23. MG to JH, n.d.

24. MG to JH, n.d.

25. JH to MG, Wednesday night.

26. MG to JH, November 19, 1932.

27. November 19.

28. MG to JH, n.d.

29. This larger sense of the Americas that Marion and other artists and intellectuals embraced refers to people anywhere on the continent. But the use of "American" for residents of the United States dominated Marion's time and is still widely accepted.

CHAPTER 8

1. *New York Times*, April 15, 1933, 12, quoted in Helen Delpar, *The Enormous Vogue of Things Mexican: Cultural Relations Between the United States and Mexico, 1920–1935* (Tuscaloosa: University of Alabama Press, 1995), "Rising hum," 26; "the Enormous vogue," 54; original publication.

2. *New York Times*, May 30, 1920, sec. 2, 2, quoted in Delpar, *The Enormous Vogue of Things Mexican*, 5; original publication.

3. MG to Musy, December 27, 1932.

4. Marion Greenwood Interview by Dorothy Seckler, January 31, 1964, Archives of American Art, 3.

5. "Sent me off with smiles" and advice about Theosophical meetings, MG to Musy, December 17; "I long for my little sweetie," December 30, 1932.

6. MG to Musy, December 30, 1932.

7. MG to Musy, January 8, 1933.

8. James Oles, *South of the Border: Mexico in the American Imagination / México en La Imaginación Norteamericana, 1914–1947* (Washington, DC: Smithsonian Institution Press, 1993), 131.

9. Sue Vogel discusses O'Higgins's name at length in *Becoming Pablo O'Higgins* (Pince-Nez Press: San Francisco/Salt Lake, 2010). James Oles's cites his name change in "Walls to Paint On," 200.

10. Oles, "Walls to Paint On," 233.

11. MG to Musy, January 8, 1933.

12. Folgarait, *Mural Painting and Social Revolution in Mexico, 1920–1940*, 1998, 18.

13. Jennifer Jolly points out that the creation of *mestizaje* ignores the contributions of Africans brought to Mexico with the slave trade. See *Creating Pátzcuaro, Creating Mexico: Art, Tourism, and Nation Building under Lázaro Cárdenas* (Austin: University of Texas Press, 2018), 133–34.

14. See Robin Adèle Greeley, "Muralism and the State in Post-Revolution Mexico, 1920–1970," *Mexican Muralism*, 19–22.

15. José Clemente Orozco, *An Autobiography*, trans. Robert C. Stephenson (Austin: University of Texas Press, 1962), 40–41.

16. Plate, biographical sketch, 17.

17. MG interview with Seckler, 9.

18. James Oles, "The Mexican Experience of Marion and Grace Greenwood," in *The Eagle and the Virgin: Nation and Cultural Revolution in Mexico, 1920–1940*, ed. Mary Kay Vaughan and Stephen Lewis (Durham, NC: Duke University Press, 2006), 79.

19. MG to Musy, January 14, 1933.

20. MG to Musy, January 14, 1933.

21. MG to Musy, January 8, 1933.

CHAPTER 9

1. Wittner Bynner, *Selected Letters*, ed. James Kraft (New York: Farrar, Straus and Giroux, 1981), 136–37.

2. MG to Musy, January 25, 33. This letter states seventy-five dollars a month, but a February 7 letter mentions Moisés Sáenz's reduction to thirty-five dollars.

3. MG to Musy, n.d.

4. William Spratling, *File on Spratling: An Autobiography* (New York: Little, Brown & Co., 1967), 16–38.

5. Delpar, *The Enormous Vogue of Things Mexican*, 62.

6. Spratling, *File on Spratling*, 37–38.

7. Delpar, *The Enormous Vogue of Things Mexican*, 67.

8. Spratling, *File on Spratling*, 67.

9. Oles, *South of the Border*, 1993, 133.

10. Descriptions of Spratling's complex personality from W. Kenneth Holditch, "William Spratling, William Faulkner and Other Famous Creoles," *Mississippi Quarterly* 51, no. 3, Special Issue: William Faulkner (Summer 1998): 423–34; Spratling quote, Penny C. Morrill, "Renaissance Transformation," in *William Spratling and the Mexican Silver Renaissance: Maestros de Plata* (New York: Harry N. Abrams, in Association with the San Antonio Museum of Art, 2002), 20.

11. MG to Musy, January 25 and 27, 1933.

12. MG to Musy, n.d.

13. MG to Musy, March 4, 1933.

14. MG to Musy, n.d.

15. MG to Musy, n.d.

16. MG to Musy, n.d.

17. MG to Walter Greenwood ("Papa"), February 28, 1933.

18. Dina Comisarenco Mirkin, *Eclipse de Siete Lunas: Mujeres Muralistas en México* (Mexico City: Artes de México y del Mundo, 2017), 38.

19. Oles, "Walls to Paint On," 90.

20. *Mexican Life,* 9, no. 7 (July 1933): 19–21.

21. Dulze Pérez Aguirre, "La educación socialista en México y el mural 'Atentado a las maestras rurales de Aurora Reyes,'" *Revista Internacional y Comparada de Derechos Humanos* 2, no. 2 (July–December 2019): 219–49. Dina Comisarenco Mirkin devotes a chapter to Reyes in Eclipse de Siete Lunas, 72–83; a detail, "El ataque a la maestra rural," appears on 204.

22. Art historian Bridget Quinn points out that art historians assume that men created early Mesoamerican wall paintings, but art history is replete with overturned assumptions.

23. JH to Musy, March 7, 1933.

24. MG to Musy, March 16, 1933.

25. Langer, *Josephine Herbst,* 139.

26. Langer, *Josephine Herbst,* 140.

27. Langer, *Josephine Herbst,* 138.

28. MG to Musy, April 15, 1933.

29. MG to Musy, April 6, 1933.

30. MG to Musy, May 14, 1933.

31. All quotes from MG to Musy, February 24, 1933.

32. MG to Musy, April 30, 1933; MG to Musy, March 24, 1933.

33. MG to Musy, March 24, 1933.

34. Langer, *Josephine Herbst,* 141.

35. Langer, *Josephine Herbst,* 141.

CHAPTER 10

1. James Oles, "Walls to Paint On," 122.

2. MG to Musy, April 28, 1933.

3. "I'd go crazy," MG to Musy, April 28, 1933; "stop suggesting men," MG to JH, June 17, 1933.

4. MG to Musy, April 28, 1933.

5. MG to Musy, April 30, 1933.

6. See Jolly, *Creating Pátzcuaro, Creating Mexico.*

7. Jolly discusses Quiroga's regulation of indigenous craft production and, with it, a view of Indians as "subservient, indebted, and devoted to beneficent outside authority figures"; Jolly, *Creating Pátzcuaro, Creating Mexico,* 164–66.

8. JH to MG, June 11, 1933.

9. JH to MG, June 30, 1933.

10. JH to MG, n.d.

11. JH to MG, n.d., envelope marked June 10, 1933.

12. MG to JH, May 27, 1933.

13. June 8, 1933.

14. Jolly, *Creating Pátzcuaro, Creating Mexico*, 25–30.

15. MG to JH, May 27, 1933.

16. MG to JH, August 9, 1933.

17. June 8, 1933.

18. June 1, 1933.

19. June 17, 1933.

20. For a thorough study of the Corpus festival in pueblos around Lake Pátzcuaro, see Aída Castilleja, "La Cha 'nantskua o Fiesta del Corpus en Pueblos Purépechas," in *Historia y vida ceremonial en las comunidades mesoamericanas: Los ritos agrícolas, eds. Johanna Broda and Catherine Good* (Primera edición, México, Instituto Nacional de Antropología e Historia, Universidad Nacional Autónoma de México, Instituto de Investigaciones Históricas, 2004), 38–414.

21. MG to JH, June 17, 1933.

22. MG to JH, June 17, 1933.

23. MG to JH, June 8, 1933.

24. Oles, "Walls to Paint On," 30.

25. MG to JH, June 27, 1933.

26. JH to MG, n.d.

27. JH to MG, June 20, 1933.

28. MG to JH, July 28, 1933.

29. Oles, "Walls to Paint On," 142.

30. MG to JH, July 7 or 9, 1933.

31. JH to MG, Friday morning and afternoon, n.d.

32. JH to MG, Friday afternoon.

33. MG to JH, July 12, 1933.

34. MG to JH, July 18, 1933.

35. MG to JH, July 28, 1933.

36. MG to JH, June 17, 1933.

37. MG to JH, July 31, 1933.

CHAPTER 11

1. MG interview with Seckler, Smithsonian, 4.

2. MG to Musy, August 16, 1933.

3. MG to JH, July 7, 1933.

4. MG to Musy, June 4, 1933.

5. MG to Musy, n.d.

6. MG to JH, August 9, 1933.

7. MG to JH, August 11, 1933.

8. MH to JH, August 7, 1933.

9. MG to JH, August 11, 1933.

10. MG to JH, August 7, 1933.

11. MG to JH, n.d.

12. MG to JH, July 26, 1933.

13. MG to Musy, September 12, 1933.

14. MG to JH, June 22, 1933.

15. Jolly, *Creating Pátzcuaro, Creating Mexico*, 85.

16. MG to JH, July 3, 1933.

17. MG to JH, August 15, 1933.

18. Musy to JH, Sunday, no year.

19. See Oles, "Walls to Paint On," 144, for Marion's description of the process.

20. Oles, "Walls to Paint On," 146.

21. Comment about Grace, MG to Musy, September 26, 1933; quote about Hans Hoffman, MG to JH, September 13, 1933.

22. "Old hags," MG to JH, November 21, 1933; "I wake in the morning," November 8, 1933.

23. MG to JH, October 15, 1933.

24. MG to Musy, October 28, 1933.

25. MG to JH, October 26, 1933.

26. Oles, "Walls to Paint On," 153.

27. Comisarenco Mirkin, *Eclipse de Siete Lunas*, 41; Oles, "The Mexican Experience of Marion and Grace Greenwood," 82.

28. MG to JH, January 7, 1933.

29. Oles discusses these articles in "Walls to Paint On," 156n107. Marion cited the "international artist" description from "Dos Hermanas Pintoras, de Mucho Talento," undated clip, MGA. The first US coverage of Grace's mural was Jack Star-Hunt, "Brooklyn Girls Delight Mexico with Eight Murals," *New York Herald Tribune*, np, March 4, 1934. Oles points out that the writer misidentified Marion's mural as seven paintings.

30. Herbst, "The Artist's Progress," 24.

31. Francisco Antuñez, "El México de Marion Greenwood," undated clipping, MGA, cited in Spanish in Oles, "Walls to Paint On," 56–157. The English translation follows in footnote 110. Quote about "long division," MG to JH, October 15, 1933.

32. MG to JH, December 3, 1933.

33. MG to JH, September 13, 1933.

34. MG to Musy, November 21, 1933.

35. MG to Musy, "Thinks it's swell," January 12, 1934; "a mouthful," January 4, 1934.

CHAPTER 12

1. Lola Alvarez Bravo interview with James Oles, 1990. Cited in "Walls to Paint On," 159.

2. MG to Musy, September 26, 1933.

3. MG to Musy, September 18, 33; August 16, 1933.

4. Musy to JH, n.d.

5. MG to JH, January 17, 1934.

6. Comisarenco Mirkin, *Eclipse de Siete Lunas*, 47.

7. Note in Beinecke File, Yale, n.d., File 3, 58.

8. GG to Musy ("Ma"), December 26, 1933; letter cited in Oles, "Walls to Paint On," 161 and footnote 123.

9. MG to JH, n.d.

10. Oles, "Walls to Paint On," 165.

11. MG to JH, December 3, 1933.

12. "Echoes of an Extraordinary Lady," interview with Jim Reed, *Woodstock Times*, August 2, 1979, 24.

13. MG to JH, January 4, 1934.

14. MG to JH, February 23, 1934.

15. MG to JH, January 17, 1934.

16. "Splendid," Pablo O'Higgins to MG, December 14, 1933; "stepping in," February 23, 1934.

17. JH to MG, n.d.

18. MG to Musy, September 4, 1933.

19. MG to JH, March 14, 1934.

20. MG to Musy, November 28, 1933.

21. MG to JH, n.d.

22. MG to JH, n.d.

23. JH to MG, n.d.

24. "Wrong, all wrong," "You seem to utterly ignore," MG to JH, n.d.

25. Oles, "Walls to Paint On," 226.

26. See Alma M. Reed, *Peregrina: Love and Death in Mexico*, ed. Michael Schuessler (Austin: University of Texas Press, 2007).

27. MG to JH, May 11, 1934.

28. Pablo O'Higgins to MG, June 12, 1934.

29. Oles, "Walls to Paint On," 239.

CHAPTER 13

1. The descriptions of events appear in "The Battle of the Century," Emanuel Eisenberg, *New Masses* 17:11, December 10, 1935. For another overview of the debate, see Acevedo, "Young Muralists," in *Mexican Muralism*, 125–47.

2. David Alfaro Siqueiros, "The Counter-Revolutionary Road of Rivera," *New Masses*, May 29, 1934.

3. Eisenberg, "Battle of the Century," *New Masses*, 18.

4. Edward Weston, *The Daybooks of Edward Weston* (New York: Aperture, 1990), 35.

5. Eisenberg, "Battle of the Century," *New Masses*, 18.

6. MG to JH, December 15, 1934.

7. Pablo O'Higgins to MG, n.d., MGA.

8. Barry Carr, "Mexico: Radicals, Revolutionaries and Exiles: Mexico City in the 1920s," *Berkeley Review of Latin American Studies* (Fall 2010): 26–30.

9. See Jennifer Jolly, "Animating Internationalism," 800.

10. Oles, "Walls to Paint On," 234. Oles covers the entire market project in detail in this dissertation.

11. MG to Musy, April 30, 1933.

12. MG to Musy, "All communists and for good reason," May 9, 1933; "a wonderfully hopeful slant," April 30, 1933.

13. MG to Musy, April 30, 1933.

14. Acevedo, "Young Muralists," in *Mexican Muralism*, 129.

15. Pablo O'Higgins to MG, June 12, 1934.

16. Oles, "Walls to Paint On," 232. See also Acevedo, "Young Muralists," 125–42.

17. MG interview with Seckler, 10.

18. MG to JH, December 15, 1934; science as the basis for socialism, see Oles, "Walls to Paint On," 250.

19. MG to JH, February 23, 1934.

20. MG to JH, December 15, 1934.

21. MG to JH, December 26, 1934.

22. "Born remembering"; "perfectly awful," MG to JH, December 26, 1934.

23. Notebook in the MGA.

24. Oles, "Walls to Paint On," 287–88.

25. Oles, "The Mexican Experience of Marion and Grace Greenwood," 86. Also Oles, "Walls to Paint On," 284.

26. Brenner, *Idols Behind Altars*, 246–47.

27. Oles, "Walls to Paint On," 304.

28. Herrera, *Listening to Stone*, 143.

29. Oles, "Walls to Paint On," 375. For an overview of the Noguchi sculpture, 374–99.

30. Herrera, *Listening to Stone*, 147–48.

31. Herrera, *Listening to Stone*, 151.

32. Herrera, *Listening to Stone*, 152–43.

33. Amy Wolf, introduction, "On Becoming an Artist: Isamu Noguchi and His Contemporaries, 1922–1960," Isamu Noguchi Foundation and Garden Museum, November 17, 2010–April 24, 2011.

34. Guillermo Rivas, "Mexican Murals by Marion Greenwood," *Mexican Life* 12, no.1 (January 1936, 24–25): 61.

35. Guillermo Rivas, "The Murals of Grace Greenwood," *Mexican Life* 12, no. 12 (December 1936): 28–30.

36. "Mexican Market (Art)," *Time* 26, no. 4 (July 22, 1935): 26.

37. MG to JH, October 26, 1935.

38. MG to JH, February 2, 1936.

CHAPTER 14

1. MG to JH, December 28, 1935.

2. MG to JH, February 2, 1936.

3. MG to JH, December 28, 1935.

4. Oscar Stonorov (OS) to MG, September 29, 1934.

5. OS to MG, April 11, 1935; "Since I've come," MG to JH, October 26, 1935.

6. See "Artists Here in Serious Straits: PWA Art Official Pleads for Federal Aid Program During the Winter," *New York Times*, September 23, 1934, n.p. MGA.

7. Programs included the Federal Art Project (FAP), the Public Works of Art Project (PWAP), and the Treasury Department's Section of Fine Arts (previously called

Painting and Sculpture). The section, which hired established artists for federal projects, sometimes clashed with the FAP, which focused on the unemployed regardless of reputation. Marion and Grace worked on projects via the section and the FAP. See A. Joan Saab, *For the Millions: American Art and Culture Between the Wars* (Philadelphia: University of Pennsylvania Press, 2004), 18–19.

8. Julia Jacobs, "The Virus Won't Revive F.D.R.'s Arts Jobs Program. Here's Why," *New York Times*, April 22, 2020.

9. Charlotte Streifer Rubinstein, *American Women Artists: From Early Indian Times to the Present* (Boston, MA: G.K. Hall & Co., 1982), 215.

10. Saab, *For the Millions*, 15.

11. James Oles, review of "Vida Americana: Mexican Muralists Remake American Art, 1925–1945," Whitney Museum of American Art, *Panorama: Journal of the Association of Historians of American Art* 6, no. 2 (Fall 2020).

12. Barbara Haskell, *Vida Americana: Mexican Muralists Remake American Art, 1925–1945* (New York: Whitney Museum of Art, February 17–May 17, 2020), 118–19.

13. Cited in Herrera, *Listening to Stone*, 142.

14. Langa, *Radical Art*, 132.

15. Saab, *For the Millions*, 44.

16. Herrera, *Listening to Stone*, 140.

17. Herrera, *Listening to Stone*, 146.

18. MG interview with Seckler, 9.

19. In 2001, the building was torn down, destroying the murals. The housing project's history is recounted in a website compiled by Phil Cohen. J. Richard Altieri took photos of the murals in the "Social Room (probably building 9)" for the US Housing Authority on February 6, 1939. Those match Marion's description of her work. Another building, no. 22, possibly housed Grace's mural.

20. OS to MG, June 23, 1936.

21. ALP member, *Daily Worker*, September 28, 1939, MGA.

22. Ralph M. Pearson, "The Artists Point of View," *Forum*, December 19, 1936.

23. *Bulletin of the Museum of Modern Art* 4, no. 6 (July 1937).

24. OS to MG, n.d., MGA.

25. MG to JH, July 12, 1933.

26. Sylvan Cole interview with Elinor Langer, New York, April 1978, Beinecke Library.

27. MG to JH, February 2, 1936.

CHAPTER 15

1. Charles Fenn (CF) diary entry written when he was ninety-five and living in Schull, Ireland, October 29, 2002. The reference to the song is from Fenn's unpublished memoir, *Life Begins at Eighty-Seven*, 1993, 16.

2. Fenn, diary.

3. Alyn Fenn interview with the author, Schull, Ireland, October 4, 2019.

4. Fenn, *Life Begins at Eighty-Seven*.

5. "Unbelievable slavery" and Story of Cobh Harbour from "Odyssey which ended in west Cork," Charles Fenn Obituary, *Irish Times*, Saturday June 19, 2004.

6. Bathtub gin, Alyn Fenn interview, 2019; burning taste story, Charles Fenn, *Journal of a Voyage to Nowhere* (New York: W. W. Norton, 1971), 98. The novel is based on Fenn's experience.

7. Fenn, *Journal of a Voyage to Nowhere*, 100.

8. Charles Fenn, *At the Dragon's Gate: With the OSS in the Far East* (Annapolis, MD: Naval Institute Press, 2004), 1.

9. Wedding stories from Fenn's diary.

10. Preston J. Hubbard, *Origins of the TVA: The Muscle Shoals Controversy, 1920–1932* (Tuscaloosa: University of Alabama Press, 2nd edition, 2006).

11. MG to Edward B. Rowan (ER), January 9, 1939.

12. ER to MG, January 16, 1939.

13. T. W. Forbes to ER, March 23, 1939.

14. ER to MG, March 30, 1939.

15. MG to ER, April 1, 1939.

16. ER to MG, April 12, 1939.

17. Howard Hull, "Crossville: Marion Greenwood, the Partnership of Man and Nature, 1940," *Tennessee Post Office Murals* (Johnson City, TN: Overmountain Press, 1996), 40.

18. Reference to trip, Catherine MacKenzie, "Place Really Does Matter: Marion Greenwood's 1947 'China' Exhibition," *RACAR: Revue d'art Canadienne/Canadian Art Review* 25, no. 1/2, Producing Women/Ces Femmes que produisent, 1998, 58–72, footnote 9. Description of the Italian frescoes, Seckler, Smithsonian interview, 11.

19. Heather Mullinix, "Post Office Mural on Loan to UT," *Crossville Chronicle*, June 2, 2014.

20. MG interview with Seckler, 16.

21. MG to Julian Huxley, January 17, 1940.

22. Julian Huxley, *Essays of a Biologist* (New York: Knopf, 1923), 112–13.

23. Deborah Straw, Review of *Dear Juliette: Letters of May Sarton to Juliette Huxley*, "Language is a virus" blog.

24. MG to Huxley, January 17, 1940.

25. Julian Huxley, *Essays of a Humanist* (Middlesex, England: Penguin Books, 1966), 227.

26. Huxley, *Essays of a Biologist*, 106.

27. Jiddu Krishnamurti, *International Star Bulletin* 8, August 1930, 2.

28. MG to Huxley, May 7, 1940.

29. Interview with Brodsky, August 12, 2019.

30. "Red Hook gets Mural Praising Planned Living," *New York Herald Tribune*, November 28, 1940.

31. Agnes Adams, "Painting Murals Is This Woman's Work," *New York Post*, November 27, 1940.

32. Catharine Blanck, "Muralist Enjoys Her Work at Red Hook Development," *Brooklyn Eagle*, Sunday, April 14, 1940, 10A.

33. MG to Huxley, January 17, 1940.

34. MG to Huxley, May 7, 1940; "Why aren't they smiling?" Seckler interview, 17.

35. MG to JH, Sunday night, n.d.

36. MG to CF, August 24, 1938, MGA.

CHAPTER 16

1. MG to EA, June 25, 1940.

2. EA to MG, July 15, 1940; July 19, 1940.

3. MG to EA, July 17, 1940.

4. MG to CF, September 24, 1940.

5. MG to CF, August14, 1940.

6. MG to CF, August 14, 1940.

7. "Fine rare person," MG to CF, n.d.; "well-seasoned Yaddonians," EA to Rebecca Pitts (RP), April 26, 1940, Yaddo files, NYPL.

8. RP to EA, n.d., NYPL.

9. MG to CF, n.d.

10. MG to CF, Friday night, n.d.

11. MG to CF, Sunday, n.d.

12. Drag "I love you," MG to CF, September 24, 1940; "erratic, temperamental," n.d.

13. MG to CF, n.d.

14. MG to CF, n.d.

15. All quotes in paragraph from MG to CF, 1941.

16. Saab, *For the Millions*, 149, 129–56, for an overview of the fair.

17. Bohrod quote, Gail Windisch, "Delivering Art to American Homes: Associated American Artists and the Two Men Who Shaped it, 1934–84," *Art for Every Home: Associated American Artists 1934–2000*, ed. Elizabeth G. Seaton, Jane Myers, and Gail Windisch (Manhattan, KS: Marianna Kistler Beach Museum of Art, 2015), 31; MG quote, 40.

18. Windisch, "Delivering Art to American Homes," 34.

19. *New Masses*, July 3, 1934.

20. Gabriel, *Ninth Street Women*, 52.

21. Fenn, *Journal of a Voyage to Nowhere*, 86.

22. *New York Times*, September 20, 1940.

23. CF to MG, October 0? [*sic*], 1941.

24. MG to CF, March 18, 1941.

25. Fenn, unpublished memoir, 87.

CHAPTER 17

1. William Maxwell, *So Long, See You Tomorrow* (New York: Vintage Books, 1996), 131.

2. MG to CF, May 3, 1941.

3. MG to CF, June 7, 1941.

4. The painting, now at the University of Arizona Museum of Art, was widely exhibited from the 1940s to the 1980s.

5. "My own little fingers," MG to CF, June 7, 1941; "Swanky Chevrolet," June 24, 1941.

6. CF to MG, October, 1941.

7. "Bone-shaking lorries," Fenn, *Journal of a Voyage to Nowhere*, 101; "I've bitten off more," CF to MG, October 0 (possibly typo for 10), 1941.

8. MG to CF, June 7, 1941.

9. CF to MG, October, 1941.

10. *New York Times*, December 7, 1941.

11. MG to CF, December 17, 1941.

12. Fenn, *At the Dragon's Gate*, 2.

13. Fenn, *At the Dragon's Gate*, "ignorance is bliss," 3; "subservient," 19; story of the blazing vehicles from Fenn's memoir, 96.

14. Fenn, memoir, 98.

15. MG to CF, June 24, 1941.

16. Note regarding the novel, MG to CF, February 25, 43.

17. MG to CF, December 15, 1942.

18. MG to CF, February 16, 1943.

19. Florence Cramer diary, September 4, 1941, Archives of American Art, Smithsonian Institution.

20. MG to CF, February 25, 1943.

21. Fenn, *At the Dragon's Gate*, 3.

22. R. Harris Smith, *OSS: The Secret History of America's First Central Intelligence Agency* (Berkeley: University of California Press, 1971), "eccentric schemer," 3; "I'd rather," 6.

23. Smith, *OSS*, "I know," 11; "Wobblies," 9–10; International Railway, 15.

24. MG to CF, May 16, 1943.

CHAPTER 18

1. Fenn, *At the Dragon's Gate*, 7.

2. Smith, *OSS*, 12.

3. Fenn, *At the Dragon's Gate*, 8–9.

4. MG to CF, September 18, 1943.

5. Marcel Proust, *In Search of Lost Time*, Vol. 1, *Swann's Way*, trans. Lydia Davis (New York: Penguin Books, 2004), "attentive to," 45; "like souls," 47; "I was born remembering," MG to CF, December 26, 1934.

6. All quotes from MG to CF, September 24, 1943.

7. Jennifer Jolly suggests that *New Year's Eve* reproduces the "classic melancholia iconography" of genius awaiting inspiration. She suggested that Marion's depiction of an African American couple as "melancholic" was "radical." Personal correspondence, August 2023.

8. MG to CF, August 9, 1941. *New Year's Eve* is sometimes called *Midnight Show*.

9. MG to CF, October 15, 1943.

10. "Thrilling," MG to CF, December 7, 1943; Other quotes from Robert Henkes, "Marion Greenwood," *American Women Painters of the 1930s and 1940s: The Lives and Work of Ten Artists* (Jefferson, NC: McFarland and Co., 1991), 55.

11. Marcel Proust, *In Search of Lost Time: The Captive and the Fugitive*, vol. 5, trans. C. K. Scott Moncrieff and Terence Kilmartin, rev. D. J. Enright (New York: Modern Library Edition, 1992), 129.

12. MG to CF, December 7, 1943.

13. Fenn, *Journal of a Voyage to Nowhere*, 75.

14. MG to CF, "black haunted self," n.d.; "What a family," October 15, 1943.

15. MG to CF, December 1, 1944.

16. MG to CF, January 23, 1944.

17. MG to CF, January 23, 1944, for all quotes related to this incident.

18. CF to MG, January 29, 1944.

19. Fenn, *At the Dragon's Gate*, 14.

20. CF to MG, n.d.

21. MG to CF, February 25, 1944.

22. MG to CF, n.d.

23. MG to CF, "new slim figure," March 21, 1944; "treatments," March 10, 1944.

24. *New York Times*, March 26, 1944, Section X, p. 7.

25. MG to CF, June 16, 1944.

26. MG to CF, December 6, 1943.

27. Douglas Gilbert, *New York World Telegram*, November 3, 1944.

28. MG to CF, December 1, 1944.

CHAPTER 19

1. These paintings and sketches are held in the US Army Museum Enterprise Art Collection, the US Army Center of Military History, Ft. Belvoir, Virginia.

2. Brian Lanker and Nicole Newnham, *They Drew Fire: Combat Artists of World War II* (New York: TV Books, 2000), 1.

3. Lanker and Newnham, *They Drew Fire*, 6.

4. Estelle Mandel, Associated American Artists press release, March 1944, MGA.

5. Langer, *Josephine Herbst*, 250–60.

6. Lanker and Newnham, *They Drew Fire*, 7.

7. Elizabeth G. Seaton, Gail Windisch, and Jane Myers, "Art of Every Possible Service": Associated American Artists and Corporate Commissions During the War Decade," in *Art For Every Home*, 123.

8. Seaton, Windisch, and Myers, *"Art of Every Possible Service,"* 124.

9. All quotes from MG to CF, June 29, 1944.

10. Stansell, *American Moderns*, 295.

11. "The male in one form," MG to CF, August 18, 1947; "so-called neurotics," July 24, 1944.

12. MG to CF, July 24, 1944.

13. Atlantic City descriptions, MG to CF, July 24, 1944; DeWitt Mackenzie, *Men Without Guns* (Philadelphia: Blakiston Company, 1945).

14. On the neglect of women participants, see Joanne Mulcahy, "Marion Greenwood and Anne Poor: The Women Artists of the WWII Art Program," *Hyperallergic*, June 4, 2019.

15. "rather cloistered life," Sylvia Moore, *Woman's Art Journal* 2, no. 2 (Autumn, 1981–Winter, 1982), 50; "Fort Totten for me," from Poor's diary.

16. MG to George Biddle, April 10, 1943; MG to Mrs. Henry Morgenthau Jr., April 28, 1943, both in the Marion Greenwood file, US Army collection, US army history

unit, Ft. Belvoir, VA, cited in Catherine Speck, *Beyond the Battlefield: Women Artists of the Two World Wars* (London: Reaktion Books, 2014), 254.

17. Paula E. Calvin and Deborah A. Deacon, *American Women Artists in Wartime: 1776–2010* (Jefferson, NC: McFarland, 2011), 4; Speck, *Beyond the Battlefield*, 60.

18. MG to CF, May 9, 1944. A lithograph of *Mississippi Girl* is now in the collections of the Hood Museum, the Yale University Art Gallery, San Francisco's Fine Art Museums, among others.

19. John O'Connor Jr., "Painting in the United States, 1944," *Carnegie Magazine*, 1944, 143; Walter Read Hovey, "The 1944 Carnegie from the Pittsburgh Point of View," *Art News*, October 15, 1944, 12.

20. Hovey, *Art News*, 12.

21. "I was not just American," Herrera, *Listening to Stone*, 173; overview of his experience in Arizona, 179–185.

22. MG to CF, September 5, 1944.

CHAPTER 20

1. Description of Captain Toman, Fenn, *At the Dragon's Gate*, 21; other details, CF to MG, November 3, 1944.

2. "Bathhouses," Fenn, *At the Dragon's Gate*, 26; medal for valor noted on the book's jacket; other descriptions, 30.

3. Fenn, *At the Dragon's Gate*, 23.

4. Barbara W. Tuchman, *Stilwell and the American Experience in China, 1911–1945* (New York: Random House, 2017, first edition 1971), 421.

5. "The US government," Tuchman, *Stilwell and the American Experience in China*, 546–47; "reporters finally accessed," 570–71.

6. Tuchman, *Stilwell and the American Experience in China*, 194.

7. Tuchman, *Stilwell and the American Experience in China*, 42.

8. MG to CF, August 5, 1944.

9. MG to CF, August 5, 1944.

10. "The deep piano notes," MG to CF, November 3, 1944; "The most wondrous husband," December 23, 1944.

11. MG to CF, November 3, 1944.

12. CF to MG, December 6, 1944.

13. MG to CF, May 4, 1945.

14. Story of Pop, Fenn, *At the Dragon's Gate*, 62; the court-martial, 138.

15. CF to MG, December 6, 1944.

16. "Quite disagreeable," CF to MG, November 3, 1944; "Were we crazy?" MG to CF, January 7, 1945; "You have never bored me," MG to CF, July 10, 1945.

17. CF to MG, n.d.

18. MG to CF, August 18, 1944.

19. MG to CF, July 14, 1945.

20. All quotes, MG to CF, July 10, 1945.

21. Smith, *OSS*, 325.

22. Fenn, *At the Dragon's Gate*, 32; in Chinese philosophy, *Hsu* is often spelled Shu,

a basis for leading a virtuous life and a concept Westerners often describe as akin to the Golden Rule.

23. "Alert, eager," "*Hsu* from the start," Fenn, *At the Dragon's Gate*, 139; Baudelaire quote, 140.

24. "Lucias" code name and the meaning of "sincerely," from an interview with Charles Fenn as part of the 1998 BBC documentary, *Uncle Sam and Uncle Ho*.

25. Smith, *OSS*, 331.

26. Fenn, *At the Dragon's Gate*, 220.

27. Dixee R. Bartholomew-Feis, *The OSS and Ho Chi Minh: Unexpected Allies in the War Against Japan* (Lawrence: University of Kansas Press, 2006), 96.

28. Charles Fenn, *Ho Chi Minh: A Biographical Introduction* (New York: Charles Scribner's Sons, 1973), 47.

29. MG to CF, August 15, 1945. Truman's formal announcement of V-J Day was on September 2, 1945.

30. MG to CF, January 7, 1945.

31. CF to MG, n.d.

32. MG to CF, July 10, 1945.

33. Telegram in Charles Fenn's correspondence, MGA.

34. MG to CF, September 15, 1945.

35. Douglas Gilbert, *New York World Telegram*, November 3, 1944.

36. CF to MG, n.d.

CHAPTER 21

1. CF to MG, October 25, 1945; November 11, 1945.

2. CF to MG, "Dose of Confucian," October 25, 1945; "Let the past be dead," October 15, 1945.

3. Fenn, *At the Dragon's Gate*, 97.

4. MG to Emanuel Redfield, April 21, 1946; MG to Musy, November 16, 1946.

5. MG to Musy, June 1, 1946, cited in MacKenzie, "Place Really Does Matter," *RACAR*, 60.

6. MacKenzie, "Place Really Does Matter," 58.

7. MG to Musy, August 8, 1946, cited in MacKenzie, 71, note 62.

8. Description of Marion's immersion in the art scene, MacKenzie, "Place Really Does Matter," 60; "Rhythm and vitality," Wambly Bald, "An Artist Views the Smiling Poor of China," *New York Post*, July 25, 1947.

9. CF to Marshal Chang Fa-Kwei, April 14, 1947; quotes in MacKenzie, "Place Really Does Matter," 60.

10. Invitation included with a letter from Catherine MacKenzie to Robert Plate, June 16, 1996.

11. MG to CF, "I lie there," June 10, 1947; "three old," June 7, 1947.

12. "Why can't we," MG to CF, June 7, 1947; "We will always," June 12, 1947.

13. CF to GG, no date but written the day after Marion sailed in June 1947.

14. Description of Ah Sung, Fenn, memoir, no page number; "male craving" memoir, 126.

15. All quotes from CF to GG, n.d.

16. MG's musings on her year in Hong Kong, Seckler interview, 1964.

17. MG to CF, June 30, 1947.

18. CF to MG, "It is a sin," September 19, 1947; "That you should sacrifice," August 26, 1947; Charles calculated the value of the ring at $1,500. A potential buyer had offered $800 years before. CF to MG, November 8, 1947.

19. CF to MG, September 24, 1947.

20. MacKenzie, "Place Really Does Matter," 63.

21. Pegeen Sullivan and Julian Huxley statements from the exhibit catalog, "Marion Greenwood: Paintings, Gouaches, Drawings From China," Associated American Artists, December 1–December 20, 1947.

22. Bald, "Smiling Poor," *New York Post*, July 25, 1947.

23. "Water carrier," Margaret Breuning, "Return from China, *Art Digest*, December 15, 1947, 21; "Lives with insight," *New York Times*, "On View," December 7, 1947.

24. Harry Salpeter, "Marion Greenwood: An American Painter of Originality and Power," *American Artist* 12 (January 1948); "outcasts and peasants," 14; "better than nothing," MG to CF, January 13, 1948.

25. "Attractions in the Galleries," *New York Sun*, Friday, December 5, 1947.

26. H.D., *New York Times*, "On View," December 7, 1947, 16x.

27. "Fu Manchus," Bald, "Smiling Poor," July 25, 1947; PM's *Picture News*, Sunday August 31, 1947.

28. Notes on Luce as publisher, MacKenzie, "Place Really Does Matter," 66; "Just an island," MG to GG, September 1, 1946, cited in MacKenzie, 70, endnote 32.

29. "In all matters," CF to MG, November 26, 1947; "your oil technique," December 14, 1947.

30. Seckler interview, 1964.

31. Tentative plan for London, CF to MG, November 8, 1947.

32. CF to MG, January 6, 1948.

33. MG to CF, February 22, 1948.

CHAPTER 22

1. MG to CF, January 5, 1948.

2. MG to CF, description of arts opportunities, January 29, 1948; joking promises, February 4, 1948.

3. "New York after World War II," PBS American Experience, linked to *The Center of the World: New York*, a documentary film aired on September 8, 2003.

4. MG to CF, "There is nothing," January 29, 1948; details of Josie's offer, MG to CF, March 3, 1948.

5. MG to CF, "I can of course," July 31, 48; "Any straw," February 22, 1948.

6. MG to CF, February 8, 1948.

7. MG to CF, "Marion looks tonight," March 10, 1945; "everyone thinks," March 3, 1948.

8. Brodsky interview with the author, Woodstock, October 14, 2013.

9. Nickolas Muray to MG, May 6, 1949.

10. MG to CF, January 29, 1948.

11. CF to MG, "desert of American Art, July 17, 1949; "told Reeves off," July 30, 1949.

12. Frank Holland, "Marion Greenwood's Paintings of Chinese Scenes Win Acclaim," *Chicago Sun Times*, April 18, 1948, 80; "Marion Greenwood," *Art News*, December 1947.

13. "At the Moment," *Chicago Sun Times*, 1948, clip from MGA.

14. Emily Markert, "Alice Neel Didn't Work Alone," *Hyperallergic*, August 31, 2021.

15. *The Pantagraph*, Sunday, November 14, 1948, Bloomington, IL, no byline.

16. MG to Marc Sandler (MS), March 7, 1948. For more on Sandler's art collecting, see MacKenzie, 71, note 48.

17. MS to MG, January 12, 1948, Marion Greenwood Collection, courtesy of University of Tennessee Libraries.

18. MG to CF, June 16, 1948.

19. MG to CF, March 30, 1948.

20. The note on Charles asking Josie for advice on leaving Marion appears in the Josephine Herbst papers, Beinecke Library; "You have made it," "I now ask you again," MG to CF, March 30, 1948.

21. Fenn, memoir, 176.

22. Loan documents from Savings and Loan Association of Kingston, MGA.

23. MG to CF, June 10, 1949.

24. May 29, 1949.

25. MG to CF, June 23, 1949.

26. CF to MG, September 13, 1949.

27. "Brushes Hubby," *New York World-Telegram and Sun*, January 25, 1950; "Woman Artist Wins Divorce," *New York Journal-American*, January 22, 1950, 10-L.

28. MG to Huxley, March 8, 1950, Juliette Huxley papers, Woodson Research Center, Rice University.

29. MG to CF, February 25, 1948.

CHAPTER 23

1. Dane Rudhyar to MG, May 23, 1948.

2. MG to CF, September 25, 1950.

3. MG to CF, "a great help," June 3, 1950; "God, how I need," November 30, 1950.

4. Elizabeth (Betty) Trivell interview with the author, November 1, 2017.

5. Background on Bob Plate and letter on the MacArthur parade, Bob Plate (BP) to MG, April 20, 1951.

6. MG to CF, August 3, 1950.

7. MG to CF, January 21, 1953. Fenn recounts losing then regaining his citizenship in *Ho Chi Minh*, 1973, appendix D.

8. MG to CF, "I never did," "anti-everything," "a good old American," April 16, 1952.

9. MG to BP, April 14, 1952.

10. MG to CF, January 28, 1951.

11. "Unless," MG to CF, November 30, 1950; "My best things," Seckler interview, 1964; "This sort," MG to CF, February 8, 1951.

12. Reeves Lewenthal, "To Whom It May Concern," April 9, 1951.

13. DeWitt Peters, "Haitian Art . . . How It Started," in *Readings in Latin American Modern Art*, ed. Patrick Frank (New Haven, CT: Yale University Press, 2004), 70. The editor cautions that Peters overstates his importance in "starting" Haitian art but acknowledges his role.

14. MG to CF, March 13, 1953.

15. "Hopelessly narrow minded," MG to CF, April 11, 1952, to CF; "private kingdom," MG to BP, March 15?, 1952.

16. MG to BP, March 12, 1952; MG to CF, April 11, 1952.

17. *Haiti Sun* 1, no. 33, April 29, 1952; MG to CF, April 11, 1952.

18. *The Lamp*, March 1955; "dare to have a cow," and "fake it later," MG to BP, n.d.

19. Karen McCarthy Brown, *A Vodou Priestess in Brooklyn* (Berkeley: University of California Press, 1991), ix.

20. Laënnec Hurbon, "American Fantasy and Haitian Vodou," in *Sacred Arts of Haitian Vodou*, ed. Donald J. Cosentino (Los Angeles: UCLA Fowler Museum of Cultural History, 1995), 184.

21. King, *Gods of the Upper Air*, 275–301.

22. MG to BP, March 12, 1952.

23. Plate diary, "With her usual," April 9, 1951; "great vitality," December 3, 1951.

24. MG to CF, July 22, 1952.

CHAPTER 24

1. MG to CF, March 24, 1951.

2. MG to CF, October 7, 1952.

3. Both quotes, Robert Plate diary, July 15, 1952.

4. Plate diary, April 16, 1953.

5. BP to Irwin Greenwood, December 31, 1953; BP uses "Muzzy," an alternate spelling of "Musy."

6. Advertised in the *New York Times*, June 20, 1954.

7. MG to CF, July 29, 1954.

8. C. Kermit Ewing to MG, July 6, 1954.

9. MG to CF, "fears of," July 29, 1954; "almost had," December 4, 1954.

10. MG to CF, December 4, 1954.

11. "Mural Artist Ready for Work at UT Center," n.d., MGA.

12. "Close your eyes," news clip, n.d., courtesy of MGA; "still wrestling," from "Tennessee Mural to be Unveiled," *Knoxville Journal*, June 5, 1955; "serious beauty," Jack Neely, "The Singing Mural: Marion Greenwood's Long-Concealed Masterwork in a Rare Public Display, *Metropulse*, June 11, 2014.

13. Martha Lee Osborne interview with the author, Knoxville, TN, June 5, 2014.

14. "Panel to Discuss Controversial UC Ballroom Mural," *Metropulse* news release, March 23, 2006.

15. *Metropulse*, March 23, 2006.

16. Descriptions of the mural and the painting process from Frederick C. Moffatt, "Marion Greenwood in Tennessee," forward by Sam Yates, exhibition catalog, TRACE: Tennessee Research and Creative Exchange, 2014.

17. *Knoxville News-Sentinel*, Monday, June 6, 1955.

18. Details of the mural, including the reference to El Greco, from Moffatt, "Marion Greenwood in Tennessee," 5.

19. "Wonderfully alive," LeRoy P. Graf to MG, June 8, 1955; confessed to feeling empty, *Knoxville Journal*, "TN Mural To Be Unveiled," June 5, 1955.

20. MG to CF, January 29, 1956.

21. Jack Neely, "Will UT's Greenwood Mural Go into Hiding Again? Its Fate Remains Unclear," *Metropulse*, Wednesday, July 24, 2013.

22. Eric Harkness, phone interview with the author, August 9, 2013.

23. I attended the opening in 2014. All quotes are from my interviews with guests that night, an event the following night, and with UT gallery manager Mike Berry.

24. "Humanizes," Moffatt, 3; Liv McConnell, "Controversial Mural Seen in New Light," *Daily Beacon*, June 25, 2014.

25. Fred Moffatt, interview with the author, Knoxville, June 6, 2014.

26. BP to C. Kermit Ewing, July 24, 1970.

27. Brodsky interview with the author, October 14, 2013.

CHAPTER 25

1. MG to CF, January 29, 1956.

2. *Metropulse*, March 23, 2006.

3. MG to CF, January 29, 1956.

4. Marion Greenwood, "Form and Content," in *The Art of the Artist: Theories and Techniques of Art By the Artists Themselves*, ed. Arthur Zaidenberg (New York: Crown Publishers, 1951), 106–107.

5. CF to MG, March 5, 1959.

6. Gabriel, *Ninth Street Women*, xv.

7. "The So-called Woodstock School," Bruce Weber, "Making It Permanent: Community, Family, Friendship, and the Building of the Collection of the Woodstock Artists Association," in *Woodstock Artists Association: One Hundred Years of Community and Art*, ed. Natalie Chapman, 102 (Woodstock, NY: WAAM, 2019); For another discussion of Woodstock art movements and styles, see Tom Wolf, "Historical Survey," *Woodstock's Art Heritage: The Permanent Collection of the Woodstock Artists Association* (Woodstock, NY: Overlook Press, 1987), 17–29.

8. Karal Ann Marling, "Introduction," *Woodstock: An American Art Colony: 1902–1977*, Vassar College Art Gallery, January 23–March 4, 1977, 20.

9. Weber, "Making It Permanent," 122; "The Mayor of Woodstock," from a phone conversation with Bruce Weber on December 5, 2022.

10. Email exchange with Bruce Weber, December 7, 2022.

11. Plate diary, July 25, 195; regarding the different artists groups, Sal Sirugo's wife, Irene, remembers the abstract camp as separate from the realist.

12. Details of Bud Plate's life from Marc Plate, "My Father, Walter Plate," exhibit catalog.

13. Conversation with Marc Plate, July 27, 2022.

14. Brodsky interview, October 14, 2013.

15. Plate diary, "mustached artist," May 18, 1952; "the usual crowd," Sunday, June 1, 1952.

16. Brodsky interview, October 14, 2013.

17. MG to CF, June 26, 1956.

18. Unnamed publication in BP to MG, July 28, 1956.

19. Willard W. Beatty to MG, June 10, 1936, MGA.

20. "My very darling," Diego Rivera to MG, August 6, 1949, MGA; "absolute no," MG to BP, November 5, 1956.

21. Seckler interview, 8.

22. MG to CF, January 29, 1956.

23. Louise Reisman to MG, August 7, 1956.

24. BP to MG, August 11, 1956.

25. BP to MG, July 26, 1956.

26. MG to CF, June 26, 1956.

27. Judith Shea phone interview with the author, October 29, 2021.

28. "Talented Woman Artist," *Waterloo (Iowa) Daily Courier*, December 20, 1950.

CHAPTER 26

1. Summary of the trip, MG to CF, October 21, 1962.

2. MG to BP, "Washington Square Types," June 16, 1962; "thinks he's James," June 18, 1962.

3. MG to BP, June 28, 1962.

4. Plate diary, August 12, 1961.

5. Card in the MGA, n.d.

6. All letters from Verna Carleton Millan to MG in the MGA, n.d.

7. Plate diary, August 20, 1962.

8. BP to Adolf and Virginia Dehn, July 27, 1964.

9. Susan Teller, "At Associated American Artists with Sylvan Cole, Jr.," *Art for Every Home*, 2015, 221; "Sylvan loved women," Susan Teller phone interview with the author, Monday, September 24, 2018.

10. Sylvan Cole, "Oral History Interview with Sylvan Cole," by Avis Berman, Sylvan Cole Gallery, New York, Smithsonian Archives of American Art, June through October 2000, transcript, 35.

11. "The Maine Campus," (Orono), February 18, 1965, clip from MGA.

12. Greenwood, "Form and Content," 106.

13. Syracuse University Archives, News Release, March 16, 1965.

14. Richard G. Case, "Syracuse University Gives Birth to a Mural," *Empire: The Magazine of Central New York*, September 26, 1965.

15. *Marion Greenwood's mural statement*, n.d., MGA.

16. *Syracuse University News*, March 16, 1965, SU archives.

17. *Daily Orange*, September 29, 1965, *Daily Orange* [microfilm], Syracuse University Libraries.

18. "Readers Sound Off on Campus Problems," *Daily Orange*, October 19, 1965.

19. Syracuse University Record, September 15, 1983.

20. "There is nothing," BP to William Plate, June 23, 1967; "He has compassion," MG to CF, November 9, 1968.

21. Sylvan Cole to BP, August 3, 1967; Letter from Artists' Fellowship, E. Raymond Kinstler to MG, April 1, 1968.

22. Mac to Zaddo (Grace to Marion), September 30, 1969.

23. Georges and Lilly Schreiber to MG, n.d.

24. Walter Greenwood to Lester Greenwood, April 25, 1967, MGA.

25. GG to MG, n.d., MGA.

26. BP to "Gladdie and Bud," February 13, 1969.

27. MG to CF, May 1, no year.

28. BP to art critic Emily Genauer, n.d.

29. Marion Greenwood interview with Karl Fortess, Woodstock, NY, June 1969.

CHAPTER 27

1. BP to Amy and Walter Charak, December 27, 1969.

2. Raymond Kinstler to BP, October 2, 1969, MGA.

3. Response to Käthe Kollwitz, BP to CF, March 6, 1970; response to Bud's provocation, Brodsky interview, October 14, 2013.

4. Albany Medical Center to Commissioner Joseph Fitzsimmons, Ulster County Department of Social Services, December 3, 1969, MGA.

5. Plate diary, January 1, 1970.

6. "M weak," January 14, 1970; "My darling Marion," diary, n.d.; "Oh my darling," Wednesday, January 7, 1970.

7. Plate diary, February 5, 1970.

8. BP to Kinstler, February 11, 1970.

9. Plate diary, February 19 and 20, 1970.

10. Plate diary, August 12, 1970.

11. "Frightful," BP to Aileen, April 8, 1970; "the most alive"; Plate diary, March 7, 1970.

12. Plate diary, March 19, 1970.

13. "Touching," Plate diary, May 1, 1970; "a mixed bunch," BP to Virginia Dehn, n.d.; list of lovers and friends, Plate diary, March 26, 1970.

14. BP to CF, March 6, 1970.

15. June Sandler to BP, February 20, 1970.

16. Plate diary, April 26, no year.

17. Plate diary, January 18, 1970.

18. "She is very," Jessie Greenwood to BP, March 12, 1970; "I'd be happy," BP to Jessie, March 16, 1970.

19. In a diary entry, Bob described how Grace told him about Marion's "abortion from Pacheco, weird relationships with [John] Hermann & [Josephine] Herbst and the lesbian Helen Fisher." It's unclear whether the judgment of "weird" was Grace's or Bob's. March 3, 1970. In my 1969 interview with Gladys Brodsky, she also mentioned an abortion Marion had in Mexico or upon her return to New York, but I found no other evidence of a third abortion or any other mention of Helen Fisher.

20. "Marion, there is no," Plate diary, April 5, 1970; "my extraordinary," diary, April 6, 1970.

21. BP to CF, March 6, 1970.

22. Letter draft in MGA, n.d.

23. Jaime Plenn, "'Everywhere She Saw Beauty': An Epitaph for Marion Greenwood," *News, Mexico City*, Tuesday, March 26, 1970.

24. Plate diary, April 19, 1970.

25. Plate diary, September 17, 1970.

26. "The Ultimate Mystery: Strauss's Death and Transfiguration," Houston Symphony website, October 30, 2019.

27. MG to JH, November 19, 1932.

CHAPTER 28

1. Stansell, *American Moderns*, 151.

2. "Excavated from beneath," Ralph M. Pearson, "Marion Greenwood," *The Modern Renaissance in American Art: Presenting the Work and Philosophy of 54 Distinguished Artists* (New York: Harper and Brothers, 1954), 257–59.

3. Cath Pound, "Why Portraits Have Fascinated Us for Millennia," BBC Culture, February 6, 2022.

4. Kelli Morgan, "Blowing Holes in Traditional American Portraiture," *Hyperallergic*, March 10, 2023.

5. MG interview with Karl Fortess, Woodstock, 1969.

6. Peter Schjeldahl, "Shapes of Things: The Birth of the Abstract," *New Yorker*, January 7, 2013, 68–70.

7. "Reputational caprice" and "Vermeeromania," Jason Farago, "The Absolute Vermeer, in a Show More Precious Than Pearls," *New York Times*, February 9, 2023.

8. Lucy R. Lippard, "'19th-Century American Women Artists' at the Whitney Downtown, and '7 American Women: The Depression Decade' at Vassar College Art Gallery," *Art in America* (September–October 1976): 113.

9. Lippard, *Art in America*, 113.

10. Salpeter, "Marion Greenwood," *American Artist*, 1948, 14.

11. "Bloom of pulchritude," Salpeter, *American Artist*, 1948; he cites the "sheaf of wheat" description from Gilbert, *New York World Telegram*, 1944.

12. "At the Moment," *Chicago Sun Times*, 1948, clip from MGA.

13. Brodsky interview with the author, Woodstock, October 14, 2013.

14. Brodsky interview, 2013.

15. In a biography of Calder, Jed Perl speculates about an affair between Marion and Calder. AAA director Sylvan Cole also mentions it in an interview, but I found no evidence in Marion's letters or papers. See Jed Perl, *Calder: The Conquest of Time, the Early Years: 1898–1940* (New York: Knopf, 2017), 208–9.

16. Nicholas Jeeves, "The Serious and the Smirk: The Smile in Portraiture," *Public Domain Review*, September 18, 2013.

17. Richard Brilliant, *Portraiture* (London: Reaktion Books, 1991), 156.

18. Janet Malcolm, "Edward Weston's Women," *New York Review of Books*, December 5, 2002.

19. MG to CF, n.d.

20. Joanna Woods-Marsden, *Renaissance Self-Portraiture: The Visual Construction of Identity and the Social Status of the Artist* (New Haven, CT: Yale University Press, 1998), 191–213.

21. Higgie, *The Mirror and the Palette*, 16.

22. Schjeldahl, "Shapes of Things," 70.

Bibliography

ARCHIVAL SOURCES

Alfred Honigbaum Archives, Kirshenbaum Family Collection

Archives of American Art, Smithsonian Institution, Washington, DC

Art Students League (ASL) of New York Archives, New York

Beinecke Rare Book and Manuscript Library, Elinor Langer Collection of Josephine Herbst, Yale University, New Haven, Connecticut

Grace Greenwood Archives (GGA), Carol Lee and Irene Sirugo Collection

Historical Society of Woodstock Archives, Woodstock, New York

Marion Greenwood Archives (MGA), estate executor Marc Plate, Woodstock, New York

New York Public Library (NYPL), Marion Greenwood guest file, Yaddo records, Manuscripts and Archives Division, Astor, Lenox, and Tilden Foundations

New York Public Library (NYPL), Lionel Pincus and Princess Firyal Map Division

Rice University, Woodson Research Center, Fondren Library, Juliette Huxley papers, 1895–1994, MS 474

Syracuse University Libraries, Syracuse, New York

University of Tennessee Libraries, Betsey B. Creekmore Special Collections and University Archives, Marion Greenwood Collection, Knoxville

PRINT AND OTHER SOURCES

Acevedo, Esther. "Young Muralists at the Abelardo L. Rodríguez Market." In *Mexican Muralism: A Critical History*, ed. Alejandro Anreus, Robin Adèle Greeley, and Leonard Folgarait, 125–47. Berkeley: University of California Press, 2012.

Adams, Agnes. "Painting Murals Is This Woman's Work." *New York Post*, November 27, 1940.

"Artist to Talk at Her Exhibit." *Pantagraph*, Bloomington, IL, Sunday, November 14, 1948.

"Brushes Hubby." *New York World-Telegram and Sun*, January 25, 1950.

"At the Moment." *Chicago Sun Times*, 1948.

Babcock, Barbara. "'A New Mexican Rebecca': Imaging Pueblo Women." *Journal of the Southwest* 32, no. 4, Inventing the Southwest (Winter 1990): 400–37.

Bald, Wambly. "An Artist Views the Smiling Poor of China." New York Post, July 25, 1947.

Baldwin, Neil. *Martha Graham: When Dance Became Modern*. New York: Alfred A. Knopf, 2022.

Barnieck, Jens. "Sonata for Winold Reiss." In *The Multicultural Modernism of Winold Reiss, 1886–1953, Transnational Approaches to His Work*, ed. Frank Mehring, 206–17. Berlin: Deutscher Kunstverlag, 2022.

Bartholomew-Feis, Dixee R. *The OSS and Ho Chi Minh: Unexpected Allies in the War Against Japan*. Lawrence: University of Kansas Press, 2006.

Berman, Avis. *Rebels on Eighth Street: Juliana Force and the Whitney Museum of American Art*. New York: Atheneum, 1990.

Blanck, Catharine. "Muralist Enjoys Her Work at Red Hook Development." *Brooklyn Eagle*, Sunday, April 14, 1940, 10A.

Bohm-Duchen, Monica. *Art and the Second World War*. Princeton: Princeton University Press, 2013.

Boyer, Paul S., ed. *The Oxford Companion to United States History*. Oxford: Oxford University Press, 2006.

Braude, Mark. *Kiki Man Ray: Art, Love, and Rivalry in 1920s Paris*. New York: W.W. Norton, 2022.

Brenner, Anita. *Idols Behind Altars: Modern Mexican Art and Its Cultural Roots*. Mineola, NY: Dover Publications, 2002.

Breuning, Margaret. "Return from China." *Art Digest*, December 15, 1947.

Brilliant, Richard. *Portraiture*. London: Reaktion Books, 1991.

Bulletin of the Museum of Modern Art 4, no. 6 (July 1937): 7–8.

Bynner, Wittner. *Selected Letters*, ed. James Kraft. New York: Farrar, Straus and Giroux, 1981.

Calvin, Paula E., and Deborah A. Deacon. *American Women Artists in Wartime, 1776–2010*. Jefferson, NC: McFarland & Co., 2011.

Caro, Julie Levin. "The Winold Reiss Studio and Art School as a Hub of Transcultural Modernism." In *The Multicultural Modernism of Winold Reiss, 1886–1953, Transnational Approaches to His Work*, ed. Frank Mehring, 190–205. Berlin: Deutscher Kunstverlag, 2022.

Carr, Barry. "Mexico: Radicals, Revolutionaries and Exiles: Mexico City in the 1920s." *Berkeley Review of Latin American Studies* (Fall 2010): 26–30.

Case, Richard G. "Syracuse University Gives Birth to a Mural." *Empire: The Magazine of Central New York*, Sunday, September 26, 1965.

Castilleja, Aída. "La Cha 'nantskua o Fiesta del Corpus en Pueblos Purépechas." In *Historia y vida ceremonial en las comunidades mesoamericanas: Los ritos agrícolas*, ed. Johanna Broda and Catherine Good, 387–414. Primera edición, México, Instituto Nacional de Antropología e Historia, Universidad Nacional Autónoma de México, Instituto de Investigaciones Históricas, 2004.

Chapman, Natalie, ed. *Woodstock Artists Association: One Hundred Years of Community and Art*. Woodstock, NY: Woodstock Artists Association, 2019.

Cole, Sylvan. Interview by Avis Berman, Smithsonian Archives of American Art, June–October 2000.

Comisarenco Mirkin, Dina. *Eclipse de Siete Lunas: Mujeres Muralistas en México*. Mexico City: Artes de México y del Mundo, 2017.

Corn, Wanda M. *The Great American Thing: Modern Art and National Identity, 1915–1935*. Berkeley: University of California Press, 1999.

Delpar, Helen. *The Enormous Vogue of Things Mexican: Cultural Relations between the United States and Mexico, 1920–1935*. Tuscaloosa: University of Alabama Press, 1995.

Donohue, Mary V. *Marion Greenwood: A Global Artist, 2018. Self-published.*

Doss, Erika. *Benton, Pollock, and the Politics of Modernism: From Regionalism to Abstract Expressionism*. Chicago: University of Chicago Press, 1991.

Douglas, Ann. *Terrible Honesty: Mongrel Manhattan in the 1920s*. New York: Farrar, Straus and Giroux, 1995.

Eakin, Hugh. *Picasso's War: How Modern Art Came to America*. New York: Crown, 2022.

Eisenberg, Emanuel. "Battle of the Century." *New Masses*, December 10, 1935.

Evers, Alf. *Woodstock: History of an American Town*. Woodstock, NY: Overlook Press, 1987.

Faderman, Lillian. *The Gay Revolution: The Story of the Struggle*. New York: Simon & Schuster, 2015.

Farago, Jason. "The Absolute Vermeer, in a Show More Precious than Pearls." *New York Times*, February 9, 2023.

Fenn, Charles. *At the Dragon's Gate: With the OSS in the Far East*. Annapolis, MD: Naval Institute Press, 2004.

———. "Life Begins at Eighty-Seven." Unpublished memoir, 1993.

———. *Ho Chi Minh: A Biographical Introduction*. New York: Charles Scribner's Sons, 1973.

———. *Journal of a Voyage to Nowhere*. New York: W. W. Norton, 1971.

Franck, Dan. *Bohemian Paris: Picasso, Modigliani, Matisse, and the Birth of Modern Art*. New York: Grove Press, 2003.

Ferriero, David S., and Elaina Richardson. "Forward." In *Yaddo: Making American Culture*, ed. Micki McGee. New York: Columbia University Press, 2008.

Folgarait, Leonard. *Mural Painting and Social Revolution in Mexico, 1920–1940: Art of the New Order*. Cambridge: Cambridge University Press, 1998.

Fondation Richard Walker. Première exposition annuelle d'un nouveau groupe internationale de peinture moderne, du 30 septembre au 14 octubre inclus, a La Galerie René Zivy, 57, Avenue Montaigne, Paris.

Gabriel, Mary. *Ninth Street Women: Lee Krasner, Elaine de Kooning, Grace Hartigan, Joan Mitchell, and Helen Frankenthaler: Five Painters and the Movement that Changed Modern Art*. New York: Little Brown and Co., 2018.

Gallagher, Catherine. "Winold Reiss." In *Woodstock Portraits*, May 8 through June 28, Woodstock Artists Association, 1999, 31–32.

Gallt, Frank A. *Picturesque Catskills Official Guide*. Catskill, NY: Catskill Mountain Resort Co., 1922.

Gilbert, Douglas. *New York World Telegram*. November 3, 1944.

Goldman, Emma. "Love and Marriage." In *Anarchism and Other Essays*, third revised edition. New York: Mother Earth Publishing, 1917.

Greeley, Robin Adèle. "Muralism and the State in Post-Revolution Mexico, 1920–1970." In *Mexican Muralism: A Critical History*, ed. Alejandro Anreus, Robin Adèle Greeley, and Leonard Folgarait, 13–36. Berkeley: University of California Press, 2012.

Greenwood, Marion. "Form and Content." In *The Art of the Artist: Theories and Techniques of Art by the Artists Themselves*, ed. Arthur Zadenberg, 106–7. New York: Crown Publishers, 1951.

———. Interview by Dorothy Seckler. Smithsonian Institution Archives of American Art, December 31, 1964, 1–14.

Gottlieb, Robert. "'Dah-ling': The Strange Case of Tallulah Bankhead." *New Yorker*, May 8, 2005.

Haskell, Barbara. "América: Mexican Muralism and Art in the United States: 1925–1945." In *Vida Americana: Mexican Muralists Remake American Art, 1925–1945*, ed. Barbara Haskell, 14–45. New York: Whitney Museum of Art, February 17–May 17, 2020.

Henkes, Robert. *American Women Painters of the 1930s and 1940s: The Lives and Work of Ten Artists*. Jefferson, NC: McFarland and Co., 1991.

Herbst, Josephine. "The Artist's Progress." *Mexican Life* 11, no. 3 (March 1935): 24–26.

———. "Marion Greenwood." *Mexican Life* 9, no. 7 (July 1933): 19–21.

Herrera, Hayden. *Listening to Stone: The Art and Life of Isamu Noguchi*. New York: Farrar, Straus and Giroux, 2015.

Higgie, Jennifer. *The Mirror and the Palette: Rebellion, Revolution, and Resilience: Five Hundred Years of Women's Self-Portraits*. New York: Pegasus Books, 2021.

Hills, Patricia. "Paul Kellogg, Alain Locke, Winold Reiss, and the Survey Graphic March 1925 Issue Harlem: Mecca of the New Negro." In *The Multicultural Modernism of Winold Reiss, 1886–1953, Transnational Approaches to His Work*, ed. Frank Mehring, 120–39. Berlin: Deutscher Kunstverlag, 2022.

Holditch, W. Kenneth. "William Spratling, William Faulkner and Other Famous Creoles." *Mississippi Quarterly* 51, no. 3, Special Issue: William Faulkner (Summer 1998): 423–34.

Holland, Frank. "Marion Greenwood's Paintings of Chinese Scenes Win Acclaim." *Chicago Sun Times*, April 18, 1948.

Hovey, Walter Read. "The 1944 Carnegie from the Pittsburgh Point of View." *Art News*, October 15, 1944.

Hughes, Robert. "The Wave from the Atlantic." *American Visions*, Episode 5, BBC, February 5, 2002.

Hull, Howard. "Crossville: Marion Greenwood, the Partnership of Man and Nature, 1940." In *Tennessee Post Office Murals*, 39–44. Johnson City, TN: Overmountain Press, 1996.

Hurbon, Laënnec. "American Fantasy and Haitian Vodou." In *Sacred Arts of Haitian Vodou*, ed. Donald J. Cosentino, 181–97. Los Angeles: UCLA Fowler Museum of Cultural History, 1995.

Huré, M. Fernand. *Ambassades et Consulats, Revue Mondiale Illustrée*. Paris: Diplomatie Mondanites Actualites, 1928.

Huxley, Julian. *Essays of a Humanist*. Middlesex, England: Penguin Books, 1966.

———. "Marion Greenwood: Paintings, Gouaches, Drawings From China." Associated American Artists. December 1 through December 20, 1947.

———. *Essays of a Biologist*. New York: Knopf, 1923.

Indych-López, Anna. "Celluloid América: Siqueiros, Hollywood, and Plástica Fílmica." In *Vida Americana: Mexican Muralists Remake American Art, 1925–1945*, ed. Barbara Haskell, 188–95. New York: Whitney Museum of Art, February 17–May 17, 2020.

Jacobs, Julia. "The Virus Won't Revive F.D.R.'s Arts Jobs Program. Here's Why." *New York Times*, April 22, 2020.

Jeeves, Nicholas. "The Serious and the Smirk: The Smile in Portraiture." *Public Domain Review*, September 18, 2013.

Jolly, Jennifer. "Animating Internationalism: David Alfaro Siqueiros and Antifascist Art in the 1903s." *Art History* 45, no. 4 (2022): 798–831.

———. *Creating Pátzcuaro, Creating Mexico: Art, Tourism, and Nation Building under Lázaro Cárdenas*. Austin: University of Texas Press, 2018.

King, Charles. *Gods of the Upper Air: How a Circle of Renegade Anthropologists Reinvented Race, Sex, and Gender in the Twentieth Century*. New York: Doubleday, 2019.

Krishnamurti, Jiddu. *International Star Bulletin* 8 (August 1930).

Langa, Helen. *Radical Art: Printmaking and the Left in 1930s New York*. Berkeley: University of California Press, 2004.

Langer, Elinor. *Josephine Herbst: The Story She Could Never Tell*. Boston: Little, Brown and Co., 1983.

Lanker, Brian, and Nicole Newnham. *They Drew Fire: Combat Artists of World War II*. New York: TV Books, 2000.

Lippard, Lucy R. "'19th-Century American Women Artists' at the Whitney Downtown, and '7 American Women: The Depression Decade' at Vassar College Art Gallery," *Art in America* (September–October 1976): 111–13.

MacKenzie, Catherine. "Place Really Does Matter: Marion Greenwood's 1947 'China' Exhibition." *RACAR: Revue d'art Canadienne/Canadian Art Review* 25, no. 1/2, Producing Women/Ces Femmes que produisent (1998): 58–72.

———. "Marion Greenwood: American Painter and Graphic Artist: 1909–1970." *International Dictionary of Women Artists*, vol. 1, 616–18. London: Fitzroy Dearborn Publishers, 1998.

Mackenzie, DeWitt. *Men Without Guns*. Philadelphia: Blakiston Company, 1945.

"Marion Greenwood, Muralist. 60. Dead." *New York Times*, February 21, 1970.

McCarthy Brown, Karen. *A Vodou Priestess in Brooklyn*. Berkeley: University of California Press, 1991.

McConnell, Liv. "Controversial Mural Seen in New Light." *Daily Beacon*, June 25, 2014.

Marling, Karal Ann. "Introduction." In *Woodstock: An American Art Colony: 1902–1977.* Vassar College Art Gallery, January 23–March 4, 1977.

———. "American Art and the American Woman." In *7 American Women: The Depression Decade*, 7–15. Poughkeepsie, NY: Vassar College Art Gallery, 1976.

Malcolm, Janet. "Edward Weston's Women." *New York Review of Books*, December 5, 2002.

Mathews, Marcia M. "George Biddle's Contribution to Federal Art." Records of the Columbia Historical Society, Historical Society of Washington, DC, 1973/1974, 49:493–520.

"Marion Greenwood Applauded for Steady Rise to Mural Fame." *New York Post*, April 12, 1936.

Maxwell, William. *So Long, See You Tomorrow.* New York: Vintage Books, 1996.

Mehring, Frank, ed. *The Multicultural Modernism of Winold Reiss, 1886–1953, Transnational Approaches to His Work.* Berlin: Deutscher Kunstverlag, 2022.

———. "How Silhouettes Became 'Black': Winold Reiss and the Visual Rhetoric of the Harlem Renaissance." In *The Multicultural Modernism of Winold Reiss, 1886–1953, Transnational Approaches to His Work*, ed. Frank Mehring, 140–57. Berlin: Deutscher Kunstverlag, 2022.

———. *The Mexico Diary: Winold Reiss Between Vogue Mexico and Harlem Renaissance.* Tempe, AZ: Bilingual Press, 2016.

Markert, Emily. "Alice Neel Didn't Work Alone." *Hyperallergic*, August 31, 2021.

"Mexican Market (Art)." *Time* 26, no. 4 (July 22, 1935): 26.

Midorikawa, Emily. *Out of the Shadows: Six Visionary Victorian Women in Search of a Public Voice.* Berkeley, CA: Counterpoint Press, 2021.

Millan, Verna Carleton. *Mexico Reborn.* Boston: Houghton Mifflin, 1939.

"Montparnasse to Mexico." *Brooklyn Daily Eagle*, March 1, 1936: F8–F9.

Moffatt, Dr. Frederick C. "Marion Greenwood in Tennessee." Forword by Sam Yates, TRACE: Tennessee Research and Creative Exchange, UT Downtown Gallery, Knoxville, TN, June 6–August 9, 2014: 1–19.

Moore, Sylvia. *Woman's Art Journal* 2, no. 2 (Autumn 1981–Winter 1982).

Morgan, Kelli. "Blowing Holes in Traditional American Portraiture." *Hyperallergic*, March 10, 2023.

Morrill, Penny C. "Renaissance Transformation." In *William Spratling and the Mexican Silver Renaissance: Maestros de Plata.* Harry N. Abrams, in association with the San Antonio Museum of Art, 2002: 12–69.

Mulcahy, Joanne B. "Marion Greenwood and Anne Poor: The Women Artists of the WWII Art Program." *Hyperallergic*, June 4, 2019.

———. "How the Art Students League Shaped the Life of Twentieth-Century Artist Marion Greenwood." *Linea: Studio Notes from the Art Students League of NY*, October 15, 2020.

Mullinix, Heather. "Post Office Mural on Loan to UT." *Crossville Chronicle*, June 2, 2014.

Neely, Jack. "The Singing Mural: Marion Greenwood's Long-Concealed Masterwork in Rare Public Display." *Metropulse*, June 11, 2014.

———. "Will UT's Greenwood Mural Go into Hiding Again? Its Fate Remains Unclear." *Metropulse*, Wednesday, July 24, 2013.

"New York after World War II." PBS. *American Experience: The Center of the World; New York,* aired on September 8, 2003.

Nochlin, Linda. "The Realist Criminal and the Abstract Law." *Art in America,* September 1, 1973.

O'Connor, John Jr. "Painting in the United States, 1944." *Carnegie Magazine, 1944,* 143–47.

"Odyssey Which Ended in West Cork." Charles Fenn Obituary, *Irish Times,* June 19, 2004.

Oles, James. Review of "Vida Americana: Mexican Muralists Remake American Art, 1925–1945," Whitney Museum of American Art. *Panorama: Journal of the Association of Historians of American Art* 6, no. 2 (Fall 2020).

———. "The Mexican Experience of Marion and Grace Greenwood." In *The Eagle and the Virgin: Nation and Cultural Revolution in Mexico, 1920–1940,* ed. Mary Kay Vaughan and Stephen Lewis, 67–78. Durham, NC: Duke University Press, 2006.

———. "Walls to Paint On: American Muralists in Mexico, 1933–1936." PhD dissertation, Department of Art History, Yale University, 1995.

———. *South of the Border: Mexico in the American Imagination/México en La Imaginación Norteamericana, 1914–1947.* Washington, DC: Smithsonian Institution Press, 1993.

Orozco, José Clemente. *An Autobiography,* trans. Robert C. Stephenson. Austin: University of Texas Press, 1962.

"Panel to Discuss Controversial UC Ballroom Mural." *Metropulse* news release, March 23, 2006.

Patterson, Jody. "Modernism and Murals at the 1939 New York World's Fair." *American Art* 24, no. 2 (Summer 2010): 50–73.

Peatross, C. Ford. "Stepping Out in Winold Reiss's New York, 1915 to 1952." In *The Art of Winold Reiss: An Immigrant Modernist,* ed. Marilyn Satin Kushner, 29–48. New York Historical Society, 2021.

Pearson, Ralph M. "Marion Greenwood." *The Modern Renaissance in American Art: Presenting the Work and Philosophy of 54 Distinguished Artists,* 257–61. New York: Harper and Brothers, 1954.

———. "The Artists Point of View." *Forum,* December 19, 1936.

Pérez Aguirre, Dulze. "La educación socialista en México y el mural: Atentado a las maestras rurales de Aurora Reyes." Revista Internacional y Comparada de Derechos Humanos 2, no. 2 (July–December 2019): 219–49.

Perl, Jed. *Calder: The Conquest of Time, the Early Years: 1898–1940.* New York: Knopf, 2017.

"Personality of the Week." *Haiti Sun* 1, no. 33 (April 29, 1952).

Peters, DeWitt. "Haitian Art . . . How It Started." In *Readings in Latin American Modern Art,* ed. Patrick Frank, 67–72. New Haven, CT: Yale University Press, 2004.

Plate, Robert. "Marion Greenwood." Biographical sketch: 1–17, Marion Greenwood Archives.

Plenn, Jaime. "'Everywhere She Saw Beauty': An Epitaph for Marion Greenwood." *News,* Mexico City, March 26, 1970.

Pound, Cath. "Why Portraits Have Fascinated Us for Millennia." BBC Culture, February 6, 2022.

Price, Ruth. "'The Longest Stay': Agnes Smedley, Yaddo, and the 'Lowell Affair.'" In *Yaddo: Making American Culture,* ed. Micki McGee, 79–94. New York: Columbia University Press, 2008.

Proust, Marcel. *In Search of Lost Time.* Vol. 1, *Swann's Way.* Translated by Lydia Davis. New York: Penguin Books, 2004.

———. *In Search of Lost Time.* Vol. 5, *The Captive and the Fugitive.* Translated by C. K. Scott Moncrieff and Terence Kilmartin, revised by D. J. Enright. New York: Modern Library Edition, 1992.

Rago, Louise Elliott. "An Interview with Marion Greenwood." *School Arts Magazine,* June 1961.

"Readers Sound Off on Campus Problems." *Daily Orange,* October 19, 1965.

"Red Hook Gets Mural Praising Planned Living." *New York Herald Tribune,* November 28, 1940.

Reed, Alma M. *Peregrina: Love and Death in Mexico,* ed. Michael Schuessler. Austin: University of Texas Press, 2007.

Rubin-Dienstfrey, Sydelle. "Transcultural Readings of Winold Reiss, Franz Boas, and Miguel Covarrubias: Art and Ethnography of the Harlem Renaissance." In *The Multicultural Modernism of Winold Reiss, 1886–1953, Transnational Approaches to His Work,* ed. Frank Mehring, 106–19. Berlin: Deutscher Kunstverlag, 2022.

Rivas, Guillermo. "Mexican Murals by Marion Greenwood." *Mexican Life* 12, no.1 (January 1936): 24–25, 61.

———. "The Murals of Grace Greenwood." *Mexican Life* 12, no. 12 (December 1936): 28–30.

Rubinstein, Charlotte Streifer. *American Women Artists: From Early Indian Times to the Present.* Boston: G. K. Hall & Co., 1982.

Saab, A. Joan. *For the Millions: American Art and Culture Between the Wars.* Philadelphia: University of Pennsylvania Press, 2004.

Salpeter, Harry. "Marion Greenwood: An American Painter of Originality and Power." *American Artist* 12 (January 1948): 14–19.

Sampson, P. W. "A Modern Cellini—Winold Reiss." *Du Pont Magazine* 25, no. 3 (March 1931): 4–6.

Schjeldahl, Peter. "Shapes of Things: The Birth of the Abstract." *New Yorker,* January 7, 2013.

Seaton, Elizabeth G., Jane Myers, and Gail Windisch, eds. *Art for Every Home: Associated American Artists 1934–2000.* Marianna Kistler Beach Museum of Art, 2015.

———. "'Art of Every Possible Service': Associated American Artists and Corporate Commissions During the War Decade." In *Art for Every Home: Associated American Artists 1934–2000,* 121–24, 130–39. Marianna Kistler Beach Museum of Art, 2015.

"Sees Artists Here in Serious Straits: PWA Art Official Pleads for Federal Aid Program During the Winter." *New York Times,* September 23, 1934.

Siqueiros, David Alfaro. "The Counter-Revolutionary Road of Rivera." *New Masses,* May 29, 1934.

Smith, Anita M. *Woodstock: History and Hearsay.* Catskill Mountains Publishing Corporation, 1959.

Smith, R. Harris. *OSS: The Secret History of America's First Central Intelligence Agency.* Berkeley: University of California Press, 1971.

Solomon, Deborah. *American Mirror: The Life and Art of Norman Rockwell.* New York: Farrar, Straus, and Giroux, 2013.

Speck, Catherine. *Beyond the Battlefield: Women Artists of the Two World Wars.* London: Reaktion Books, 2014.

Spratling, William. *File on Spratling: An Autobiography.* Boston: Little, Brown, 1967.

Stansell, Christine. *American Moderns: Bohemian New York and the Creation of a New Century.* New York: Henry Holt, 2000.

Star-Hunt, Jack. "Brooklyn Girls Delight Mexico with Eight Murals." *New York Herald Tribune,* March 4, 1934.

Stewart, Jeffrey C. "Winold Reiss's American Studies." In *The Art of Winold Reiss: An Immigrant Modernist,* ed. Marilyn Satin Kushner, 49–55. New York Historical Society, 2021.

———. "Winold Reiss as a Portraitist." *Journal of the Cincinnati Historical Society* 51 (Summer–Fall 1993): 3–19.

———. *To Color America: Portraits by Winold Reiss.* Washington, DC: Smithsonian Institution Press for the National Portrait Gallery, 1989.

Straw, Deborah. Review of *Dear Juliette: Letters of May Sarton to Juliette Huxley.* "Language is a virus" blog, n.d.

Sweet, Jill D., and Ian Berry. *Staging the Indian: The Politics of Representation.* The Tang Teaching Museum and Art Gallery at Skidmore College, 2001.

"Talented Woman Artist Changes Technique Often." *Waterloo (Iowa) Daily Courier,* December 20, 1950.

Teller, Susan. "At Associated American Artists with Sylvan Cole, Jr." In *Art for Every Home: Associated American Artists, 1934–2000,* ed. Elizabeth G. Seaton, Jane Myers, and Gail Windisch, 221–24. Marianna Kistler Beach Museum of Art, 2015.

"Tennessee Mural to Be Unveiled." *Knoxville Journal,* June 5, 1955.

Tuchman, Barbara W. *Stilwell and the American Experience in China, 1911–1945.* New York: Random House, 2017.

Tully, Judd. "The Art Students League of New York." *American Artist* 48, no. 505 (August 1984): 52–53, 74–76.

Uncle Sam and Uncle Ho. BBC documentary, 1998.

Vogel, Susan. *Becoming Pablo O'Higgins.* San Francisco: Pince-Nez Press, 2010.

Weber, Bruce. "Making It Permanent: Community, Family, Friendship, and the Building of the Collection of the Woodstock Artists Association." In *Woodstock Artists Association: One Hundred Years of Community and Art,* ed. Natalie Chapman, 68–145. Woodstock, NY: WAAM, 2019.

———. "In Quest of Harmony: The Founding and Early Years of the Woodstock Artists Association." *Hudson River Valley Review* 36, no. 1 (Autumn 2019): 35.

Wellensky, Elliott. *When Brooklyn Was the World: 1920–1957*. New York: Harmony Books, 1986.

Werth, Barry. "Refuge and Crucible: Newton Arvin's Yaddo." In *Yaddo: Making American Culture*, ed. Micki McGee, 17–30. New York: Columbia University Press, 2008.

Weston, Edward. *The Daybooks of Edward Weston*. New York: Aperture, 1990.

Wierich, Jochen. "Painting the Old West New: Winold Reiss' Blackfeet Portraits." In *The Multicultural Modernism of Winold Reiss, 1886–1953, Transnational Approaches to His Work*, ed. Frank Mehring, 94–105. Berlin: Deutscher Kunstverlag, 2022.

Wilson, Elizabeth. *Bohemians: The Glamorous Outcasts*. New Brunswick, NJ: Rutgers University Press, 2000.

Windisch, Gail. "Delivering Art to American Homes: Associated American Artists and the Two Men Who Shaped it, 1934–84." In *Art for Every Home: Associated American Artists 1934–2000*, ed. Elizabeth Seaton, Jane Myers, and Gail Windisch, 23–31, 40–45. Marianna Kistler Beach Museum of Art, 2015.

Wolf, Amy. "Introduction." In "On Becoming an Artist: Isamu Noguchi and His Contemporaries, 1922–1960." Isamu Noguchi Foundation and Garden Museum, November 17, 2010–April 24, 2011.

Wolf, Tom. "The Centennial of the Woodstock Artists Association." In *Woodstock Artists Association: One Hundred Years of Community and Art*, ed. Natalie Chapman, 16–67. Woodstock, NY: WAAM, 2019.

———. "Introduction." In *Woodstock Portraits* exhibition, May 8 through June 28, Woodstock Artists Association, 1999: 3–5.

———. "Historical Survey." In *Woodstock's Art Heritage: The Permanent Collection of the Woodstock Artists Association*, 17–29. Woodstock, NY: Overlook Press, 1987.

Woods-Marsden, Joanna. *Renaissance Self-Portraiture: The Visual Construction of Identity and the Social Status of the Artist*. New Haven, CT: Yale University Press, 1998.

Index

Associated Artists Gallery, 146
Atentado a las maestras rurales (Attack on the Rural Schoolteachers) (Reyes), 89–90
Atlantic City (New Jersey), 192, 194–96, 203, 210

Babcock, Barbara, 51
Bacon, Francis, 295
Bacon, Peggy, 29, 166, 168, 197
Baillot, Juliette, 156
Baker, Josephine, 36, 182
Band, The, 282
Bankhead, Tallulah, xv, 280
Bara, Theda, 17–18
Bard College, 276–77
Barr, Alfred, Jr., 262
"Battle of the Century," 127
Baudelaire, Charles, 208
Bautista, Fulgencio, 245
Beals, Carleton, 83
Beatty, Willard W., 266
Bellows, George, 29
Belmaison Galleries, 48
Benga, Ota, 48
Benton, Thomas Hart, 21, 142, 166, 194, 215, 256; *Burlesque*, 58
Bernard, Harry, 206–7
Bernhardt, Sarah, 190–91
Bernstein, Leonard, 227
Berry, Mike, 258
Besant, Annie, 18
Biberman, Edward, 50, 52, 109
Biddle, George, 141, 193, 197
Big Spring, William "Billy," 310n14
Billy the Kid (Copland), 61–62
Bishop, Isabel, 276
birth control, 22
Bishop, Isabel, 166
Bisstram, Emil, 52
Blackfeet, 45–46, 56, 310n11, 310n14
Blake, William, 151, 193
Blanch, Arnold, 204, 282; as "Mayor of Woodstock," 263

Blavatsky, Madame, 14, 49
Blom, Frans, 84
Blue Circle (Kandinsky), xiii
Boas, Franz, 46, 48, 259
bohemian movement, 18–19
Bohrod, Aaron, 167, 230–31, 294
Bolio, Antonio Mediz, 130
Bolivar, Simón, 128
Boston marriages, 66
Boswell, Helen, 252
Boswell, Peyton, 252
Boyington, Pappy, 186
Brancusi, Constantin, 38
Braque, Georg, 37, 223
Brennan, Frances, 193
Brenner, Anita, 6, 78, 99, 119
Breton, André, 189, 243
Brett, Dorothy, 49
Bridgman, George B., 23–24, 31–32, 35
Brilliant, Richard, 295
Britain, 157
Brodsky, Gladys, xiii, 17–18, 157, 229, 256, 259–60, 263–65, 280–81, 284, 294–95, 332n19
"Broken Appointment, A" (Hardy), 210
Brown, Bolton, 28
Brown, John, 75
Brown, Karen McCarthy, 247
Brown v. Board of Education, 256
Bry, Edith, 311n21
Buffalo Bill's Wild West Show, 49
Burke-Wadsworth Act, 169
Burlesque (Benton), 58
Burma, 176
Butler Institute of Art, 241
Bynner, Witter, 83
Byrdcliffe (artist's colony), 27, 29, 33

Café Society (club), 182
Cahill, Holger, 141, 143
Calder, Alexander "Sandy," xv, 36, 38, 295, 333n15
California, 48
California School of Fine Arts, 141–42

and Machine), 116; human labor and industrialization, theme of, 116; lack of ambition, 115; Mexico City social life, 118; *Mining*, 134–35; murals of, 116, 134–37; New Deal programs, 140; Public Works of Art Project (PWAP), 123; social consciousness of, 128
Greenwood, Irwin, 11, 16, 26, 83, 86, 122, 217, 250–52, 273, 286
Greenwood, Jessie, 217, 250–51, 273, 287
Greenwood, Lester, 11, 16, 58, 91, 217, 234, 250–52, 268, 280–81, 286
Greenwood, Marion, 3, 6–8, 13, 15–16, 23, 30, 35, 39, 52, 121–22, 143–44, 149–51, 170, 174–76, 178–79, 193, 200–201, 205, 286, 289, 309n9, 312n17, 312n18, 323n7; abortion of, 59, 64, 69, 313n20, 332n19; affairs of, 40, 63, 66, 256, 333n15; anti-colonialism of, 246; anti-Soviet, 240; at Art Students League, 17, 22, 25, 32, 37, 88, 127, 197; Ashcan School training, 24, 37; Associated American Artists (AAA), joining of, 166–68; Associated American Artists (AAA) exhibit, 217–18, 220–23; in Atlantic City, 192, 194–96, 203, 210; aura of, 4; auto accidents, 269, 275, 280; background of, 11–12; beauty of, xiv, 189–90, 230, 294–95; as bohemian, xv, 19, 288, 294; in Canton (China), 214–15; *Carnival (Festival) at Kripplebush*, 182; cerebral hemorrhage, 283–84; charm of, 231, 290; *China Granite Quarry*, 218; *Civil War in Austria*, 168; cocktail glass, tipping of at Guggenheim Museum, xiii–xiv, xvi, 270; communism, turn toward, 106, 112, 129, 131; contradictions of, 185–86; *Coolie*, 230; creative process, 276; critical and commercial neglect of, 230–31; in Cuba, 244–45; dark side of, 68; death of, 285, 298; dependence, on Charles, 216; divorce, 235–36; in Dominican Republic,

244–45; egalitarian society, faith in, 209; *Elegy*, 241–42, 246, 265, 297; "ethnic types," devotion to, 24; *Exile*, 188; expressionistic style, turn to, 241; faltering confidence of, 210–11; *Fan Girl* (Greenwood), 214, 233; feminist principles, embodying of, 279; as femme fatale, xiv–xvi, 295; Fenn, marriage to, 152; Fenn, separation from, 161–62; *Fish Market, Nazaré*, 273; as forthright, 259–60; frescoes, 9, 10, 17; *Gazing Children*, 277; gender boundaries, ignoring of, 294–95; *Gene at Work*, 56; as jealous, 216; financial worries, 171, 229, 251; frescoes, 86–87, 165, 167; "good art," definition of, 138, 270; in Haiti, 243–49, 259; *Haitian Dancers*, 247; *Haitian Market Women*, 246–47; *Haitian Musicians*, 247; having children, mixed feelings of, 274; health issues, 210, 227–28, 251; Herbst, relationship with, 64, 67–71, 93, 97–98, 102–3, 125, 132, 138–39, 146, 160, 185; *Heretic, Martha Graham*, 57–58, 144–45; holidays, despising of, 131–32; in Hong Kong, 212–17, 222–24; Hong Kong art, 230, 243, 259; *hsu* (heart songs), 211, 213, 217–18; Huxley, relationship with, 155–57, 160; ideological statements, resistance of, 112; *Industrialization of the Countryside, The*, 132–34; Indigenous peoples, romantic attitude toward, 103–4; *Ink Grinder*, 220; *Invocation* (Greenwood), 241–42, 246, 256; Irish sense of tragedy, 296; Jekyll and Hyde persona, 216, 235; *Jockey, The: Portrait of Eddie Arcaro*, 163; in Knoxville, 252–56, 259, 261; at Kripplebush, 181–82; *Lament*, 241, 256, 297; leftist politics of, 72, 137–38; lesbian relationships, 312n11; *Lisbon Woman*, 273; *Little Tailor*, 24, 29; lithographs, 28–29, 168, 276, 281; loneliness of, 102, 104, 106, 109, 118,

185–87, 204; marriage as institution, disdain for, 94; *Mary in Black*, 295; meteoric rise of, 5; *Mexican Harvest*, 167–68; *Mexican Life*, 88, 112; in Mexico, 51, 71–72, 75–82, 124–25, 127–28, 140, 255, 259, 265–68, 281, 288; in Mexico City, 93–94, 125, 127, 138; Mexico City social life, 118; *Mexico of Today and Tomorrow*, 134; *Mississippi Girl*, 56, 197, 199, 244, 294, 297; in Morelia, xv, 5, 94–95, 102, 104, 105–11, 113, 115–16, 118, 120, 123–24, 127, 132, 167, 211, 253, 297; *Mother and Child*, 86; *Mountain Family*, 168; as muralist, 82, 107, 112, 257, 266, 288; murals of, 9–10, 87–91, 94, 103, 109, 112–16, 123, 132–37, 140, 153–55, 157–60, 211, 252–56, 258–59, 268, 279, 281, 288, 291, 297; National Academy of Design, elected to, 269–70; Native Americans, depictions of, 45–46; *Navajo Boy*, 50, 76, 104; *Neurosurgery*, 192; New Deal programs, 140–41; *New Year's Eve*, 182; *Night Song*, 273; *Night in Spain*, 164; *Notre Vendeuse de Journaux*, 37; "Now I'll be all alone," 97; outsider status of, 104; "out of tune" with art trends, fear of, 262–63, 266, 269–70, 292; *Paisaje y economía de Michoacán—Landscape and Economy of Michoacán*, 112; in Paris, 36–38; *Partnership of Man and Nature*, 153–55, 258; *Peon's Funeral*, 86; Plate, relationship with, 237–41, 243, 248–53, 259; political contradictions of, 160; poor, sympathetic to, 240; *Portrait of Verna*, 56; in Portugal, 272; poverty of, 165, 169; pregnancy of, 59; as prodigy, 20; Proust, obsession with, 181, 184–85, 190, 191, 206, 210, 223, 228–29, 236, 238; public art projects, wearing her down, 159; Pueblo peoples, portraits of, 49–50; Public Works of Art Project (PWAP),

123; radicalism, embrace of, 130; realism of, 241–42, 277, 291, 292; Red Hook Housing Project mural, 157–58, 160; *Rehearsal for an African Ballet*, 184, 188; Reiss, tutelage of, 40–42; *Rendezvous*, 188; resilience of, 296; and Rivera, 120, 132, 267; Rivera, influence on, 134; Rodríguez market murals, 129–31; romantic primitivism, 86; self-portraits of, 44–45, 231, 270, 274–75, 287, 295–96; as sensualist, 66, 146; serendipity, dependence on, 252; sexism toward, 194, 230; *Simple Confession*, 172; *Singing Mural, The*, 254–56, 257, 258, 259, 279; and Siqueiros, 81, 127–28; social consciousness of, 21, 31, 128–29; socialism, passion for, 151; social realism of, 145; in Southwest, 48–51; in Spain, 272–73; Spanish Civil War, effect on, 163–64; spiritualist leanings, 18; stability, need for, 177; *Street Meeting*, 142; suicide, thoughts of, 228; in Taxco, 83–84, 86–87, 92, 123; *Taxco Market*, 88–89; temperament of, 70; Theosophy, 92, 157, 189, 275; time, motif of, 180–81, 210; *Toilers, The*, 218, 221; transient quality of things, awareness of, 180; *Tribute to Woman*, 277–79; in Trinidad, 244, 246; trust in own judgment, 26; as unhinged, 217; Virgin of Guadalupe celebration, 131; voice of, comparison to Tallulah Bankhead, xv, 280; *Voodoo Ritual*, 247; as war artist, 194–97, 199, 230–31; *Water Carrier*, 220; weight, concern over, 188, 210; *Woman of Nazaré*, 273; at Woodstock, 37, 180, 204, 233–35, 263–64; at Woodstock music festival, 282; Woodstock images, 29; working people, dignity of, 108; at Yaddo, 32–34, 37, 59–62, 66–70, 104, 140, 161–63, 169, 181

Greenwood, Caroline Henshaw, 12

Mendez, Leopold, 78–80, 129
Metropolitan Museum of Art, 23, 78, 165, 231
Mexican American War, 79
"Mexican Arts" (exhibition), 78
Mexican Folkways (journal), 78
Mexican Harvest (Greenwood), 167–68
Mexicanicity, 85
Mexican Life (Greenwood), 88, 112
Mexican muralism, 81
Mexican Revolution, 142
Mexico, xiv, xvi, 3–6, 9–10, 51, 71, 79, 88–90, 92, 169–70, 211, 259, 273; Africans in, 314n13; "enormous vogue of things Mexican," 75–76; *indigenismo*, 96; Maximato ("puppet presidencies," 128; *Mexicanidad*, 96; New Deal, influence of, 141; "romantic anticapitalism," 76; strikes in, 133
Mexico City (Mexico), 3, 6, 9–10, 76–78, 81–82, 93, 126, 134, 138; Jamaica Terminal, 131, 132; as place for artists, 4; as radical scene, 128
Mexico of Today and Tomorrow (Greenwood), 134
Michelangelo, 159
Michoacán (Mexico), 96
Milch Gallery, 265, 276
Millan, Ignacio, 78, 80–82, 94, 101, 120–21, 274
Miller, Arthur, 252
Millman, Edward, 263
minimalism, 282
Mining (G. Greenwood), 134–35
Mirkin, Dina Comisarenco, 88, 112, 116
Miró, Joan, 192
Mississippi Girl (Greenwood), 56, 197, 199, 244, 294, 297
Mistral, Gabriela, 128
Mitchell, Joan, 262
Modern Art Collector (magazine), 44
modernism, 24–25, 28, 37, 44
Modotti, Tina, 78, 99
Moffat, Fred, 256, 258

Mohr, Lillian Homen, 279
Mona Lisa (da Vinci), 292
Mondrian, Piet, 15, 57
Montenegro, Robert, 129
Monument to Ben Franklin (Noguchi), 143
Moreno Sanchez, Manuel, 102–3, 106–7, 146
Morgan, Kelli, 292
Morgenthau, Henry, Jr., 197
Morris, Henry, 151
Morrow, Dwight W., 84–85
Morrow, Elizabeth, 84–85
Motherwell, Robert, 262
Museo Michoacano, 116
Mother and Child (Greenwood), 86
Mountain Family (Greenwood), 168
Mountbatten, Louis, 187
Munich (Germany), 44
muralism, 80–81, 96, 118, 128
Muray, Nickolas, 53, 229
Murillo Coronado, Gerardo, 84
Museum of Modern Art (MoMA), 142, 145, 155, 165, 243

Nanking, 174
National Academy of Design, 20, 23, 241, 269–70
National Association of Women Artists, 269
National Fine Arts School, 129
National Institute of Arts and Letters, 285
National Museum of the American Indian, 310n7
National Palace, 7
National Recovery Administration (NRA), 143
Native Son (Wright), 182
Navajo Boy (Greenwood), 50, 76, 104
Navarrete, Artemio, 85
Nazis, 169
Neel, Alice, 231, 292
Neely, Jack, 258
Neurosurgery (Greenwood), 192
Nevelson, Louise, 197